The American Exploration and Travel Series

ADVENTURE IN THE WILDERNESS
THE AMERICAN JOURNALS OF
Louis Antoine de Bougainville
1756–1760

ADVENTURE
IN THE
WILDERNESS

THE AMERICAN JOURNALS OF
Louis Antoine de Bougainville
1756–1760

Translated and Edited by
EDWARD P. HAMILTON
Foreword by Colin G. Calloway

Norman and London UNIVERSITY OF OKLAHOMA PRESS

BY EDWARD P. HAMILTON

A History of Milton (Milton, 1957)

The French and Indian Wars: The Story of Battles and Forts in the Wilderness (New York, 1962)

(Translator and Editor), *Adventure in the Wilderness: The American Journals of Louis Antoine de Bougainville, 1756–1760* (Norman, 1964)

Library of Congress Catalog Card Number: 64–11318
ISBN: 0–8061–2248–X

Adventure in the Wilderness: The American Journals of Louis Antoine de Bougainville, 1756–1760 is Volume 42 in The American Exploration and Travel Series.

Copyright © 1964 by the University of Oklahoma Press, Publishing Division of the University. All rights reserved. Manufactured in the U.S.A. First edition, 1964. First paperback printing, 1990.

Contents

Foreword, by Colin G. Calloway	xi
Bougainville and His Journal	xvii
The Seven Years' War in America	xxi
Journal for 1756	3
Journal for 1757	77
Journal for 1758	195
Journals for 1759–60	316
Memoir Since November 15, 1758	322
Appendix	330
Index	335

Illustrations

Louis Antoine de Bougainville	*Facing page* 12
Portaging	13
Oswego	28
Dispositions at Fort Carillon	29
The Marquis de Vaudreuil	124
The Marquis de Montcalm	125
Bougainville Around 1758	140
French Vessel of the Period	141
Diorama of French Defenses at Fort Carillon	252
Montcalm Congratulating His Troops	253
The Montcalm Cross	268
Fort Ticonderoga Today	269

Maps

New France and the British Colonies, 1756 — xxii
The Champlain Valley — 128
Fort William Henry, 1757 — 161
Bougainville's Sketch of the Louisbourg Landing — 217

Foreword
By Colin G. Calloway

A CENTURY AGO, the Canadian historian, Abbé Casgrain, made a transcript of the journal of Louis Antoine de Bougainville, but chose not to include it in his *Collection des Manuscripts du Maréchal de Lévis* (12 vols. Quebec, 1889–1895). That was a mistake because Bougainville's journal is a gem. It contains the observations and insights of a French officer who was aide-de-camp to the Marquis de Montcalm and active in a key arena of the Seven Years' War in North America. In its pages the reader will find valuable material on military affairs, Indian relations, and life in New France in the closing years of the contest for continental hegemony waged between Britain and France.

Bougainville was short, overweight, and asthmatic, but Montcalm recognized him as a man of courage and talent. He was an educated man who knew ancient history, could quote the classics, and had written a book on calculus by the time he was twenty-five years old. In later life he traveled around the world and published an account of his voyages, was made a member of the Académie des Sciences, and after a spell in prison during the Terror, became a count of the Empire in 1808.[1] He also sat at Indian coun-

[1] For further details on Bougainville's career, see *Dictionary of Canadian Biography*, vol. 5 (Toronto: University of Toronto Press, 1983), 102–106.

cil fires, sang the war song with Indian warriors, and was an adopted Nipissing and Caughnawaga of the Turtle clan.

When he arrived in Canada in 1756, Bougainville had no combat experience, but Montcalm said that he had "a military mind indeed" (p. 334). Bougainville's journal is a valuable record of the war from the perspective of a French officer who knew both his British enemies and his Indian allies. It is rich in daily details of the struggle for North America and contains the author's reflections on the war, the country in which it was fought, and the people who fought it.

Bougainville saw at firsthand the guerrilla warfare that typified so much of the contest. He was present at the capture of Oswego in 1756, when the French secured control of Lake Ontario, and at the siege of Fort William Henry in 1757, where Indian allies slaughtered English prisoners. He was wounded at Ticonderoga in 1758, when Montcalm's troops repulsed General James Abercromby's bloody assault. After a brief return to France, he came back to Canada as a colonel and knight of St. Louis. His journal becomes much more brief at this time. Although he was unable to participate in the historic clash on the Plains of Abraham, he witnessed the fall of Quebec in 1759. The following winter he commanded at Ile aux Noix, on the Richelieu River, and in September 1760, at Montreal, he carried the French articles of capitulation to General Amherst. Taken prisoner along with the rest of the army, he was shipped back to France.

He conveys the problems of supply in a country where war is dictated by the seasons, where French soldiers wait each year for the opening of the rivers, and where starving citizens in Quebec watch anxiously for the first ships from the home country. When he can get it, he adds news of the war in Europe and of developments deep in Indian country. He comments on the workings of the French military, criticizes the waste and corruption inherent in the French system, and laments the rivalry between Governor Vaudreuil and Montcalm. His lists of French and English forces in North America illustrate the disparity in numbers and reflect the polyglot composition of the French army, made up of regular troops, Canadian militia, volunteers, mission Indians from the

Foreword

St. Lawrence, and warriors from as far away as the western Great Lakes. He voices his concerns about the effects of the North American service on discipline and morale: French officers gamble without restraint, and regular troops seem corrupted by the example of Indians and Canadians "breathing an air permeated with independence" (p. 51).

Perhaps most interesting and valuable are Bougainville's observations on Indians and the inner workings of the Franco-Indian alliance. Indians dominate the journal. Indian war parties come and go; Indian wampum belts circulate; Indian chiefs and French officers hold innumerable councils; Indians frequently dictate strategy; and Indians often interest and always frustrate Bougainville. The English saw the Indians as pliant tools in the hands of the French, but Bougainville reveals the difficulties and complexities inherent in Franco-Indian relations and details the careful management and attention to forest protocol by which the French maintained the alliance of independent-minded warriors.

He recognizes that the French rely on the Indians: "In the midst of the woods of America one can no more do without them than without cavalry in open country" (p. 149). Like British officers in the Revolution and the War of 1812, he feels compelled to justify their employment, pointing out time and again that they are "a necessary evil." But he also resents the dependence and regrets that the French must pander to the whims and wishes of Indian allies who seem to him to be mercenary, bloodthirsty, and unreliable.

Bougainville shares the prejudices and ethnocentrism of his countrymen and his class. He has little derogatory to say about his British enemies, perhaps because he lived for a time in London, but he regularly describes Indians and Canadians in negative terms. In Bougainville's view, Indian scouts cannot be trusted, Indian warriors cannot be controlled, and Indian behavior cannot be predicted: "the caprice of an Indian is of all caprices the most capricious" (p. 37). He expresses disgust at the Indians' love of alcohol, abhorrence at their methods of waging war, and dismay at their continual demands for supplies.

At the same time, however, Bougainville proves himself an ethnographic observer of some value. The list of Indian nations that appear in the journal includes Mohawks, Oneidas, Onondagas, Cayugas, Senecas, Caughnawagas, Hurons, Algonkins, Nipissings, Abenakis from Missisquoi, Penobscot and St. Francis, Maliseets, Ottawas, Menominees, Chippewas, Mississaugas, Iroquois from the Lake of the Two Mountains, Delawares, Potawatomis, Shawnees, Catawbas, Cherokees, and Sauks and Foxes. Bougainville comments on intertribal relations and the diplomatic tug-of-war that the British and French wage for the allegiance of key tribes. He finds the endless councils tiresome and dismisses one condolence council as "much repetition and useless words from all quarters" (p. 247), but he records the formalities of council fire diplomacy and notes the importance of women in Iroquois councils (p. 104).

As a French officer he is primarily concerned with the Indians' role as warriors, but he also displays more than passing interest in their cultures. While he complains that all Indians are alike in their cruelty and lack of reliability, he does make distinctions in the character and customs of the various nations and recognizes the different bands within them. He describes Indian villages at Caughnawaga and Lake of the Two Mountains. He identifies prominent war chiefs, such as the Nipissing Kisenik, whom he describes as "a rare bird in the land" (p. 160), but recognizes that Indian leaders had little authority and that their leadership depended upon the "voluntary subordination" of their followers (p. 134). He describes Indian war customs and medicine making, and his ear catches differences in the music of Winnebagoes and Ottawas (p. 118). He watches traditional Indian religious observances, such as offering tobacco to Rock "Rozzio" in Lake Champlain, and sees Catholic Indian converts at mass. While he suspects that an Indian in a surplice is "a wolf in sheep's clothing" (p. 76), he nevertheless provides insights into the syncretism of Indian and Catholic beliefs: Hurons hang a wampum belt in a chapel dedicated to the archangel Michael in the hope that he will accompany them on the warpath (p. 190). Though Bougainville denounces Indians as barbarians in war, he also shows them to be human beings who, for example, stop to pick blueberries on their way to a fight (p. 146).

Bougainville's journal presents a view from the inside of a crumbling empire. Travel is hazardous, news is infrequent, supplies are uncertain, and famine and disease stalk the land. "The Acadians die in crowds," he writes in 1757 (p. 194). The French lack the manpower and the resources to hold back the British, and they are unsure of their Canadian militia and their Indian allies. Warriors ignore their chiefs and treat the French with little respect, even as they make endless demands on their allies' limited supplies of goods, alcohol, and patience. Interpreters make things worse. Waste, inefficiency, and peculation plague the system. Petty jealousies divert the talents and sap the energies of the men at the top. Officers grope their way to bed for want of candles. A courier who arrives in Montreal after more than three months' travel from Louisiana is kept waiting at the governor's door with no more attention paid to him than if he had come to Paris from Versailles. As the tide turns in Britain's favor, Bougainville's criticisms of the conduct of the war mount: "What a country! What a war!" (p. 222).

Editor Edward P. Hamilton provides annotations on people and places but basically leaves Bougainville to speak for himself. The journal is neither a lengthy and rambling discourse nor simply a dry record of daily entries. Bougainville emerges as an intelligent observer, blinkered by his share of prejudices and, as a dedicated officer, frustrated at serving his country in trying circumstances. He has a scientific curiosity in the world around him and an enduring interest in the human condition. *Adventure in the Wilderness* is a valuable eyewitness account of the French war effort by a man who was a scholar and something of an ethnographer as well as a soldier and a diplomat. The paperback edition will be welcomed by students of military history, colonial history, and Indian history and culture.

Bougainville and His Journal

LOUIS ANTOINE DE BOUGAINVILLE was born in 1729, the son of Pierre Yves de Bougainville, a well-to-do lawyer of Paris. He thus was a member of the upper level of the *bourgeoisie* and of good social standing, although not of the noblesse. We know little of his early activities, except that he originally studied law but apparently never practiced it. He must, however, have devoted considerable study to higher mathematics, for at the age of twenty-five he produced a book on integral calculus. About this time he served as an officer in the Picardy militia, and he later spent several months as secretary to the French ambassador in London, where he perfected his English and apparently made many friends. By 1755 we find him in the French Army as a lieutenant of dragoons, and he had a second volume on calculus ready for the press. In January, 1756, he was elected a member of the British Royal Society, an extraordinary honor for so young a man, and a foreigner at that. Early in this same year he was appointed aide-de-camp to the Marquis de Montcalm with the rank of captain, and in April the two left for Canada.

Bougainville then commenced a journal and continued it throughout his stay in North America. It is the frank and detailed story of the activities, thoughts, and observations of an educated French gentleman who knew the English and their language and was a member of the French high command in Canada. Montcalm and Bougainville each thought very highly of the other, and the two remained close friends until the death of the Marquis.

By the end of the war, Bougainville was a colonel, and he shortly transferred to the navy. In 1766 he led a scientific expedition around the world and explored the South Pacific. He published a book of his travels in 1771. The story of his discovery of Tahiti and his descriptions of that region excited considerable public interest. It was he who introduced the Bougainvillea flower to Europe. Bougainville served under Admiral de Grasse during the American Revolution and became a commodore in 1779. By 1790 he commanded the Brest fleet, but resigned soon after. He was made a member of the Institute and served in the Bureau of Longitude. Under Napoleon he became a senator and a count.

Bougainville was short and plump, almost fat, and he suffered badly from asthma except when at sea, probably one of the reasons for his transferring to the navy. He died in 1811.

The journal remained in the hands of his family, and a transcript was apparently made for the French Archives. Abbé Casgrain, the Canadian historian, while gathering material for the Lévis papers, published by the Province of Quebec between 1889 and 1895, made a transcript of the journal when it was in the possession of the Marquise de Bassignac, Bougainville's eldest granddaughter. Despite the great interest of Bougainville's journal, Casgrain failed to use any part of it, probably because, as an ardent French-Canadian patriot, he felt that the author had a bias against the inhabitants of the country.[1] I prefer, however to believe that Bougainville, an intelligent observer, was an honest reporter and that he did not distort the facts. His journal closely parallels Montcalm's but differs very materially at times. I believe that much of Montcalm's journal was actually written by Bougainville.

[1] See Edward P. Hamilton's "Parkman, Abbé Casgrain, and Bougainville's Journal," *Proceedings* of the American Antiquarian Society for October, 1961.

Bougainville and His Journal

So far as I have been able to determine, this journal has never been translated into English. I have worked from Parkman's transcript of the copy in the French Archives, sent him by his friend, Pierre Margry, and have collated it with the journal as printed in French by the Archivist of Quebec in 1924. The latter was also transcribed from the Paris Archives and collated with Abbé Casgrain's transcript. The original journal must still be somewhere in France, but several copies exist elsewhere. The New York State Library has a few Bougainville manuscripts, and the Burton Historical Collection of the Detroit Public Library has recently acquired a number, one or two of which are either copies or the originals of a portion of the present translation. Such differences as I have found are all quite minor in nature. The journal in many places consists of a series of disjointed notes; at others it is written in more finished form. I have attempted to make as literal a translation as possible, diverging from such course only when it seemed necessary in order to make the passage clear. French place names, although many could be put into English, have in most cases been retained. This translation as far as the journal entry for October 18, 1757, has been made with the kind permission of the Massachusetts Historical Society, the owner of the Parkman transcripts, and the subsequent portion through the kindness of the Archivist of Quebec, who has custody of the longer transcript. I owe thanks to Professor Mason Hammond for his kind assistance in translating many of Bougainville's Latin quotations, to William N. Fenton for help on matters concerning Indians, to Michel Bevillard for verifying the accuracy of my translation, and to Mrs. Thomas V. Lape, Librarian of Fort Ticonderoga, for the laborious work of deciphering and typing my manuscript.

Edward P. Hamilton

FORT TICONDEROGA
JANUARY 6, 1964

The Seven Years' War in America

THE LAND UPON which Bougainville first set foot in May of 1756 was again at war after the few years of tenuous peace resulting from the Treaty of Aix-la-Chapelle in 1748. Both France and Britain had realized that the war for empire must be resumed, and each made preparations. The conflict was inevitable, and it was expedited and made still more certain by the French encirclement of the British western frontiers through their ever increasing chain of posts and little forts, while the westward push of British fur traders exasperated the French. Armed clash was bound to come, and it came at last in 1754 when French troops drove the British away from the Forks of the Ohio, present Pittsburgh, where the British had started to build a trading post at that strategic point, considered by both nations to belong to themselves alone. Washington's little skirmish with Jumonville spilled the first blood of the new war, and was followed by the former's surrender at Fort Necessity. Peace continued officially between France and Britain, but both nations sent regular troops and skilled professional officers overseas, and these, not the colonial levies and militia, bore the brunt of the coming war.

The first real battle came in July, 1755, when Braddock's march

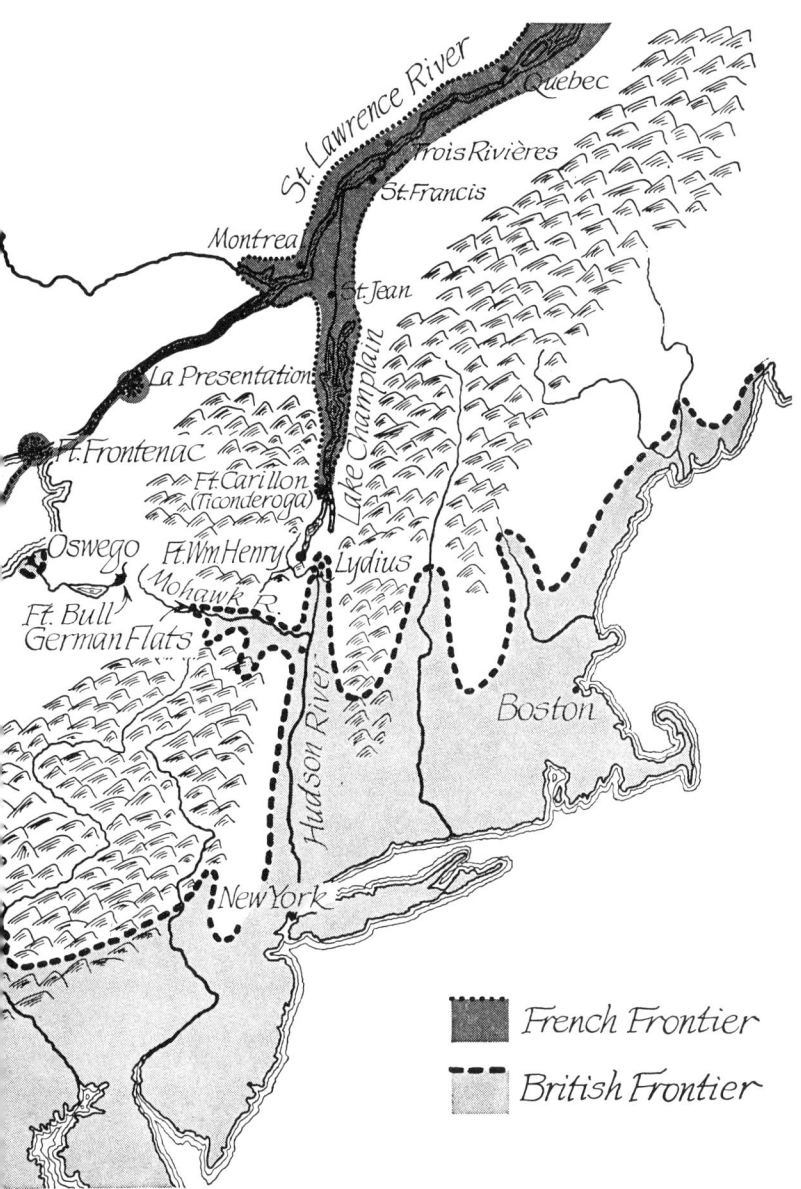

New France and the British Colonies, 1756

against the Forks of the Ohio, then held by France's Fort Duquesne, was ambushed while but a few miles from its objective. The British did not consider Braddock's expedition an act of war, but merely a police action against unwarranted intruders. A little later that summer Baron von Dieskau led a French force of regulars and Canadian levies south against the new British Fort Edward on the Hudson, some twoscore miles north of Albany. Meanwhile, William Johnson, one of the great men of colonial North America, was sent to seize the French post at Crown Point on Lake Champlain. The two forces met in battle at the head of Lake George, and the French withdrew north in utter defeat, their general captured. Johnson then started construction of Fort William Henry near the site of his victory. The year ended with a major defeat and a material victory for each side, but the pretense of peace was still maintained.

May of 1756 saw the arrival of Montcalm in America. Figure 1 shows the approximate frontiers of the two nations at that time, and it seems appropriate at this point to devote a paragraph or two to the effect of the geography of North America on Montcalm's impending campaigns.

In colonial days there were, practically speaking, almost no roads, and both trade and war moved by water. Thus the water routes of the country were of vast importance. Save for the Mohawk corridor running west from near Albany, the British had no access westward by water; all their other rivers faded away on the eastern slopes of the Appalachians. Note how this great mountain chain isolated the British colonies from the West, while the St. Lawrence gave France unlimited access, even to the Mississippi. Foot travelers and pack trains could gain the western plains with difficulty, but until wagon roads penetrated the mountains, access to the British west remained extremely limited. General Braddock succeeded in driving through a military road, a tremendous achievement that has largely been overlooked because of his defeat at Turtle Creek. Braddock was a competent officer, but he had bad luck.

Dutch traders of Albany tried to divert as much as possible of the furs of the French Far West from the St. Lawrence to the Hudson. To expedite this purpose, the British post of Oswego was established, first only as a seasonal trading camp, and then by 1727 as a permanent fortified post. For years the government of Canada had considered the destruction of this place, but had never attempted it. Oswego became a troublesome thorn in the flank of New France, an intrusion that could not be endured. In 1756 it was inadequately garrisoned by British and short of supplies, and the little Lake Ontario navy was still largely on the stocks in the shipyard instead of cruising the lake to add security to the important post. Oswego became Montcalm's first objective, and Bougainville tells us the story of its seizure. The only thing he does not mention is the partially successful attempt of the Indians to massacre the surrendered British garrison, dire forewarning of the sad massacre that followed in the course of the next year.

Lord Loudoun came from England in 1757 to take over the command from Massachusetts Governor Shirley, who had inherited it on the death of Braddock. The Scottish peer attempted a naval expedition against Louisbourg, the fortified port on Cape Breton Island that guarded the approaches to the St. Lawrence and threatened those to New England and New York. Largely because of conditions for which Loudoun was not to blame, the attempt failed. While too large a part of the British were away on this abortive foray, Montcalm struck in the Champlain Valley and overwhelmed Fort William Henry. Bougainville tells of this affair in great detail in his journal. The year 1757 was a sad one for the British cause.

The turn of the tide came in 1758, although it was ushered in by Abercromby's unhappy defeat by Montcalm at Ticonderoga. This was one of the great and bloody battles on our continent and one which was hardly exceeded in losses before the contests of the Civil War. Bougainville was in the thick of the battle, and he devotes many pages to its telling. This debacle was, however, more than balanced by the great victories gained by Britain over the French, who were rapidly becoming exhausted. Bougainville's journal is full of references to lack of men and supplies. He, perhaps, failed to realize clearly that once formal warfare had started in Europe, the American conflict became of much less importance, a side show as it were, and men and munitions were not available without end for all the theaters of war. The loss of Canada would be minor and only temporary if the war could be won in France.

Lieutenant Colonel Bradstreet's dashing foray against Fort Frontenac, main depot of supplies for the French West, was the first British success, but Louisbourg shortly fell to Amherst's methodical siege. Then a third victory crowned the year as the ailing Brigadier Forbes avenged Braddock by driving the enemy from Fort Duquesne, thus initiating the collapse of French Trans-Appalachia. Only Niagara, the true key to western waters, held out for another year, though cut off from most supplies through the fall of Frontenac. Late autumn of this year, 1758, saw Bougainville sail to France to beg for additional aid, and his journal really ends with his description of the terrors and the hardships of this voyage. He returned the next spring, promoted full colonel, and exercised an independent command during the remainder of the war, first during Wolfe's siege of Quebec, which ended in the loss of the city and the deaths of both Wolfe and Montcalm. During the next and final campaign Bougainville attempted to hold the Richelieu Valley against the steady British advance, but was forced to fall back on Montreal, and the eventual surrender of all Canada followed. The latter portion of his journal consists of relatively short summaries of his activities rather than the lengthy day-to-day record he had formerly kept.

Bougainville had intended to publish his journal at the end of the war, and much of it was recorded only as notes or brief sentences which he planned to expand into a more finished form. In my translation I have made no attempt to do this, but have followed the text literally, deviating only when expansion or substitution seemed necessary for the sake of clarity.

ADVENTURE IN THE WILDERNESS
THE AMERICAN JOURNALS OF
Louis Antoine de Bougainville
1756–1760

"Taken from M. Margry's private collection and sent to Mr. Parkman as a souvenir of friendship with the reservation that he will not publish it. It will serve for his Montcalm. M. Margry does not wish him to be deprived of this document, so interesting for the composition of his book. He trusts that he can depend upon his friend for this act of discretion. This journal is often only a memento where the facts and thoughts are only indicated with abbreviations, with the view of using it later."

In pencil in Parkman's hand: "This journal is in Archives de la Guerre somewhere."

Journal for 1756

ARRIVED AT QUEBEC May 12, 1756. Left Quebec in one of the King's canoes Saturday, May 22, at nine o'clock in the morning, spent the night five leagues on the way at St. Augustin. M. de Montcalm[1] left the same day by chaise.

Left St. Augustin at eleven o'clock in the morning, at five in the evening reached Pointe aux Trembles, two and a half leagues from there. Reached Montreal the following Saturday at five o'clock in the evening.

M. de Bourlamaque[2] left for Frontenac on June 21.

M. de Montcalm left for Carillon[3] on the twenty-seventh with the Chevalier de Lévis[4] and M. de Montreuil.[5] I remained at Montreal until M. Doreil[6] arrived with the attached instructions.

---

[1] The Marquis de Montcalm (1712–58), brigadier general in command of the French regular troops in Canada.
[2] Colonel François Charles de Bourlamaque, third in command of French regulars.
[3] Later named Fort Ticonderoga by the British.
[4] Brigadier François de Lévis (1720–87), second in command. He later became a duke and a marshal of France.
[5] The adjutant general.
[6] Commissary of war, the officer in charge of military supplies.

§ June 22 : The Chevalier de Tourville left in the frigate *Sauvage* to carry word to the Court of the arrival of the reinforcements in Canada.

§ June 27 : Orders sent to M. Descombes, chief engineer, to join from Frontenac[7] the detachment of M. de Villiers and to go to reconnoiter Oswego.[8] M. Desandrouins[9] asked to plan this trip.

The same day I wrote M. de Montcalm and sent him a package of letters.

§ June 29 : Indians from M. de Villiers' detachment arrived at Montreal with three deserters from Oswego. An officer of La Sarre Regt. dead here of the sickness contracted on the *Leopard*.

§ July 1 : Deputies came from the Nipissings who have deserted M. de Villiers, who with about twelve hundred men holds a flying camp of observation in the Oswego region. They were ordered to return, as were the Indians of all the other tribes who have deserted in the same way.

M. Beaussier left with two ships of seventy-four and seventy guns and two frigates of thirty and thirty-six guns to cruise in Louisbourg waters.

The English have three armed craft on the lake [Ontario]. Three others, more powerful than these, are about to be launched. If nothing happens before then, they will have control of the lake.

§ July 2 : Received news of the taking of an English shallop, armed with nine swivels, on Lake Ontario. Our armed craft met those of the English on their first reconnaissance. The English maneuvered to give chase, but, seeing us advance instead of turning tail, they fled. Maxim of the English at sea: avoid combat when only on equal or slightly superior terms on the same principle that one gives one's purse without any resistance to any thief who demands it, even in a public place and within reach of help.

[7] Fort Frontenac at present Kingston, Ontario.
[8] British fortified trading post on Lake Ontario, a great threat to the French fur trade with the West.
[9] A capable French engineer officer (1729–92). Served under Rochambeau here during the Revolution.

Journal for 1756

The crew, to the number of sixteen men, has been sent to Quebec. A petty victory like all those achieved in this country, but interesting because of the impression of superiority that it gives our Indians.

JULY 3 : News from Presque Isle,[10] almost all the Indians from the back country have got there, but, because they have been told that there is smallpox at Frontenac and Niagara, they do not wish to go farther; most of them have gone back. One hopes, however, to lead a few of them on. Through interrogation of prisoners and captured English papers it still appears that the enemy have all their forces assembled at Albany and its vicinity. At the Albany camp they have in abundance all the food and supplies that one could wish for in a camp. A great number of them desert, all marching away in spite of their attempts to hold them. It is believed that their main effort will be by way of Lake St. Sacrement.[11]

One of the papers states that they have about one thousand regulars under General Braddock.

A prisoner reported that recently the English general received a special messenger at Fort Edward[12] and that, in consequence, he had left posthaste for Boston, probably because of the arrival of reinforcements from England at that town. M. Dieskau[13] is in New York, but not cured of his wounds.

I wrote M. de Montcalm, and sent him his letters.

M. de Bourlamaque arrived at Frontenac.

Our engineers, busy at fortifying this place, complain of the lack of almost all the things necessary to advance the work.

Note regarding this fortification on the change that M. de Bourlamaque has had made in the plan, making everyone quit work at four o'clock so that the workers may drill. Five new ves-

---

[10] Present Erie, Pa., then an important Canadian post on Lake Erie.

[11] Lake George.

[12] British fort on the Hudson where the portage to Lake Champlain started.

[13] Baron Von Dieskau, commander of the French Army, who was captured by General William Johnson at Lake George in 1755.

sels and two of the King's flutes,[14] the *Outarde* and the *Anna Sophia*, arrived in the harbor of Quebec carrying food and munitions.

From all our posts great complaints of the bad quality of the food.

ࡿ JULY 8 : M. Godet left for Frontenac as a special messenger.

ࡿ JULY 9 : The Intendant[15] arrived at Montreal.

ࡿ JULY 10 : A Canadian officer arrived here with ten English, as much prisoners as deserters, reports news of successful action carried out by M. de Villiers on the Oswego River. With four hundred men he attacked a convoy of three or four hundred bateaux, each with two men, and three companies of soldiers. The English companies here are of one hundred men. Some have been reduced to sixty-two. [They were] returning from Oswego, where they had carried food and munitions, and had gone up again after more provisions. Villiers put them to flight and knocked off a great number, and would have knocked off a lot more were it not for the poor quality of the tomahawks furnished by the King's Store, took twenty-four scalps and killed or wounded in their flight, according to his estimate, about three hundred men. We lost in this affair a colony officer, six Canadians and colony soldiers and one Indian.[16]

The victory would have been greater except for the precipitation of the Indians who attacked too soon, and I would add, also that of the chief, for I have seen him in a similar situation.

As for the rest of it, his detachment, according to what he wrote M. de Vaudreuil,[17] is not capable of undertaking anything at present, the Indians have all left him, the Canadians and soldiers are

[14] Warships with part of armament removed to allow use as transports or supply ships.

[15] François Bigot (1703-77), the corrupt economic czar of Canada.

[16] This convoy was led by Lieutenant Colonel John Bradstreet, a competent British officer. He actually lost between sixty and seventy men and brought back eighty French muskets and two prisoners.

[17] The Marquis de Vaudreuil (1698-1778), governor of Canada.

Journal for 1756

almost all sick, a sickness occasioned by the terrible quality of the rations, just as bad as at the Point[18] and in all the posts. Nevertheless he is maintaining his camp of observation. M. de Vaudreuil is sending a reinforcement of men and supplies. M. de St. Luc[19] left Tuesday with a troop of Indians to rejoin him. The quantity of munitions sent several days ago to Lake Ontario, the detachments of Canadians which left for the same place, the refusal of M. de Vaudreuil for me to rejoin M. de Montcalm, although M. Doreil arrived at this city today, and consequently my duties here cease, the report received by M. de Montcalm that the English no longer appear to be in the neighborhood of the Point; all these reasons make me believe that M. de Montcalm will be recalled here to go to make an attempt on Oswego. This evening a messenger carries him an order to return to Montreal.

Besides, according to the reports of prisoners and deserters, this undertaking will be easy to accomplish. The fort which on this side of the Oswego River is only a stockaded fort with eight guns of very small caliber; there are only 250 men in the garrison. This fort once taken, the batteries that would be put in position there would breach the big fort on the other side of the Oswego, which is a simple loopholed rampart. Its strongest point is a sort of earthen hornwork which envelops all the right flank and rear of the fort. There are scarcely six or seven hundred men in the garrison, badly fed, low in spirit, discouraged, ready to desert at the first chance. Two engineers who have been there the last two months have built no new works at the place. That is what they say of the condition of the fort, the importance of which to the English makes me doubt that it may not be in a better state of defense. My guess as to the return of M. de Montcalm in the near future and his destination was verified this evening by the departure of a courier carrying orders for him to return to Montreal.

All these days here there have been Indian councils.

Today I wrote M. de Montcalm and sent him a package of letters.

---

[18] Probably *Pointe à la Chevelure*, Crown Point, where Fort St. Frederic was.
[19] St. Luc de la Corne, famous Indian leader.

I send off tomorrow forty-three men to Frontenac and thirty-eight to the Point. The *Leopard*'s sickness has started to subside; there are scarcely any soldiers in the hospital sick with it. It carried off the captain, first lieutenant, an ensign, the chief surgeon, the chaplain and about sixty men, both soldiers and sailors, of this ship, three officers and about thirty regular soldiers who were on board, a sickness coming, they say, from the antiquity of the ship and the captain's lack of maintainence and provision for ventilation, an unusual sickness in its symptoms and its effects. Several people who have been attacked and cured have remained out of their head. M. Gautier, a skilled doctor, zealous citizen, good physician, correspondent of the Academy of Sciences, died of it, a victim of the care and diligence he gave to the sick.[20]

JULY 11: At noon there arrived at Montreal M. Marin, a colony officer who spent the winter at the post at Stinking Bay,[21] and who led five hundred Indians to Presque Isle, the rendezvous assigned for all the Indians from the Far West.[22] All have decamped, having heard it said that there was smallpox at all our forts. The Indians fear nothing so much as this disease; in fact it treats them cruelly when they are attacked by it, either because of lack of proper care, or because of a susceptibility in their blood. Only the Indians of the Menominee tribe, or the Wild Oats people, to the number of about forty, have, according to their expression, closed their eyes and risked death to come with M. Marin, first to join M. de Villiers, with whom they were in the attack on the English bateaux, and afterwards to go downriver to Montreal. Wild oats are a kind of grain resembling oats, which are used just like rice and which are a very healthful form of nourishment. This plant forms the totem of this nation. The Menominees are always strongly attached to the French. They came in five great birch-bark canoes with six scalps and several prisoners. Arrived opposite to Montreal, the canoes were placed in several lines, they lay to for

[20] This sounds like some sort of influenza brought from France.
[21] Green Bay, Wis.
[22] Bougainville wrote *"pays d'en haut,"* the "country above" or the "high country." Since it was the Far West of those days, I have used this expression.

8

some time, the Indians saluted with a discharge of guns and loud cries to which three cannon shot replied. Afterwards they came ashore and went up to the Chateau in double file, the prisoners in the middle carrying wands decorated with feathers. These prisoners were not maltreated, as is customary upon entering into cities and villages. Entered into M. de Vaudreuil's presence, the prisoners sat down on the ground in a circle, and the Indian chief, with action and force that surprised me, made a short enough speech, the gist of which was that the Menominees were different from the other tribes which held back part of their captures, and that they always brought back to their father all the meat they had taken. Then they danced around the captives to the sound of a sort of tambourine placed in the middle. Extraordinary spectacle, more suited to terrify than to please; curious, however, to the eye of a philosopher who seeks to study man in conditions nearest to nature. These men were naked save for a piece of cloth in front and behind, the face and body painted, feathers on their heads, symbol and signal of war, tomahawk and spear in their hand. In general these are brawny men, large and of good appearance; almost all are very fat.[23] One could not have better hearing than those people. All the movements of their body mark the cadence with great exactness. This dance is [like?] the pyrrhic [dance] of the Greeks. The dance ended, they were given meat and wine. The prisoners were sent off to jail with a detachment to prevent the Algonquins and the Iroquois of the Sault[24] who were at Montreal from knocking them on the head, these Indians being in mourning for the men they had lost.

&· JULY 12 : More bread and wine was given the Menominees. In the evening there arrived a band of ten Chippewas.

&· JULY 13 : The Menominees had a public audience at the

[23] One transcript says "*gais*"—merry, cheerful. The other says "*gras*"—greasy, fat.

[24] Sault St. Louis, or Caughnawaga, a Jesuit mission where dwelled Indians of the Five Nations who had been converted by Jesuit missionaries in the Mohawk Valley and persuaded to move to Canada. Caughnawaga was the center of the smuggling trade between Albany and Canada.

Chateau during which the orator made a long harangue to M. de Vaudreuil to tell him that they alone of all his children had carried out his orders and risked the smallpox and the enemy, that the other nations had held back, perhaps as much because of not wishing to strike at the English at Oswego, for whom they still held a secret inclination, as through fear of the disease. As for them, nothing could have kept them back, despite the fact that they had not been the best treated of the Indians. They complained that in a visit made the previous year to carry presents to the nations of the back country they had been neglected. The answer to this speech was put off until the next day, and they were given bread and wine. On their own initiative they stationed two Indians as sentries at the Chateau door with orders to stop all Indians of their nation from entering while the General was at table.

M. de St. Luc gave them a belt of wampum[25] in the name of the Abnakis, Algonquins, and Iroquois of the Sault to exhort them to come with them to strike the English at Oswego. They accepted the belt and declared that they would come with them to partake of this meat which they had already tasted. M. de St. Luc left this evening.

Yesterday there arrived another band of twelve Chippewas, who were given an immediate audience.

JULY 14 : News was received from the Point that two boats loaded with wheat had been attacked at the extremity of Lake Champlain and at Otter Creek by a party of English, perhaps with a few Indians included. There were six men in each boat, who probably were made prisoners except for one found dead and scalped in one of the boats. Complaints continue more loudly than ever about the lack of provisions and of the bad quality of the little that there is at Fort St. Frederic.[26] M. de Montcalm is expected by the end of the week.

[25] The word *collier* is used—collar, but usually a belt is meant, although wampum collars were also used.
[26] At Crown Point.

Journal for 1756

JULY 15 : M. de Rigaud[27] left today with MM. de Lévis, de Courtemanche and de Ligneris to take command of the camp of M. de Villiers where the Indians and the Canadians who have been sent daily are supposed to go. The body which constitutes this camp will be an army of observation, if they lay siege to Oswego.

In the afternoon the Menominees came to hear the answer to their speech of the thirteenth and to take their leave. The answer consisted of thanks for their zeal in coming despite the smallpox, eulogies of their valor in M. de Villiers' last stroke, for which those who had distinguished themselves would receive medals and gorgets, word of presents which would be sent to their villages, exhortation to follow M. de Rigaud on his expedition, claiming that they would go very little out of their way if they returned by way of Toronto, and, lastly, prayers that they should not respond to the bad advice of those who wished to destroy their obedience to their fathers' orders. To confirm these last two propositions, they were given two wampum belts which were put at the feet of the two principal chiefs.

The Menominee orator then got up, gave thanks for the presents, accepted the belts, and promised that all would follow M. de Rigaud except a few who would stay behind to take care of their wounded and sick. He asked for new canoes, for food to take them to Toronto and from there to the Bay, and an outfit such as they were usually given. All these were granted to them. M. de Vaudreuil then gave two medals, one larger and the other smaller, and consequently one more honorable than the other, to two warriors, and himself put the ribbon around their necks; he also gave eight gorgets. The medals carried one one side the imprint of the King with the ordinary exergue, on the other a French warrior and an Indian shaking hands with these words [*omitted in MS*]:

This ceremony accomplished, M. Marin, gathering up the belts, sang the war song for M. de Vaudreuil, the Indians keeping time with a guttural inhalation. Then he gave the belts back to the two first chiefs, who had also sung their war songs one after the other.

[27] Rigaud de Vaudreuil (1703–79), brother of the governor of Canada.

A third sang after them, the assembly was over, and the Indians withdrew, carrying away the scalps, the wands decorated with feathers, a kind of trophy, and the banners they had stored with M. de Vaudreuil. They will be outfitted tomorrow and will leave the next day under the leadership of M. Marin.

JULY 16: M. Mercier, the Canadian artillery commander, arrived this afternoon from the Point, having left Carillon yesterday morning. He reported that M. de Montcalm slept today at St. Frederic, so he should be expected on Sunday evening or Monday. No news that the English are making any move in this area. They sent a small detachment in pursuit of a party which stopped two bateaux on Otter Creek.[28] It appears certain that General Johnson[29] has gone to the Five Nations to try to get them to raise the hatchet against us and to come to war with him. The General has been adopted by these tribes, speaks their language, has their manners and style, is painted in war paint like them. He even has a cabin in their villages. It is to be feared that part of the warriors will follow him.

JULY 17: Received news from Frontenac. Our sailing vessels left Sunday to go to Niagara to hunt for a party of the Béarn regiment and of the artillery, the rest will come in the bateaux that have been sent for that purpose. Sunday a detachment of two hundred men and five lieutenants of La Sarre, Guyenne and Béarn left Frontenac to join M. de Villiers. M. Descombes, engineer, went with this detachment. His mission is to reconnoiter Oswego and to report on its condition, if he can get near to it.

The Canadians at M. Villiers' camp are almost all sick. The greater part are already in the hospital at Frontenac and more come there every day. This sickness is caused by the bad quality of the salt pork and flour. Moreover, not having at Frontenac enough ovens, nor bakers to make biscuits ahead of time, they can only make them in accordance with their immediate needs. Thus they

---

[28] River entering Lake Champlain at Vergennes, Vt.
[29] Sir William Johnson (1715–74).

Courtesy McCord Museum of
McGill University, Montreal

Louis Antoine de Bougainville—
"I shall always ask for first call on him
whenever I am charged with a particular task."

Portaging, an important aspect of the campaigns.

Journal for 1756

are put in barrels while still warm and reach M. Villier's camp all moldy. The Intendant in order to remedy this inconvenience should always issue out a sufficient number of portable ovens. The works at Frontenac progress slowly. Since nothing is in shape, neither storehouses, nor artillery, nor fortifications, nor timber cut, everything distracts the workmen, who are very few in number. While waiting, the wheat, the grain, and the powders are divided up. The hospital perhaps will not be finished this year. Altogether everything appears to be little advanced. May God grant that the expedition they propose shall succeed. The enemy will be chased away from a post very advantageous to them both for war and as a depot for trade, and especially we shall be rid of great source of embarassment.

JULY 18 : M. Marin left with the Menominees; all wished to follow him except the wounded. Today a deputation of Iroquois from the Sault came to compliment the Intendant on his arrival at Montreal.

JULY 19 : The Marquis de Montcalm arrived at Montreal this morning. He has made complete dispositions for defensive action in the region of Carillon. The Chevalier de Lévis commands there. His position is a touchy and delicate one, for he should have five thousand men in order to make a good defense, and he has at most only two thousand, of which fourteen hundred are regulars, the rest militia and Indians. There are now four hundred on the way to reinforce him. The fort at Carillon will not be safe to risk a garrison in for another six weeks.

M. Mercier left this morning for Frontenac to get the artillery prepared.

JULY 20 : Received news from Quebec that MM. de Brugnon and de la Rigaudière, one commanding the frigate *Sirène*, the other the *Licorne*, have been ordered to sail and attack two English frigates in position at Isle St. Jean.

JULY 21 : I left Montreal with the Marquis de Montcalm at

half-past four this evening. We reached Lachine, where we spent the night, at half-past seven. Lachine is three leagues from Montreal. It is the place where one embarks for all voyages to the west, the river not being navigable from Montreal to this place. A canal from Montreal to Lachine has been proposed to supply this deficiency.

July 22 : Left Lachine at half-past five in five bateaux, each with a crew of ten men, halted at eight at the Dorval Islands in Lachine Parish, which is two leagues long, then made the passage of Châteauguay, and of Isle Perrot, on which league-long island we dined. Made the Cascade passage on foot through undergrowth, and slept at Pointe à Coulonge, after making eight leagues during the day.

For all this distance the navigation is very difficult, but there is the most beautiful scenery in the world. The river is full of well wooded islands and its channel obstructed with rocks as well as restricted by these islands. There are waterfalls and almost continuous rapids for nearly forty leagues. At the Cascades the river divides into two branches, the northern one called "La Grande Rivière" or "River of the Ottawas," and it is by following it that one goes to Michilimakinac; the other branch leads to Frontenac and to the Illinois country by way of the lakes. The land which separates the two branches is a great peninsula three hundred leagues long, which extends as far as Detroit. This land at its greatest width is twenty-four leagues wide.

At the Cascades there is a parish called St. Joseph, some twelve leagues long, extending to Pointe au Baudet. It is a manor belonging to M. de Longueuil; the land is excellent. On the south side of this same island starting also at the Cascades is a manor belonging to M. de Vaudreuil, which has the same extent as that of M. de Longueuil. There is no church; the inhabitants go to that of The Lake of the Two Mountains, a journey of a league. From Lake St. Francis up to Isle Perrot this branch of the river, full of waterfalls and rapids, never freezes. The lake and the continuing river extend up to the foot of the Long Sault, which is six leagues long. Lake

Journal for 1756

St. Francis is seven leagues long and is seven leagues from the Cascades. The trees in all these parts are admirable, many of them suitable for ship building. It is a shame that so fine a countryside should be without cultivation.

Arrived at our sleeping place at half-past four. It is a very hard day's journey and one that they usually take two days to make.

JULY 23: Left Pointe à Coulonge at six and on foot as far the head of the Cedars portage, a distance of three-quarters of a league. The portage is covered by a little stockaded fort called the "Fort of the Cedars" and almost abandoned. Continued on foot as far as Pointe au Bluet.

Re-embarked and proceeded to Coteau du Lac where there is a portage of two or three arpents[30] past Pointe au Diable. The waterfall at Coteau du Lac is one of the hardest to pass. It is three leagues from Pointe à Coulonge. We arrived there at half-past eleven and dined. Started off again at half-past two, got on to the lake again a league from Coteau du Lac at quarter of four; passed by the painted[31] trees. We set our sails upon entering the lake, with a light wind from the northeast. Passed by Bateaux Cove and Pointe aux Foins. The inhabitants of the Cedars come here to make hay, which they come for during the winter over the ice. Baudet River and Baudet Cove where we camped, a nice camp site even for three battalions. We got there at a quarter-past six in the evening. From this cove to the end of the lake it is three leagues. Made eight leagues today.

JULY 24: Left at half-past four, passed Anchorage Point, Pointe à la Morandière, Isle au Raisin, stopped to dine at Les Chenaux, about three leagues from the entrance of the Lake. From there one could see Fort St. Regis, which is on Rivière à la Mine. This fort is stockaded, built last year. There is a Jesuit mission there where some of the Iroquois have started to come. Left at two,

---

[30] An arpent was 190 feet. It was also a measure of area, about one and one-half acres.

[31] "*Matachés*"—war painted. Probably trees with trunks painted with Indian symbols.

passed Pointe Molène, Pointe au Mai, the ⸺ River, Isle à la Savate, camped at six above Les Milles Roches, made ten leagues during the day.

JULY 25 : Passed Le Moulinet at five o'clock, Isle aux Têtes, so called because of an execution M. de Frontenac had carried out there, the big shallow, the little channel of Long Sault, the Rigolet, walked the Long Sault while the bateaux were hauled up, then passed the Great Camp, Fer à Cheval Pointe, the big eddy, St. Marie Stream and Point, dined by Isle aux Chats. Left at half-past two, passed the great rocks, many nameless points, the flat rapid and camped there, made nine leagues.

JULY 26 : At five o'clock passed Pointe à Colas, One Eyed Man's Point, St. Marie Stream, Iroquois Point, Presque Isle, Cardinal's Point, Les Galops, where we dined. Started again at half-past two, passed Pole Cove, so named because the river is now free from rapids as far as Frontenac so the boatmen no longer need poles and throw them away here. Drunkard's Point, Isle aux Galops, Pointe Galette, Fort Presentation,[32] where we arrived at half-past four and where we spent the night.

The King had forbidden any French post being built above the Long Sault. The Abbé Piquet,[33] able missionary, known for a voyage he made to France with three Indians, obtained a twelve-arpent concession above La Galette. Five years ago he built a fort of squared posts, flanked by four strong bastions, palisaded without and with a water-filled ditch. Beside the fort is the village of a hundred fires, each that of an Iroquois chief, all warriors. Each of these chiefs costs the King about one hundred crowns. They have made a clearing, have cows, horses, pigs, and hens. They plant Indian corn and last year sold six hundred minots[34] of it.

[32] Present Ogdensburg, N. Y.

[33] François Piquet (1708–81), a most energetic Sulpician missionary to the Indians. In 1749 he established the mission and military post of La Présentation and was virtually both its clerical and its military commander. Six times he accompanied his Indians to battle.

[34] A minot was slightly over a bushel.

Journal for 1756

Abbé Piquet teaches them and drills them in the French military exercises.

His assistant is Abbé Chevalier Terley, called Chevalier Terley because of his warlike disposition. There is in the fort a captain of colonial troops as commander, but all real control is ecclesiastical. They plan to transplant here all of the Five Nations that can be won over to France.

There arrived at the fort at the same time as we did seven of this fort's Indians, sent last year as deputies to the Five Nations. They brought back with them forty ambassadors of the Oneidas and Onondagas, who came, I believe, to assert their neutrality. Every day is passed in council with one or the other. They will leave day after tomorrow for Montreal. There have arrived at Niagara deputies of the Cayugas and the Senecas. They came with M. de Joncaire,[35] an officer of colony troops, our ambassador to these tribes.

The Menominees have joined us here and follow us as far as Frontenac and farther if we can make them stay with us.

JULY 27: This morning the Presentation Indians sang the war song, and were given a cow and a cask of wine for their war feast.

We left at half-past eight. The Iroquois were lined up under arms in the French manner, one of them beating a salute very well, and saluting the General with a triple discharge of musketry.

Passed Pointe au Baril three leagues from La Galette and dined.

Camped about five leagues from Pointe au Baril, made eight leagues.

JULY 28: Left at five o'clock, passed Toniato Peninsula, The Little Narrows, or Pointe au Baptême, so called because of a baptism carried out there as they do on the Grand Banks[36] (notice in

---

[35] Son of a French officer and a Seneca mother, he was skilled as an ambassador to the Indians and as an interpreter.

[36] French naval ships, when reaching the Grand Banks, had a ceremony like that of crossing the Equator. Father Neptune came aboard, neophytes got a dunking, and the captain ransomed his ship with wine for the crew.

passing all the naval customs established in this colony), the Thousand Islands, dined half a league from Corbeau Bay. Then passed Corbeau Bay, Isle aux Citrons, where we stopped until six in the evening because of the heat. Camped at Cochois Island at half-past eight.

᚛ JULY 29 : Left at four o'clock, passed the little rock, Isle aux Cèdres, where there is a guard, Montreal Point, where there is another, entered Catarakoui Bay,[37] and reached Fort Frontenac at ten in the morning.

List of Guards

On road to Little Cataraqui	1 Capt., 1 Sgt., 20 men.
At Pointe Montreal	1 Lieut., 1 Corp., 12 men.
At Little Cataraqui	1 Sgt., 1 Corp., 8 men.
At storehouses	1 Corp., 8 men.
At Isle aux Cèdres	1 Corp., 4 men.
At headquarters orderly room	1 Corp., 4 men.

Camp Frontenac
Orders and Journal, 29–30 July
St. Charles and Milan
Regular Duty

The brigade major tomorrow will report the condition of all posts, the strength of troops, and the number of bateaux. He will assign all militiamen to brigades and report their strength.

The artillery commander will report the state of the party held for M. de Montcalm. The brigade major will have the militia units equalized to simplify distribution of rations. The part of the Béarn regiment now here will tomorrow draw bread for three days, Guyenne day after tomorrow.

M. de Rigaud's camp will be rationed through August 8. La Sarre regiment, which marches this morning to join it, is rationed to the thirteenth. M. Landrieff, commissary for rations, to work diligently on the two ovens that he has promised to finish by Monday.

The four ovens now working [are] to make 3,500 rations per day, the six which cannot start until Tuesday will make 5,500. There are 120 sacks of biscuit, making 4,000 rations of a pound and a half each.

---
[37] Site of present Kingston, Ontario, and at this period of Fort Frontenac.

Journal for 1756

M. Landrieff will report tomorrow evening on the required daily rations including officers, servants, and Indians.

M. Descombes will present a signed report of the necessary tools that he expects to load. M. Arnoux, surgeon major, will report the sick and the convalescents and a memorandum of his plans for the hospital at Frontenac and for the field hospital, as well as the number of bateaux which he requires.

[The Journal resumes]

M. de Montigny, officer of colonial troops, is in charge of so-called *Voyageurs* of the West who have come here for the expedition.

M. de Rigaud, who commands the observation camp, has been notified of M. de Montcalm's arrival at Frontenac, directed to build ovens and bake plenty of biscuits, to have war parties, without getting himself committed, attack or harry every convoy going to Oswego, and asked where the two parties will join, whether by Isle aux Galops or at Niaouré Bay,[38] and told to send the bateaux, and that if the sailing vessels arrive the thirtieth or thirty-first, it will be possible to leave Frontenac on the fifth.[39]

M. de Rigaud in his letter of the twenty-seventh said that he had 152 sacks of biscuits which should make 5,000 rations, 70 kegs of salt pork of 45 pounds apiece, 30 bags of peas, and 38 quarters[40] of flour. He had 589 men, colony troops and militia, 120 Indians, and three light companies[41] from La Sarre, Guyenne, and Béarn.

Reached Frontenac at half-past ten. We found that La Sarre regiment had left that morning to join M. de Rigaud's camp at Niaouré Bay. M. Descombes returned here yesterday from his reconnaisance to Oswego. He made it without any opposition on the enemy's part. Part of the Béarn regiment, although it left Niagara a week ago, has not got here yet, which commences to be disturbing.

---

[38] Sackets Harbor, N. Y.

[39] For some reason several orders of the day were copied into the journal.

[40] A quarter (*quart*) was about 250 pounds. It probably can be best thought of as a barrel.

[41] At this period each battalion usually had one company of grenadiers and one light company used for scouting and similar purposes.

🙵 July 30–31 : St. Roch and Montpellier. Rallying cry for the posts: Victory.

Continuing assignment of the militia by brigades and as much as possible by parishes, counted guns in bad condition, convalescents, sick, [and] cripples, in both the militia and the Guyenne regiment, destined to remain at Frontenac. The state of the artillery and the munitions has been settled this evening with M. Mercier.

> 14,400 cannon shot
> 270,000 musket shot for 1,200 Frenchmen
> 400,000 musket shot for 1,800 militia and Indians

On departure the soldiers will have only full cartridge boxes, the militia and the colony troops are to have half a pound of powder and a pound of balls each.

> Provision for field hospital   2 bateaux
> For the artillery   101 bateaux on which

will depart 400 troops as well as the 400 militia who man them.

M. de la Pauze tomorrow will make a count of all the workers, carpenters, armorers, joiners, pit sawyers, and will form them into companies. He will take care to arrange with Sieur Pilet for the assembly of the ten artillery wagoners in order to send them the day after tomorrow along with the horses to Niaouré Bay.

Order to M. Landrieff to arrange for the rations and the ovens for the expedition up to September 1, and to make a signed report on this matter to M. de la Pauze.

It is forbidden to give a gun even to those without one until after landing. Then the 150 grenadier muskets for the militia and colony troops, the 200 muskets of ordinary caliber for the soldiers and French troop [may be issued].

Sieur Godin will leave tomorrow at nine o'clock to carry dispatches to the Marquis de Vaudreuil in a six-man canoe, and he will take back two English deserters.

M. de Aubesprie, captain in Béarn regiment, will leave tomorrow at daybreak in a canoe with six men and six soldiers to go as

Journal for 1756

far as Baie de Coui[42] to make a reconnaisance in the lake and look for news of the Béarn regiment.

JULY 30 : The eight sailors from the *Leopard*, come from Quebec, [assigned] to M. Mercier to act as cannoneers, and all the calkers employed on the repair of the boats to be distributed among the batteries.

Bateaux as of morning of 30th	137
Arrived that day	14
Canoes for carrying messages, not including those of 165 *voyageurs*	6

In the morning an Indian council to [try to] hold the thirty Menominees. Pork, wine, tobacco, vermilion, and eighteen strings of wampum, to a value of forty pistoles, since yesterday. They will end up by leaving after all. In the afternoon they sang the war song and have qualified this ceremony by praying to the Master of Life. They asked for a dog, because they dreamed that one would bring them good luck in war. A child of six danced without a breechclout because they do not give one until a child is ten. After the defeat of the barges,[43] his parents gave him an Englishman to kill to stop him crying. Three days ago they took an Englishwoman prisoner. Her reception was to be turned over to the Indian women, who treated her humanely enough, only giving her a shower of blows with sticks.

[Order of the Day]
From 31 July to 1st August
St. Jacques and Madrid

Colonel for Picket Duty: ——
M. de Bourlamaque proposed once for all for Lieutenant Colonel. M. de l'Hôpital, who will go off picket duty when the guard is relieved.

The officers are warned that upon leaving they will carry only a two-by-two tent, a portmanteau or a small chest, a single mattress, one sheepskin per officer, and one kitchen hamper for at least four

[42] Near Picton, Ontario, and some thirty-five miles southwest of Frontenac.
[43] This is probably Bradstreet's battle mentioned in the July 10 entry.

officers, wine for twenty days. No hen or turkey coops to be taken.

For the hospitals only freshly salted beef will be taken, as well as rice, wine, brandy, lard, brown sugar, prunes, and with medicines, linen, bandages, and eight large duck tents for the field hospital. M. Arnoux will go with the three regimental surgeon majors and a surgeon's boy.

Tomorrow at five in the morning the militia to be reviewed. Béarn regiment tomorrow will report its effective strength, its sick and convalescents, its munitions, and its arms that need repairs.

All troops, including the militia, tomorrow will take four days' bread, provided that all shall be paid up to July 4.

JULY 31 : The Béarn regiment arrived at three o'clock. The cause of its delay was heavy winds, which obliged them to give up at Toronto and return to Niagara, which they left yesterday morning.

The navigation of Lake Ontario is quite dangerous and difficult. The least wind makes it rough, the waves are short and frequent, and in heavy weather one gets tireder than on the open sea. Besides there are almost no harbors or sheltered places.

M. Godet left at eight this morning to carry dispatches to Montreal.

Fourteen bateaux *"du cent"*[44] arrived here.

     Order of 1–2 August
     St. Pierre and Pézenas
Officers of the Picket Guard
     M. de Bourlamaque, colonel
     M. de Fonbonne, lieutenant colonel

Tomorrow all the habitants who have been reviewed will assemble, namely, the four brigades of artillery, the first two at five in the morning, the other two at six. M. Mercier will have them taken opposite the works, will examine their arms, have each fire one shot, and see that each brigade chief makes a record of the arms of his brigade.

M. Wolf, officer of partisans, will assemble his three brigades at five o'clock for the same purpose. M. Carpentier, the other partisan

---

[44] "Of the hundred"–? Perhaps a definition of size.

officer, at the same time will form up his two along the exterior front of the works.

At one in the afternoon the officers and sailors attached to the artillery park will be assembled for the same arms inspection.

M. de Portneuf, officer of colonial troops, at seven o'clock will assemble his detachment which was on the barges for this same inspection, which he will make himself. He will make a report to the brigade major.

Each of these detachments will be dismissed after inspection. All colony troops and militia tomorrow will take three days' rations, the cannoneers, workers, and sailors attached to the artillery at five, at six the detachment of M. Portneuf, Sieur Laforce's men, the detachments of MM. de Montigny and Marin, at seven the two first brigades attached to the artillery, at nine the other two, at eleven M. Wolf's three brigades, which he will lead himself with his sergeant, at one in the afternoon the last two brigades lead by M. Carpentier.

The Guyenne and Béarn regiments will assemble at seven at the head of their camps to pass in review. The Menominees will be alerted to be on the left where they will also pass in review. All soldiers and militia are forbidden to fire their weapons on the pretext of emptying them. They must unload with a worm.[45]

Each brigade commander will assign his bateaux in accordance with the list given him.

Since the magazine guards are essential, they will be increased by eight men and a lieutenant.

᚛ AUGUST 1 : Left Catarakoui for M. de Rigaud's camp, which is twelve leagues away, on August 1 at half-past eight and proceeded until midnight.

᚛ AUGUST 2 : Left at three o'clock, stopped at six at Isle aux Chevreuils. Started again at eleven and reached camp at four.

Found M. de St. Luc, just returned from the south.

At nine o'clock the Indians reported two English vessels in the vicinity of Isle aux Galops. Eight canoes and 140 Canadians and

---

[45] A corkscrew-like attachment which fastened to the end of the ramrod and allowed removal of the charge from a muzzle-loading weapon. Worms were also made in large sizes for use in cannon.

Indians went to look for them but found nothing. Passed the night among the islands and returned to camp at eight in the morning of August 3.

🦢 August 4 : Left at nine in the morning for Catarakoui and continued without stopping. Set sail at three leagues from Catarakoui and reached the fort at half-past four.

Left at nine in the evening with M. de Montcalm, the *voyageurs*, Montigny at their head, and the engineers. Stopped at midnight at Isle aux Chevreuils.

🦢 August 5 : Remained on the island until three in the afternoon, along with the Guyenne regiment, an artillery brigade. M. de Bourlamaque and M. de l'Hôpital left this morning at half-past four.

Started off again at three and arrived alone at the camp at nine in the evening.

🦢 August 6 : M. de Montcalm arrived at seven o'clock with M. de Montigny, the *voyageurs*, and the Menominees.

In the afternoon a council of the Nipissing, Abnaki, Algonquin, and Iroquois nations, united in a war feast. Then they sang the war song.

🦢 August 7 : At nine in the morning the first division of the army, which had left Catarakoui on the fifth, reached here. At ten an Indian war party set out.

At four a detachment of twenty Indians left for the Oswego River to try to intercept couriers using this route between Oswego and Albany.

🦢 August 8 : At eight departed the army's advanced guard composed of four hundred colonial troops and all the Indians under the orders of M. de Rigaud. They are to go part way by land.

At two the second division of the army and the heavy artillery arrived.

A canoe sent off to Frontenac.

🦢 August 9 : The first division of the army left at five to cook

Journal for 1756

rations at the Rivière aux Sables, five leagues from Niaouré Bay. Arrived at two o'clock this morning at Cabin Bay where the advanced guard of the army arrived at two o'clock this morning. This bay is three leagues from Oswego. MM. Mercier and Desandrouins have returned from a reconnaissance for a proper place for a landing at a place called La Petite Anse, half a league from Oswego. I have always gone with the advance guard of Indians, Kisensik[46] at their head.

AUGUST 10 : Canoe arrived from Montreal, another sent to M. de l'Hôpital, who today should have left Niaouré with the second division and the artillery, telling him to come as far as Rivière à la Famine, six leagues from Oswego, and to await orders there.

The advance guard, still under the orders of M. de Rigaud, left at ten on foot to go through the woods without being seen to take a position at La Petite Anse to cover the landing of the first division, which should start moving at seven this evening in order to arrive during the night.

Canadian and Indian canoes sent to lie in wait at the great point of Oswego to observe the movements of the English barges.

Their return at two o'clock was at the same time as that of a party of Indians who went on the war path a few days ago. Toward eleven o'clock today they made a coup between the two forts, that is to say, killed two men whose scalps they brought back. The officer who was with them reported that the English were working to build embankments around Fort Ontario and that they also were doing much digging at the other fort.

Another canoe sent to M. de l'Hôpital to tell him to come forward with the artillery to join us at La Petite Anse.

Eight pieces of cannon.

[There is a gap in the journal for August 11–13, and the following is a brief summary of events during that period. There were three forts at Oswego, the old fortified trading post on the bank of the Oswego River, the poorly designed palisaded Fort Ontario, built in 1755, and the only partially completed Fort Oswego on the high

---

[46] Chief of the Nipissings.

ground west of the river. On August 11 the Canadian troops and the Indians invested Fort Ontario, and the next day the regular troops arrived with the artillery train. The trenches were commenced that night, and the following day was devoted to a brisk artillery fire by the British, the French artillery not yet being in position. Just before nightfall the British abandoned Fort Ontario and retreated to the unfinished Fort Oswego. On the fourteenth the French commenced cannonading the ramshackle old blockhouse, and succeeded in killing Colonel Mercer, the commanding officer.]

᪷ August 13 : Workers have been ordered immediately to build a road for the artillery and to start building a battery to fire against Oswego. They are to work on this battery all night.

᪷ August 14 : The enemy fired briskly during the entire night and especially towards morning. Our battery was very late in firing and then only with very few pieces. M. de Rigaud ordered to go with the Canadians and Indians and cross the river three-quarters of a league upstream and to harass the enemy. I have been detached to cross the river with him and at noon to summon the enemy to surrender.

At nine Colonel Mercer who commanded at Oswego was killed.

An hour later the enemy hoisted a white flag and two officers came to make proposals for surrender. I have been sent to propose the articles and to remain as a hostage. The articles are that the garrison will be prisoners of war, that the officers and soldiers take away their baggage and will be taken to Montreal to be exchanged. The place to be evacuated at once and the garrison placed inside Fort Ontario. M. de Bourlamaque named commander at Oswego with a garrison of three hundred men.

Taken at this place ——— cannon, ——— mortar, three armed vessels of ——— and ——— cannon and two armed bateaux, much provisions, munitions of all sorts, and about 1,700 prisoners. About 80 English killed and 30 of ours.[47]

---

[47] The Indians massacred the wounded and some of the prisoners to a total of from fifty to perhaps almost one hundred, but both Bougainville and Montcalm failed to record the fact.

Journal for 1756

ಶ್ AUGUST 15 : Two hundred and twenty-eight prisoners left [today].

The officers and the women sent to Montreal in forty bateaux. Action taken to demolish the forts and to take away the artillery and all munitions.

News brought by Indians that an English relief force was on the way to Oswego. Observers sent to reconnoiter the enemy and verify this news.

Our two armed vessels appeared this morning off Oswego and entered the port at four o'clock.

ಶ್ AUGUST 16 : Continued the demolition and the loading of the artillery and munitions into the vessels. We have moved and now have our right on Fort Ontario and the left slanting across the woods, a position taken more suitable for our needs and more prepared for the enemy should they wish to come.

ಶ್ AUGUST 17 : I was sent this morning to reconnoiter the road through the woods which leads to the Five Nations. Found several brushed out, but one which I followed for some distance was well marked with wheel tracks and seemed to me to be the true road.

32 prisoners left today. Abbé Piquet arrived with several Indians. The Menominees left this morning.

M. de Langy has returned from his reconnaisance. He went five or six leagues beyond the portage and saw nothing.

Three of the captured vessels took off this evening loaded with artillery and shot.

ಶ್ AUGUST 18 : I have been sent to explore the coast the other side of the Oswego River, to sound the anchorages and bays suitable for a landing. Several Indians of the Five Nations have arrived, presumably to observe our movements. They only learned upon their arrival here of the capture of Oswego.

Fort George[48] burned as well as a vessel still on the stocks. The entrenched camp destroyed, all vessels taken off, and all loadings completed. Prisoners left for Montreal.

[48] The old fortified trading post.

◈ August 19 : Today all the rest of the prisoners were sent away. All the vessels have gone off with their cargoes. Fort Ontario was destroyed during the night.

◈ August 20 : The stockade of the fort has been set on fire and the stone house of Oswego filled with wood and combustible material.

This morning they planted a cross with this inscription:
In hoc signo vincunt
and a post with the arms of France with this:
Manibus date lilia plenis.[49]

At noon Chabert de Joncaire arrived with fifty Indians of the Five Nations, coming from Niagara with the intentions of hitting the English. They will come, I think, to the Point. Today they completed all demolitions and set fire to everything that had not been demolished, to a bark still on the ways and to all the barges and bateaux that could not be taken away.

◈ August 21 : The departure of all the army at seven o'clock in the morning to return to Montreal; proceeded as far as Rivière Au Sable. Camped at this river, La Sarre being the regiment on the right of this river and Guyenne and Béarn on the left.

◈ August 22 : The weather being very bad, we were not able to leave before nine o'clock. The lake was very rough. The last bateaux were very late in arriving at Niaouré Bay. At seven o'clock in the evening the troops were ranged in order of battle at the head of their camp and the *Te Deum* was sung, followed by three rounds of musketry. It is at Niaouré Bay that the different bodies of troops must assemble before leaving for their respective destinations.

◈ August 23 : Béarn left at nine o'clock to go to Montreal, leaving a detachment to go to Frontenac. We left at noon and the violence of the wind forced us to go ashore that evening at Isle aux Chevreuils; we spent the night in bivouac.

[49] "Give lilies freely."

Oswego, scene of Montcalm's first victory.
From an old print.

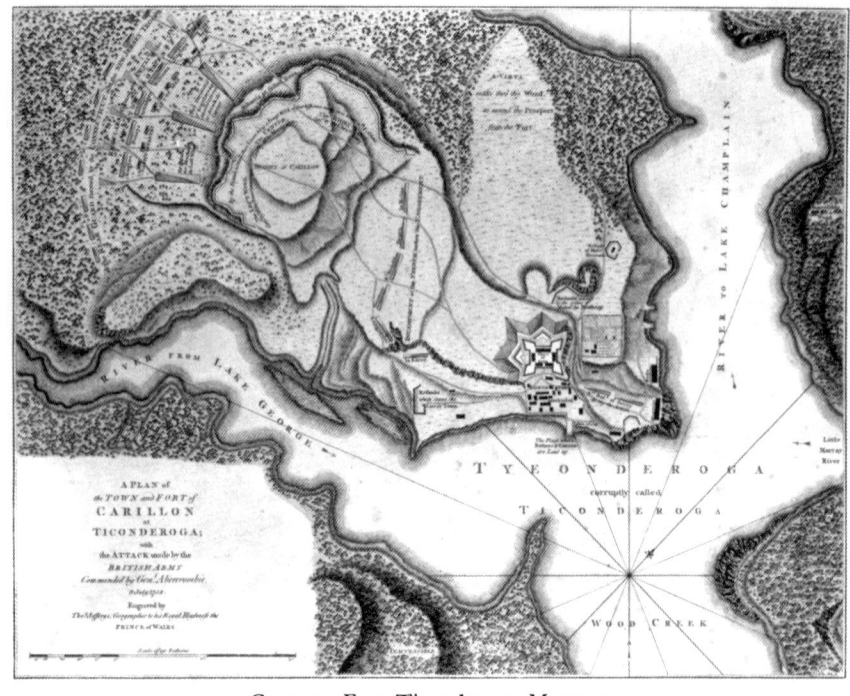

Courtesy Fort Ticonderoga Museum

French and English dispositions at Fort Carillon.
From an old print by Jefferys.

Journal for 1756

&❧ AUGUST 24 : Left at four o'clock in the morning with a good southwest wind; at nine o'clock met a canoe sent by M. Vaudreuil. Stopped an hour to answer his dispatches. News from France of the battle of our fleet in the Mediterranean, of the singular fight of the ship *Aquilon* and the frigate *Fidele* against an English sixty-four and a frigate of thirty guns near the tower of Chassison; of the declaration of war made by the English King; of the treaty concluded with the Queen of Hungary.

News of English preparations aimed at Lac St. Sacrement, of the arrival of Lord Loudoun[50] with five hundred Scotsmen at New York who were proceeding, they say, in this same direction, obliging us to speed up our march towards this frontier. There are only two hundred leagues to go. At ten o'clock reached La Presentation and had supper with Abbé Piquet.

&❧ AUGUST 25 : I left all alone, sent on ahead at one o'clock; took an Indian for a guide through the falls. I proceeded without stopping as far as the Buisson where I slept, nightfall not permitting me to pass the rapids.

&❧ AUGUST 26 : Left at daybreak, reached Montreal at ten-thirty, the wind being northeast and of great violence.

M. de Montcalm arrived at six o'clock in the evening; Béarn reached La Chine at seven o'clock where it camped. Guyenne reached there the next day.

&❧ AUGUST 27–SEPTEMBER 4 : The regiments of Guyenne and Béarn have passed La Prairie in succession. Two hundred men of Béarn have repaired the road from La Prairie to St. John and these two battalions embarked there for Carillon.

The Indians of all the tribes have come to Montreal and left for the Point.

&❧ AUGUST 30 : They sang the *Te Deum* at Montreal for the taking of Oswego; two English flags destined to be hung up in

---

[50] The new British commander in North America. He replaced Massachusetts Governor Shirley, who had succeeded to the command upon the death of General Braddock.

the parish church were presented there by M. de Rigaud and M. de Bourlamaque, after which they were paraded [through the streets].[51]

News received on September 2 of M. Beaussier's fight. The *Héros* alone against two English, one of sixty-four and one of sixty-two guns. He remained master of the field of battle through the flight of the others, which, being disabled, he could not follow. The *Illustre* engaged in the action and went in pursuit of the snow,[52] which it lost in the fog. The *Licorne* and the *Sauvage* were separated by this same fog.

All the English prisoners sent to Quebec.

ಕ್ಕು [SEPTEMBER, 1756] : After M. de Dieskau's affair[53] the Five Nations, seeing how the Mohawks had been treated and fearing resentment from the French, sent ambassadors who went to La Presentation. They made excuses and disavowed the actions of their young men. They were received with firmness by the Marquis de Vaudreuil who assured them that he would treat as enemies all those he found dealing with the English. They gave him belts to insure their neutrality and told him that he should not carry the war to them, that he could carry it to Oswego but not farther. These words were accepted and answered with two belts. Abbé Piquet and M. de Joncaire have been the intermediaries in this negotiation.

Since then, during the whole winter the Marquis de Vaudreuil has had ambassadors among the Five Nations. The Oneidas accompanied M. de Lévis and appeared well disposed towards us. For three months we have been waiting for a reply from some one of our ambassadors. M. de Joncaire is charged with countering Colonel Johnson's negotiations.

The Marquis de Montcalm should not ignore the fact that the

---

[51] Four years later General Amherst recovered these flags at the surrender of New France at Montreal.

[52] A snow is a vessel similar to a brig, but differing in having a trysail mast close abaft the mainmast.

[53] The defeat of the French by William Johnson's army at Lake George the previous year.

Journal for 1756

Iroquois are not favorably disposed towards the English because they have maltreated the Delawares, their nephews.

[There follows a report of the activities of the year 1756 and the taking of Oswego. Both of these have been printed elsewhere in English, and neither adds to the interest of the journal. Also omitted is a list of names of forty-eight bateau men.]

ᛞ SEPTEMBER 4 : Left Montreal at three in the afternoon with M. de Bourlamaque. Reached La Prairie on the other side of the river at seven. There is a badly made stockaded fort there, which is falling in ruins. The day before, a scalp was taken within two leagues of La Prairie. This caused M. de Montcalm to take an escort of fifteen colony soldiers and thirty Ottawa Indians when he went to St. Jean.

ᛞ SEPTEMBER 5 : Left at six in the morning, on foot, on horseback, and by carriage. Reached St. Jean, which is five leagues, at one in the afternoon. The road across the flat land is very bad. It is necessary to rebuild it entirely, drying it out by [drainage] ditches on both sides and by raising the road surface. The cleared lands in this region would appear to be excellent. It is only a matter of employing the ordinary methods of drainage.

St. Jean is a fort built of squared posts with four bastions. The fort is badly built, cost 96,000 francs, and is in bad condition. There is normally a garrison of a captain of colony troops and fifty men. In the port there is a vessel which goes back and forth as convoy to St. Frederic and Carillon.

The Guyenne regiment left at three for Carillon.

ᛞ SEPTEMBER 6 : Order given to hold 12 bateaux for us ready to start at any time. A company of grenadiers with a light company[54] of the Sarre regiment arrived last evening at St. Jean to serve as escort to M. de M[ontcalm].

---

[54] *"Piquet"* in MS, but this refers almost certainly to the light-company concept then in its early days. The *piquet*, while perhaps not so formally organized as it was or soon came to be in the British service, certainly functioned as light infantry.

At eight a habitant living half a league from the fort brought in a Scottish Highlander who came to surrender to him. When questioned, this man stated that he left Albany six weeks ago, passed by Schenectady, Johnson's house,[55] and Fort William [Henry?], from which a detachment of about fifty, four Scots, the rest Indians, had come. They were lost in the woods for ten days, and he was wounded in the leg and abandoned by his people, and hunger had compelled him to come and surrender. This man said that five hundred Scots had come two months ago from O——'s [Otway's?] regiment and that five hundred more were on the way to New York, that Lord Loudoun would arrive three weeks after them to be governor general of the English colonies and commander of all the troops. He [the Scot] was sent on to Montreal.

Indians sent to chase the people who attacked La Prairie returned without finding anything.

Iroquois Indians living at the Sault[56] are suspected to be in communication with the Mohawks.

An ox given to about one hundred and fifty Indians, Iroquois, Chippewas, Ottawas, for a feast and to sing the war song.

꙳ SEPTEMBER 7 : Left St. Jean at seven, stopped at four leagues at Boileau's camp. The General's bateau leaked and was sent back to St. Jean to be exchanged. Storm and rain all day.

꙳ SEPTEMBER 8 : Left at three in the morning, stopped at nine to cook a meal, left again at eleven, reached camp at six. Some Iroquois who accompanied us found signs of Mohawks. They were sent ahead to look for them. They found a dugout and a fire which these Indians had just left and the tracks of three Mohawks. They followed them for a distance of about three leagues. Darkness made them come back without catching any.

Left at nine in the evening, leaving the Indians to beat the woods, proceeded all night, meeting the Guyenne regiment.

[55] At Fort Johnson, near Amsterdam, N. Y.
[56] These were the Caughnawaga Indians, largely Mohawks converted to Christianity by the French and persuaded to move to the Jesuit mission on the south bank of the St. Lawrence, just above Montreal. They were active in smuggling furs to Albany and thus in constant touch with the Iroquois in New York.

Journal for 1756

September 9: Stopped at nine in the morning to eat. At six reached Fort St. Frederic,[57] where the Guyenne regiment had arrived two hours earlier.

The fort is stone with a great redoubt, also of stone, inside it. It is badly located, there being several heights which command it. Within musket range on these heights they have built a redoubt and defensive works of horizontal timbers, works badly made and more harmful than useful. Moreover there is here ground which would make an excellent establishment and one which could be the key point of this frontier. There is normally a garrison of fifty men with a captain. There are several sheds around the fort and below the fort.

Received news that two officers of La Reine regiment were scalped while hunting on the opposite shore at Carillon.

Fort St. Frederic is on Lake Champlain where it contracts.[58]

Now there is a hospital there which takes the sick from the camp at Carillon.

September 10: The Guyenne regiment left at six in the morning for Carillon.

We left at noon and reached Carillon, which is five leagues away, at six in the evening.

September 11: Fort Carillon, commenced last fall, is situated almost at the head of Lake Champlain on a peninsula pointing south which divides the lake from the south bay, and to the north [of] the outlet of Lake George. The fort is square with four bastions of which three are in a defensible state. It is of horizontal timbers. The position is well chosen on a rugged rock formation, but the fort is badly oriented and is not far enough out on the north point of the lake, which has obliged them to make a redoubt at the place where the fort should have been. As for the rest of it they

---

[57] At the west end of present Champlain Bridge, a little north of present Crown Point. Ruins of the base of its walls still remain.

[58] French records often refer to Lake Champlain south of this fort as *La Rivière aux Chicots*, the River of Tree Stumps. Wood Creek at present Whitehall, N. Y., was also so named.

would have done better to take advantage of the rock, breaking it up with a pickaxe and using it for the parapets.

The camp is on the river's edge at the foot of the rocky formation. It is presently composed of the battalions of La Reine, Languedoc, Royal Roussillon, and some colony troops. Guyenne and Béarn are camped half a league away at the Falls of Lake St. Sacrement. From there two roads built through the woods, one on the right, the other on the left, the first leading to the end of the Portage[59] where the Chevalier de la Corne is camped with 600 men. That of the left leads to the same camp and to that of M. de Contrecoeur, 400 men strong, which is half a league beyond the Portage on the left bank of Lake St. Sacrement with a post of 120 men in between. Two well armed bateaux leave this camp every day to watch the movements of the enemy on the lake.

The English have two large camps, one at Fort Lydius[60] on the Hudson River with a water battery, the other at Fort George[61] at the head of Lake St. Sacrement, the two connected by a great road, and consisting [in all] of ten to twelve thousand men of whom the regular troops are five hundred of Colonel Otway's regiment, four hundred and eighty Scottish Highlanders of Murray's regiment with Lieutenant Colonel Grant commanding this corps in America, nine hundred of Abercromby's, eight hundred of Webb's, the rest militia, all under the orders of General Winslow.

They are also raising a regiment which will be commanded by Lord Loudoun, general of all of English North America.

The regiment will be four hundred strong, officers and soldiers almost all Pennsylvania Germans. It will be a royal regiment.[62] According to the reports of prisoners the recruiting has been suc-

---

[59] The portage, or carry, between Lake Champlain and Lake George was about a mile long. The French referred to the upper end at Lake George as the "Portage," the Champlain end as the "Falls."

[60] Fort Edward.

[61] Fort William Henry.

[62] The Sixtieth, or Royal Americans, the only British regiment in which a foreigner could hold a commission. It had many excellent German and Swiss officers in its ranks.

Journal for 1756

cessful. Lord Loudoun has brought the principal officers of this regiment with him. Otway's and Murray's regiments were expected six weeks ago, the one four hundred, the other five hundred men from old England.

The English also have posts at Albany, Schenectady, Johnson's house, Half Moon,[63] and Fort Edward, and they have accumulated a great store of munitions and rations at Fort George.

Johnson concerns himself only with Indian affairs, he is the chief of that department. He has gathered together four or five hundred Indians from the regions of the Delaware, the Susquehanna, Seneca, etc., that we call Moraigans [Mahicans]. We do not know the destination of the Mohawks, to the number of one hundred, who have taken up the hatchet against us.

The enemy occupy almost all the islands in Lake St. Sacrement by entrenched posts. They say that they are making many beams, planks and such. I suspect them to be preparing all the material for a fort to be built at the Portage as soon as we fall back, or early next spring. They have two armed vessels on the lake, two others on the ways, and about two hundred bateaux.

They have little parties of Scottish Highlanders[64] and a few Indians continually observing from the heights and the woods that surround Carillon. I suspect that they have established a flying camp behind the mountains north of the lake which supplies and shelters all these little parties.

In this position of the enemy, we being so much inferior in number, without vessels or boats and no fort on Lake St. Sacrement, it would appear to me to seem impossible to undertake anything of consequence against troops three times greater in number, well established everywhere, and having the support of very good forts. We content ourselves with continually harassing them by raiding parties who recently have succeeded in taking prisoners almost within sight of Boston, by putting ourselves in a state to resist an attack on their part. Our order of battle is laid down in advance,

---

[63] Waterford, N. Y.
[64] Actually Rogers' Rangers.

all orders given for the march and disposition of the various troops, the signals are agreed upon, and I believe that the enemy would be well blocked if he came to attack us. We all wish that he would come, but there is no sign of it.

We have about 180 Indians, all at the Portage and at M. de Contrecoeur's camp.

At six this morning we inspected the posts at the Falls,[65] at the Portage, and those of MM. St. Martin and de Contrecoeur. At this last one there was a council of Indians who leave tomorrow for a raid to make a coup or a reconnaissance. All the country that we have been over, going by the right-hand road and returning by the left, is a country of mountains, precipices, entirely a tricky and dangerous country. Returned to Carillon at two o'clock.

At six the Iroquois who left us on the evening of the eighth to follow the trail they had discovered, returned with two prisoners, a Scottish cadet and a militia captain.

I questioned the former, his deposition is attached below. [*Omitted in MS*] The two men were of the same party as the other Scot brought to St. Jean on the ninth.

About three hundred Indians arrived at the camp this evening, Iroquois, Chippewas, Ottawas.

Indian council of the usual sort. Some reports of Indian scouts seem to confirm what I had suspected and said to the General of a flying camp behind the mountains to the northwest.

SEPTEMBER 12–13 : Nothing new, a few Indians scouting on the lake.

Every day 480 workmen are ordered for the fort of Carillon.

We now have six hundred Indians, and hold a council to send them off in detachments, but it is a long job to get them to make up their minds. It requires authority, brandy, equipment, food and such. The job never ends and is very irksome.

SEPTEMBER 14 : Usual work details and camp services. It had at last been arranged with the Indians that one party would

---

[65] The lower end of the portage at the foot of the discharge of Lake George, where the French built a sawmill.

Journal for 1756

proceed by the bay[66] and the other by Lake St. Sacrement to strike Lydius, George, and the road between the two forts. They were to leave this evening. Several Iroquois who for two days have been out on a scout came back with seven deer they had killed. They invited their brothers to a feast, and behold, everything is off and the departure can wait.

Two pickets of the Béarn regiment arrived from St. Jean.

SEPTEMBER 15 : I have been detached, along with MM. Desandrouins and Mercier[67] to reconnoiter, under the escort of a large party of Indians, the English position in the islands of Lake St. Sacrement and to get as near their forts as possible. Ordered to return if the Indians show signs of slackening and our observations cannot be made with safety.

We returned at six in the evening to M. de Contrecoeur's advanced camp.

The Indians who were supposed to leave this evening did not go, even the destination of the detachment has been changed. None of it goes by the bay. They wish to go all together and by Lake St. Sacrement. The whole detachment, both Frenchmen and Indians, amounts to seven hundred men. If they find some operation to do as a unit, they will not separate, if not, they will break up into little groups, each of which will make a separate strike. It is said that departure is set for tonight, but it is only a rumour, and the caprice of an Indian is of all possible caprices the most capricious.

SEPTEMBER 16 : Indians again determined to leave tonight. At M. de Contrecoeur's camp about one hundred Canadians and four hundred Indians under the command of M. de la Périère, captain of colony troops, embarked at six o'clock. The canoes, thirty-four in number, waited in line behind a point until dusk had fallen.

Indians determine the route, the halts, the scouts, and the speed to make, and in this sort of warfare it is necessary to adjust to their ways.

---

[66] South Bay of Lake Champlain, near Whitehall, N. Y.
[67] M. Mercier, chief of Canadian artillery. He was one of Bigot's crew of grafters.

Went ashore beyond Isle La Barque[68] on the north side. Passed the night in bivouac at the head of the boats. Sent a canoe to reconnoiter in the channel through the islands. It met a small English bateau which was cruising about. It was moonlight. Our canoe lay hidden in shadows cast by the trees and watched the movement of the enemy boat, which almost immediately returned without having seen us. Upon the return of our first canoe another departed at once and did not come back until daylight.

SEPTEMBER 17 : At daybreak a council of the war chiefs of the nations, at the end of which 25 Indians were sent along with three Frenchmen, with orders to separate at a certain distance and one party to go along the shore, the other along the mountains. The Indians were given a telescope to reconnoiter the islands among which they pretend the enemy is established.

We entered the edge of the woods, the canoes remaining on the shore.

On the report of an Indian that he had seen smoke far off, two Abnakis were sent around eleven o'clock to look over the place it came from. They returned at two and reported that after going about a league and a half they had seen several fires on a fairly large island.

At three a part of our first exploring party came back and reported to the chiefs that they had found only old tracks, a fairly good road beyond the first range of mountains and that, having come within sight of Fort George, they only saw the fort imperfectly from a distance.

At half-past five the rest of our scouts returned without having discovered anything except smoke in several of the islands.

After their return a herald went along the shore and summoned the chiefs of the nations to a council. All went to the camp of the Iroquois, who being the greatest in number took the lead without even learning the wishes of the French commander. The chiefs, blankets on their backs and lance in hand, gravely advanced, took

---

[68] Identified by Parkman as Odell Island opposite Sabbath Day Point on Lake George.

Journal for 1756

their places, and smoked the council pipe. The orator explained the purpose of the detachment, the reports of the scouts, and on these matters they deliberated for a long time in the constant presence of a French interpreter. The result was that they sent two canoes out scouting with orders to search the islands, and at nightfall the whole fleet of canoes would leave and camp two leagues beyond on the south shore, and this was done. As for the rest of it, the Indians treated us imperiously, made rules for us to which they did not conform, and one suspected that the Iroquois were not acting in good faith.

SEPTEMBER 18 : Nothing new during the night's march, the islands have been searched, and traces found of old fires. Halted. Stopped toward two in the morning about four leagues from Fort George. Spent most of the night in the canoes. At daybreak sent out scouts as usual.

The council which was held at daybreak decided to make neither any fires nor the least noise. As soon as it broke up the Indians at once did both.

At ten I was with MM. Mercier and Desandrouins and an escort on top of a mountain near our camp from which we saw the whole length of Lake St. Sacrement and the location of Fort George. After this scout we could well believe that it is almost impossible for the enemy to prevent us passing through the lake even if they should set up posts in the islands scattered through it, but we have observed the fort and the entrenched camp from too great a distance to have any certain ideas about them.

The Iroquois appear still to wish to pass the night here and consequently tomorrow's daylight hours. The other nations do not like it. Discord is introduced into the camp of Agramont.[69]

Scouts have come to report that they had seen a canoe go ashore on the north side at a point where they thought they had also seen several tents or huts.

---

[69] A proverbial expression. The Lord is supposed to have ordered St. Michael to sow discord in the army of Agramont, an able chieftain who was attacking Charlemagne.

Resolved to send two canoes at nightfall to reconnoiter this point. They returned at eleven and confirmed the first report. Embarked at once, crossed the lake in complete silence, and halted behind a point a league and a half above where it was believed that the enemy post was.

ᗞ SEPTEMBER 19 : An hour before daybreak we left through the woods to make an attack, leaving a few with the canoes with orders to put out into the lake and to come to us when they heard the first shots. We marched through the woods in several files, the Indians almost naked, all in black and red war paint. We surrounded the suspected point, but found nothing except old fires smoldering in the roots of trees and a few abandoned huts. We at once returned, suspecting that the Iroquois had deceived us, more especially since in order to cut off the retreat of the enemy, if there had been any, it would have been necessary to go ashore beyond the point and not this side of it.

Because of the grumbling of the other nations the Iroquois were deprived of command, and with a common accord 110 Indians, the most nimble of all the detachment, were chosen, who left with a score and a half of the most active Canadians with the intention of going as far as the fort and not returning until they had made a coup.

The canoes were put in the woods with the rest of the detachment to guard them. It was agreed that if the warriors had not returned in two days, it would be proof that they had been hotly pursued and had taken the course of going back to Carillon through the mountains and hence that the canoes could return. They left at eleven o'clock.

Around two o'clock, at about a league and a half from the fort, they suddenly ran into a detachment of thirteen English, whom they immediately attacked. All except one, who [by now] will have carried the news to the enemy, were killed or captured. The Iroquois had two killed or wounded. The Indians on the field of battle performed cruelties even the recital of which is horrible.

Journal for 1756

At noon MM. Mercier, Desandrouins, and I left in a canoe. We reached Carillon at seven.

Lake St. Sacrement runs almost in a straight line from northeast to southwest. Since it is incased within two mountain chains, there are neither waves nor ground swells. Sailing is pleasant there, the shore safe almost everywhere. The mountain chain on the south side continues to the end of the lake. That on the north is interrupted about three leagues from the fort. The country then becomes flat, the woods open, and the English have made a very good trail which continues on behind the mountains.

᠅ SEPTEMBER 20: The Indians returned tonight to M. de Contrecoeur's camp, making a continuous fusillade on the lake. Opposite the camp they lay to and uttered cries of mourning. A canoe going out to them asked the reason for their grief. "Marin is dead (for when they have several dead the head of the party is deemed dead), we are dead." Some words of consolation. Then they made death cries and came ashore shooting off their guns.

At seven M. de Montcalm held a troop review and inspected the camp of M. de la Corne and that of de Contrecoeur.

The Indians have seventeen prisoners; they have already knocked several of them on the head. A detachment of a lieutenant and thirty men ordered to bury the two dead. The cruelties and the insolence of these barbarians is horrible, their souls are as black as pitch. It is an abominable way to make war; the retaliation is frightening, and the air one breathes here is contagious of making one accustomed to callousness.

According to the prisoners' depositions it would appear that the English have not two thousand men at their fort, all militia, many sick, no plan for an offensive, fear of being attacked, that they have had some communication with our Iroquois, that the fort is not finished. That M. Loudoun has not yet come, that they will winter there about one thousand men of which three or four hundred will be regulars, that they have designs for an establishment at the foot of the bay, but that they have put it off for this year, that there is unrest, particularly among the Dutch, and that the regulars do not get along with the militia and Indians.

Two canoes of Indians went off today without telling anyone.

🦢 SEPTEMBER 21 : At five in the morning council held with the Ottawas and the Chippewas; the former, having four prisoners and about five hundred leagues to go to get home, left this evening; the Chippewas say that they have not seen the enemy close to enough and have agreed to leave this evening to make a raid toward Lydius.

At ten o'clock, a council with the Iroquois. At first words of condolence over the losses they have suffered; two complete outfits, called "ouapons," and on each eight strings of beads, called "wampum," covered the dead and dried their tears.

All the Indians, I believe, want to leave, Iroquois, Abnakis, Hurons, Five Nations. Of 450 scarcely 30 will remain. They have made a coup. It is necessary to seek their native hearth. The Canadians feel the same way.

It has been exceedingly hot for several days. It is 27½ degrees [Reaumur=94°F.] at Carillon today. The greatest heat has been 35 degrees [111°F.] at this fort at 43 degrees of latitude. It is surrounded by mountains and rocky cliffs, which concentrate the heat and reflect it back. All this country is full of rattlesnakes; they do not do any harm unless one walks on them or on branches [of bushes] which touch them.

I have had a count made these last few days. We are in all 5,300 men at Carillon and the advanced posts.

🦢 SEPTEMBER 22 : A convoy of some thirty bateaux arrived with M. Bleury, who is the head of the ferrying service. Because of this convoy we are now provisioned up to the tenth of the month. M. de Vaudreuil proposes to form a detachment of two thousand men to engage the enemy in combat in the Canadian manner. I do not know what bait can make people leave a fort who are determined to stay shut up in it, and come out into the woods to fight Canadian style. Our general seems to me to pursue a wiser

Journal for 1756

course, that of not exposing himself to a material set-back or the embarrassment of an enterprise which, undertaken with éclat and ending in nothing, would rate as a defeat in the eyes of friendly and enemy Indians, not suspending for even a month [the work at] Fort Carillon, on the contrary making haste, so that these works will not be the principal occupation of the army next campaign, and at the same time increasing the ferrying of convoys so that this post will have sufficient munitions and supplies so that a lack of them will not hinder an offensive that circumstances might make practicable in the early spring, and so that in case of a forced defense, the enemy, who would then be in force, by intercepting the convoys on Lake Champlain could not make an army camped at Carillon die of hunger.

The *Dunkerquois* should have set sail on September 11. They say that several merchant vessels loaded for Canada have been captured, that by June 7 they had not had news at Bordeaux of the capture of Fort St. Philippe at Mahon, that we have sixty ships at Brest, that the English have fifty in the Channel, that the Prince of Conti at the head of eight thousand men is within reach of Holland, but what trust should one put in these rumours that come from eighteen hundred leagues away?

The battalion of La Sarre goes, says M. de Vaudreuil, to build the road from St. Jean to La Prairie.

At two o'clock nine Indians, who left a day before the big detachment, returned with a scalp taken at Fort George. The Indians are of the Five Nations. They left, and we have here not more than about sixty Indians, Iroquois, Abnakis, and Amalecites. These last are Abnakis established on the River St. Jean.

The news from La Belle Rivière[70] is good. It is not true that the English have evacuated Fort Cumberland,[71] but they have all the country for more than forty leagues beyond this advanced post.

The Chevalier de Villiers has taken Fort Granville,[72] sixty miles

---

[70] The Ohio country, of which Fort Duquesne at the forks of the Ohio was the headquarters.

[71] At the junction of Wills Creek and the Potomac. Present Cumberland, Md.

[72] On the Juniata near Lewistown, Pa.

from Philadelphia. In this fort there was a garrison of sixty men and supplies for six months. The Indians continue to carry consternation into Virginia, Pennsylvania, Maryland, and Carolina. Although they today have more than one hundred leagues to go to find any scalps to lift, this distance does not stop them. The Delawares have burned one of the prisoners taken at Fort Granville to punish him for having several years before assassinated one of his comrades in order to marry his widow. The English have enlisted one thousand men to paint themselves like Indians and make raids into this country.

Today there arrived a reinforcement of twenty-four Iroquois and Nipissing Indians, lead by several officers of colony troops.

All the sick of the army left this evening for the Montreal hospitals.

There was a fire in the camp around four o'clock, but it was put out before night.

SEPTEMBER 23 : The Chippewas who wished to go and see the enemy at close quarters have slunk back, having been only within two leagues [of them].

SEPTEMBER 24 : Cold and rainy weather, the work slowed down. Great negotiations towards sending some Abnakis on a scout to the foot of the bay.

SEPTEMBER 25 : Eighteen Abnaki Indians at last left this morning for the head of the bay; about fifty others, Iroquois and Nipissings, all that are left with us, went forward to M. de Contrecoeur's camp.

SEPTEMBER 25–29 : Nothing new. The weather has become fine and warm.

This evening the Abnakis who had gone on a scout have returned. Nine gave out on starting and took the road to Montreal. The other nine divided into two little parties, one of which found on the Chicot River two dogs which made them suspect that there had been a detachment there or some hunters, and so they came back as fast as they could.

Journal for 1756

Today there arrived at the camp twenty Potawatomis, a nation living near Detroit.

In the spring there are famous foot races at that place. It is the Newmarket of North America. The bets are made with packs of furs by the Indians and merchandise by the French. Sometimes they have as many as two thousand Indians there, some of whom come from six or seven hundred leagues. That is the way to build up a good wind.

SEPTEMBER 30 : Council held with Potawatomis. They have told of all they have done since they left home, the hatchet given them three years ago by M. Péan,[73] their voyage to Niagara, to Frontenac, Montreal, of their scouting trips on Lake Champlain, the intention they have of doing their Father's will here. A council indicated for tomorrow to get down to business.

OCTOBER 1 : Nothing decided in this council. A small party of six Iroquois has gone to make a strike near Fort George and to carry to within sight of the fort letters from prisoners made at Oswego. The custom of bugles or drums [for a parley] is unknown here. It would even be dangerous because of the Indians.

OCTOBER 2 : Seven Nipissings arrived today. The Potawatomis have had their farewell audience. They are due to leave this evening, but several Abnakis who wish to join them have begged them not to leave before tomorrow. It is a consequence of the laziness of this nation, brave it is true, and implacable against the English, but one of the most unmanageable and insolent of all.

The nations of the Far West are, in general, easier to lead than our domesticated Indians. They have greater respect for the French whom they see less often, moreover their great distance from home is a reason why they do not relax everytime they have made a strike.

The Potawatomis are different in council from the other nations I have observed. In council their orators do not make all their speech at once. Each sentence is a unit that the interpreter trans-

---

[73] Town major of Quebec and one of Bigot's evil crew.

lates before the orator proceeds farther. As for the rest, they speak with that warmth and vehemence that I have noticed in Lamotte, chief of the Menominees. It has been agreed in council that the Nipissings should leave with the Potawatomis, four Iroquois, and seven Abnakis and a few Canadians. This detachment will go by the foot of the bay, reconnoiter and try to make a strike on the road between Fort George and Fort Lydius. If they find nothing, they are to split up into little detachments which will raid into New England.

M. de Bleury arrived this evening with seventy bateaux loaded with food and munitions. Three Abnakis came back with him. As they were returning to Montreal, they saw in Lake Champlain at about a league and a half from Fort St. Frederic on the north shore four barges abandoned in a little cove. They went there and found one of the barges mounted with three swivels, and in it a barrel of powder, some balls and grenades, about forty oars, and many tracks on the shore and at the edge of the woods. They brought back the barge that had the artillery and sent from the fort a lieutenant and thirty men to look for the other three. The barges presumably belonged to a party which had for its object the capture or harrying of some of our convoys.[74] It is still to be learned by what route these barges got to Lake Champlain. Five roads, two to the north and three to the south. The first is marked out through the woods behind the mountains north of Lakes St. Sacrement and Champlain, passes through the woods of Fort George to the heights of St. Frederic. To the north of these mountains, the Indians say, there is a lake on which the British have been able to build barges for a long time, for they appear to be old. The lake probably stretches to the Bouquet River or to some other that

[74] These barges, probably actually whaleboats, were almost certainly abandoned by members of Rogers' Rangers. Rogers himself appears to have abandoned some very near this place when returning from his scout toward St. John August 16–September 2. The boats had been carried six miles over the mountains east of Lake George, a most arduous task, launched in Lake Champlain, and hidden somewhere south of Carillon until used in the July raid. They, of course, were rowed by the fort at night.

Journal for 1756

empties into Lake Champlain. It does not appear probable that they portaged these barges either from Fort George or even from La Barbue River.[75]

Or, secondly, they may have gone up a little river which flows into the Hudson River, gone on beyond Fort St. Frederic, then portaged either as far as Lake Champlain or as far as this lake whose existence the Indians assure us of, but the location and size of which no one can determine.

Or, thirdly, they may have built these barges on the Chicot River, the mouth of which is in the great bay, have passed by Forts Carillon and St. Frederic by night, and gone cruising on the lake, or have followed the bay up to Diamond Point,[76] portaged through the great marsh, thus avoiding Carillon, continued on up the lake, portaged across the peninsula above St. Frederic behind M. Hocquart's farm,[77] re-entered the lake opposite Montreal Point.

Or, fourthly, they may have followed Chicot River and the bay to about a league from Fort Carillon, where there is a sort of little bay to the south and at the end of this bay a three-mile portage which goes to a lake that discharges to the south of Lake Champlain about four leagues below Fort St. Frederic.[78]

Or, fifthly, come by La Loutre River that the English call Otter Creek which has its source close to Connecticut and flows into a little lake with which it enters Lake Champlain.[79]

To learn what they can in this respect, two detachments will leave tomorrow, one from M. Contrecoeur's camp going north of the mountains to reconnoiter what roads there may be in this area, the other, composed of eighty Canadians and twenty French volunteers, will leave Carillon and will go to the same bay where the

---

[75] Put's Creek at Crown Point.

[76] Diamond Point, or Cape Diamond—Mount Independence on the Vermont shore opposite Ticonderoga. During the Revolution the Americans had defensive works there.

[77] Hocquart owned the land on the east side of the lake across from Crown Point and, apparently, also some on the western shore south of the fort.

[78] This does not agree with the geography of the region. Probably based on Indian reports.

[79] See footnote 78 above.

barges were, go up Bouquet River, search all this area, cross Lake Champlain, and reconnoiter beyond La Loutre River.

I have for the first time received letters from France, dated June 6. They tell us of the opening of the trenches before Fort St. Philippe the night of May 9–10, that by June 6 this fort was not yet taken, of the treaty of alliance with the Queen of Hungary, and that of neutrality with Holland, of the arrival of the Danish and Swedish ships at Brest, of M. de la Galissionere's fight, May [*blank*], and several other bits of news.

We know that at least four merchant vessels loaded for Canada, two of which carried workmen, have been taken and a fifth one sunk by the English on leaving French ports. An English squadron is cruising around Gaspé; fortunately the fogs will be becoming heavier and heavier.

OCTOBER 3 : The detachment of thirty Indians and thirty-six Canadians headed for Fort Lydius left this morning as well as the seven Nipissings who go with two weeks' supplies to strike a blow in the direction of Boston.

At four in the evening the detachment of one hundred men sent to look for the roads that the English might have to the north and south of our lakes left for Fort St. Frederic, where eight Iroquois will join them tomorrow.

Seventy sick sent away this evening by M. Bleury's bateaux which are going back. All the rest will remain in the field until it pleases our governor to cease to fear lest the enemy come to attack us, something they have not thought of for the last two or three months.

OCTOBER 4 : Nothing new. Ordinary work going on.

OCTOBER 5 : The five Iroquois who went to raid around Fort George came back without having made a strike. They deposited some letters of English prisoners within sight of the fort. They pretend to have heard Indians singing the war song inside the fort, and dedicating to hell the head of the chief of the French. I very much doubt that they heard anything at all.

Journal for 1756

☙ OCTOBER 6 : I have been to Cape Diamond, which is just opposite Fort Carillon. This cape is so named because they have found pieces of quite beautiful rock crystal there. They also have found a number of rattlesnakes, but since they give warning of all their movements, and besides only strike at those who tread on them, it is very easy to avoid them. The country people claim that by crushing the head of the serpent on the bite one prevents any bad effect.

This evening at eight several discharges of muskets were heard far off in the bay, followed by five cries of mourning which announced bad news to us and were repeated several times. It was three canoes of Indians and Canadians. Before coming ashore, an Indian in a very loud voice and one which could be heard all over the camp announced that they were killed and had lost an Abnaki. Here is the story:

Our party left on the third and left its canoes on this side of Twin Rocks,[80] took the Chicot River road through the woods, saw a little river flowing to join it at the place where they had seen the two dogs on the twenty-eighth. From a little distance they sent forward nine scouts, five of whom held back, the others, a Frenchman, an Abnaki, a Nipissing, and a Potawatomi scouted ahead. (They sent one of each nation.) They had arrived near the place in question, when, passing by the foot of a rocky cliff, two gunshots were fired from the rocks. They retraced their steps. The Abnaki was not seen again after sixty paces. They ran and rejoined the rest of the detachment, received from the Potawatomi and Nipissing two belts of wampum to wipe away their feeling of loss, and at once the entire party without stopping made seven or eight leagues to the rear. Then they held a war council, with the result that the Abnakis, the Iroquois except two, and all the Canadians and colony soldiers came back to Carillon. The Potawatomis and the Nipissings, making nineteen warriors with M. de Langis at their head, remained with the intention of flanking the post on the rock cliff and finding out what it might be, a simple reconnaissance detachment or a grand guard of a considerable body of troops

[80] About halfway between Ticonderoga and the southern end of the lake.

which perhaps was building a fort at the end of the bay on the Chicot River, or one which covers the road from Fort Lydius to Fort George, and is also intended to give warning if the French should come to make an attempt against them again this year, following the road that M. de Dieskau had taken.[81] Whatever this post may be, if it exists at all, what may be its size and objective, whatever may be the plans and movements of the English in these regions, it seems to me that, the season being much advanced, the campaign, which has been very brilliant, since we have had only great successes without any loss on our part, is drawing to the end, peace could be made this year.

The improvement of the works of Fort Carillon being an important objective, we should not attempt any offensive act at the end of the bay, unless it was only a matter of a little post easy to seize. Any material check would be of the greatest consequence, would perhaps render us unable to carry out next year's campaign. Men are scarce here and more precious than one can say. They come from a great distance and the road that brings them is not easy.

OCTOBER 7 : This morning they dried the tears of the Abnakis (Note: It is not certain that he was killed.), a belt of two thousand beads, two strings of wampum, several drinks of brandy, and a "ouapon" covered the dead man, loosened the throat, swept away the clouds that obscured the view, freed the tongue, and made it possible to have ideas and plans. The Indians held a council among themselves to learn whether they should go at once to avenge the dead man.

M. de Lévis has returned to Fort St. Frederic, having looked over the trails to the north of Lake Champlain. No bateau could be taken over these trails, they are practicable only for those who are fleeing or are on a raid. This river flowing into Hudson River of which I spoke previously is initially only a trickle and further on it is full of falls and rapids, consequently it is not navigable.[82]

[81] He went by water to South Bay at the end of Lake Champlain and then marched cross-country to the southern end of Lake George.
[82] Probably the Schroon River is meant.

Journal for 1756

It is very likely that the armed barges came from the Chicot River, passing under the forts of Carillon and St. Frederic by night. This idea is made more likely because several of the oars were bound with cloth.

OCTOBER 8 : Rainy day, the work interrupted. These works go very slowly, the soldiers, corrupted by the great amount of money,[83] by the example of the Indians and Canadians, breathing an air permeated with independence, work indolently. The engineer[84] is almost never at the works. It is not to his interest that the fort should be completed quickly. He has the exclusive privilege of selling wine (It sells for 55 sous a bottle.), and all the money of the workmen, and even the pay of the soldiers, goes to the canteen. Moreover he has built this fort of horizontal timbers in a country where stone, limestone and sand are found in abundance, where in getting the stone to face [the walls], the ditch is made at the same time, where there is doubtless wood, but men are lacking to cut it, square it, haul it, where there are neither wagons nor horses. It is an odd thing, this engineer gives the workers certificates which have the value of money, without anyone controlling their issue, and all of these certificates come back to him.

They believe that they have found fresh tracks in the vicinity of M. de Contrecoeur's camp.

The Indians go hunting every day, proof that the English Indians have gone back to their villages. When these Indians believe themselves safe from attack there certainly is no danger to fear. Those who remain here get drunk and, since they have lost all their spirit, everything is permitted them.

OCTOBER 9 : The end of the campaign review has been made of the regiments of Guyenne and Béarn. The two battalions are one of 513, of which only 387 men are here, and the other 512 men. Four Indians of the Five Nations from La Presentation have come here to make a coup.

---

[83] French soldiers were given extra pay for working on the fort.
[84] Michael Chartier de Lotbinière, a young Canadian engineer officer, relative of Governor Vaudreuil.

ಶ OCTOBER 10 : Nothing new. Ordinary work.

ಶ OCTOBER 11 : This morning the Marquis de Montcalm passed in review the battalion of La Reine which has 356 men, having only nine companies and a tenth one provisional, formed out of the nine others. Four were taken [by the enemy] crossing the ocean.

A soldier of the Béarn regiment, lost in the woods south of the falls of Lake St. Sacrement, met three Mohawks, one of whom gave him a blow with a tomahawk that he parried with his hand. They immediately stripped him and made him flee with them. After passing two mountains they stopped and sat down. A deer passed by and two of them went off to chase it. The third one getting up to light a fire, our prisoner took his gun, the wound in his hand not allowing him to use it, and threw it into the thick underbrush and took to his heels, fear giving him legs like wings. For a long time he heard the woods ring with the cries the Indians uttered. At last he reached the main guard of the camp at the Falls, more dead than alive.

M. de Bleury arrived at three with a convoy of thirty-five bateaux. He did not bring any wine. The army has been on water and beer for two weeks. This beer, or rather spruce beer, is made from molasses or brown sugar and spruce, which is a kind of fir. They boil branches of it when the sap is running.[85] The canteen of M. de Lotbinière is the only place that has wine, even the hospital is out of it.

No news from France. Three English vessels are cruising off Gaspé. I doubt if they can keep station there very long.

A letter of M. Dumas[86] of September 9 informs us that upon receiving the news of the siege of Oswego he got together all the Indians of the region of Fort Duquesne in order to put on a powerful diversion. The conduct of this siege being so brisk that this

---

[85] This is the *sapinette* of the French. It can be made in a very few days with the simplest of facilities, and is a palatable and warming beerlike drink.

[86] Commander at Fort Duquesne. An excellent and humane officer, he was active throughout the entire war.

diversion did not take place, he turned loose this pack against the southern provinces of New England. This same letter of M. Dumas adds that during the first part of September a body of three hundred English came to burn the village of Attigué.[87] The party arrived without being discovered and made its attack at daybreak. A French officer who was in the village to recruit warriors made a stand with his Frenchmen long enough for the Indians to put their women and children in a place of safety. These then immediately attacked the English and put them to flight. They killed seven of our people and lost eighteen of theirs, two of whom were taken prisoner. They were not immediately pursued because the Indians lacked powder, two barrels of which blew up during the action. M. Dumas has replaced this loss and the Indians did not delay in leaving to take revenge. Retaliation will be prompt and bloody.

I doubt very much if the English will find this sort of business to their taste. According to the report of prisoners, half of the detachment became scattered in the woods. Terror and ignorance of these places will make them perish.

Upon the departure of this detachment Fort George[?] was abandoned. They have sent a party from this direction and another from that of Fort Cumberland. M. de Ligneris, captain of La Marine, has gone to relieve M. Dumas.

OCTOBER 12 : The Marquis de Montcalm passed in review the battalion of the Royal Roussillon which has 503 men and thirteen companies.

This morning a soldier of Béarn and a servant girl[88] had their scalps taken on the road from M. de St. Martin's camp to that of M. de Contrecoeur. At the sound of the shots people ran out from the two camps, but the Indians took a hurried departure without having stripped the bodies, leaving some spears and blankets behind.

They pursued them and kept them in sight as far as the mountains; they noted about a score of them. Several detachments have

---

[87] On the Allegheny River near Kittanning, Pa.
[88] Another transcript says "manservant."

been sent to try to cut off their retreat. I doubt that they will succeed. We have no Indians at all in these two camps and it is just like chasing deer with neither dogs nor horses.

M. de Contrecoeur's post has been withdrawn today back to that at the Portage.

Two hundred soldiers at La Marine regiment, due to occupy the posts in the Far West, left this morning.

OCTOBER 13 : This morning the battalion of Languedoc was reviewed. It has 353 men, having only nine companies and a tenth one of provisional grenadiers drawn from the other nine. Four companies are in England [as prisoners].[89]

The weather, which has been very fine up to the present, appears to be setting in to snow and cold. The east, north, and northeast winds are the ones that bring rain and fog in this country. It is the contrary in France and this difference comes from the situation of this country with respect to the sea.

Eleven Iroquois who left here three days ago to go and reconnoiter the end of the bay returned today. They reported that they had found only trails still quite fresh. Say what you will, the wisest thing to do is to put no trust in the reports of Indians and half-breeds.

Just the same, this talent they have of finding tracks in the woods and of following them without losing them, a talent one cannot dismiss in doubt without refusing to accept the evidence, can be regarded as a perfection of the instinct. They see in the tracks the number that have passed, whether they are Indians or Europeans, if the tracks are fresh or old, if they are of healthy or of sick people, dragging feet or hurrying ones, marks of sticks used as supports. It is rarely that they are deceived or mistaken. They follow their prey for one hundred, two hundred, six hundred leagues with a constancy and a sureness which never loses courage or leads them astray. As regards their sense of direction in the woods, it is of a complete sureness. If they have left a place where they put their

---

[89] They were captured in 1755 when their transports fell prey to the British Navy.

Journal for 1756

canoes, whatever distance they may have gone, whatever turns they may have made, crossing rivers, mountains, they come directly back to the place where their canoes were left. Observation of the sun, the inclination of trees and of leaves that they look at, a long practice, and finally an instinct superior to all reasons, these are their guides, and these guides never lead them astray.

OCTOBER 14 : Indian council indicated for tomorrow to decide about a score who came here to go and make a strike.

The soldiers have too much money. A soldier of Languedoc yesterday lost one hundred louis. This country is dangerous for discipline. Pray God that it alone suffers from it.

OCTOBER 15 : The number of workmen increased. If the skill in using them increased in proportion to the number of workmen, the fort would soon be in good shape. Our general's plan is not to withdraw the army until the fort is completely free from any risk, that to effect this they will have palisaded that part of the ramparts which are not yet as high as they should be, and that they have built inside the fort sufficient barracks to lodge the garrison which will be [*blank*].

The troops work with ardor. There is at the Falls a sawmill which under the direction of M. de L[otbinière] never was got in shape to make planks, they had even decided to abandon it. M. de la P[ause] was put in charge of the mill, and he got it in shape to get out 150 planks in twenty-four hours. It cost the King [*blank*] crowns and yet could not run; five hundred francs and one of our officers has accomplished what this great sum and the Vauban of Canada could not achieve. Unfortunately it is to the interest of this Vauban that the work should drag out. The canteen must have its business. Wine here is six livres a quart; I note this difference in price, it is the thermometer of peculation in this country.

The Potawatomi old men who remained here yesterday made medicine to learn the news of their brothers. The hut shook, the medicine men sweated drops of blood, and at last the devil came and told them that their brothers would return shortly with scalps and prisoners. A medicine man in the medicine house is just like the priestess of Delphi on her tripod or Canidie[90] evoking the shades.

Eight Indians and as many Canadians left this evening from the portage camp in two canoes to go and make a strike at Fort George.

🕮 OCTOBER 16 : We now have been without candles for two weeks, the officers grope their way to bed. It is an inconvenience, but a greater one is that the bakery and the hospital will be without them. To make up for it, they melt salt pork into tin lamps and use it instead of oil. I admire with what persistence and what industry they use all means here to squander the King's money. Candles which come from France with much difficulty are frightfully expensive here, oil which is made from fish in this country, and for which because of the war there is very little demand, goes almost for nothing. So in all the posts they burn candles and do not send oil there at all, although our general has often asked for it. Another colony like this and the king of the sea would destroy that of the land.

Four Indians who went hunting saw fires in the big marsh behind Cape Diamond and at once came back.

🕮 OCTOBER 17 : The Iroquois who left the day before yesterday sent back two Indians to report that they had found between Isle la Barque and Sugerloaf[91] one of the English vessels with three bateaux with a crew of seven men each. The detachment continued on its way.

🕮 OCTOBER 18 : The Potawatomi medicine man made medicine again. He came this morning to find the Marquis de Montcalm. He brought him a stick marked with sixteen notches and four crosses on the last quarter which said that his brothers left sixteen days ago, made a coup four days ago, and that they would return today with scalps and prisoners. Our prophet was pale and wasted. He had fasted for forty-eight hours, accordingly he devoured everything they gave him to eat.

[90] Canidia was a sorceress of Naples mentioned by Horace.
[91] Sugarloaf Mountain near Huletts Landing, N. Y.

Journal for 1756

At three the Potawatomis arrived. They signaled from a point about a quarter of a league from the fort to have boats sent to them; they had not gone back for their own canoes, fearing to find an ambush at the place where they had left them. They brought back one prisoner taken within a few leagues of Albany. This man is a New Englander who for three weeks was carting provisions from Albany to Fort Edward or Lydius. The prisoner said that there were no more than about 150 Scottish Highlanders at Albany, and that they were working to make this place safe on the side toward the woods, that all the troops, both regulars and militia, have been brought away from the Lake St. Sacrement region and have been distributed between Fort Edward and Fort George, that they have brought up a very great quantity of munitions and rations, that almost two thousand carts had been kept busy carrying them, each cart being escorted by two soldiers, that the last of the artillery consisting of many cannon and mortars was put in position three weeks ago, that Lord Loudoun left Albany on October 3 to go to Lake St. Sacrement, where General Johnson had also gone with his Indians, that at first they had believed that the militia would be sent home, but that they had only sent back the sick, that they had even sent up more recruits as replacements, that there had been thought of building a fort at the end of the bay but that Lord Loudoun had not approved, wishing to build it on the point[92] at the end of the campaign, that his [the prisoner's?] only son had been killed at Saratoga at drill, a musket being found loaded.

This deposition, the contents of which are either true or false, will, I believe, make us keep in the field longer. Perhaps the enemy general is making these movements in fear of some enterprise on our part? Or perhaps he waits until our troops have gone before he attacks Fort Carillon, or rather comes to grab the Portage and make a fortified position there, perhaps all these moves merely come down to provisioning his fort for the winter, perhaps there is no truth in what the prisoner said of ending the campaign later?

It would be of an advantage to them because we have to move our troops out before the English do. Passage to Montreal and

[92] This location cannot be definitely identified.

Quebec is open only until ice closes the roads. The English have winter a month later and spring a month earlier than we. Moreover, their troops in going into winter quarters go from a warm country into one which is no less so, and their route is by way of the King's Highway in which two carriages can go abreast, and the rivers are navigable at all times. The prisoner said the enemy have twenty thousand men. Take off a half or even two-thirds and it is still much more than the some three thousand that we have here.

ОСТОBER 19 : Money changing goes on here just as in la Rue Quincampoix.[93] M. de L[otbinière]'s certificates are in poor repute. A man who has silver or gold changes it for colony paper notes at 12 per cent profit. Then he changes for those of Lob——, sometimes at a quarter, a third, or even a half of their value in profit. He sends these L—— to Montreal and the treasurer gives colony notes in exchange at no other cost than four deniers for the livre. The colony notes come back to camp and the circuit starts again. It is a shuttle which produces great profits. M. de L[otbinière] makes no difficulty in taking up the notes, he even, they say, has exchange agents to take them back.

The weather has been warm all this time, this morning we had a thunder and rainstorm. The west wind is whistling with great violence.

By a letter dated at River St. Jean,[94] October 17, Father Germain, missionary attached to the Acadians scattered along the banks of this river, reports that he cannot come to Quebec this winter, that two Acadians who arrived from Boston that very day reported that there was rumored among the English that a French fleet was sailing toward Louisbourg, that it had taken three English ships, one of which was commanded by Rous,[95] a privateers-

---

[93] A street in Paris where John Law had the Banque Générale of the Mississippi bubble.

[94] In present New Brunswick.

[95] Captain John Rous commanded one of the Massachusetts warships at the 1745 siege of Louisbourg so ably that he was given a commission in the Royal Navy.

man famous in these waters. Father Germain did not go into any detail as to what had happened this year in Acadia, nor as to the state of our affairs on the St. Jean River.

The commander at Presque Isle also wrote that the news of the taking of Oswego created a sensation in the western country, that a great number of Indians appeared full of ardor to come next season and hit the English. It is especially of the Indians that he speaks truth:

Donec eris felix, multos numerabis amicos. Tempora si fuerint nubila, solus eris.[96]

Today a party of thirty men was sent to the end of the bay.

OCTOBER 20: At four in the evening three Canadians going to the camp at the Portage met an English party which they thought consisted of ten men. A Canadian fired and killed one. The English then fired and slightly wounded two of ours, and [then] fled at once. Thirty grenadiers have been sent to pursue them.

Some Indians who were sent hunting on the other side of the lake have come back to say that they have seen at a short distance from Hanged Men's River,[97] behind Cape Diamond, the tracks of a dozen men. Tomorrow before daybreak a party will go over from this shore.

It would appear that the English very much wish to take a prisoner in order to learn the time fixed for our departure. Up to now these attempts have not succeeded, but they are not discouraged, and moreover they doubtless know that we have almost no Indians left. Immediately after their departure three or four Iroquois took a turn around in the direction of Fort George.

I do not believe that it is a good policy in the case of a defensive such as we are conducting today to send to the army at any one time a large number of Indians, such as M. de Vaudreuil sent us the end of last month. They gather together in mobs, argue among themselves, deliberate slowly and all want to go together to make a strike and at the same place, because they prefer big war parties.

[96] "When you are fortunate, you will have many friends. If conditions are gloomy, you will be alone."
[97] Probably East Creek in Orwell, Vt.

Between the resolution made and the action taken there passes considerable time, sometimes one nation stops the march, sometimes another. Everybody must have time to get drunk, and their food consumption is enormous. At last they get started, and once they have struck, have they taken only a single scalp or one prisoner, back they come and are off again for their villages. Then for a considerable time the army is without Indians. Each one does well for himself, but the operation of the war suffers, for in the end they are a necessary evil. It would be better to have on hand only a specified number of these mosquitoes, who would be relieved by others, so that we would always have some on hand. In general it does not seem to me that we are getting all the use we can out of these Indians. With less servile compliance for their caprices, less respect for the silly things they do, less outward indifference toward the service expected of them, one would accustom them to consideration toward the French, to obedience, I would say even to a kind of subordination. Finally, if they believe that they can be dispensed with, they should seek to make themselves of value through real services. Some companies of volunteers who through living in the woods would know them and serve as guides would be a marvelous spur to prick the honor of these barbarians, for self-love is everything, and pride is the only wealth of every Indian.

OCTOBER 21 : The party of Iroquois who left the evening of the sixteenth returned this morning. They reported that they had taken the road to the south, that on the seventeenth two English vessels and two bateaux had passed the heights of Sugar Loaf, that at three leagues from Fort George they had dropped off an Indian and a Canadian on the road from Fort George to Fort Edward, and that several other Indians with Pertuis had been on top of the mountain nearest Fort George, that the first two had heard on the road the noise of a great many men and wagons which seemed to be returning to Fort Edward, that the scouts on top of the mountain had seen the fort, which appeared to them to be finished, the entrenched camp in which they had counted about fifty tents

Journal for 1756

across and twelve deep with little movement in either place and the anchorage, where they saw two vessels and about one hundred bateaux. On their way, both going and returning, they found many tracks, mostly of Indians and all of little parties of eight or ten men, except for one track of a party of about sixty, all Englishmen.

OCTOBER 22 : The Potawatomis left today. They are going to Montreal to look for their women and children, to drink their Father's milk, to get drunk, to get re-equipped. Afterwards they will come with arms, baggage, and family to Carillon for the winter.

The cold has been very sharp these days. It has frozen quite hard the last two nights. This evening the wind shifted and the weather became mild. The conical tents and huts are no longer very habitable.

OCTOBER 23 : They are awaiting the arrival of M. de Bleury's convoy with the greatest of impatience. The strong winds which have been whistling the last few days have doubtless slowed him down.

OCTOBER 24 : Nothing new. Some boats came from the point but they have not yet seen M. de Bleury.

OCTOBER 25 : Today, at last, this long-hoped-for Bleury has arrived. His convoy consists of fifty-four bateaux, and he brings twenty-four hogsheads of wine. It is a fine graft that this admiral of Lake Champlain has. He gets eighteen sous a pound for what he carries for the King, and each bateau is loaded with three tons. Add to that what he brings on his own account in wine, brandy, and poultry which he sells at an excessive price.

News from France has come to us by way of Louisbourg[98] which informs us of the surrender of Port Mahon[99] on June 29,

---

[98] The great French naval base on Cape Breton Island which guarded the approaches to the St. Lawrence.

[99] British naval base on Minorca in the Mediterranean.

that the English squadron was reinforced to eighteen vessels, that M. de la Galissonnière[100] captured a merchant fleet coming from Smyrna. This prize was valued at twelve millions, that Spain had equipped eighteen warships, several of which entered the port of Majorca, that the English had taken from the Dutch eleven ships leaving le Havre.

This same Louisbourg letter tells us that they are actively continuing the works to put this place in a defensible condition, that eighteen French sailors, escaped from Halifax, report that our prisoners there are suffering much, that our ships taken in those seas were the *Arc en Ciel*, the *Pontchartrain*, and the *Equité*, that seventeen armed ships, both great and small, had left Halifax, the first of which were cruising around in order to intercept anything heading for this colony, and the others were disturbing things along our shores, that they have barges by means of which they grab up the schooners and shallops which their masters run ashore in order to save their crews, that the Indians had decoyed four ashore in the Fronsac[101] thoroughfare, had taken one in which were five men and a wounded naval lieutenant, that they killed twenty-six others who were trying to reach safety in the anchorages of the great cove.

The winter quarters assignments of the four battalions came today. Guyenne goes to Quebec, La Reine to Pointe aux Trembles, seven leagues from this capital, La Sarre to Trois Rivières, St. Anne, Batiscan, and Champlain, Royal Roussillon to Chambly and the River Sorel, Languedoc to Boucherville, Longueuil, and la Prairie, Béarn to Montreal. Consequently Guyenne will leave for its quarters on November 1, La Reine, the second, Béarn, the third, Royal Roussillon and Languedoc the eleventh. There will remain as a garrison for Fort Carillon a picket of La Reine, one from Languedoc, and one from Royal Roussillon, making 150 men, 100 colony troops and about 50 workmen. M. de Lusignan,

---

[100] A former governor of Canada.
[101] Cape Fronsac was at the northern end of the Gut of Canso between Nova Scotia and Cape Breton.

without question one of the best of the colony troop's officers, who now commands at Fort St. Frederic, is assigned to come and take command this winter of Carillon and all the Lake St. Sacrement frontier. He will have a garrison of ——— men at Fort St. Frederic.

OCTOBER 26 : The Marquis de Montcalm left Carillon this afternoon. We went in M. de Bleury's bateaux. We have with us the grenadier company and a light company of La Sarre, officers from each battalion sent to arrange billets for their troops. Nineteen Indians also go with us. The Chevalier de Lévis remains at Carillon until the eleventh, the day set for the departure of the last of the troops.

We reached St. Frederic at nightfall. We had calm weather on the way. The Marquis de Montcalm ordered a detachment that was gathering fodder for M. de Lotbinière's horses to return to Carillon. Collecting forage is a most useless task since it had been necessary to send back M. de L[otbinière's] horses, which will do nothing all winter and for which he is paid not less than six livres a day. It is now a matter of getting the wood supply for the two forts cut. At St. Frederic for a garrison of one hundred men and the necessary noncombatants they will need fifteen hundred cords of firewood. There are some forts where the King gives six livres a cord for wood to the commander who makes himself responsible for cutting and hauling it. It is thus that it costs the King so much to keep his troops warm in the midst of forests.

On the eleventh of this month the Marquis de Montcalm received an order from the Marquis de Vaudreuil, dated the third, to change the field ration in this garrison immediately. This decrease was because of the lack of provisions in the storehouses, this year's poor harvest, the feeble resources of the colony, and the uncertainty of help from France. The Marquis de Montcalm took it upon himself to delay this operation, fearing that such [a reduction], made almost at the end of the campaign, would expose our poverty and could even make it known to the enemy. Besides, the French troops have never drawn more than a pound and a half of bread and a half-pound of salt pork, the surplus being credited to them in money. On a repeated order from the Marquis de Vaudreuil, our general decreed that the reduction will be effective the first of November, which is a time which can be taken as marking the end of the campaign. Actually the troops started to move back today.

ಜ಼ OCTOBER 27 : Left St. Frederic at half-past nine, reached Isle au Chapon[102] at six in the evening. Bivouacked in the open, something a bit unpleasant at this season.

ಜ಼ OCTOBER 28 : Set sail at five in the morning with a southwest wind that failed us at noon. Kept on without stopping as far as St. Jean, which we reached at half-past eleven at night.

The Marquis de Montcalm here found a letter from the Marquis de Vaudreuil which informed him that the Marquis de Vaudreuil had changed the winter quarters assignments which he himself had decreed. He pretends that if his initial assignments were followed, the troops would not be able to live in the places he sent them. If this is so, this uncertainty shows a serious fault in the internal government of the colony. If the Governor General knew the state of his colony, the strength of each parish, how many buildings, what each area produces in provisions year after year, he would be in a position to make a prompt and firm decision concerning the quarters for the troops, and directions for the militiamen would be made with more order and justice. But it is necessary to come to Canada to see things of exactly another world. When I reflect on the methods of governing this country, for which the King pays out enormous sums, I recall the way Jupiter ruled the world, as described at Lucien's feast.[103]

According to the new assignment to quarters, La Reine goes to the area of Beaupré, Guyenne still at Quebec, Royal Roussillon at Chambly, Béarn at La Prairie, Longueuil and Boucherville, where this battalion had been last winter. La Sarre goes to Pointe aux Trembles from Montreal, Languedoc to Montreal.

[102] Schuyler Island near Port Kent, N. Y.
[103] Probably refers to one of the works of Lucian, the Greek satirist.

Journal for 1756

According to the first arrangements proposed by M. de Montcalm, the battalions which had the worst quarters last winter and those which had suffered most in this campaign would have had the best quarters. A spirit of justice dictated this arrangement. They changed it, and in this change there is a marked intention of thwarting the French General and of making the troops discontented. One must be blind not to see it, and that we are treated here the way the Lacedaemonians treated the Helots.

OCTOBER 29 : We passed the day at St. Jean. The fort could very easily be burned by a winter raiding party. It has a stockade of very dry posts, and there is nearby a number of birch-bark canoes. Moreover, it is badly supplied with the things necessary for its defense. It is, nevertheless, one of the colony's most important posts for all the convoys which pass to the Lake Champlain frontier. At present there is a garrison of thirty-five men who will perhaps be increased up to sixty and have a drummer at M. de Montcalm's solicitation, for last winter there were only fourteen there. I do not at all like it that all the powder is in the cellar where they go morning and night to get the wine. There is a ship builder with twenty carpenters to build between now and summer a schooner of eighty tons, which will be armed with ten four-pound guns. We already have on the lake a much smaller schooner, armed only with four swivels.

OCTOBER 30 : We left at seven this morning on horseback. The road from St. Jean to La Prairie is six leagues long and it is abominable. There is in this region a little river whose waters inundate the entire area. Until they give it a place to drain off, the road will always be impracticable. The regiment of La Sarre, which is camped at La Sahvane, three leagues from St. Jean, has built about two hundred toises[104] of road commencing at a point which is on the river to the right of their camp. The location of this river is excellent to stop an enemy who might have taken St. Frederic and who was pushing a body of troops overland from St.

---

[104] A toise is an old French unit of linear measure equivalent to 2.1315 yards.

Jean. M. de Vaudreuil sent a sculptor to direct the work on the road. I doubt that even Phidias could build a road from Montreal, but, since the sculptor has returned to his regular trade, the work has stopped.

We dined at the camp at La Sahvane, where the Marquis de Montcalm reviewed the La Sarre regiment, which has five hundred men in thirteen companies. It lost twenty-five men. The battalion has a picket detached for the Niagara garrison this winter.

Reached La Prairie at seven in the evening and slept there.

Left La Prairie at seven in the morning, and reached Montreal at nine.

This morning there was an audience given the Ottawa Potawatomis, and this afternoon to the Ottawas and the Chippewas. The Indians will winter at Carillon. A few of them have gone back to their towns to bring back all their young men in the early spring, to relieve those who winter here and then will return to their villages.

NOVEMBER 1 : The latest news from Acadia informs us that the Acadians to the number of about two thousand, men, women, and children, and six or seven hundred Indians of the Huron nation still live on the river and the island of St. Jean.[105] They have taken a great quantity of cattle from the English, but they have neither flour nor biscuits. They will be sent some, but if they lack them I doubt if the enthusiasm of Father Germain, missionary, who is at their head, can prevent great numbers of them from going to throw themselves into the arms of the English, whatever conditions they may have imposed upon them. We have a small stockaded fort on Isle St. Jean.

The English have twice tried a descent on Gaspé. They have taken several prisoners, but they have been forced back to their shores, and the force of two hundred men that we have at this bay are doing as well as we could expect. The essential point is that the English should not establish any post there.

[105] Prince Edward Island. The St. John River, if that is what he means, is in New Brunswick.

Journal for 1756

᠅ NOVEMBER 2–4 : The King having sent orders to the Marquis de Vaudreuil to proceed in the trial of MM. Stobo and Wanbram [van Braam]—hostages given by the English as a guarantee for the capitulation made at Fort Necessity, convicted, almost, at least in the case of the first, of having been in correspondence with the enemy—they have been brought from Quebec to Montreal, where the court-martial is to be held. A letter of Sieur Stobo, found in General Braddock's papers, in which he told them the condition, strength, and size of the garrison of Fort Duquesne and of the best time and way to surprise it, appears to furnish sufficiently damning proof against him.[106] As for the rest of it, this question pertains to the law of nations, and if, as the Roman law puts it, the word hostage, *obses*, is derived from *hospes*, guest, the principles which should decide this question seem to me clear and simple. What are hostages when the promises of which they are the pledge have been violated? It is true that England pretends that Major Washington did not have the right to promise to restore prisoners who belonged to that country, and that she refused to recognize the validity of the capitulation. In this case these hostages become no more than ordinary prisoners, who are not, I believe, subject to any punishment for trying to serve their country. It is up to those who hold them to see that they do not have the means.

᠅ NOVEMBER 4 : The battalion of La Sarre today went into quarters around Montreal.

᠅ NOVEMBER 5–7 : It is said here that the English have evacuated and burned Forts Bull[107] and William,[108] and they add that they were forced to it by the Five Nations, to whose ambassadors M. de Vaudreuil declared that he returned to them the lands of Oswego, stolen from them by Corlar[109] and conquered by Onon-

---

[106] Stobo also included a map of the fort.
[107] At the carrying place between the Mohawk and Wood Creek flowing into Lake Oneida.
[108] Fort Williams at the other end of the carry. General Webb abandoned and burned these forts after the fall of Oswego.
[109] Name used by Indians for both Schenectady and the Governor of New York. Arent Van Curler was the founder of Schenectady.

thio's[110] arms, upon the condition that they would not suffer the English to establish themselves there again. This news, which has no other source than the report of a few Indians, requires confirmation. Pyrrhonism[111] here is necessary and most sensible.

  NOVEMBER 7 : The Marquis de Montcalm has ordered me to go to Quebec to carry dispatches for the last departing ships. At three in the morning I went on board a schooner which goes down to Quebec loaded with furs. The wind being southwest, we went down as far as this side of Trois Rivières where we anchored at seven in the evening.

  NOVEMBER 8 : The wind having swung around into the north and become quite violent, I got myself put ashore to continue my way by land. I proceeded day and night.

  NOVEMBER 9 : I reached Quebec at ten in the morning, traveling by carriage, on foot, and by wagon. This trip is quite difficult, especially at this season. The *Deux Frères*, the *Beauharnois*, a brigantine, a schooner, and the King's frigate the *Abénakis*, pierced for ——— guns, with eighteen mounted, of which two are twelve-pounders, have not yet sailed. This frigate, built here, was on the ways for three years because of the short working season. She lies well in the water and has a fine appearance. They say that she is not low built enough and too narrow [crank?]. The ships delay sailing, waiting for the dispatches and orders of the Marquis de Vaudreuil.

The ground is starting to be covered with snow and the edges of the rivers are frozen.

  NOVEMBER 10–13 : The merchants here are very busy making up their last parcels, completing their orders for the goods they want sent, and all that concerns their commercial relations. They will have nothing to do all winter, for there is not enough internal business to keep them occupied. One finds that M. de Vaudreuil's

---

110 Indian name for the Governor of Canada.
111 A form of extreme skepticism.

dispatches arrive very late. Formerly they did not let the ships remain beyond the end of October, and there are several cases of ships departing in November and being caught in the ice or dashed ashore by violent winds, which are only too common at this season. Such is the inconvenience of this river. No vessel can winter here. The ice does not allow it. The little boats that stay here during the winter are hauled ashore. There is, however, a league from Quebec a bay called ——— where they have passed the winter, but not in safety. Besides there is no port at Quebec, the ships there have no shelter from squalls, and several have dragged their anchors or broken their cables and smashed up on the shore.

&~ NOVEMBER 13 : M. de Vaudreuil's dispatches have come at last, and the departure of the vessels expedited. The brigantine left on the twelfth, between ten and eleven in the morning. The *Deux Frères* is going to leave with the tide today. The *Beauharnois* and the frigate are still in the roads. The ships carry some English prisoners to France. Seven hundred more of them remain here. The rest have been sent off, part to France and part to England.

The court-martial for the trial of the hostages was held the eighth. It was composed solely of officers of the colony troops. Sieur Wanbram [van Braam] is acquitted. Sieur Stobo, having admitted in his interrogation that he had had correspondence with the English and that the letter found in the papers of General Braddock was his, has been unanimously condemned to have his head cut off. He will be reprieved from execution of the sentence in accordance with the order of the King.

The Marquis de Vaudreuil asks the King for an increase of ten companies of the Marine troops, three hundred recruits for our six battalions, and that there should be a replacement for the eight companies lacking to La Reine and Languedoc, and that all companies of the six battalions should be brought up to fifty men. This increase will give us the equivalent of two more battalions, without increasing the number of officers, something most costly to the King and most burdensome for the colony. But what he insists on most is the sending of foodstuffs. It is the most essential thing of all. The harvest has been bad, and henceforth it will be necessary to mix oats with the flour in the bread.

He declares that unless they send foodstuffs in abundance, not only is it useless to send troop reinforcements, but also he will send back two of the battalions now here. For the rest of it, he asks that they get the convoys destined for this colony started by the end of February. The requests made by M. Bigot are curious because of their immensity.

NOVEMBER 14: The *Beauharnois* and the frigate are still here, each has lost an anchor; wind northeast; one fears for these vessels.

The battalion of La Reine which left Carillon on the second arrived this evening at its quarters which extend from the Beaupré region, which is on the south shore a league below Quebec, as far as the parish of St. Joachim, the extremity of which is nine leagues away. The battalion has suffered a great deal from cold and from ice, and especially from hunger, having often been without bread.

NOVEMBER 15: The Guyenne battalion today reached Quebec, where it will be in garrison this winter. Leaving Carillon on the fifth, it found no bread at either St. Jean, Chambly, or Trois Rivières. Contrary winds kept it ashore in deserted regions for several days, and on the twelfth, in the evening, a sudden squall threw it into the River St. Anne, which is twenty leagues from Quebec. It there found itself caught in the ice, and was able to free only a dozen bateaux, into which they put what little food remained for all the troops and which continued the journey by water. The others came on foot, finding bread only with the greatest of difficulty, obliged to bivouac at night in the midst of ice and snow. They arrived yesterday, almost all with colds, wasted and emaciated. This march has been only too laborious, coming as it did at the end of a campaign as rough as that we have just had. The battalions started too late to reach quarters so far off.

The *Abénakis* and the *Beauharnois* set sail at one in the afternoon with a good southwest wind. Pray God that this wind will soon carry them out of the river.

Journal for 1756

NOVEMBER 16: All day there has been a very strong northeast wind, which brought with it thirteen inches of snow. The *Beauharnois* got through the Traverse[112] yesterday. The *Abénakis* did not make it. Ships cannot proceed in this wind, and will be lucky if they do not drag their anchors.

NOVEMBER 17: The frigate yesterday made the Traverse at four in the evening. She will be able to go and anchor at the Isle aux Coudres,[113] which is the best anchorage in the river.

NOVEMBER 18: The wind, which has been northeast all day, will not, I believe, let them proceed. I took medicine today.

NOVEMBER 19: The winds have been calm all day. I sent M. de Montcalm a model of an extension ladder suitable for an escalade [of the wall of a fort], which remedies the inconvenience of having too short ladders when in action. I note the proportions here [*omitted in MS.*].

NOVEMBER 20: Southwest wind all day. They think that the frigate will be able this evening to be clear of the roadstead. Fine weather, temperature minus seven and one-half degrees [15°F.].

NOVEMBER 21: Fine weather, southwest wind, minus eleven degrees [7°F.]. The Intendant received a letter from M. Pellegrin that in passing the Traverse, the wind had suddenly quit, that his ropes being frozen, he had not been able to drop his anchor at once, and the current had driven him onto a shoal where he remained for three hours. As he commenced the passage at half-tide, high tide refloated him.

NOVEMBER 22: Southwest wind until three, then north. Minus twelve degrees [5°F.].

As the year has been a very bad one, they are mixing peas with the flour in making bread, two quarts of peas to two quarts of

---

[112] The difficult passage through the shoals by the eastern end of the Isle of Orleans.

[113] An island sixty miles downstream from Quebec where the river pilots usually took over.

flour; at first they wanted to mix oats with it. The mixture worked well and the bread was better. But the oats produced almost no flour, it only gave bran. A police regulation has ruled here that bread will be distributed to the public only in the afternoon. I went to see this distribution. It presents the image of a famine. They fight to get near the wicket through which they pass the bread. Those who cannot get near hold out their permits on the end of a stick. It is a sight to keep away from, especially the English prisoners, who come every day to look on and who do not fail to draw their conclusions from it.

News from Montreal. The Chevalier de Lévis, after having seen the last of the troops into their winter quarters, arrived the seventeenth. No news of the enemy.

NOVEMBER 23: Northeast wind. It snowed all night and part of the day. ——— degrees. The river St. Anne ———.

NOVEMBER 24: Fine weather, southwest wind.

NOVEMBER 25: Strong north wind that the local people call St. Catherine's Gale, and which they have observed to come regularly at about this time.

I went in a sleigh to St. Foix, two and one-half leagues from town. The women of this country take pleasure in winter in going in a sleigh over the snow and ice in weather in which it would seem that they should not go outdoors at all, even in cases of necessity. St. Catherine's Day is one of dancing and feasting here.

NOVEMBER 26: Continuing northeast wind which was very violent tonight. The river is already very much filled with drift ice. The captain of the Port of Quebec believes that the frigate has not gotten beyond Le Bic.[114] If this is so, they will have suffered much and will continue to.

NOVEMBER 27: Today M. Péan and I were godfathers to a child of M. DeVienne.[115]

---

[114] On the south shore of the St. Lawrence some forty miles east of Tadoussac.
[115] Bougainville's cousin, a Canadian official.

Journal for 1756

ಜೊ NOVEMBER 28 : A tax of four livres and ten sous per minot of wheat decreed until the harvest.

ಜೊ NOVEMBER 29 : Fine weather with southwest winds. News has been received, they say, that the frigate was still at Pot à l'Eau de Vie.[116] One should note that she carries food for only forty-five days.

ಜೊ NOVEMBER 30 : Took medicine today. Pretty strong northeast wind since night. Snow and powdered snow; the little river in front of the Intendance[117] is frozen over.

ಜೊ DECEMBER 1 : It has been very windy all day. We fear for the frigate.

This evening a courier arrived from Montreal. He told us that on November 26 one hundred Indians of the Five Nations, including women and children, arrived at Sault St. Louis. They are Onondagas and Cayugas. They expect still a few more who should also winter at Montreal. These guests would be more welcome if it were not necessary to feed them, but they are ambassadors who come only for this.

ಜೊ DECEMBER 2 : Northeast wind and snow. There is now as much on the ground as there was all last winter.

ಜೊ DECEMBER 3 : Dry northeast wind, minus 9 degrees [12°F.] in the evening.

ಜೊ DECEMBER 4 : At eight in the morning the thermometer was at minus 11 degrees [7°F.]. Southwest wind. In the evening minus 10 degrees [10°F.].

ಜೊ DECEMBER 5 : At eight in the morning minus 11½ degrees [6°F.]. It was that cold in 1742. Southwest wind.

ಜೊ DECEMBER 6 : At eight in the morning minus 17 degrees [−6°F.]. The record year of 1709 was only minus 15 degrees

---

[116] Unidentified, but by inference near Bic.
[117] Residence of Bigot, the Intendant.

[−2 °F.]. Northwest winds, which are the coldest and dryest of the winds here.

❧ DECEMBER 7 : At seven in the morning the thermometer was at minus 19 degrees [−11 °F.]. Northeast wind and snow all day. Thermometer at minus 15 [−2 °F.] at twelve in the evening.

❧ DECEMBER 8 : At eight in the morning minus 7½ degrees [15 °F.], wind from southwest, at eleven minus 12 degrees [5 °F.].

❧ DECEMBER 9 : In the morning minus 14½ degrees [0 °F.]. During the day the cold decreased noticeably. It rained and melted. The wind was south.

❧ DECEMBER 10 : In the morning 4 degrees [41 °F.]. During the day it thawed.

❧ DECEMBER 11 : Rain and continued thaw. The weather is as mild and gentle as in the springtime. This difference of 19 degrees [43 °F.] of temperature in three days should not be healthy. Thermometer at zero [32 °F.].

❧ DECEMBER 12 : Heavy rain and thawing all day. South wind. Zero degrees [32 °F.].

❧ DECEMBER 13 : Same weather as yesterday. Northeast wind. It is as mild as spring. The sleighs are beginning to proceed with difficulty. Thermometer ½ degree [33 °F.].

❧ DECEMBER 14 : In the afternoon the wind shifted and it started freezing again. Northwest wind. Received news from Montreal this morning. They are holding councils with the Iroquois. No news of the English. Thermometer minus 3½ degrees [24 °F.].

❧ DECEMBER 15 : Southwest wind, violently cold. A courier left for Montreal. Minus 21 degrees [−15 °F.].

❧ DECEMBER 16 : Fine weather. Extreme cold continues, minus 19½ degrees [−12 °F.]. Southwest wind.

❧ DECEMBER 17 : A little snow fell. Very windy[?].

Journal for 1756

ᗷ᛫ DECEMBER 18 : Calm weather, very cold. Southwest wind. They are about to send off a party of four hundred Missisaugas, Iroquois, and Canadians to go and strike at Fort George and look it over. Minus 17 degrees [−6°F.].

ᗷ᛫ DECEMBER 19 : Gentle southwest wind and very cold. Minus 16 degrees [−4°F.].

ᗷ᛫ DECEMBER 20 : Snow and powdered snow. Northeast wind. The powdered snow is an extremely fine snow which, falling from the sky and combining with that which the wind raises from the roofs and roads, envelops you, blinds you, and leads astray one who knows the way very well. When one is overtaken in the open by this powdered snow, one must realize that he is really in danger. There are instances of people who in the night, a hundred paces from their houses, have perished without being able to reach them.

ᗷ᛫ DECEMBER 21 : Calm weather, southwest wind, cold not too bad.

ᗷ᛫ DECEMBER 22 : Fine weather, sharp cold. Southwest wind.

ᗷ᛫ DECEMBER 23 : Northeast wind. Cloudy weather, light fall of powdered snow.

ᗷ᛫ DECEMBER 24 : Northeast wind, cloudy weather, a little snow. Courier came from Montreal. Many are dying in the hospitals. It is the result of a campaign such as we have just made.

ᗷ᛫ DECEMBER 25 : Calm weather, pleasant and gentle. Southwest wind.

ᗷ᛫ DECEMBER 26 : Snow and pleasant enough weather. Northeast wind.

ᗷ᛫ DECEMBER 27 : A windy day. I went today to hear mass at Lorette. It is a village of Huron Indians two leagues from Quebec. Their houses are built of stone. They hold their lands with the same rents and rules as do the French inhabitants. They are all Catholics, good or bad, for they are always savages just as much as those who have been the least tamed. They have a Jesuit missionary at their head. They regularly attend the services. The women in the church are separated from the men. The women sing after the men, and the women's choir is quite harmonious. They sing in unison. One would take them for a choir of our nuns, except that almost all of our Indian women have singularly melodious voices. What struck me most was an Indian who assisted at the mass in a surplice. I thought I saw the wolf in sheep's clothing. 3 degrees [25°F.].

We dined with a habitant in whose house I saw some superb wool. If they would interest the habitants in raising sheep, they would get from Canada a great quantity of wool of the most beautiful kind. The ewes very often have two lambs, a fecundity they do not possess in France. This article of wool is important in trade and deserves particular attention. 3 degrees [25°F.].

DECEMBER 28: Cloudy weather, very mild in the morning, 0 degrees [32°F.], colder in the afternoon, minus 3 degrees [25°F.]. West wind.

DECEMBER 29: Snow all day, northeast wind. A ship intended for Gaspé, where it is supposed to leave some foodstuffs and take on a load of salt cod and set sail for France, has been caught in the ice at the heights of Cape Chat.[118] It is locked in there. Three men of the crew froze and the rest mutinied. This ship is considered as lost. It left a few days after the *Abénakis*, but it rejoined it at the last anchorage and the frigate set sail only three hours before it. The frigate was obliged to cut her cable, which was frozen.

DECEMBER 30: Fair and pleasant weather, rather cold in the evening. Southwest.

DECEMBER 31: Clear and quite cold. Southwest.

[118] On the south shore of the St. Lawrence one hundred miles west of the west end of Anticosti Island.

Journal for 1757

&~ JANUARY 1 : A considerable amount of powdered snow. This evening there was a very heavy snowfall. Had news from Montreal. Minus 13 degrees [3°F.]. Northeast.

&~ JANUARY 2 : Mild weather. Zero degrees [32°F.]. Northwest wind.

&~ JANUARY 3 : Snow and powdered snow all day long. Already more snow has fallen than in a whole ordinary winter. This one is extremely harsh. Minus 9 degrees [12°F.]. Northeast wind.

&~ JANUARY 4 : The Marquis de Vaudreuil arrived today, accompanied by the Chevalier de Lévis. Calm and pleasant weather. Minus 11 degrees [7°F.]. Southwest wind.

&~ JANUARY 5 : Unsettled weather. It snowed during the evening. The Marquis de Montcalm got here at eleven in the evening. Minus 10 degrees [10°F.]. Northeast wind.

&~ JANUARY 6 : Fair and pleasant enough weather. Minus 6 degrees [18°F.]. Southwest wind.

&~ JANUARY 7 : It snowed hard this night, powdered snow,

morning and evening. Minus 5 degrees [21°F.] and minus 11 degrees [7°F.]. Variable winds.

ଛ୬ JANUARY 8 : A violent powder snowstorm this morning. It lasted all day in a horrible fashion. It is impossible to conceive of a viler sort of weather. Minus 14 degrees [0°F.] and minus 17 degrees [−6°F.]. Northeast wind.

ଛ୬ JANUARY 9 : This morning there fell a freezing rain accompanied by an icy wind which bit deep. The roads are impassable. One could not understand how frightful this country is if he has not been here. Minus 14 degrees [1°F.]. Northeast wind. Great ball and faro at the Intendant's house.

ଛ୬ JANUARY 10 : Fair and pleasant weather. Southeast wind. Minus 9 degrees [12°F.].

ଛ୬ JANUARY 11 : Very cold, with powdered snow. The roads are almost impassable. Carriages do not keep the snow out. It is torture to expose oneself in the open. Minus 14 degrees [1°F.]. Northeast wind.

ଛ୬ JANUARY 12 : Northeast wind and snow. Minus 13 degrees [3°F.].

ଛ୬ JANUARY 13 : Pleasant weather, snow without wind. Minus 5 degrees [21°F.]. Northeast wind.

ଛ୬ JANUARY 14 : Fine clear weather. Minus 9 degrees [12°F.]. Southwest wind.

ଛ୬ JANUARY 15 : Very cold weather, frightful in the afternoon. Violent wind and powdered snow. Minus 21 degrees [−15°F.]. Northeast wind.

ଛ୬ JANUARY 16 : Fine enough weather. Minus 16 degrees [−4° F.]. Northeast wind.

ଛ୬ JANUARY 17 : This morning the thermometer was at minus 24 degrees [−22°F.]. The great cold does not prevent one going out about as usual. Northwest. It is said that the river froze across

Journal for 1757

this night, but this news was found to be false. It was bridged across only for a few hours. They say that there is a bridge when the river freezes opposite the Pointe de Lévis. Its width would be two hundred toises.[1] For this to happen one must have cold enough weather with a calm and a low tide. Fourteen or 15 degrees [0°F.] is enough, along with the other two requirements that we have just mentioned. There is rejoicing when the ice bridge forms. The country to the south then is in touch with that to the northwest of the city. Firewood and provisions move easily and the inhabitants of Quebec go in their sleighs over to this point, which is a great diversion. Northwest wind. Minus 24 degrees [−22°F.].

JANUARY 18: Clear and frightfully cold weather. Everyone who comes from even a short distance has his nose, ears, or chin frozen. At the lower city it is always 1½ to 2 degrees [3–4° F.] less cold than at the upper. The cape breaks the force of the northwest wind. Minus 27 degrees [−29°F.] and minus 25 degrees [−24°F.]. Northwest wind.

JANUARY 19: The coldest part of the day is just at dawn. After that it lessens during the day by 4 [9°F.], 5 [11°F.], or even 6 [13°F.] degrees. It then gets colder during the nights. Minus twenty-four degrees [−22°F.]. Northwest wind.

JANUARY 20: The cold lessened. Southwest wind.

JANUARY 21: The cold wave is completely broken. Rain and thawing since noon. Zero degrees [32°F.]. Northeast wind.

JANUARY 22: Fair and pleasant weather. Minus 6 degrees [18°F.]. Southwest wind.

JANUARY 23: The weather which had been so mild for three days became very cold again. The wind has swung into the northwest. This night there was an earthquake at Montreal at fourteen minutes past midnight, and it lasted seven or eight seconds. Minus 18 degrees [−8°F.]. Northwest.

---

[1] The Quebec transcript says 800 toises. Actually the river is about 1,300 toises wide at Point Lévis and 450 at its narrowest at the city.

ᘌ JANUARY 24: Clear weather. Minus 12 degrees [5°F.]. Southwest wind.

ᘌ JANUARY 25: Cloudy weather with snow. Powdered snow in the evening. Minus 6 degrees [18°F.]. Northeast wind.

ᘌ JANUARY 26: Windy and snowy weather. The Marquis de Vaudreuil left today to return to Montreal. Minus 5 degrees [21°F.]. Northeast wind.

ᘌ JANUARY 27: Mild weather and very pleasant all day. Minus 4 degrees [23°F.]. Northeast wind.

ᘌ JANUARY 28: Calm weather. Minus 10 degrees [10°F.]. Southwest.

ᘌ JANUARY 29: Calm weather. We have news that the Marquis de Vaudreuil is ill at Trois Rivières. It is yet uncertain what his sickness is, but it nevertheless can be dangerous. It is, they say, a pleurisy. Minus seventeen degrees [−6°F.]. Southwest wind.

ᘌ JANUARY 30: M. de Rigaud left this morning for Trois Rivières. The bishop has exposed the Host and held a procession to re-establish M. de Vaudreuil's health. There is much talk about what would happen to the government in case he who today is at its head should be lost. M. de Rigaud is the senior, in fact the only civilian governor, and by a decree of the council command in the country devolves upon him. The Marquis de Montcalm is a brigadier general and would not know how to be under his orders. Northeast wind.

ᘌ JANUARY 31: The Marquis de Montcalm left this morning for Quebec. I went with him. We spent the night at St. Anne, sixteen leagues. Northeast wind.

ᘌ FEBRUARY 1: We reached Trois Rivières at ten. M. de Vaudreuil is still sick with a false pleurisy. There is every reason to believe that he will recover.

At noon a courier arrived from Carillon who brought us word

of an affair which took place two leagues from the fort on January 21.

M. de Lusignan, who commands there, had sent off several sleighs escorted by a sergeant and fifteen men to go and get certain provisions from St. Frederic. At about halfway between the two forts an English detachment dashed out of the woods in four places, cut off our little convoy, took three sleighs and seven soldiers. The rest took off as fast as their legs would carry them for Carillon, and M. de Lusignan at once sent off one hundred men of the regulars and the colony troops, along with a few Indians and Canadian volunteers under the orders of M. de Basserode, captain of Languedoc, and M. d'Astrel, lieutenant in the same regiment. M. de la Granville, captain in the regiment of La Reine asked leave to go along as a volunteer. M. de Langlade, half-pay ensign of La Marine, was at the head of the Indians, almost all Ottawas. The detachment went to lay an ambush on the road of the English, whose advance guard appeared three hours after midday. After one discharge of musketry, which did not have the effect that one would expect, the rain which had been falling all day having wet the guns, our troops pounced upon the enemy with the bayonet and overwhelmed them. Their rear guard gained a height which overlooked that upon which our people were. They shot it out until nightfall, when the English seized the opportunity to retire in disorder, leaving food, snowshoes and forty-two dead, three of them officers, on the field of battle. Our people made eight prisoners and retook four of the seven they had taken that morning. They [the English] had killed the other three. We lost nine soldiers, one Indian and a Canadian killed in the action and twenty-seven wounded, three of whom died from their wounds. Our detachment passed the night on the field of battle and received a reinforcement of twenty-five men and a convoy of food and munitions, a surgeon and a chaplain. Our soldiers, who had no snowshoes, fought at a disadvantage, floundering in the snow up to their knees. M. de Basserode was wounded in the leg. Five commissary clerks who volunteered for the action behaved wonderfully. One of them got a musket ball through his throat and died the next day. In Canada everyone is a soldier, but every soldier is not equally brave. The English detachment consisted of seventy-three men, six of them officers, and ten sergeants, commanded by Robert Rogers, captain of one of the four companies of forest runners that the English call "Rangers," whose mission is to go scouting in the woods. The companies consist of fifty men, with three officers and four sergeants. Two are in garrison on a little island in the Hudson River, opposite Fort Lydius, or Edward. The other two in a little stockaded fort which is near the ditch of Fort George, or William Henry, to the south of this fort. The success of this affair cannot excuse M. de Lusignan from having weakened his garrison considerably and thus running the risk of being taken by a surprise attack.[2]

We left Trois Rivières at four and spent the night at Isle au Castor,[3] crossing Lake St. Pierre and the river on the ice. The sleighs go unbelievably fast on the ice.

༄ FEBRUARY 2 : We reached Montreal at three in the afternoon. By letters from M. de Ligneris, commandant of Fort Duquesne, we learn that this winter an English party of thirteen men, eight of them Indians of the Chien[4] nation came and took three scalps from a party of Shawnees who were hunting. M. de Ligneris had them pursued. They got back the three scalps and made six prisoners. The Chien nation lies near to the Flat Heads [Choctaws]. It is numerous and warlike. When the Indians sink their tomahawks in the post, a warrior who has not been to war against the Chiens does not dare appear in the ranks of the others who have. According to the reports of prisoners there are only two hundred

---

[2] Rogers, with his party of 74 all bunched together, walked, according to his own statement, right into an ambush of about 250 French and Indians. He lost 14 killed, 6 wounded, and 6 prisoners. The French force actually consisted of 89 regulars and 90 Canadians and Indians.

[3] Unidentified, but probably one of a group of islands at the western end of Lake St. Pierre.

[4] Unidentified. The French sometimes called the Cheyennes by this name, but they were western Indians, far from the area of the Choctaws. Possibly the Creeks or Chickasaws, who were constantly at war with the Choctaws, were meant.

Journal for 1757

men at Fort Cumberland, and, as there has been no build-up of provisions at this place, it would appear that the English plan nothing against the Belle Rivière.

&~ FEBRUARY 3 : We shall be very much inconvenienced next campaign if the help from France does not arrive promptly. Despite all the pains of Sieur Cadet,[5] commissary general, the Intendant has been able to promise only forty days of supplies for four thousand men. The circumstances are difficult and critical. The enemy apparently wish to start the campaign early. The poor administration and the greed of officials and a few private individuals are the cause of this scarcity which has been building up for several years.

The Marquis de Vaudreuil has received representatives from the Abnakis of St. Francis[6] and Bécancour[7] that the Jesuits wish to move their village to the lands of the Belle Rivière. The pretext of these zealous missionaries was to get them away from commerce with the French and the use of brandy, and their object to profit from the lands which the Indians had cleared. They have already done this in regard to the Hurons whom they have moved from Vielle Lorette to La Jeune Lorette.[8] The Abnakis do not wish at all to consent to this change of abode. Beholding them [considered] Jansenists,[9] and the Jesuits have refused them the sacraments and even entrance into the church. Well and good, say the Indians to their missionary, you are the father of prayer, the prayers, the sacraments, and the church all belong to you, but it is we who have built your house, it is ours, and we are going to close its door to you. Jerome, the chief of the village, also presented a note to M. de Vaudreuil, conceived in these terms: "I, Jerome, chief of the villages of the Abnakis, say to you, my father, that the black

---

[5] One of Bigot's gang. Son of a butcher, he became the richest man in Canada through his peculations.

[6] A mission near the mouth of the St. Francis River.

[7] Near Trois Rivières.

[8] The original La Lorette Mission was about eight miles due west of Quebec. The New Lorette was on the St. Charles River some four miles north of the older mission.

robes wish to make us leave our native hearthstones and carry our council fire elsewhere. This land we inhabit is ours. What it produces is the fruit of our labor. Dig into it and you will find the bones of our ancestors. Thus, it is necessary that our ancestor's bones rise up from the ground and follow us into a foreign land." The Jesuits finally renounced, at least for the present, this enterprise.

ᗣ FEBRUARY 4–6 : I questioned two English prisoners taken in the action of January 21. According to their report, the garrison of Fort Lydius consists of six hundred men detached from the three regiments of troops of Old England. There are moreover, as we have said, two companies of rangers whose sole mission is to make frequent patrols in the woods beyond the fort. The garrison of Fort George consists of four hundred men, detached from the same regiments as above, and two similar irregular companies who perform the same service as at Fort Lydius. The two forts are stocked with provisions sufficient for a large army for a whole campaign. The regular troops and the militia, which has not been allowed to go home, are distributed in Saratoga, Stillwater, Halfmoon, and Albany. One-third of all those able to bear arms in New York, New England, and Pennsylvania have been ordered to hold themselves ready to march on short notice. They say among the English that Lord Loudoun will assemble at Lake St. Sacrement in April an army of twenty thousand men, and that an English fleet will come to seize the River St. Lawrence.

The last detachment has come from Lake St. Sacrement, which is all frozen over, the ice, however, being still thin. Hudson River as far as Albany, where the tide is felt, and the creeks that flow into it are also frozen over and ordinarily remain so until the end of March. In these, the most northern parts of the English provinces, there is enough snow for sleighs and sledges. In accordance with the depositions of the prisoners, I made a plan of Forts George and Lydius.

We are having a great number of grappling hooks made here, and have sent from Quebec to St. Jean winter provisions, sleds, snowshoes. The fourteen carpenters have left for Carillon. These movements give rise to all sorts of conjectures.

Someone stole the royal money chest from M. Varin's house. There is little that one will say here about this theft. Pray God that the King this year loses only this which amounts to fifty-four thousand francs.

᛫ FEBRUARY 7 : By letter dated January 13 Abbé Piquet informs us that he has sent an express to the Five Nations to see how matters stand and to learn if, in case we wish to attack New England from their direction, they would allow us free passage through their lands and furnish food, of which the Indians have a considerable accumulation.

᛫ FEBRUARY 8 : A letter of January 5 from Sieur Pouchot,[10] captain in the Béarn regiment, who commands at Niagara, tells us that the Delawares are always [there] in great numbers. They seem well-intentioned and expect to be there next spring to the number of four hundred. Sieur Pouchot continually entertains parties carrying on little wars. He was visited on their return by sixty Senecas who had killed twenty men and made three prisoners in Virginia.

A letter from M. de Ligneris of the twentieth gave details of the little adventure described under February 2. Only the Indians who came to attack the Shawnees were not of the Chien nation, but of that of the Catawbas. The commandant hopes to keep conditions at La Belle Rivière in the good state which they now enjoy, provided that he is kept supplied with food, munitions, and trade goods.

᛫ FEBRUARY 6-16 : The Marquis de Vaudreuil arrived at Montreal today completely cured of his illness. A party of 300 regulars, 50 of whom will be grenadiers from the 4 companies in this country, and 896 men making 16 companies, each formed by 17 soldiers of La Marine regiment, 33 militiamen, 2 officers of La

---

[9] Jansenism was an anti-Jesuit heresy resembling Calvinism in some ways.
[10] An excellent officer who gave fine service throughout the war.

Marine, 1 from the militia, a cadet and 2 sergeants, are to be at St. Jean by the twentieth under the orders of M. de Rigaud and M. de Longueil, King's lieutenant at Quebec, and in this capacity acting as lieutenant colonel. The first has gone to sing the war song with the Abnakis at St. Francis, and the second with the Iroquois at the Sault. M. Poulharies, captain of grenadiers of the Royal Roussillon, commands the French detachment. Sieur Dumas, captain of Marine troops, acts as brigade major. The objective of this expedition is still uncertain. What is certain is that it will use up the few eatables that we have been able to get together, that it will prevent us from starting an early campaign, and that this movement will perhaps get the English in motion a month earlier than otherwise. It would seem that they have the idea of surprising Fort George, an undertaking which, judging by the statements of the prisoners made January 21, seems impossible, lacking one of those miracles which happen only in Canada, and, if they do not take this fort, no other of those bits of luck which are called successes here will make up to the colony for the consumption of the few foodstuffs that we still have, or to the King for the almost million of expense that this enterprise will cost. Besides one would wish to secure surprise, and a crowd of English who freely walk in the city and the suburbs are witnesses of all the movements which take place, hearing all the talk that goes on, and being able to know with precision the number of troops, the time of departure, and the place of assembly. Sieur Mercier has left for Carillon and Sieur Lotbinière is due to go there immediately. The Marquis de Montcalm has several times made in writing all the remonstrations that his office and the King's orders to him allow him to make, and for which the present conduct of affairs gives only too much reason, but his warning suffers the fate of those of Cassandra, and no one does him the honor of consulting with him. He most often learns from public talk of the operations ordered by M. de Vaudreuil. The sovereign council of Quebec has sent a commissioner here to enquire into the theft made at the treasury. On the fourteenth the house of Sieur Martel, who has just retired as storehouse keeper, caught fire. It is certainly odd that at almost the same time, both

Journal for 1757

the treasury was robbed and the storehouse keeper's house burned, and this just before the time the accounts were to be presented, but this fire was put out at once.

❧ FEBRUARY 17–28: On the eighteenth at St. Jean the equipment was issued. It is well to list here of what this equipment consists. This list will show once and for all how these winter expeditions are equipped. (The money value of part of this equipment may be taken instead, if one chooses.)

EQUIPMENT

One overcoat	25 livres
One blanket	9 "
One wool cap	3 "
Two cotton shirts	16 "
One pair mitasses[11]	5 "
One breechclout	2 livres, 10 sous

(A soldier has breeches and drawers instead of a breechclout.)

Two hanks of thread	One waistcoat
Six needles	Two pair of deerskin shoes
One awl	One dressed deer skin
One tinderbox	Two portage collars[12]
One butcher's knife	One drag rope
One comb	One pair of snowshoes
One worm	One bearskin
One tomahawk	One tarpaulin per officer, one large one to every four men.
Two pair of stockings	
Two siamese[?] knives	
One pair of mittens	

Twelve days rations have been issued, bread, salt pork, peas on the basis of field ration. Each officer has in addition three pints of brandy and two pounds of chocolate. Each of them has assembled his dog team to draw the sleds, some have even taken horses. Dogs, at the time of departure, cost up to one hundred livres.

---

[11] Loose leggings made of coarse, heavy cloth, fastened with garters at ankle and knee.

[12] Probably some sort of breast strap to attach to a rope when hauling.

The expedition left St. Jean in four divisions on the twentieth, twenty-first, and twenty-second, and the fourth division which should have left on the twenty-third was held up until the twenty-fifth by bad weather and a thaw. Lake Champlain was largely open water. It was necessary to send back horses, dogs, and part of the provisions, and each officer had to drag his own sled. M. de Bleury has been sent to carry the detachment in boats to the southern part of the lake, opposite Pointe à Fer.[13] They say that the ice is safe from there as far as Carillon. The staff and the grenadiers go with the fourth division. In truth they have been promised that they will be the advance guard on the return trip. What I notice here is that the foolish errors are made in a big way, both as to means and to extent. Behind the expedition there march 350 domesticated Indians, who will help the consumption [of provisions].

During the last days of this month it froze again very hard. Several officers of colony troops came back sick. The French officers set an example of steadfastness and even of good grace in enduring the hardships of the march.

We have had news from M. Boishebert, commander at River St. Jean, dated January 15. As he was marching to surprise the fort at Gaspereau,[14] taken from us in 1755, the English evacuated and burned it on October 12. Sometime previously they had captured or killed sixteen men of this garrison. M. de Boishebert has withdrawn to Miramichi and its vicinity for the winter with his Acadians to the number of fifteen hundred, not including women and children. He has orders to remain at this post and to proceed to Isle Royale[15] immediately upon call by M. de Drucour, who commands there. Besides, he feels the scarcity common to all Canada. The Acadians exist with ten pounds of beef and ten pounds of peas. They also eat seal meat and a few skinny horses. This poor nourishment gives rise to much sickness. On the twenty-seventh a com-

---

[13] Some three miles south of Rouses Point, N. Y.

[14] The fort on the northern side of the Isthmus of Chignecto in Nova Scotia. The English, however, kept possession of the much more important Fort Cumberland on the Isthmus.

[15] Cape Breton Island.

Journal for 1757

mand of the bishop was published, ordering public prayers to continue until the end of the campaign.

The Indians did not leave St. Jean until the twenty-eighth.

MARCH 3 : A deputation of Iroquois from the Lake and the Sault arrived today to warn the Marquis de Vaudreuil that they suspected the fidelity of the Oneidas, who last year made us take Fort Bull. M. de Vaudreuil has not given any credit to this advice which he believes to be advanced by the Five Nations, who are jealous of the credit and consideration enjoyed by the Oneidas among the French. He has reassured the domesticated Iroquois.

The institution of army field hospitals has been approved. They can only gain by this change.

MARCH 4 : The Intendant has bought from four private citizens five hundred quarters of Nerac[16] flour. He proposes to make bread from it for the officers. It would be more human and more military to mix this excellent flour with other of lesser quality and to make bread from it for both soldier and officer.

It has been decreed in order to conserve food, that henceforth, all Canadians who leave Quebec, Trois Rivières, and Montreal to go to war will take with them food for their trip and their stay at St. Jean, and that the commissary clerk will then pay them for it in cash.

All the storehouse keepers at the private posts have been charged with receiving and examining their accounts. There is always an appearance of reform.

MARCH 5 : News from Detroit has been received. The Choctaws and the Acapas or Catawbas, Carolina Indians, seek peace with the Indian nations who are our allies and offer to fight the English. The Cherokees have sent word by Sieur Decoigne, a Canadian captured and adopted by them ten years ago, that they will come in the spring to Detroit to hear the words of Ononthio and that they will go wherever he wishes.

---

[16] Unidentified.

The inhabitants of Detroit expect to be able to furnish Fort Duquesne with five hundred hundredweight of flour, maize, and salt pork. If they were assured of being able to sell their crops to the posts in their area, they would pay more attention to cultivating their land.

At the same time we had news from Niagara as of February 7. They had a big council there with the Cayugas, the Delawares, and the Shawnees. They reported what had happened at the council held at Colonel Johnson's house. They have renewed their assurance of attachment to the French. The Delawares have threatened the Five Nations with war if they do not come out in our favor. This nation unceasingly has before its eyes the ignominious stain of wearing the "machicoté,"[17] with which the Iroquois branded them after conquering them. It is like the day of the Caudine Forks which the Romans never forgot.

They said that the English had sent an officer to them from Virginia, exhorting them to take up the hatchet, but they refused. The Cayugas reported that at Albany there was a sharp dispute between the Scottish Highlanders and the New England militia, that they had come to sabre blows, and that several hundred men were left [dead] on the ground. This news doubtless has some foundation. I do not doubt the lack of understanding which will always exist between troops of different kinds, but I very much doubt that there was so much blood spilled.

The Indians say that according to reports circulating among the English that they will make efforts in the direction of La Belle Rivière and that an English squadron will come soon to block the St. Lawrence River.

Sieur Pouchot, although a Frenchman, seems to have won the affection of the Indians who have given him the name of Gategayogen, that is to say the "Center Of Good Fortune."

The Marquis de Vaudreuil has decided to have the fortifications at Niagara done over in stone.

---

[17] Technically, this word has some connection with choral singing, but here it obviously refers to the woman's skirt which the Delawares were forced by the Iroquois to wear figuratively after their defeat in 1720.

Journal for 1757

§➳ MARCH 8 : By the latest news from Fort Duquesne one learns that the Catawbas scalped a Canadian and took another prisoner. This news appears to contradict what we said above, that they had sent deputies to Detroit. But this contradiction is only apparent. It is the majority of the nation that wishes to make peace with us, but there are some among them who live with the English and, consequently, cannot help from following them.

We have also had news from Niagara as of February 14. MM. de Chabert and de Joncaire left there on the thirteenth to go as ambassadors to the Five Nations. A council was held with the Onondagas and the Iroquois of La Belle Rivière. These last have reproached the Onondagas that the ground was covered with their dead who demanded vengeance against the English. Upon which a chief got up, sang a war song and was followed by 60 warriors. This crew sang, drank, and beat the drum all night. The party grew larger the next morning and they expect that there will be 120 warriors. It should go through the country of the Delawares, in the direction of Tioga.[18]

The Delawares said in council with more emphasis than truth that they were five thousand, and that should even twenty thousand English come from Europe they would exterminate them in the forests.

§➳ MARCH 10 : For a week the cold has been very sharp. The thermometer is always between minus 18 degrees[−8°F.] and minus 20 degrees [−12°F.]. The sun, however, already has power enough to melt the ice.

§➳ MARCH 12 : According to news just received from St. Frederic, under the date of the seventh, M. de Rigaud, with his last division, left St. Jean the twenty-fifth and spent the night two leagues from St. Jean. The order of march was a company of Canadians, commanded by M. de Godefroy, at the head. M. Dufy, merchant of Montreal, commanding the volunteers; the grenadier company, the rest of the Canadians, and the Indians with M. de Longueuil.

[18] On the Susquehanna River near Elmira, N. Y.

February 26: A day's march of six leagues in two divisions, one through the woods, the other by the shore of the lake.

February 27: Halted on account of snow.

February 28: The weather was fine; they profited by it by making seven leagues.

March 1: Eight to nine leagues.

March 2: Halted because of wind and fear of powdered snow.

March 3: Difficult march, there being much water on the ice. However they made seven leagues.

March 4: Equally difficult march because of thaw; made only five leagues.

March 5: Left at half-past one in order to arrive early at St. Frederic and camped half a league from the fort on the north side.

March 6–7: Halted. Orders to the Canadians to make deerskin shoes, both for themselves and for the soldiers, to repair the sleds and to make ready sledges in case there was water on the ice.[19] They were obliged to issue supplementary rations, much having been spoiled on account of the rain. They started to proceed with caution and to mount guard after the third. And at St. Frederic the officers were ordered to camp with their men.

At St. Frederic M. de Rigaud found M. Mercier, who assured him that all was ready at Carillon, ladders, combustible materials, and food, so that they could leave with fifteen days rations.

One-half of the detachment was to leave St. Frederic on the eighth with M. de Rigaud, the other half the ninth with M. de Poulhariez. The Indians, some hours later, with M. de Longueil.

Note: There have been omitted from this journal two little letters which deserve attention and which will serve to prove more and more both the bad administration and the lack of faith that must be added to what those say who are charged with various details, and how much this country is ruled by Providence. First, at the time they were assuring the Marquis de Vaudreuil that no food supplies were lacking at Presque Isle, M. Benoit, who commanded there, a most truthful man, if there is any such in Canada, informed me that except for the food supplies from Oswego, which had been

---

[19] The sleds ("*traînes*") were made like a great ski with lacing thongs along the edges, and their loads would get wet if there was much water over the ice. By "sledges" is probably meant the addition of runners to raise the ski-like affair and make it into what we call a sled.

Journal for 1757

sent there, he would have been forced to evacuate the fort through lack of supplies. The second fact is that M. Mercier, commanding the artillery, responsible for inventorying the powder and munitions found at Oswego, charged his inventory with only twenty-three thousandweight of powder, and M. Jacob, artillery officer, a very honest and very exact man, *rara avis in terris et presertim in America septentrionale*,[20] has by his exact inspection of the boats put into store an additional ten thousandweight of powder and ——— of ball.

Note: In calculating the leagues made each day one will find that they are less than one ordinarily makes from St. Jean to Fort St. Frederic; this happens because Canadians always differ as to leagues and distances, and because they were able to go direct from point to point on the ice without any detours.

MARCH 15 : M. de la Pauze, major of the Guyenne regiment, has ruled jointly with the commissary general that they will not[?] establish the ration allowance, be it for garrison or for field duty, at eleven sous per soldier and fourteen sous per officer. The ration is composed of two pounds of bread, half a pound of salt pork or a pound of beef and four ounces of peas. The allowance of last campaign was on the basis of twelve sous per pound for salt pork for officers and ten sous for soldiers, two sous, six deniers a pound for bread for officers and two for soldiers, six livres the hundredweight for peas.

MARCH 18 : M. Desandrouins, engineer officer, left this morning for St. Jean to look into the methods of repairing this fort, the palisades of which have partly fallen down through decay, as well as the gallery, and of rendering it safe from a surprise attack by building a moat and a drawbridge, an enlargement of the magazine and lodgings for 150 men.

The four battalions of regulars have been asked the number of carpenters they have so that they can be sent next week to work at getting the wood ready while waiting the time in early spring when work can get under way.

---

[20] "A rare bird in the land and especially so in North America."

The Marquis de Vaudreuil appears to fear through Indian warnings an invasion by way of Les Cédres.[21] It has been proposed to him to re-establish the palisades of a sort of fort which is there and to put a colony ensign and twenty-five or thirty soldiers there with signals to communicate with Isle Perault and other neighboring parishes, the militia of which would turn out promptly if any expedition should appear.

MARCH 19 : According to news from Carillon M. de Rigaud's detachment remained there from the ninth to the fifteenth. This delay was occasioned by the rations not being ready and by the bad weather. It got under way the fifteenth by the south side of Lake St. Sacrement. They issued rations for twelve days and distributed ladders five feet, eight inches long, three of which fit together and make one of thirteen and one-half feet[?]. They have given one to every fourth soldier. The ladders conform closely enough to the model which was given to the Marquis de Vaudreuil. They are a little heavy, having been made of green wood. This sort of preparations should always be made in advance and they always should have a supply in the arsenals, something they forget as easily in Europe as in America.

A large part of the Canadians were badly armed. It was necessary to get busy repairing their arms while they were at Carillon, and this will always happen so long as the militia officers are not held responsible and punished when they bring badly armed men.

MARCH 25 : The Marquis de Vaudreuil, having sent the Oneida, whose attachment to our interests is known, with the younger M. Lorimier, and several Indians to sound out the dispositions of the Five Nations and of the village of the Palatines,[22] they returned on the twenty-fourth and had a private and secret

---

[21] A village on the north bank of the St. Lawrence about thirty miles above Montreal.

[22] At German Flats on the Mohawk. The settlers at this little village believed that they could remain neutral, but the place was destroyed by a party of French and Indians in November, 1757. On the south and opposite side of the river was Fort Herkimer, called Fort Kouri by the French.

audience on the twenty-fifth. The result is that the Palatines disavow what the Oneidas said at the great council, perhaps because they fear the English or because they are ignorant of the secret negotiations since the English captured one of their principal men, named L'Ours, and have established a garrison of two hundred men in his house and have fortified it. They also reported a sort of council held at Albany where Colonel [Sir William] Johnson has asked their aid and given them a hatchet. The result was that all this came to no conclusion and that they went away saying that they wished to consult with their elders who had gone to hold a big council at Montreal. It would seem that the Cayugas are those who have shown the greatest attachment at this council to the interests of their father Ononthio and have spoken most haughtily to their brother Corlar.

Twenty carpenters and a sergeant of the Béarn regiment were sent off this morning to prepare the timber necessary to repair the fortifications at St. Jean and to enlarge the storehouses.

ೀ MARCH 29 : M. Mercier has brought the news and the details of the expedition of M. de Rigaud de Vaudreuil, Governor of Trois Rivières. The detachment of sixteen hundred men, under the orders of M. de Rigaud, left on the fifteenth and camped on the right of Lake St. Sacrement, opposite M. de Contrecoeur's old camp. On the sixteenth at daybreak they sent off a scouting party of seventy-five Indians and twenty-five Frenchmen, commanded by MM. Hertel, de Louisbourg[?], and St. Simon. The detachment proceeded down the middle of the lake in five columns, those of the right and the left composed of Indians commanded by MM. de Longueil, father and son. The center three, that of the regulars, commanded by M. de Poulharies, captain of grenadiers of the Royal Roussillon, and the other two of colony troops commanded by MM. St. Martin and St. Ours, lieutenants of colony troops. The volunteers formed the advance guard and they all camped at Sugar Loaf. On the seventeenth they proceeded in the same order and went into camp on the ice near the Bay of Kalouské, where they had to sleep on the ice without any fires. The eighteenth they reached the Bay, and, after having made a division of the sleds, they remained there all day and in the morning sent MM. de Poulharies, Dumas, Mercier, Savournin, and Raymond with a detachment to reconnoiter the fort, which was a league and a half from the camp, under the escort of fifty Indians and fifty Canadians, commanded by MM. de Langy, Senior, Longueil, Junior, and Pontleroy. In the evening they issued orders for an escalade attack in three columns of which the French [regulars] would form the right, and they got under way for the Bay of Niacktaron, which is only a league from the fort and which would be the depot for sleds and provisions. They left at eleven in the evening in order of march. MM. Dumas, Mercier, and Savournin, who had been sent a second time to examine the fort, having reported that it was not possible to attack it, they determined to limit themselves to burning everything outside, and they worked vainly at it during the night of the eighteenth to nineteenth. The wood they used was wet and the combustibles made of Sieur Mercier's composition were useless.

MARCH 19 : The Indians started to set fire to a few bateaux. Two Indians were wounded and a colony soldier wiped out by a bomb. The English made a sortie to put out the fire in the bateaux. They were driven back with a loss of a dozen men. The same day the pickets of Royal Roussillon and Languedoc were ordered to go to watch the movements of the enemy on the road to Lydius. A colony soldier who got mixed up with them had his foot carried away by a cannon ball. At evening the pickets of La Sarre and Béarn with two hundred men of the colony troops were ordered to help those who were trying to burn the vessels, bateaux, and huts, and this was achieved with some degree of success.

MARCH 20 : The entire detachment was marched across the lake in full view of the English, parading the ladders ostentatiously, and M. Mercier was sent to the commander of the fort to demand that he surrender. M. Mercier told him that it was the custom of civilized nations to give warning before an escalade in order to avoid bloodshed, that he should surrender and not persist in defending a place belonging to the King of France. The Englishman could smile, for the Frenchman ignored the fact that an escalade is a surprise action, and that once war started, property rights and claims no longer exist. To avoid being ridiculous when at war, one must be more than just a man of spirit.

The English commander, after assembling the officers of the garrison in order to gain time and to have time to empty part of the outer storehouses, answered that he would defend himself. The troops returned to their original positions, and they again sent off the light companies of Royal Roussillon and Languedoc on the road to Lydius, and at nightfall some grenadiers and pickets of La Sarre and Béarn were ordered to support the men who had been ordered to keep on setting fires. They burned the sheds, the little fort. The English had profited by our negligence during our demand for surrender by pulling the roofs off the storehouses, so that the fire should not spread to the Fort.

MARCH 21: The bad weather forced inaction. Only a few Indians were sent scouting.

MARCH 22: Orders were given to start back, but the bad weather prevented. There still remained to be burned a vessel pierced for sixteen guns, which was on the stocks at fifteen paces from the fort and under its fire. M. Wolf, half-pay officer of the Bentheim Regiment, who was accompanying the regulars, asked permission to go and burn it at nightfall with twenty volunteers from the regulars. It was not until eleven at night that he succeeded in his operation, in spite of the enemy's continuous fire. Only two soldiers of Languedoc were killed and three wounded from Royal Roussillon, Languedoc, and Béarn. Such was the end of this expedition; they burned the enemy's three hundred bateaux, four vessels, two storehouses, and left one other which they believed too exposed to burn. They burned the little fort where they kept their volunteers, the huts, the saw mill, a lot of wood planks and fire wood. One must hope that this loss will delay the operations of the enemy, who were able and wished to get started ahead of us in this area. The success they had in this expedition is proof that the Marquis de Montcalm was entirely right in wishing for a detachment of only six to eight hundred men at most. They would have accomplished the same objectives with more glory, have cost less in money and food, and we would have been able to get started as soon as the ice went out. It seems to me that they should not have summoned the commander to surrender until after they had burned all the surrounding structures, but should have taken a firmer tone, not speaking of an escalade but of reducing the fort to ashes and putting the garrison to the sword.

The English will not fail to try to make it appear in public papers that this [affair with its] summons to surrender, made by so large a body of troops and followed by two days of inaction in front of the fort, was really the raising of a siege. It is even to be feared that, such is the importance of the operation, they will believe it in Europe, in view of the expense and what a detachment of sixteen hundred men, which for America should be regarded as a real army, should have been able to accomplish.

MARCH 23: The detachment left Fort George and camped at Sugar Loaf.

MARCH 24: At Carillon.

MARCH 26: The expedition left Carillon after having left there the four pickets of Languedoc, Béarn, La Sarre and Royal Roussillon. They sent the Chevalier de Langy off to get news of the enemy and to make some prisoners. The expedition went into camp the same day, the twenty-sixth, at St. Frederic. It had to remain the twenty-seventh and twenty-eighth and to leave as reinforcements for the garrison the pickets of the companies detached from La Marine regiment, and will take away with it the grenadier company, and all the Canadians that must be sent when the snow melts to prepare their fields and sow their crops. The Indians that have been let loose keep coming away. The time of release should be determined when the Indians are invited to an expedition by giving them belts, and when they accept these it is a pledge that they bind themselves to follow the general in whose name they are presented and for the [entire] expedition proposed to them.

Since the ice in Lake Champlain has started to break up toward Pointe aux Fer, thirty bateaux have been ordered to meet our detachment.

The English have asserted that of the seventy-seven men in the party defeated by M. de Basserode, captain of the Languedoc regiment, all but three escaped.[23] Those who did not remain on the field of battle died of their wounds.

[23] The ambushing of Rogers. See the entry for February 1, 1757.

Journal for 1757

The Indians are very discontented over the last expedition, and, since they are not courtiers, they complain loudly. They even go so far as to express their thoughts in full council, but the interpreters only translate what is agreeable to the assembly.

᠅ APRIL 1–13 : The thaw seemed to start seriously on the fourth. By the sixth it was dangerous to cross the river in a sleigh or even on foot. All the crossings are no longer about the same. It has been necessary to be familiar with them and to choose your way; some, even the most daring or the most unfortunate, have perished. Since the sixth it has been the most beautiful weather in the world. In this city the sidewalks by the buildings are all bare. The mass of snow and ice in the streets decreases noticeably every day; also it is warm. One could say that in this country there truly are only two seasons, winter and summer. On the eighth the sleighs were put away and the carriages brought out.

On the ninth a man arrived from Louisiana. He left there on July 1 with the convoy which is sent from that colony every year to the posts we have in the Illinois country. He left the Illinois country Christmas Eve, and at last got here, having had as guides through the forests and lakes some Indians that he changed at each post [on the way]. I was astonished to see this courier who came from so far, in so uncomfortable a fashion, waiting neglected at the door of M. de Vaudreuil's office and paid no more attention than if he were one who had come to Paris from Versailles.

According to the news he brought from Louisiana, they there enjoy a complete peace. The fortunate inhabitants of that beautiful country as late as the month of July did not know that war was declared. May they always be ignorant of it!

We learned at the same time of the death of the chief of the Caitas[?], a nation located between Carolina and Mobile, near Alibamans, the last post we have in this region.[24] These Indians can turn out sixteen hundred warriors. Since their chief was strongly attached to us, it is suspected that an English traitor killed him with

---

[24] Fort Toulouse in the country of the Alibamons, a Creek tribe. It was about ten miles north of present Montgomery, Ala.

a poisoned lancet. The chief bears the title of emperor, his son has been elected in his place and they have named a regent to govern during his minority. Thus, as one approaches Mexico, he again finds traces of civilized customs. The Natchez of Louisiana have a king, temples, a religion marked by initiations, etc.

᚛ APRIL 10 : Easter. An order of the bishop's has been published which decrees that next Sunday a *Te Deum* will be sung in thanks for the fortunate success of the last expedition. It is to be noted that the bishop did this public act without either the orders or the participation of the Governor General, who had not dared to ask for it. The bishop's order is just as ridiculous as the object of the *Te Deum*.

᚛ APRIL 19 : What ice was left on the river went out this night. It is now navigable. A canoe came from the south shore. The first troops are preparing to start the campaign. The weather continues to be very fine. However the ground is still too wet to allow them to start sowing except on the high land. Thus in three months the land is sowed and produces the crop.

This evening we had news from France by way of Louisbourg under the date of October 28. The ship left La Rochelle November 6 and reached Isle Royale January 30. The Louisbourg courier was sent on February 3. The privateer captains of this place are very good. They have brought back some one hundred thousand crowns worth of prizes. The place is in good condition and fears nothing. The English have sent M. de la Grive, military commissary, and eighty soldiers from Halifax to be exchanged for a like number of those captured at Oswego.

The European news is of the invasion of Saxony by the King of Prussia, the action between the Prussians and Saxon troops, which was indecisive, the march of twenty-five thousand French troops into Germany as auxiliaries for the Queen,[25] and commanded by the Prince de Soubise, the army which is to assemble in Flanders under the orders of the Prince de Conti, the indecision

---

[25] Maria Theresa of Austria.

of the Dutch, insulted by the English, and to whom the French do not wish neutrality to be permitted, and who, realizing that the ruin of their commerce is inevitable whichever side they declare for, do not know what to do. Finally the troubles which still continue in France between Parliament and the clergy. At Rome, at least, the soothsayers would not let them be spoken of when the state was at war. Despite this ferment, which seems to threaten Europe with a general conflagration, I see the Prussian monarch, who, put perhaps under the ban of the empire and who, finding himself to have got involved in too violent a game, concluding in a moment his own private peace. The Queen who, profiting by our alliance, made her son King of the Romains, and then regaining the spirit and the methods of her house, is ready to declare against us. Spain remains in position to be a mediator and to profit by these troubles, more perhaps than any other country. And finally England, the sole cause of this war, soon exhausted by a violent crisis which annihilates her commerce, wearies her existence, increases her public debt, and makes the nation insolvent and in ruins, demands before two years the peace which she has so madly wished to break, and well resolved to take every measure to break it again with advantage when one expects it least; and France victorious, but worn out by these very victories, governed moreover by political principles, making peace and not gaining from this war the advantages that she should.

APRIL 24 : Abbé Piquet, missionary of La Presentation, a post due to his efforts, arrived this morning with sixty Indians who come to demand an explanation on the matter of the proceedings of an Onondaga chief who took them belts in the name of the Marquis de Vaudreuil, pretending that the Governor General had made him chief of the [Long] House, which appeared to them contrary to the rights of a warlike and free people who acknowledged as chiefs only those they gave themselves and for the period they wished. They brought with them the Onondaga chief to be present at the explanation of the words of their father. They reiterated that they were the only Indians who in M. Duquesne's time had been willing, while kneeling, to take an oath of fidelity to the great Ononthio, a ceremony performed by no other Indian nation, save on this occasion, and that they believed that this injury to their rights freed them from this oath. Besides they complained that this Onondaga chief was not yet of the Faith and that we [the French] wished them to trust too much and too soon in the Five Nations whom they were constantly advised to mistrust.

Note: I will observe that in the estimation of the Five Nations, the Onondagas hold first place. It is at their [Long] House that the general councils must be held, since the defection of the Mohawks, and, to use the metaphorical expression of these Indians, it is among the Onondagas that the council fire must be kept forever burning, just like that of the Vestal Virgins in ancient times.

Note: I forgot in speaking of M. Rigaud's expedition to say that M. de Lusignan, commander of the fort at Carillon, one of the senior officers of the colony troops and one of those who has the most reputation, has profited by the sad situation of finding himself in an uninhabited country to have wine sold at the rate of 1200 livres per hogshead, while it is worth only 100 crowns [300 livres] at Montreal, which comes to 10 livres per jug, and brandy which is worth 15 livres per velte,[26] or four jugfulls at 50 livres, and an inspector of works has profited by the circumstances to have a skinny cow killed, and sold her at 30 sous [1½ livres] per pound. One must agree that this spirit of greed, of gain, of commerce, will always destroy the spirit of honor, of glory, and military spirit. All that happens in the colonies is critical of gentry[27] in trade, and confirms the system of the Marquis de Lassay and of the Baron de Montesquieu for a monarchial state.

APRIL 25: Ten Iroquois went on the warpath toward Fort George. They were advised to bring back some live letters, in other words, prisoners.

Several Ottawas and Potawatomis also went to make a strike in

---

[26] About one quart.
[27] "*Noblesse*" in text, but "gentry" is a better term when applied to Canada.

Journal for 1757

the same region. They ask for Aouschie [Aoussik?], Nipissing chief, always filled with the idea of perishing or of avenging as much as he can M. Descombes whom he killed unintentionally.

APRIL 26 : M. de Pommeray, officer from Isle Royale, left this morning to take advantage of a ship that must hurry from Quebec to carry food to Miramichi for M. de Boishebert and the Acadians. This officer has been charged to give to M. de Drucourt[28] the packets containing the details of what happened here during the winter. The Governor of Louisbourg will send them on to France.

The council with the Iroquois from La Presentation was held this morning; the two Indians that Abbé Piquet had sent to Paris were present, dressed like Frenchmen from head to foot. Pierre, one of them, wore the jacket that the Dauphin had sent him. He seemed to me a savage harlequin in blond wig and lace-covered garb. The Iroquois orator expounded at length upon the attachment of their House for the religion and the King; that only they among all the Indians had, in the presence of M. Duquesne, sworn an oath of fidelity to the great Ononthio; that this governor general had given them the accolade with the sword which he had promised to use to protect them; [that] he had spoken of the form of government established over them, consisting of twelve village chiefs, six war chiefs, and twelve council women. But, he added, "Although we have been reborn through this same baptismal water which has washed the great Ononthio, we have not renounced our liberty or the rights we hold from the Master of Life. The pledge works both ways. If one wishes to try it he may free us from the oath we have made. It is only we who can give ourselves chiefs. What is this order that has brought us this Onondaga who is not of the Faith and who lays claim to be our chief? Father, explain this order. It has troubled our spirit."

The council women were present at the sitting. They presented some sentiments in their [own] name. The Marquis de Vaudreuil promised his answer the next day.

---

[28] Governor of Louisbourg.

ಳು APRIL 27 : The Marquis de Vaudreuil replied to the Iroquois of La Presentation. He confirmed all that the Marquis Duquesne had said to them when he received their oath of fidelity. He gave them a new belt to bind them with a still stronger chain, and declared to them that his intention in sending them this Onondaga who was the source of their dissatisfaction had not been that of violating their privileges in introducing him into their [Long] House against their will, but of making them understand that this warrior was of proven value and attachment to France. They would do well to take him into their village as soon as he had been baptized, and to give him the place of their famous chief, Callure, killed in the attack on Fort Bull. The sitting ended with the presentation of wampum belts to the council women. The gravity with which they attended the deliberations deserves to be noted. They have, moreover, the same standing among the Indians that the matrons formerly had among the Gauls and Germans.

ಳು APRIL 28–MAY 4 : The La Presentation Indians received from the Marquis de Vaudreuil seven gorgets and seven spontoons. This preferment was made in favor of the war chiefs. They all went back to their village.

It has been like summer for several days. They have sent off from Lachine sixty bateaux manned by 240 Canadians to carry provisions and trade goods to the posts in the West. The government should stock these posts in such a manner that the Indians will not have cause to regret Oswego, where they found in abundance and at a low price the goods necessary for their needs and for their luxuries. These posts are the only instruments which can in any way maintain a hold over these ferocious people. Moreover, this matter of Indian trade deserves a whole study by itself.

ಳು MAY 4 : The battalion of Royal Roussillon has received orders to assemble at Chambly on the eighth, camp at St. Jean on the ninth and leave on the tenth with the Béarn regiment to go and occupy Carillon under orders of M. de Bourlamaque.

Journal for 1757

᠙ MAY 5 : A few Potawatomis, who wintered here, left this morning to return to Detroit.

We have just received news from Fort Duquesne, dated March 8. Small war parties in the field all the time; one of them brought back four English prisoners who said that the garrison at Fort Cumberland was stronger than last year, and that they expected one hundred Catawbas, Indians who bear the name of a Cherokee village and live among the English.

The same report announces an embassy of ten Delaware chiefs and as many Shawnee chiefs, who come to Montreal to hear the words of Ononthio. M. de Ligneris asks for a missionary to establish himself with the Delawares and also for a few domesticated Abnakis. The Delawares regard the Abnakis as their brothers, they speak the same language. As regard to the Iroquois, whom they call their uncles, they fear them more than they love them.

There is word from the Illinois country that they can supply Fort Duquesne with two thousand hundredweight of flour and five hundred quarters of salt pork, considered to be sufficient provisions for five hundred men for six months, including extra employees and the visits of Indians.

There is also news from Niagara, dated April 11.

M. Pouchot reports a council held on January 30 between the Iroquois, the Shawnees, and the Delawares. These last spoke at length of the chiefs of their nation formerly hanged by the English, this is and always will be their excuse for making war. They have reproached the Iroquois bitterly for the failure of the Five Nations to declare themselves openly. They also said that they would no longer wear the "machicoté." This is a piece of cloth that women wear and which is to them what the breechclout is to men. The Iroquois imposed this disgraceful rule upon the Delawares after defeating them, thus degrading them from their status of men. The Delawares added that the Iroquois had [better] wear this "machicoté" themselves, that they [the Delawares] wished to strike the English, that they called the Abnakis their brothers, and that perhaps they would become crazy, or in other words, even raise the hatchet against their uncles, the Iroquois.

The latter replied that the "machicoté" which the Delawares had worn for so long a time was too filthy for them to wish to wear in their turn, that it was necessary to refer the decision on this matter to the general council which would be held immediately at the Onondaga town,[29] and that while waiting they could continue to make war against the English who had insulted them.

MM. de Chabert and de Joncaire have returned from their mission to the Senecas and the Cayugas. Immediately after their departure there were formed in these two villages four parties that reached Niagara on March 17. Sieur Pouchot held council with them. The council women begged him to have pity on them, that, since their young men had gone to war, he must supply their needs, that their hands were not big enough to cover their nakedness and that it would not be proper for them to let it be seen. After this council other war parties were formed and they think that now there are a score of them in the field. Their attempts should fall upon Ménade,[30] a province which being, as it were, their native land, had up to the present been respected by them.

Colonel [Sir William] Johnson has sent belts to all the villages of the Five Nations by a Mohawk, an Onondaga, and an Oneida, who are his emissaries. It would seem that his negotiations have been fruitless up to the present. But to be in a position to judge which side the Five Nations will take, it is necessary to know what will happen at the great council appointed to be held at the Onondaga village. M. de Joncaire does not believe that he can attend it. The sacred character of ambassador does not appear to him to be a certain enough guarantee to give him shelter in a council house to which he is not as well accredited as to that of the Senecas and the Cayugas, whose adopted son he is.

When I think of the actual position of the Five Nations, undecided between Ononthio, their father, and Corlar, their brother, it seems to me that it is the Dutch [of Albany] who, hard pressed by their two neighbors, each equally dreadful, very much wish to

[29] The capital of the Iroquois. It was near Syracuse, N. Y.
[30] Manhattan, i.e., to fight against the British in the province of New York.

Journal for 1757

hold themselves to a neutrality which one does not wish to permit them.

The Indians report that Colonel [Sir William] Johnson has told them that the English wish to re-establish Oswego, that this undertaking would doubtless cause much blood to flow, but that they have men enough and more than enough. Perhaps to quiet this clamor of the people and the merchants, the Court of London will send orders to Milord Loudoun to establish again, regardless of cost, a post on Lake Ontario. Perhaps equally well, the disclosure which Johnson has made to the Indians in this matter proves that the English this year have no designs in this direction.

The nations of the South have held a general council during which it was proposed to fight the English. The Chien tribe which opposed it broke up this first council. A second one was held to which it [this tribe] was not summoned and they unanimously decided to raise the hatchet against the English.

The Delawares came to say that they had seen on the Susquehanna River bateaux which the English had built at a fort called Shamoken,[31] that they were still building others, and that they talked of an invasion of ten thousand men against Fort Duquesne.

In order to judge as to the purpose of these boats it is necessary to determine just where they could be taken. This was the subject of a study given the Marquis de Vaudreuil on May 18 and which I attach here.[32]

Some Foxes living with the Five Nations came to Niagara to the number of forty, and after two councils held on April 6 and 7, they took up our hatchet and went off to raid.

The commander at Presque Isle, M. de Portneuf, preferring his own profit to the good of the service, has loaded his bateaux with brandy and merchandise instead of flour and salt pork, and so the scarcity of foodstuffs has prevented him from sending on to Niagara in early April a sergeant and forty-three men of the garrison. It is necessary to wait the melting of the ice on Lake Erie,

---

[31] Fort Augusta at present Sunbury, Pa.
[32] Omitted in the journal. Boats on the Susquehanna of course would be useless for an expedition against Duquesne on the other side of the Alleghenies.

which had not happened up to April 11, for him to forward the provisions.

ಕೆಲ MAY 6–8: MM. Stobo and Wambram [Van Braam] escaped from their badly-guarded prison. They were retaken some fifteen leagues from Quebec. This escape perhaps will make them watch more carefully this crowd [of prisoners], who are as free in Montreal and Quebec as they would be in Boston.

On the same day they heard that a party composed of sixty Indians left Carillon a few days after the expedition made against Fort George. One would wish that these Indians would proceed against the communications of Fort Lydius, but they did not wish to. They have penetrated deeply to within twenty-four leagues of Boston and burned two mills and taken six men. The prisoners know nothing of the movements or plans of the enemy. One of them that they questioned on these matters said that Lord Loudoun, when questioned by a man of importance in New England as to the plans he had for the coming year, asked him if he could keep a secret. The man assured Loudoun that he could. "And so can I," Lord Loudoun replied.

ಕೆಲ MAY 8: M. de Bourlamaque left this morning to go to St. Jean, and from there to Carillon with the two battalions of Royal Roussillon and Béarn. It will make a body of some thirteen hundred men. According to his instructions, he is to camp between the fort and the redoubt and to guard his camp with abatis.

ಕೆಲ MAY 12–15: There is great misery at Quebec. Bread is scarce, and what little there is is of the worst quality. The Intendant has been obliged to distribute two thousand minots of wheat to the inhabitants for seed. This quantity is far from sufficient and part of the land will remain unsowed. They will even have to bring from the depots food intended for the troops in order to feed the capital. No news of any ships, and this occasions much alarm. The lack of provisions prevents us from starting the campaign. All thought of offensive action is impossible for us, and even the defensive, if the enemy comes in force quickly and from several directions is scarcely less so. The battalion of La Sarre left to camp by Fort St. Jean and put this fort in condition to guard against a surprise. The battalion of Guyenne left Quebec on the thirteenth to camp at St. Therese from where it will repair the road from Chambly to St. Jean. The battalion of La Reine replaces it at Quebec, while waiting for news. Thus in case the enemy should come to lay siege to Quebec one could get to that place, in force and in very few days, the battalions of La Sarre, Guyenne and Languedoc. This last waits at Montreal.

The boat sent to Miramichi and to carry dispatches to Louisbourg set sail on the ninth.

News has been received from Fort Duquesne under the date of April 15. We there have out at all times many war parties who take scalps and bring back a few prisoners. One of these parties reported seeing near Fort Cumberland a camp of almost 150 Catawbas.

By news from Niagara under the date of May 3 and 5 we learn that many war parties of Senecas and Cayugas have gone to war against the English, that there is a great ferment among the Onondagas and the Oneidas, among whom Colonel [Sir William] Johnson has exerted the greatest effort. Several of them are extremely devoted to him. The news as to the plans and movements of the enemy continue to be very uncertain, [they are] reports of Indians who guess or who say they have seen; they speak of an operation towards La Belle Rivière, of the re-establishment of Oswego, of an expedition by sea. What it appears that we cannot doubt is that the English are assembling very considerable forces at Boston and Albany. They have reported the last attempt against Fort George as being entirely to their advantage. They say that we attacked this fort several times and that after having lost many people we were forced to retire. They should talk this way; the result of this expedition was against us.

The four hundred Canadians headed for La Belle Rivière arrived at Montreal today. They will leave the seventeenth or eighteenth.

ఎఒ MAY 16–20 : The war party of Aoussik came back with four

scalps and three prisoners from the Royal American regiment. From their depositions we have learned that the enemy is not making any move on Lake St. Sacrement. Neither troops nor convoys are moving. The English even seem not to be thinking of repairing the damage done them by M. de Rigaud's detachment. It would seem that Lord Loudoun is waiting for a squadron in order to attack Louisbourg, while two bodies of considerable size operate from the direction of La Belle Rivière and Oswego.

The Oneidas who had been sent as ambassador to the Five Nations returned and had audience on the eighteenth in the presence of the deputies from the Iroquois of the Sault and of Deux Montagnes.[33] They have given the usual complimentary belts, have excused themselves for not having executed the commission in connection with the Palatines[34] with which the Marquis de Vaudreuil charged them, have given assurances that they will embrace the Christian religion, but that they must wait for more peaceful times before doing this, and that when the ground was no longer soaked with blood they would ask for a missionary who, until then, would not be safe in their midst. They then begged the Marquis de Vaudreuil not to carry the war into their regions and to leave the road free as far as the fork which leads both to Albany and to Schenectady, and they said that they had sent the same proposition to the English.[35]

It would always seem that these Indians, divided among themselves, do not dare to take a decisive course, that, embarrassed by the nearness of the English, they wish very much to hold to a neutrality, and that at the same time they are trying to learn if we have an offensive plans in the direction of Schenectady.

Complimentary remarks from the domesticated Iroquois, exhortations to the Oneidas to continue in the desire for baptism and in their good will toward Ononthio.

[33] There was a mission of Iroquois and Algonkins some thirty miles above Montreal at the Lake of the Two Mountains, a lake in the St. Lawrence formed by the entrance of the Ottawa River.

[34] Of German Flats on the Mohawk.

[35] Naturally, the Caughnawaga Iroquois wanted nothing to interfere with their active smuggling trade with Albany.

Journal for 1757

◦ MAY 20 : The Marquis de Vaudreuil has answered the Oneidas. He has exhorted them to become converted and to continue to behave themselves. At the same time he told them that nothing could stop the hatchet, that he would attack the English everywhere, and, if the war should extend into their regions, he advised them for their own safety to join with him in fulfilling the engagements they had made with him at the famous council of last December. The Oneidas appear to wish to act accordingly.

News from Carillon. The body of troops under the orders of M. de Bourlamaque is now fourteen hundred men. Our two battalions are camped there between the fort and the redoubt. A body of Canadians hold the Portage and another the Falls. According to returns sent by M. de Bourlamaque to M. de Montcalm there are enough provisions at Carillon for fourteen hundred men for three months, and at St. Jean for one thousand for the same length of time.

◦ MAY 21 : The enterprise of Abbé Piquet has produced a secret negotiation with Thaneouneghen, famous Oneida chief who is devoted to us and to the Marquis de Vaudreuil, with the object of forcing by some striking act those of the Oneidas who still are wavering to declare for us, or those who favor the English to pick up our hatchet. As for that Thaneouneghen should first come here with his band and that of the other Oneida chiefs as a deputation to join themselves to the Iroquois of La Presentation and go secretly to strike the English. He [Piquet?] believed that before acting as an auxiliary of the French, and in order to bind the nation more solemnly and to force our other Indian allies to stand by them, it would be necessary that Ononthio should present the hatchet to them in a public council. Consequently, one was held today in the course of which the Marquis de Vaudreuil laid at the feet of the Oneidas a war belt of six thousand beads, painted red, and on which a hatchet was shown. The Oneidas raised it up both in their own name and in that of the Indians of La Presentation and of the Tuscaroras, a nation adopted by them. They then sang the war song. The Marquis de Vaudreuil promised them his help and that of all the Indians allied with France and promised to give shelter and lands to them and to their women and children wherever they wished to settle, be it at Fort Regis,[36] or at La Presentation, or at Fort Frontenac. Saregoa, great chief of Sault St. Louis, who had returned from the warpath, was at this assembly with several domesticated Iroquois. They highly applauded this course of the Oneidas, of which it will be necessary to await the results, for upon their return home they can very easily put Ononthio's hatchet under their floor mats and remain inactive. One must decide in a private council for which side these Indians will first strike.

MAY 22 : There has been a misunderstanding in the matter of the Oneidas. They pretend today that they do not wish to come out openly against the English. They have been allowed to let the hatchet remain buried until they shall find an occasion to use it without compromising themselves too much.

There arrived thirty Missisaugas of the band of a famous chief named Minabonjou.

News from Fort Duquesne, Detroit, and Niagara. They all confirm the advance of a great body of English against La Belle Rivière.

MAY 24–31 : We received a courier from Carillon. During the winter there was at this post disorder, pilferage, vexations, and all that which goes with command by a Canadian.

The English came scouting on the seventeenth to the number of twenty-four. They captured a carpenter. M. de Bourlamaque sent three detachments after them. One of these detachments, which was of only seven men, having met them, uttered the death cry and the English immediately fled, leaving their prisoner and even their arms and packs.

JUNE 1–8 : No news of ships in the river; the greatest worry on this account. They are dying of hunger at Quebec. Everyone there is on a bread ration.

---

[36] St. Regis, N. Y., nearly opposite Cornwall, Ont., where a new mission was being established about this period.

Journal for 1757

News from Niagara, dated May 23. Indian war parties constantly coming and going. One of them was pursued by one hundred English or Catawbas and lost three men. All the reports of prisoners and of Indians confirm the movements on the part of the English against La Belle Rivière.

Courier from Carillon who left on June 2. It appears that the enemy is commencing to assemble at Fort George. M. de Bourlamaque has sent a party for news. He has opened up a wide vista [in the woods] at the falls.

Five dispatches arrived from Michilimakinac which announce the impending arrival of four hundred Ottawas.

Courier from Quebec the ninth. No ships sighted.

JUNE 10 : At last we have learned that there are three merchant ships in the river, one from the Isles[37] and two from Bordeaux. These are the *David* and the *Jason*, belonging to Gradis,[38] loaded with various merchandise belonging to the King. There are on board 140 recruits, one thousand quarters of flour, and as much of salt pork. At all events, the famine at Quebec will end. They tell of fleets of merchant ships and war vessels headed for this colony. They have informed us of the attempt committed against the person of the King, the changes in the ministry, the promotion of marshals of France, the advance of one hundred four thousand men into Westphalia and the appearance of the considerable efforts that England will make in this region.

JUNE 12 : By news from Carillon, dated the eighth, the English came to the number of two hundred in eleven barges to feel out the post at the Portage. They fired from out of range and consequently we did not need [to reply]. Many Missisaugas and Ottawas have arrived. There also came three Iroquois from La Presentation who complained that the Oneidas had taken away from them a prisoner they had taken of one of the Palatines. One of the Oneida villages sent the Marquis de Vaudreuil a white belt,

---

[37] West Indies.
[38] The firm of Gradis, of Bordeaux, was hand in glove with Bigot in his operations.

that is to say, soft words to say that they had had no part in this affair.

News from Niagara of June 4. There was a sharp alarm at Toronto. Several drunken Missisaugas had threatened to destroy the fort. On receipt of the news M. Pouchot sent a picket of fifty men under the command of M. de Laferté, captain in the La Sarre regiment. Quiet was established when the reinforcement arrived. Some Potawatomis who were returning home after wintering here contributed not a little to quieting this quarrel.

The Missisaugas complained that the Oneidas have struck against them; this is an affair to conciliate promptly, for among these people the smallest altercation becomes a quarrel of the greatest consequence and one which does not end. Besides, there is, I believe, all reason to fear lest the Oneidas break their faith with us. The Senecas and the Cayugas continue to give us proofs of their attachment. The Delawares and the Shawnees have made many prisoners, brought back scalps, destroyed several houses, carried away cattle and even entire families. They have eaten an English officer whose pallor and plumpness tempted them. Such cruelties are frequent enough among the Indians of La Belle Rivière. Our domesticated Indians, softened by the glimmerings of Christianity which they have received, are no longer cruel in cold blood, but one cannot say, however, that their character is changed.

News as of May 23 has been received from La Belle Rivière. It is good, many war parties continue to desolate the English frontiers, a big convoy of provisions came from the Illinois country. The fears lest the enemy come with considerable forces against Fort Duquesne are almost dissipated. All reports of prisoners and Indians, the only spies we have here, assure us that the English have only defensive plans in this region. I do not make anything out of these contrary movements unless the inner defect of the government of the English colonies, each independent from the other, all divided in interest, government, and methods of thought, occasions this uncertainty in the movements and makes useless forces of really considerable size which would be almost enough to wipe us out. I do not doubt but that if one went about it with skill he could

Journal for 1757

get Pennsylvania and Virginia to accept such form of neutrality as he would dictate to them.

⁂ JUNE 13 : Today three hundred Indians arrived from Michilimackinac. They received an audience upon arrival, and then passed compliments in return.

A courier from Quebec reports a fourth ship seen at the great rock, forty leagues below Quebec.

The King has granted M. de Vaudreuil all the aid that he asked for this colony, to wit: an increase of ten companies for the troops of La Marine, on the basis of 65 men per company, recruits to complete the others, eight companies to replace those captured from the battalions of La Reine and Languedoc, recruits sufficient to put all the companies of our six battalions at 50 to 55 men, a detachment of royal artillery and engineers, a body of scouts, and this reinforcement amounts in all to about 3000 men. It is now only a question of their getting here.

⁂ JUNE 14 : The Michilimackinac Indians have asked for an audience with M. de Montcalm. They complimented him on the capture of Oswego. "We wished to see," said their orator, "this famous man who, on putting his foot on the ground, has destroyed the English ramparts. From his reputation and his exploits we thought that his head would be lost in the clouds. But behold, you are a little fellow, Father, and it is in your eyes that we find the grandeur of the loftiest pine trees and the spirit of the eagle." Among these savages it is nature alone that speaks. True it is that height and shape of body form the primary distinction among these people. Besides, all these Indians are fit subjects for a painting, almost all of great height. They go naked except for a breechclout. Their bearing is noble and proud. I find, however, that they have a less ferocious appearance than the Iroquois, even the domesticated ones. They spend the day singing, dancing and drinking. We now have almost four hundred of them. They use up an enormous amount of food. It is a necessary evil. They must be held here until the arrival of the necessary provisions allows us to employ them on some important mission.

ᗌ JUNE 15 : Some Ottawas from Saginaw, some Chippewas and Missisaugas who arrived yesterday evening came to pay their compliments to the Marquis de Montcalm. It seems that the capture of Oswego made a great impression on them and especially what they have heard tell of everyone there swimming in brandy.

ᗌ JUNE 16 : Courier from Quebec. The *David* and the *Jason* are in the harbor. There are three other ships in the river, one called the *President le Breton*, belonging to Gradis, one from Bayonne and a brigantine from La Rochelle.

The *David* and the *Jason* have disembarked 170 recruits drawn from a body of foreign volunteers created since we left.

There also arrived a vessel from Miramichi which brings to Quebec 120 Acadians that M. de Boishebert cannot feed. By his letters dated May 29 we learn that the famine has caused a mutiny in the troops he commands. The unhappy people, lacking everything, wished to break into the storehouses. M. de Boishebert quieted them. He lost four men in one detachment. An English prisoner taken at Annapolis [Royal] told him that Chibouctou [Halifax, N.S.] was the assembly point of a large body of troops, destined for a maritime expedition of considerable importance.[39] News from Carillon of the thirteenth and fourteenth. The English captured one of the local inhabitants. M. de Langlade at the head of about one hundred Indians took four prisoners and six scalps in front of Fort Lydius. The English made a sortie from the fort, and at the first shots fired by the enemy, the Indians fled. The hurried flight of these Indians shows a lack of discipline of which they have no idea in Europe. They returned by land to Carillon and then sent back to look for their canoes.

From the report of prisoners it would seem that Lord Loudoun embarked three weeks ago for a maritime expedition against Louisbourg or Quebec, but most likely the former place. A body of about five thousand men, all militia, is to form a defense at Lake St. Sacrement.

ᗌ JUNE 17 : News from Quebec of the fourteenth reports the

[39] Lord Loudoun's abortive expedition against Louisbourg.

Journal for 1757

arrival in the river of the *St. Antoine*, loaded with goods for the Commissary of Stores.[40] It collected ransom of eighty thousand livres from two English vessels while on the way.

Another courier left Quebec the fifteenth to say that they are scared there. But fear is an evil which has no cure. The Marquis de Montcalm has offered to go there to look over the surroundings of this place from a military point of view, and to make dispositions with respect to its defenses in case of an attack, in which I for one do not believe.

Letter from the King to the Bishop of Quebec requesting a *Te Deum* in thanks for the capture of Port Mahon.

JUNE 19 : The Marquis de Montcalm left today to look over the camps at Chambly, St. Therese, and St. Jean. He will return the day after tomorrow. Fifty Ottawas arrived and said three hundred more were coming for this year's campaign.

JUNE 20–25 : Canoe loads of Indians arrive every day. The number come from the Far West now passes a thousand. Some are come from a nation so far away that no Canadian interpreter understands their language. Two of them who killed a Frenchman thirteen months ago have been brought bound hand and foot and turned over to M. de Vaudreuil at his discretion. They left them in the guardhouse for some time. They were then brought into the council chamber. They were naked, smeared with black paint, slave sticks in their hands.[41] They were led in by the Escabian, a sort of chief who combines the functions of major-domo and cook, for he at the same time both makes the stew and assembles the warriors. Upon entering they prostrated themselves at the feet of the Marquis de Vaudreuil, who, as a sign of pardon, gave them a white shirt, advising them to have hereafter a heart as white as it was.

They also were given breechclouts, mitasses, blankets, and a present of vermilion and tobacco. They then rose up, MM. Martin and St. Luc, officers of colony troops, presented them to the na-

---

[40] Joseph Cadet of Bigot's crew.
[41] See the entry for July 11, 1756.

tions, and, this ceremony having rehabilitated them, they took their seats with their people, whose chief sang a song of thanks.

I see no difference in the dress, ornaments, dances and songs of these different nations. They are naked save for a breechclout, and painted in black, red and blue, etc. Their heads are shaved and feathers ornament them. In their lengthened ear [lobes] are rings of brass wire. They have beaver skins for covering, and carry lances, arrows and quivers made of buffalo skin. Each band goes and dances in its turn before the house of the principal citizens of the town. In truth their dances seem like the pyrrhic and the other war dances of the Greeks.

I found some difference in the music of the Winnebagos and the Ottawas. To the kind of little drum by which they mark the cadence join the voices of several men and women, and the whole forms a harmonious enough accord.

As for the rest, these Indians are erect, well made, and almost all of great height. They have cabins under the city's walls. They pass the night there drinking and singing.

News from Carillon which tells nothing concerning the war. About two hundred Indians from the Far West left to go there. The battalion of Languedoc left here the twenty-fourth. It goes into camp between La Prairie and St. Jean. It will work on the road between these two places until it goes to Carillon, which will be soon.

I at last received letters from France by the ship *Rochelois*, whose mail was sent to Quebec. When one has been away a year from his native land, he should certainly wish for news.

JUNE 26: Courier from Quebec. Statement of an English prisoner, captured by a brigantine from La Rochelle, who had left Virginia April 17. The prisoner said that the expedition of Lord Loudoun concerned Louisbourg, and that he would attack it with thirty thousand men. London demands, says he, the capture of this place in order to make peace, exchanging it for Port Mahon and Oswego. The tremblers at Quebec are now reassured. No news of any new ship at Quebec.

Journal for 1757

June 26–30: In order to take advantage of the absence of Lord Loudoun, who has lead away the best troops, regulars as well as provincials, for his maritime expedition, whatever it may be, the Marquis de Vaudreuil has determined to lay siege to Fort George, called by the English William Henry. The lack of provisions necessary to feed an army delayed the execution of this project. Sieur Martel, former keeper of the King's Montreal storehouse, is sent to examine the grain supply in the inhabitant's houses in a part of this government. He found there enough to feed an army of 12,800 men for a month. If they had made this study two months earlier, Fort William Henry would now be in our hands, and we would have been in position to thrust our advance still farther, instead of which the projected expedition today is quite uncertain. But this study of the wheat supply was against the interests of the Commissary General and his crew, of which the Marquis de Vaudreuil is himself one.[42] They then waited as long as possible, and the delay in the arrival of ships from France at last forced them to take an action which they had been advised to take as early as April. All preparations for the expedition are being hurried in all departments.

June 28: News received from Detroit under date of May 15. They expect a deputation of Choctaws and hope to persuade them to fight the English. The Catawbas are the only nation of the West who remain attached to them.

June 29: News from Niagara under date of the twenty-first. It would appear that the enemy has not the slightest thought of any operation in the region of La Belle Rivière. That assembly of bateaux at Fort Shamokin was only the arrival of people from the frontier who went there with their beasts and household effects for refuge. The continuous raids of our Indians did not allow them to remain in their homes.

The Five Nations seem always disposed to maintain neutrality and to fear lest we carry the war into their lands by way of the

---

[42] Vaudreuil must have known of the peculations of the "Grand Society," but he apparently never benefited from its operations.

Oswego River. The Onondagas have deliberated sending belts to the Mohawks in support of those sent by the Iroquois of Sault St. Louis to discourage them from going to war on the side of the English.

News from Carillon under date of twenty-fourth and twenty-fifth. They busy themselves there with arrangements in connection with the siege. The English are very active on their part. They have scouting parties out continuously to watch our movements.

Indians keep coming from the Far West. On the twenty-ninth arrived many Ottawas and a band of Delawares from Tioga. This nation has never before come to Montreal.

Orders have been sent for the departure of the regular troops from St. Jean as follows:

La Reine	July 1
La Sarre	July 2
Languedoc	July 4
Guyenne	July 6

The colony troops, militia, and Indians will leave from St. Jean the eighth to the fourteenth. In addition to the regulars, the army will be composed of about one thousand men of La Marine, twenty-five hundred Canadians, and eighteen hundred Indians, two companies of artillery, one of workmen, and an artillery train of considerable size for this country.

JULY 1–12 : Indian war council. They gave two belts, the first to the Marquis de Montcalm to thank him for leading them and praying him to take good care of them, the second to the Marquis de Vaudreuil asking him, since he did not go to war himself, that he should give of his own flesh and blood and send his brother under the orders of the Marquis de Montcalm. On this subject all the nations spoke one after the other in the following order:

> The Ottawas
> The Menominees
> The Sauks, in their own name and that of
>   the Winnebagos and the Wichitas[?]

Journal for 1757

The Potawatomis
The Foxes

Since it is not considered dignified to answer at once, the Marquis de Vaudreuil answered the next day with two belts.

The Chippewas of Pointe Chequamegon[43] did not attend this council. They are estranged from the Foxes, whom they accuse of having made the Sioux attack them. The Marquis de Vaudreuil proposes to remove this seed of discord and to reconciliate these two nations with each other before their departure.

Courier from Quebec on the second. M. de Beaufremont's squadron, coming from St. Domingo, has reached Louisbourg.

JULY 3 : The Chevalier de Lévis left to take command of the troops assembled at Carillon, while awaiting the arrival of the Marquis de Montcalm.

Courier from Quebec. Two vessels are in the harbor of this city, carrying four hundred recruits, six officers of the Corps Royal and twenty artillerymen. The squadron of M. Dubois de La Motte has also reached Louisbourg. It carries two battalions of the Berry Regiment. Louisbourg now appears safe.

The Iroquois have brought two prisoners. According to their depositions the English have seven or eight thousand men on the Lake St. Sacrement frontier.

JULY 6 : Courier from Carillon. Extract from letter of M. de Bourlamaque, dated the second. "Our detachment of 200 Indians, to which I added 25 Abnakis or Iroquois, left on June 30 with 3 colony officers and 6 cadets, in all 235 men. The Iroquois, with whom was Kametagon [Kanectagon?], lead the march. They took the road to the place where they usually hid their canoes, but upon entering the Chicot River, which is narrow and bordered with rocks, they were saluted by a volley of musketry which killed a cadet and mortally wounded several Indians. They could not get ashore on the enemy's side. It was necessary to pass the night with the river between them. At daybreak they crossed. The English

---

[43] On the south shore of Lake Superior some sixty miles east of Detroit.

were dislodged. They took up their trail and captured two Mahicans and a wounded Englishman. The Indians brought two of them to me and tore the other apart, and, as he was good, they ate him. The Englishman, whom I questioned, spoke little; he is badly wounded. The Mahican is more open. You will not get either of these prisoners. The Englishman will die, and the Mahican, whose flesh is not appetizing, will be burned. His statements have confirmed the latest news we have had as to the enemy's strength." General Webb had just arrived to command on this frontier.

JULY 9 : The Marquis de Montcalm left today with MM. de Rigaud, St. Luc, de Longueil, Junior, and Abbé Piquet to go and sing the war song at the Lake and at Sault St. Louis. We have first been to the Lac Des Deux Montagnes, which is twelve or thirteen leagues from Montreal and is formed by the Ottawa River. North of this lake is an Indian village. Indians of three different nations live there, Nipissings, Algonkins, and Iroquois. They have three separate groups of houses, although all united in the same village. They have a common church, which is attractive and properly ornamented. Two Sulpician missionaries are in charge, one for the Nipissings and the Algonkins, the other for the Iroquois.

The Indians go to pray in the church three times a day, each in his own tongue, and they attend with exemplary devotion. They serve as choir boys and chanters. The men sit on one side and the women on the other, and the choir formed by the latter is very melodious.

The cabins are well enough built but very filthy. There is a special council house for each nation and a large one, which must be three hundred feet long, for the general councils of the three nations.

Upon our arrival we were saluted by a triple discharge of two swivels and of musketry from Indians lined up on the river bank, the missionaries at their head. They led us to the church and from there to the parsonage, where the principal chiefs came to compliment the Marquis de Montcalm. In the afternoon they held a council in which the Marquis de Montcalm told the Indians that he had come to see them and to give them through this visit marks of his friendship and esteem. Then he revealed to them the project planned against Fort George, the union of all the Indians in order to co-operate in its execution, and the hope that the Marquis de Vaudreuil had that they, his children, and children of the true Faith, would help him with all their strength to destroy the common enemy. He ended by saying that he would give them three oxen for a feast and that he planned to sing the war song with them in the great council house. The Indians thanked the Marquis de Montcalm for his visit, assured him that they would follow his wishes and that in the evening they would tell him the number of warriors who would march with him.

We then visited the chiefs in their cabins. In the course of this we saw a Nipissing Indian, dishonored in the eyes of his brothers and of the Canadians because he wore breeches, covered his head, ate, dressed, and slept like a Frenchman. He goes neither to the hunt nor to war. He keeps a shop in his house filled especially with contraband goods, and he has a very lucrative business. The Indians scorn him, but do not reproach him or treat him badly. For in this place of complete liberty, *Trahit sua quemque voluptas*.[44] This man reminds me of that thought that it is trade which most of all civilizes man.

In the evening we went to the council house, the Indians were sitting there on the floor, ranged by tribes. In the middle were hung at intervals pots filled with meat destined for the war feast. A few candles lighted up this place which seemed like a witches' cavern. Kisensik spoke first. After the ordinary compliments he asked the Marquis de Montcalm for permission to give his advice on war when the occasion offered. He then outlined his tribe's requests and the number of warriors it would furnish. The chiefs of the other two nations then spoke on the same subjects. After the Marquis de Montcalm had replied to their proposals, Aoussik, seizing a bullock's head by the horns and stalking around with it, sang his war song. The other chiefs of the three nations followed him

[44] "His own liking leads each on."—Vergil.

with the same ceremony, and I sang it in the name of M. de Montcalm and was much applauded. My song was nothing else but these words: "Trample the English underfoot" cadenced to the movement of Indian cries. They then presented the Marquis de Montcalm with the first morsel, and the war feast having started, we withdrew.

The next day, the tenth, we went to Sault St. Louis. Two canoes, each with ten naked Indians, the finest men of all the villages, painted for war in red and blue, adorned with bracelets of silver and of wampum, came before us on the river a quarter league from the Sault. They brought to the Marquis de Montcalm a letter from Father la Neuville, a Jesuit, who heads this mission, in which he advised him of the ceremony about to be observed. The two canoe loads, in truth a charming sight, held the attention of all the Europeans. On the river bank we found the missionary, who received the Marquis de Montcalm upon his stepping ashore, made a short speech and lead him to the church between two rows of Indians who saluted him, the chiefs with their spears and the rest with a triple discharge from their guns. They sang the *Te Deum* in the Iroquois tongue, after which the Marquis de Montcalm was lead to the council chamber, where the chiefs joined him. The same propositions, the same answers, the same ceremonies as at the Lac Des Deux Montagnes, and moreover, that of covering, in the name of the Marquis de Vaudreuil, two dead Iroquois chiefs, and of presenting me to the nation as a candidate for adoption. Three oxen given for the war feast, which went off just like that of last night. The Iroquois adopted me during this feast and gave me the name of "Garionatsigoa," which means "Great Angry Sky." Behold me then, an Iroquois war chief! My clan is that of the Turtle, first for eloquence in council, but second for war, that of the Bear being first. They exhibited me to all the nation, gave me the first morsel of the war feast, and I sang my war song, in part with their first war chief. The others dedicated theirs to me.

I paid calls on all my clan and gave the wherewithall for feasts in all the cabins. As for the rest of it, the village at the Sault is at-

Courtesy National Gallery, London

The Marquis de Vaudreuil, last French governor of Canada—
"a man, limited, without talent, perhaps free from vice,
but having all the faults of a petty spirit."

Courtesy Fort Ticonderoga Museum

The Marquis de Montcalm, commanding general of French forces
"But behold, you are a little fellow, Father,
and it is in your eyes that we find the grandeur
of the loftiest pine trees and the spirit of the eagle."

tractive, laid out in regular form with a parade ground which divides it and serves as a riding field, for they have many horses and exercise them continually. The church is pretty and well decorated. The Indians have, as do those at the Lake, fields cultivated by their women, fowl and cattle, all individually owned. They sell, buy, and trade just like Frenchmen.

We returned to Montreal on the tenth in the evening. The same day there arrived from the post of Onyatanous,[45] M. de Mézières, captain of La Marine, with a few Indians.

JULY 12 : Left Montreal at five in the evening of the twelfth, reached La Prairie at eight, where we spent the night. Found two-score Ottawa Indians of M. Langlade's party, stragglers that he had failed to supply with bread. They had left their food for their women.

JULY 13 : Left La Prairie at half-past five, reached St. Jean at half-past ten. We made a stop here.

In the course of this day M. de Langlade's Ottawas, to the number of 150, departed, and a little later 500 Canadians led by M. de Becancourt, lieutenant of the troops of La Marine.

JULY 14 : Left St. Jean at half-past eight with MM. de Rigaud, Dumas, de St. Ours, de Bonne and several colony officers under escort of a company of grenadiers and a few Ottawa Indians.

Halted at noon at a place called Boileau's Camp, four leagues from St. Jean. There had been an establishment belonging to this Boileau who abandoned it at the start of the war, as had all those located on the shores of Lake Champlain. Camped at Foucault's mill, ten leagues from St. Jean. There we found a great number of pigeons.

JULY 15 : Left at half-past four in the morning, halted to eat at ten, started off again at noon. The heavy southwest wind forced

---

[45] Unidentified. It might be Onondaga, but there is no record of a French post there at this period.
[46] Cumberland Head near Plattsburg, N. Y.

us to stop and camp at Pointe Scononton,[46] an Iroquois word meaning deer.

We there found the Ottawas, wind-bound since yesterday evening. The Ottawas form several bands. 1. The Ottawas properly so called, who live at Michilimackinac. 2. Other nations adopted by these first and established with them at Michilimackinac, the Kishkakons, the Big Feet, the White Fish, the people of Beaver Island, who live on an island at some distance from Michilimackinac and the people of the Fork. These last frustrated a conspiracy formed in 1744 by all the Indians of the Far West to slaughter the French scattered among the different posts. They warned the Chevalier de Longueuil who commanded at Detroit, and the plot failed.

There are still Ottawas living at Detroit and at the Bay, and all the villages of this nation, which has always been attached to the French, can furnish one thousand to twelve hundred warriors.

We have moreover found with the Ottawas some Chippewas from Pointe Chequamegon, situated in Lake Superior thirty leagues beyond [Michilimackinac?], and three Micmacs.

All these Indians passed the time while they were held up in bathing and amusing themselves. They swim like fish, diving and remaining under water a long time.

The old men make medicine all night, that is to say, they consult the Great Spirit to learn of the success of their expedition. They sacrificed a dog to him today.

The Indians of the Far West are the most superstitious of all. One must be very much on his guard not to do anything which they will regard as a bad omen. For example, if one touched the weapons of a warrior who was going on a war party, he would believe himself threatened with death and would take no part in the expedition.

Met some bateaux returning from Carillon who informed us of the death of M. de L'Hopital from an attack of apoplexy and that the Indians sent after the remains of an English detachment had taken seven scalps and five prisoners.

Told this news to the Indians and held a council with them.

Journal for 1757

JULY 16: The continuing heavy wind has forced us to remain camped here all day.

The Ottawa Indians, having learned that M. Marin had left Carillon to make a raid with the Menominees, were discontented. They said that they had arrived first at Montreal, that they remained there peacefully only to obey the orders of the Governor, that of all the Indian nations [they were] the most tractable, that they made of their father's wishes a sacred duty, and that it was not fair that other Indians, arrived later than they, should make the first steps in the career of honor, while obedience alone had held them from action ever since the spring thaw. The commandant at Michilimackinac had scarcely left them time to put their cabins in order before, told by him that the French had need of their aid, they immediately rolled their blankets and hastened to Montreal, the first to get there. Thus they should be the first to drink the broth.

These moves make one appreciate the ticklishness of [dealing with] these Indians. It is a point of honor with them that anyone who offends them or appears to offend them is forever an object of reproach among them, and here is what causes murders by drunken Indians.

The Marquis de Montcalm, warned by interpreters of their discontent, summoned the war chiefs, consoled them, praised them for having followed their father's wishes, and promised them that as soon as they reach Carillon he will let them go alone to hunt a bit of meat. This promise appeased them.

Then it became a question of provisions. They had been given enough for a week, but they do not know how to husband them and are often forced to go hungry. They were given hard-pressed ship biscuits and made to understand that they could fall back on these.

Rain and storm all day long.

In the evening the young men sang the war song opposite the tents of the Marquis de Montcalm and de Rigaud, which was worth a few bottles of wine to them.

JULY 17: Left at six in the morning, stopped at Little Val-

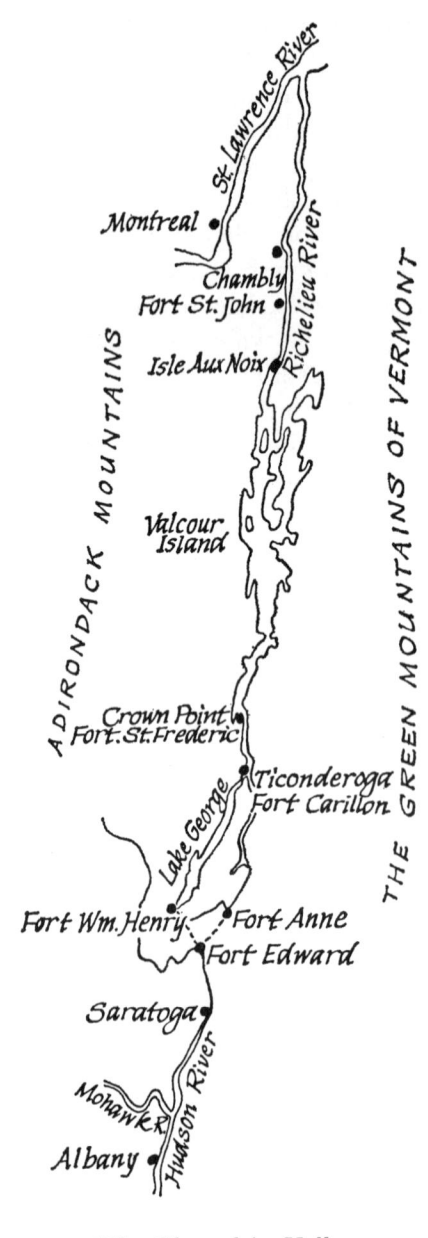

The Champlain Valley

Journal for 1757

cour Island, after having made a passage of three leagues, to hear mass. Left at once, reached Pointe aux Sables[47] to eat, and stopped [for a while] at three o'clock opposite Isle aux Morpions.[48]

Passed in sight of a mountain higher than the southern chain, high up on which is a sort of stone statue that the Indians call Rozzio,[49] regarding it as the master of the lake. They say that four islands located below it and called Islands of the Four Winds are his children. When they pass by Rozzio they send him tobacco and gun flints in order to get favorable weather.

Camped at five in the evening at Bouquet River. Our Indians, urged on by hunger, did not stop at St. Frederic. They are even bound to go on by night, if they do not arrive in the daytime.

Established a guard and a patrol.

JULY 18 : Left at half-past three and halted at Split Rock,[50] so named by the shape of the rock. It was this Split Rock which formerly marked the limits of the lands of the Five Nations in this region.

Halted at Bottle Bay.[51] It is around here that the English in the last campaign killed or captured twelve of our men. They came by way of Otter Creek, which has its source in New England.

Halted at Pointe à la Peur,[52] so named because in 1709 or '10 before Fort St. Frederic was built, which was in 1737, some fifteen hundred Canadians advancing toward Lake St. Sacrement under the orders of Sieur de Ramesay had halted at this place. They heard a great noise which was thought to be caused by a big body

---

[47] At the mouth of the Ausable River.

[48] This must be Schuyler Island, although it is also referred to in the journal as Isle au Chapon.

[49] There is confusion here. A rocky islet east of the tip of the little peninsula of Charlotte, Vt., was called Rock Roggio by the Indians. In the War of 1812 a British ship fired at it in a fog, believing it to be an American vessel. Now called Sloop Island.

[50] Off the point some three miles south of Essex, N. Y.

[51] Probably Basin Harbor in Panton, Vt.

[52] Unidentified, but somewhere between Westport and Port Henry, N. Y., on either side of the lake.

of the enemy, but which was only that of deer running through the woods. Terror seized them, they sent out no scouts, but took to their boats and went back to Montreal as fast as sails and oars could take them.

Reached Fort St. Frederic at noon and Carillon at six. We had northeast winds for two hours, the only breeze during the entire [day's?] trip. The southwest winds are, one might say, mild and gentle at this season.

M. Marin left here today with 380 men, 300 of them Indians of the Far West. They are to visit the head of the Bay, Chicot River, where Indian dreams and wild terrors have fabricated an intrenched camp of four thousand men. From there, if they meet no big enemy detachments, they go to lay an ambush between Fort George and Fort Lydius. This imaginary camp at the Chicot River has discouraged the Indians from going into this region. The Chippewas made magic and hung up a breechclout, dedicated to the Manitou, and did not wish to leave until the Manitou had carried away the breechclout. However they followed M. Marin willy-nilly.

As for the rest of it, it seems to me that we still know very little about the position of the enemy. All the Indian reports are false, they do not go where one wishes them to, but where they want to go, that is to say where there is no danger. Prisoners' statements are uncertain, contradict each other, and one cannot base any military decision on them. The trail along the shore of Lake St. Sacrement, either on the north or the south side, so far is known only to the Indians. Is the enemy dug in at Fort George, or is he not there?

Nevertheless it is necessary to act. There is a formal order to go against the enemy and attack him whether he be strong or weak, barring an impossibility as clear as the light of day, which the Montreal dreamers will not believe or will pretend that they do not believe. There is no doubt *audaces fortuna juvat*.[53]

They are making all the preparations for a siege, and the work on Fort Carillon has been stopped for two weeks. There are camped below this fort only the battalions of Royal Roussillon

[53] "Fortune favors the brave."

and of Béarn, with M. de Bourlamaque. The Chevalier de Lévis occupies the Falls with La Reine, La Sarre, Guyenne and Languedoc. M. de Rigaud commands at the Portage and at the advanced posts which are held by Marine troops and Canadians. The Indians put themselves where they please.

For ten days they have been working to get up the carry to Lake St. Sacrement the bateaux needed to carry the troops, munitions, provisions, and artillery. The carry is long and difficult. Everything is hauled by hand. It is not that there are no oxen or horses here, but that there is nothing to feed them with, and, lacking nourishment, they have not enough strength to do their job.

JULY 19: A party of Indians lying in ambush on the lake came to report that they had seen some English barges within range of our advanced posts. The enemy is very alert. They have scouting parties out all the time. The poor success of most of these detachments and the great number of our Indians do not discourage them in this petty warfare; advantage to them of having companies of volunteers, an example we should follow.

We have been to visit the post at the Falls. The Ottawa Indians who were escorting us came there to hold a council to decide whether they should proceed and along which shore. It would be better for them to wait here for the return of M. Marin. They deliberated this evening on this proposition.

The Montreal militia arrived at four, three hundred in number. They camped here this evening and will go to the Portage tomorrow. There are now 160 bateaux which have been carried up to Lake St. Sacrement. At least 250 are needed. The continual rains have seriously spoiled the road. Some hundred Indians came, eighty of them Potawatomis.

JULY 20: The Indians are not going today. They were held up and given two oxen; but as they found them skinny, they killed two others in addition.

They continue hauling up over the carry. M. Dumas, adjutant of the colony troops, is now busy putting the militia in order, forming them into brigades and attaching officers to them. He also is to organize a battalion of five hundred men from the Marine troops destined to go with the French troops. The officers to be attached to this battalion are those who would be the least fit to go with the Indians and exercise the business of harassing.

At two the barge which we send on reconnaissance every day and which carries a crew of nine Canadians and a cadet under the orders of M. de St. Ours, lieutenant of La Marine, ran into some English barges near Isle la Barque.

I do not know what the Canadians did or did not do, but what is certain is that our barge came back, M. Groisbois, the cadet, was mortally wounded, M. St. Ours was wounded in the hand, and two militiamen dangerously so.

Two councils with Indians, one with the Ottawas and the Chippewas, the other with the Potawatomis. The first decided to leave tomorrow evening, to divide their troop, part on the right shore and part on the left shore of Lake St. Sacrement, the rest on the lake itself, and to reconnoiter as far as Fort George, where they would try for a coup. I said that they had decided to go, I would prefer rather to wager that they will not leave on the day agreed upon.

The Potawatomis, the wisest and most obedient of all the Indians, will proceed tomorrow to the camp at the Portage to stay there, carry out the wishes of M. de Rigaud, and await the departure of M. de Villiers, under whose banner they wish to go. Solely to fulfill their obligations to the other nations they are sending a few of their young men with the Ottawas.

The chiefs of those who are going on reconnaissance came to bring to the Marquis de Montcalm as many sticks of wood as there were men in their party, a ceremony they always observe when they wish to strike a blow. It is a muster roll of the party. Thus in the early days of the Persian monarchy when they went to war, each warrior placed an arrow in some public place. Upon their return each took up his again, and what remained showed the loss that they had suffered.

I shall say once for all that irrespective of the obligation which one has of being a slave to these Indians, of hearing them night and day in council and in private, when caprice takes hold of them, when a dream, or an excess of vapors and the constant objective of begging brandy or wine leads them on, they are always lacking something from their equipment, their arms, or their toilet, and it is up to the general of the army to issue requisitions for the smallest of these distributions, an eternal little detail, petty and one of which Europe has no idea.

JULY 21 : The Ottawas came this morning to ask the Marquis de Montcalm for two sets of equipment, which they wished to offer in sacrifice to the Manitou at the moment when they leave.

This night one of them dreamed that Lake St. Sacrement was covered with English, a [wild] alarm in the Indian camp. It was necessary to wake up the Marquis de Montcalm who sent them back to bed, assuring them that there was nothing [to fear]. To continue, the religion of these Indians of the Far West is crude paganism and still in its infancy. Each makes a god of the object that strikes his [fancy], the sun, the moon, the stars, a snake, a moose, in fact all visible beings, animate or inanimate. They have, however, a way of determining the object of their worship. They fast for three or four days. After this preparation, calculated to make them dream, the first thing which in their sleep presents itself to their excited imagination becomes the god to which they devote the rest of their days. It is their "Manitou." They invoke it for their fishing, hunting, and war. It is to it that they sacrifice. Happy are they when the object of this important dream is of small size, a fly for example. For then "My body is a fly," say they, "I am invulnerable, what man is skillful enough to entrap [so small] a speck?"

The belief in two spirits, one good, the other bad, the one inhabiting the heavens, the other the bowels of the earth, now established among them, goes back only to the time they commenced trade with Europeans. Originally they recognized only their "Manitou." Besides they say that the Master of Life who created them was brown and beardless, while he who made Frenchmen was white and bearded.

M. de Fontenelle said, "If God made men in his image, men have well repaid Him."

They believe greatly in sorcerers, in jugglers, in all those divinations which broadly are called among them as "making medicine." They do not all believe in punishments and rewards after death, only a state like that of life, a more happy one nevertheless, for they think that the dead live in villages situated beyond the setting sun, where they have vermilion and tobacco in abundance. Before they bury them they expose them for three or four days in a sacred cabin, all warpainted and with the best of things to eat, a custom we observe in France for the royal family. Then they bury them with food and their equipment and arms. They say that on the passage [to the Happy Hunting Ground] there is a great strawberry of immense size from which the dead take a piece to serve as nourishment on the way, that moreover they will fare more or less well in the Elysian Fields, in accordance with the amount of food their relatives give them every day, but particularly on the day of the feast of the dead. The manner of their giving is to throw into the fire the first morsel, just as the ancients made libations to the shades at the beginning of a meal. Among these Indians there is only voluntary subordination. Each person is free to do as he pleases. The village chiefs and the war chiefs can have influence, but they do not have authority, still their influence over the young men depends upon how much they exert it, and upon their attention to keeping their kettles full, so to say.

As I have occasion to learn something concerning their religion, their habits, and their customs, I shall not neglect an objective important in the eyes of a philosopher, and one who studies that most essential thing of all, man.

The Indians, at last, passed this afternoon to M. de Rigaud's camp. They are portaging their canoes, provided that they will be paid for this transport.

The Marquis de Montcalm this afternoon went to the camp at the Falls and to the one at the Portage, where he gave orders for the formation of the battalion of La Marine troops, a large and difficult operation and one which those charged with are having

Journal for 1757

much trouble in accomplishing. After that he visited the advanced posts.

He made this trip from Carillon as far as the Falls in a canoe, alone with the Indians, which pleased them greatly. I made the same trip the same way in an Indian canoe. As long as it lasted a war chief standing in the canoe, "chichicoy"[54] in hand, told, in a recitative way his latest dreams. "The Manitou appeared to me," he sang, "he told me of all these young men who are following me to war. Thou shall lose none. They will succeed, cover themselves with glory, and thou will lead them all back again safely." Cries of applause interrupted him from time to time. This chief's father, a venerable old man, seated behind him, then said in a loud voice: "My son, was I wrong in exhorting you to fast? If thou had been like the others thou would have passed thy time eating, in sacrificing to thy belly, thou would not have put the Manitou in a favorable mood, and behold, he has sent thee happy dreams which bring joy to the warriors." One may see by this how much the chiefs are continually occupied in adding to their own esteem and what things enable them to do it. The bateaux of the Commissary of Stores arrived here yesterday and departed again this evening.

JULY 22 : This morning about one hundred Indians and a score of Canadians of M. Marin's party returned. They had sent scouts ahead of them in different directions. Eight of them met twenty English. Each party was seized with fear and each fled in its turn, ours, however, having fired once and killed a man. This was an event which should force some change in the party. Therefor about one hundred Indians left M. Marin, who also sent back those Canadians who had no shoes, and with the most active and best equipped he has gone to try his luck in the direction of the English forts.

Various papers have been found while following the trail of the fugitives, among which are the instructions given by General Webb to the officer commanding this party of twenty men, detached from West's company of volunteers. By these instructions

[54] A ceremonial rattle.

it would appear that the English are maintaining scouts at the foot of the bay all the time, that their post is behind the rocks alongside of which M. de Langlade was fired at. They remained in ambush there for two days. Their orders are to observe the French detachments which pass in this region, to attack them if they are weak enough, and, if they are too strong, not to reveal themselves but to send a man to Fort Edward to warn them of the road the French took. They were cautioned that friendly Indians will come to them with a red flag in hand, that they will give them the password, which is Johnson, and will show them a passport signed William.

Around eleven o'clock M. de Niverville and Father Roubaud, Jesuit, arrived with 112 Abnakis and St. François Indians, 26 from Bécancour, 18 from Misiskoui, and with M. de St. Luc, Abbé Piquet, and Abbé Matavet, missionaries, 46 Algonkins of the Lake, 53 Nipissings, 47 Iroquois of the Lake, 3 from La Presentation, and 8 Chippewas. Immediate council, nation by nation, and compliments on their arrival. They have been given the news about the state of the army, plans for departure, and the assembly ended by a drink of wine which they were made [!] to drink, while being warned that it was of no consequence.

They finally took the wise step of giving no drink at all to the army. It is the only way of getting at least some good out of a very bad wage.

M. de St. Luc brought news from Quebec and Montreal.

According to the Intendant's letters of the eleventh and fourteenth, Quebec has absolutely no bread. Everyone is in extreme misery. The small amount of provisions brought by the few ships which came is used up entirely. The Intendant has delayed having the animals killed until the four hundred hundredweight of rice from Marseilles are consumed. The King bought this rice at one hundred livres a hundredweight, and they are distributing it to the people at the rate of ten sous per pound. The country people live on a milk diet.

M. de Montbeillard, an officer detached from the Corps Royal[55]

[55] The engineer and artillery corps.

and come from France last month, remained at Quebec to reconnoiter the surroundings of that place, the river flats, to make plans and dispositions relative to the defense of this capital. One would have been able, up to now, to commence works having this objective in view, but because of lack of food they cannot get workmen. The seventeenth and no news of any ships in the river, the cause of the greatest uneasiness and with reason.

By letter from River St. Jean, dated June 20, M. de Boishebert informs us that for a quarter of the last winter at Miramichi he fed his men on ox hides, that the convoy sent by M. de Vaudreuil had at last arrived, that he would be prepared to march in the direction of Fort St. George as soon as he had received orders from M. de Drucour to leave Miramichi with his detachment, composed of one hundred French and one hundred Micmacs, to take the Indians of Ocpack on River St. Jean, who number seventy warriors, along with thirty Frenchmen and then to go to Port Toulouse,[56] to reinforce his party with the Indians and Frenchmen who occupy this post, and to go to Isle Royale with this troop which should amount to five or six hundred men.

The courier who brought M. de Boishebert's dispatches met on July 1 or 2 a few leagues this side of the village of Medocktek[57] twelve Indians of that place who were returning from Fort St. George,[58] where they had taken eight scalps and four prisoners. One of the prisoners told him that the English fleet to the number of 160 sail was before Louisbourg, but that they had learned from a small vessel just arrived at Fort St. George that this fleet had returned to Halifax and that the smallpox continued to make great ravages at this place.

In a letter from Niagara, dated July 2, M. Pouchot informs us that many Iroquois are coming to Niagara, assuring him that they are returning from the war, although they bear only few marks of it because, they say, they left their captures in their villages, that the English had abandoned their frontiers, and that everywhere one found furnished houses without any inhabitants.

[56] On the south side of Cape Breton Island, a little east of Canso.
[57] On the St. John River a little below Woodstock, N.B.
[58] Thomaston, Me.

An Iroquois came from Canestio[59] July 1, told him that the Governor of Philadelphia had sent them belts, medals, gorgets, and silver circles with a fine calumet [pipe] to invite them to come to a council with him, that these presents exhibited in the Seneca villages had produced no effect, and that they had been everywhere rejected.

At La Belle Rivière three colony officers and seven militiamen fell into an ambush and lost six, including the three officers. They had left Fort Duquesne with seventy-eight Indians who later got separated from them. On June 15 one hundred sixty Indians who left this same fort to go to war returned the next day because two Iroquois stragglers had their scalps lifted by four Catawbas. M. de Ligneris at once sent forty men out on a scout with orders to go as far as twenty leagues. On their return he proposed to send a large detachment to Fort Cumberland and even farther. In this region all the roads are empty; one meets only a few parties of English and Catawbas.

A prisoner taken to M. de Ligneris by some Delawares on June 13 has stated that the English had assembled many people, horses, artillery, munitions, and provisions with the intention of moving against Fort Duquesne. M. de Ligneris did not inform M. Pouchot of the place where this assembly was taking place.

At four o'clock forty Indians from M. Marin's party arrived here. They said that they were hungry and had no shoes.

It is said that several English barges have been seen on Lake St. Sacrement. Three hundred men, Indians and Canadians are now lying in ambush, part in canoes, part on land, and plan to capture them.

At eight there came a courier who brought us news from the sea and from Isle Royale as of June 9. Two battalions of Berry, originally destined for Louisbourg and now no longer needed there, come on to this colony. There are now six companies of them in the river in the warships the *Bizarre* and the *Célebre*, with gun powder, and the Intendant has sent four ships to take them to

[59] Probably Conestoga, near Lancaster, Pa., but there was a Canestoguine near Cohoes, N.Y.

Journal for 1757

Quebec. The *Bizarre* and the *Célebre* have orders to remain at Isle aux Coudres to dispute passage of the gulf, if they are driven away to fall back to the Traverse, and finally, under the guns of Quebec. The rest of the two battalions will come in vessels of M. d'Aubigny's squadron. The battalions are composed of nine companies of sixty men each. There also were, at the time the courier left Quebec, at St. Barnabé[60] several merchant ships, loaded with provisions, two of which at least were consigned to the Commissary General.

Three squadrons were destined for Louisbourg, two from Brest and one from Toulon. That of Beaufrement arrived first on June 2. That of M. Dubois de la Motte next and the one from Toulon last. Here is the list of warships now at Isle Royale under orders of M. Dubois de la Motte, general acting as vice admiral for this campaign.

The *Formidable*	80 guns	M. Dubois de la Motte, vice admiral's flag, Squadron Commander
The *Tonnant*	80 guns	M. de Beaufrement, carrying flag of Lieutenant General
The *Défenseur*	74 guns	M. de Blénac, Squadron Commander
The *Duc de Bourgogne*	80 guns	M. d' Aubigny, Squadron Commander
The *Héros*	74 guns	M. Chateloger, Captain
The *Diadême*	74 guns	M. Rosily, Captain
The *Hector*	74 guns	M. Curvesse, Captain
The *Glorieux*	74 guns	M. Chavagnac, Captain
The *Dauphin R.*	70 guns	M. d'Urtubie, Captain
The *Achille*	64 guns	M. de Panat, Captain
The *Eveillé*	64 guns	M. Merville, Captain
The *Vaillant*	64 guns	M. Saurin, Captain
The *Superbe*	70 guns	M. Choiseuil, Captain
The *Inflexible*	64 guns	M. St. Laurant, Captain
The *Belliqueux*	64 guns	M. d'Orvillers, Captain
The *Sage*	64 guns	M. d'Abon, Captain

[60] An island some fifteen miles downstream from Bic.

Frigates

The *Bruné*	32 guns	M. la Prévalaye, Captain
The *Fleur de Lys*	32 guns	M. Tourville, Captain
The *Abenakis*	36 guns	M. Macarty, Captain
The *Comète*	32 guns	M. de Brugnon, Captain
The *Hermione*	32 guns	M. Dubois, Lieutenant

Total sixteen ships of the line and five frigates, plus an English sixty-four, the *Greenwich*, captured by M. de Beaufremont, and the two ships the *Bizarre* sixty-four guns, Captain Montalet, and the *Célebre*, Captain la Jonquiere, that we already said were in the river.

Less than this would not put Louisbourg in condition to resist the attempts of England. The place if abandoned to its own efforts could not hold out very long. All they have done up to the present is to have put up palisades and repaired the covered ways. As to the main works of the place, neither flank nor bastion faces nor curtain walls have been repaired; it is a complete ruin. M. de Franquet, engineer officer, was sent there in 1750 to make plans and estimates of the fortifications. For four years they considered what should be done, and have only been at work the last two years, and besides, they can work during only five months in the year.

The royal order for the regulations and the increase in the artillery corps in this colony has arrived. This will consist of two companies of fifty men each, with a captain, a lieutenant, and a first and second ensign, a commander in chief at the head of the body.

☙ JULY 23: Yesterday evening the reconnaissance barge came back to report that it had seen six English barges in the vicinity of Isle de la Barque. M. de Corbière left at once with about 450 men, almost all Indians, to lay an ambush among the islands with which this part of the lake is covered. A small canoe was sent on reconnaissance from one of these islands, another was sent from a more distant island. At daybreak the first canoe returned, and the second, passing in sight of the Indians on the most advanced island, was taken for an enemy. Someone fired and his shot wounded two Ottawa chiefs, one of whom died. Great grief among the Indians.

Courtesy Fort Ticonderoga Museum

Bougainville around 1758,
the period of his service at Fort Carillon.
From an old print.

Courtesy Musée de la Marine, Paris

A vessel similar to the *Victoire*, aboard which Bougainville sailed to France in 1758. The *Victoire* was rigged with three masts instead of two and had an over-all length of seventy-five to eighty feet.

Journal for 1757

Several of them gave up. M. de Langlade, however, remained in ambush with 250 or 300 men. M. de Corbière joined and reinforced him the same evening. News is awaited. This misfortune has caused the Indians to ask that they be given a rallying cry. They ask for orders.

At noon there arrived four officers and fourteen soldiers of the Royal Corps of Artillery and Engineers. They still do not know their destination, or if they will be assigned or not, the royal orders which concern them not having yet arrived. While waiting they will serve under orders of M. Mercier.

At five a patrol of grenadiers of the Guyenne regiment returning to the camp at the Falls were fired on by some Mohawk Indians in ambush at the edge of the woods. One grenadier lost his scalp. Since this took place within 150 paces from the tents, troops turned out instantly. M. de Villiers pursued them with about 150 men, I wish that they catch them, but it is a safe bet that the men that made this strike are sure to get away. It would seem that these Indians spent the night in their ambush. They found a handful of sea biscuits there. The passage over the carry continues briskly.

༄ JULY 24 : M. Marin came back this morning with thirty-two scalps and a prisoner taken at Fort Lydius. After he was deserted by part of his people, he advanced toward this fort with the some 150 men who remained with him. He arrived there on the twenty-third at eight in the morning, ran into a patrol of ten men, who were at once knocked on the head. The main guard rushed out at the noise and met the same fate. Then all the camp got under arms. The troops left their defenses and advanced in battle formation up to the edge of the woods, firing regularly but without any effect. The Indians from the shelter of the big trees fired with a sure aim, and they said that they had killed many of them. The firing lasted for some time, after which they made their retreat, pursued for more than a league. But who can catch a fleeing Indian? They returned to their canoes without stopping. This expedition cost only one Canadian, dead of fatigue or of fear, and two Indians lightly wounded. Before they struck they had made medicine.

Such is the report of this officer. The exact truth is that only the pickets came out of the defenses at the Indians' first fusillade, that there was much firing, and that the English had eleven men killed and four wounded, two of whom since died of their wounds. The Indians, however, brought back thirty-two scalps; they know how to make two or even three out of one.

We know now through this reconnaissance of M. Marin that the end of the bay is unoccupied, that the enemy has no fort there nor any defensive works nor fixed post, but that they send scouts there from time to time to hide and watch our movements in this region, that the Chicot River is navigable, except for a very short rapid, as far as Fort Anne,[61] now abandoned, and that from this fort to Fort Lydius is an excellent road five leagues long. The prisoner taken at this fort says that the English are entrenched there and could have four to five thousand men, all militia.

Our detachment which was in ambush under Sugar Loaf returned in succession after a most fortunate action. Colonel Parker left Fort George yesterday evening with a detachment consisting of 350 men, 5 captains, 4 lieutenants, and an ensign in twenty-two barges, two of them under sail. His purpose was to test our advanced posts and to make prisoners. At daybreak three of these barges fell into our ambush and surrendered without a shot fired. Three others that followed at a little distance met the same fate. The sixteen advanced in order. The Indians who were on shore fired at them and made them fall back. When they saw them do this they jumped into their canoes, pursued the enemy, hit them, and sank or captured all but two which escaped. They brought back nearly two hundred prisoners. The rest were drowned. The Indians jumped into the water and speared them like fish, and also sinking the barges by seizing them from below and capsizing them. We had only one man slightly wounded. The English, terrified by the shooting, the sight, the cries, and the agility of these monsters, surrendered almost without firing a shot. The rum which was in the barges and which the Indians immediately drank caused them

[61] Now Fort Ann, N. Y. Stockaded forts existed here at various periods in colonial history, but never for long.

Journal for 1757

to commit great cruelties. They put in the pot and ate three prisoners, and perhaps others were so treated. All have become slaves unless they are ransomed. A horrible spectacle to European eyes.

The detachment was composed for the most part of the New Jersey regiment of militia.[62] It was the rest of those that we captured at Oswego. Colonel Parker commanded it in place of M. Schuyler, a prisoner.

According to the prisoners' reports, which essentially were in agreement, it is certain that the islands of Lake St. Sacrement are not occupied at all by the English, that they have no advanced post; that at Fort George there are not a thousand men, but that they expect within three days General Webb with a reinforcement of a size varying with the statements of different prisoners; that these troops are in camp behind the fort on an eminence which commands it, with neither ditch nor trench covering their camp; that except for five hundred regulars all the rest are militia. Names of the war chiefs who were in this party: Ottawas—La Fourche, Brisset, Pennahouel, Le Poisson Blanc, Huharnois, Le Vieux Bouchard, Makiouita, Agoda, Le Fils d'Aukameny, Ouennago, Ouenaoué, Oyuinenon, Sagné, the chief of the Saginaws of Akouoi; Chippewas—Capipoueken, Aguipemosé, Nanjeoyaky, Caouchinayé, Chabaouia; Menominees—Le Chat; Potawatomis—Millouisillyny, Ouakousy, Nanaquoibis, Oybischagamé, Nerionois.

Some of these names are Indian, the others the translation of what it means in their language.

M. de Villiers, who was in pursuit of the Indians who scalped the Guyenne grenadier, returned, having found nothing.

Today there arrived with Sieur Perthuis, interpreter, 277 domesticated Iroquois, 4 Oneidas, 5 Delawares from La Belle Rivière, 52 Hurons from Detroit and Lorette, 58 Amalecites, and 11 Abnakis from Lake St. Francis.

The day was passed in council, and the Indians, the conquerors as well as all the others in consequence of their victory, have been intolerable. One needs a head of iron to resist it.

---

[62] The Jersey Blues.

JULY 25 : Copy of deposition of Louis Vindrolette captured at Lake St. Sacrement. It is attached hereto. [omitted in MS.]

I have put this deposition here because it contains several interesting details, among others of the deceit which the English use to people their colonies with strangers imposed on by beautiful promises, from which one should conclude the discontent and bad intentions towards the war of all these colonists, made citizens at the end of four years of slavery; of the way they raise the militia regiments, and of the different intermediate posts between New York and Fort George.

The general passed the day holding council with the Indians. Several wished to return to Montreal, saying that it was tempting the Master of Life to continue to expose themselves to the dangers of war, after such a beautiful affair as they had just accomplished. The others wished to take their prisoners to Montreal. Finally everybody wanted something, everyone came at the same time, everyone shouted at once. They made very touching visits to their prisoners, caressing them, taking them white bread, wishing to see that they lacked nothing. Just the same, they ate one of them up at this camp. It is impossible to stop them.

In the afternoon they agreed that the Marquis de Montcalm should send the prisoners to Montreal. Consequently all necessary measures were taken. Two hours later they did not wish it any longer, and it was necessary to hold a council at midnight to decide this important matter. A second time they consented on condition that they would give a receipt to each band or individual for their slaves, that the Marquis de Vaudreuil would give them white bread and blankets, and that on their return they would give back [the slaves], unless they should sell them. No moderation at all in these barbarians, either unheard of cruelties or the best treatment that they can think of.

Today there arrived three officers and 150 men, recruits drawn from the regiment of foreign volunteers, and intended to fill up the companies of La Marine.

Work is always going on preparing everything necessary for the departure of the army.

Journal for 1757

ჽ﹥ JULY 26: The prisoners have at last left for Montreal, escorted by an officer and some regular soldiers. Several Indians wished to conduct their [prisoners] as far as the boats.

There also departed four Indian canoes with wounded, children, and sick.

The Marquis de Montcalm has been at the Falls to hold a council with the chiefs of the different Indian nations. He has told them his order of march, the day when he plans to start the army moving, what concerns them particularly, what is expected of them, and announced for tomorrow the grand council which will reunite and bind the nations together.

The Abnakis, speaking first, approved all that the Marquis de Montcalm proposed, as did the Algonkins and the Nipissings. The Iroquois, whose old men were not present at the council, told him: "Father, if it were a question of a sudden blow, we would soon be decided to follow thy orders, we would approve it without question, but since it is a question of business of the highest importance, since our old men are not here, it is not for us to decide. We shall render to them an exact account of what thou hast told us and we do not doubt but that they will follow thy wish."

La Motte, Menominee chief, speaking with vehemence and in the figurative style of the orientals, approved the orders. As the Marquis de Montcalm profited by the chance fall of a great tree during the council to refer to it as a certain augury of the fall of Fort George, La Motte accepted the omen in the name of the Indians of the Far West.

Pennahouel, Ottawa chief who in the war with the Foxes carried the hatchet against us, but since then always devoted to Ononthio, celebrated for his spirit, his wisdom and his conversations with M. de la Galissoniere, Pennahouel, I repeat, with the oldest of these Indians, said: "Father, I who of all the Indians have seen the most revolutions of Tibickigros (that is to say, the moon), thank thee in the name of all the nations and in my own for the good words thou hast just given us. I approve them, and no one has ever spoken better to us than thou. It is the war Manitou which inspires thee."

The army is to march in two divisions, one by land under the orders of the Chevalier de Lévis, and the other by bateaux. The land party, which has some ten leagues to make through woods and very difficult mountains, should leave two days ahead of the other in order to arrive at the same time at Ganaouské Bay.[63] It has been decided that it will start the twenty-ninth. The Indians have asked that they do not start before the thirtieth and this has been granted them.

Today our Indians thought that they had seen a white flag on a mountain at some little distance from the Portage. They thought that this might be an enemy trick, and some five or six hundred of them went there. The flag was a white rock. The Indians, in order not to waste their steps, amused themselves by gathering blueberries, a kind of berry good to eat and very healthy, and fired off their guns in the woods, which made the troops at the Portage turn out in alarm.

JULY 27: Today the Marquis de Montcalm went to camp at the Portage, where his presence was necessary to speed the arrangements for the colony troops, the brigading of the militia, the necessary distributions, and the assignment of bateaux, etc.

A grand council was held to reunite and bind together by a belt of six thousand beads the 40 nations who are here. The chiefs and orators of these nations composed the council.

Kisensik, famous Nipissing chief, opened it. "My brothers," he said to the nations of the Far West, "we domesticated Indians thank you for having come to help us defend our lands against the English who wish to usurp them. Our cause is good and the Master of Life favors it. Can you doubt it, my brothers, after the fine deed you have just accomplished. We admired it, we pay you our compliments. It covers you with glory, and Lake St. Sacrement, stained red with the blood of Englishmen, will forever attest this exploit. Let me say that it also covers us with glory, we, your brothers, and we are proud of it. Our joy should be still greater than thine, my

---

[63] Near Bolton, N. Y.

Journal for 1757

Father," said he, addressing the Marquis de Montcalm, "thou who hast passed over the great ocean, not for thine own interest, for it is not thy cause that thou hast come to defend, it is that of the great King who said: 'Go, cross the great ocean and go and defend my children.' He will reunite you, my brothers, and bind you together with the most solemn of ties. Accept this sacred bond with joy and let nothing ever break it."

This harangue was translated by the various interpreters and received with applause.

The Marquis de Montcalm then said to them, "My children, I am delighted to see you all reunited for the good work. So long as your union lasts the English will never be able to resist you. I cannot speak better to you than your brother, Kisensik, who has just spoken. The great King has without doubt sent me to protect and defend you, but he has above all charged me to see that you are made happy and invincible by establishing among you this friendship, this unity, this joining together to carry on the good work, which should exist among brothers, children of the same father, of the great Ononthio. I give you this belt as a sacred pledge of his word, symbol of good understanding and strength through the conjunction of the different beads which compose it. I bind you all together so that nothing can separate you before the defeat of the English and the destruction of Fort George."

This speech was then reported by the different interpreters and the belt thrown into the midst of the assembly.

It [the belt] was picked up by the orators of the different nations, who exhorted them to accept it, and Pennahouel, on presenting it to those of the Far West, said to them, "Behold a circle is drawn around you by the great Ononthio which none of us can leave. So long as we remain within its embrace the Master of Life will be our guide, will inspire us as to what we shall do and will favor all our enterprises. If some nation quits before the time, the Master of Life is not accountable for the evils that could hit them, but its misfortune will be its own and will not fall upon the nations who here promised an indissoluble union and complete obedience to their father's will." Once the orators had spoken in raising up the belt they put it down again in the midst of the assembly. The belt, following the custom of the nations, belongs to that one which has the greatest number of warriors in the army. It was without question granted to the Iroquois, who were and who almost always are the most numerous, and whose former victories over almost all of the nations of North America have given them a superior standing, which they continue to hold. They took the belt and their orator, addressing himself to the nations of the Far West, told them that, charmed by seeing their brothers reunited with them, and recognizing the help that they had just brought them for the defense of their lands, they begged them to accept this belt, pledge of their union, and to take it into their villages where it would be an eternal symbol of their friendship, of their common success, a witness which would keep in front of their eyes the happy results accomplished in this campaign, and would remind them to maintain forever this bond, the source of power of their warriors.

The Nipissing orator arose to tell the Iroquois: "My brothers, we are most thankful for this mark of respect you have shown to our brothers from the West. It was also our intention, and you have only anticipated us." One must note this procedure of the Nipissing. Its objective was to make the Iroquois realize that the Nipissings were the friends of all the Indians, and not to allow them to prescribe the right of precedence which their seniority gave them.

Pennahouel, in the name of the western Indians, thanked the Iroquois and accepted the belt. The different nations held a council that night to determine which one of them should keep it.

This fine affair of the belt being completed, the Marquis de Montcalm asked for the answers to the questions he had asked at last night's council with the chiefs on the subject of the march of the army, part by land, the rest by boat, of the route which must be followed in the woods, of the day of departure, and of the other similar arrangements. For it is necessary to inform them of all the

Journal for 1757

plans, to consult with them, and often to follow what they propose. In the midst of the woods of America one can no more do without them than without cavalry in open country.

The Iroquois answered that, since they were children of this country, the theater of the war, the Marquis de Vaudreuil had told them that they would serve the army as guides, and that they would with pleasure carry out the wishes of their father, and since it was necessary that one party should go by land and the other by boat, they consequently would divide up their warriors; that of 250 Iroquois of the Sault, 100 would go through the woods and 150 by canoe, that they would lead the land division by the least bad way and one which kept the lake as much in sight as possible so that, their having searched the shores, those who went by boat would fear no ambush; that as regards the day of departure they were ready at any moment that their father ordered them to start.

This answer of the Iroquois was communicated to the other nations, and at the same time all were warned that the division which went by land under the orders of the Chevalier de Lévis would assemble on the evening of the twenty-ninth in front of the camp at the Portage on the north side so as to start its march on the thirtieth at daybreak.

The nations answered that they would furnish the numbers of their warriors that they would assign to the two divisions. The report would be made by little sticks. The Iroquois, according to their custom would have ended the council by the ceremony of singing the war song, but as it is not the custom of the western nations to end councils of this nature by any war song, the object of which is to unite and bind together their spirits, their customs were followed on this point, as a courtesy to them as strangers.

The Marquis de Montcalm, before leaving the assembly, begged the chiefs to see that their young men did not continually shoot off their powder, explaining the ill consequences of doing it. The chiefs promised their best efforts toward this end.

The Menominees, Sauks, and Foxes had left the meeting because the crowd of French officers expanded the circle so that it prevented them from seeing their father and hearing his words. They were begged to return and the curiosity seekers sent away.

🙢 JULY 28 : The Indians have turned in the sticks showing the number of men they expect to go on foot. The Nipissings wished to keep their people out of this division, claiming that it was needlessly tiring; they did not succeed.

The Miamis, to the number of eight, left without telling anyone. A Potawatomi chief told the Marquis de Montcalm of it and offered to try to bring them back. He was given a belt and strings to help him succeed.

An English corpse came floating by the Indians' camp. They crowded around it with loud cries, drank its blood, and put its pieces in the kettle. However, it was only the western Indians who committed these cruelties. Our domesticated ones took no part in it; they spent all day in confession.

LIST OF INDIANS WITH THE MARQUIS DE MONTCALM'S ARMY
JULY 28, 1757

DOMESTICATED

			Officers Attached to the Indians	Missionaries	Interpreters
Nipissings—		53	M. de la Corne St. Luc, General	Abbé Matavet, Sulpician	St. Germain
Algonkins from the Lake—	24)		MM. Langis and Montegron		
From Three Rivers—	23)	47			
Abnakis of St. Francis—	104)		Chevalier de Niverville	Père Roubaud, Jesuit	Chateauvieux
of Bécancour—	80)				
of Missiskoui—	25)		M. Hertel		
of Panouameske—	36)	245			
Iroquois of Sault St. Louis—	258)		MM. de Longueuil and Sabrevois	Abbé Piquet, Sulpician	Perthuis La Force
of Lake of Two Mountains—	94)	363			
of La Presentation—	3)				
Onondagas of Five Nations—	8)				
Hurons from Detroit—	26)		De Longueuil	Abbé Piquet	St. Martin
from Lorette—	26)	52			
Micmacs from Acadia—	4)		Chevalier de Niverville and Hertel	Abbé Piquet	Launière
Amalecites—	56)	60			
Total		820			

Journal for 1757

INDIANS OF THE FAR WEST

			Officers Attached to the Indians	Missionaries	Interpreters
Tetes de Boule or Gens des Terres—		3			
Ottawas			Langlade,	Abbé Matavet	
Kiscacous—	94)		Fleurimont,	for a few	
de la Fourche—	70)	337	Herbin, cadet	from	
Sinago—	35)			Detroit	Farly,
Magnonjan—	10)			and from	St. Jean
from L'Isle au Castor—	44)			Michili-	
from Detroit—	30)			mackinac	
from Saginaw—	54)				
Chippewas					
from Chequamegon—	32)				
from Castor—	24)		La Plante,		Chesne
from Chaoschimagan—	14)	157	Loumier		
from La Carpe—	37)				
from Kakibonocké—	50)				
Missisaugas					
from Toronto—	35)		La Plante,		Chesne
from La Carpe—	43)	141	Loumier		
from La Loutre—	63)				
Potawatomis					
from St. Joseph—	70)		Marin,		Destailly
from Detroit—	18)	88	Chevalier de Langis		
Menominees					
from L'Orignal—	62)		Marin,		Reaume
from Le Chat—	67)	129	Chevalier de Langis		
Miamis of St. Joseph—	8)				
Winnebago from the Bay—	48)				
Iowas of the Western Sea—	10)	124	Marin,		Reaume
Foxes from Mississippi—	20)		Chevalier		
Sauks—	33)		de Langis		
Delawares—	5)				
Total		979			
Domesticated Indians		820			
Total Indians		1799			

From this number one must subtract some two score Ottawas or Missisaugas who left five or six days ago, and the Miamis who probably will not come back. There are a few women and children not included in this number.

The militia brigades are organized at last. There are six of them, not of equal size.

They are commanded by MM. de la Corne, 411; de Vassan, 445; St. Ours, 461; Repentigny, 432; Courtemanche, 473; Gaspé, 424. In each of these brigades there are a certain number of colony troops. M. de Villiers has besides a troop of 300 volunteers.

The battalion of La Marine is also established. It does duty like our regulars. It has 525 men.

JULY 29: The Miamis did not come back. Their example has been contagious. Several others have followed them. A few, in order not to be stopped, portaged their canoes through the woods. The deserters are Missisaugas and Ottawas. About two hundred of them have left. No way to hold them; they had made a coup, and besides they lacked everything, no blankets, no deer-skins, except very bad ones, no leggings, no vermilion. Those who send to the army Indians who lack everything, should come and command them themselves. Moreover, this inconvenience so prejudicial to the King's service results from the poor condition of the government and is the result of the greed of the leeches of the colony.

THE KING'S ARMY IN CANADA

On Lake St. Sacrement in the Camps of Carillon, The Falls, and The Portage, July 29, 1757

Marquis de Montcalm, Brigadier General
Chevalier de Lévis, Brigadier
Sieur Rigaud de Vaudreuil, Governor of Trois Rivières, commanding the colony troops.
Sieur de Bourlamaque, Colonel
Chevalier de Montreuil, Brigade Major

French Troops

La Reine	369
La Sarre	451
Royal Roussillon	472
Languedoc	322
Guyenne	492
Béarn	464
M. Desandrouins, Engineer	
Total	2570

Journal for 1757

	Colony Troops	
	La Marine Battalion	524
	Militia	
	Brigade of La Corne	411
	Vassan	445
	St. Ours	461
	Repentigny	432
	Courtemanche	473
	Gaspé	424
	Volunteers of Villiers	300
	Total	3470
	Indians	
	Domesticated	820
	From Far West	979
	Artillery	
	Sieur Mercier, Commandant	
	Officers	8
	Canoneers, bombardiers & workmen	180
	Sieur de Lotbinière, Engineer	
	Total	1979
	Total Army—	8019 men

The Chevalier de Lévis, who commands the division that goes by land, started his troops moving this evening. They are bivouacked at Burned Camp, about a half-league beyond the Portage on the left bank of Lake St. Sacrement. They will leave tomorrow at daybreak and reach Ganaouské Bay, the place designated for joining the division which goes by boat, on August 1. This latter, requiring only twenty-four hours to make the trip by water, will embark on the afternoon of the first in order to arrive on the second at daybreak.

DETACHMENT UNDER ORDERS OF THE CHEVALIER DE LÉVIS
    Chevalier de Lévis, Brigadier
      M. de Senezergues, Lieutenant Colonel
      M. de la Pauze, Assistant Brigade Major
      Six companies of Grenadiers   300
      Six pickets of Regulars   300

Two pickets of La Marine	100
De Villier's Volunteers	300
Brigade of La Corne	311
Vassan	345
Repentigny	332
Indians, about	500
	2488 men

The detachment marches without tents or baggage. It is thus that they make land marches in this country. Five hundred men ordered to work all night at the Portage.

꒰ JULY 30 : The Chevalier de Lévis left this morning, De Villier's volunteers and some Indians forming the advance guard, some other Indians marching on the flanks, and the troops in the center in three columns, that is to say, files.

The Royal Roussillon brigade, consisting of that battalion and Béarn, came from Carillon with M. de Bourlamaque to camp at the head of the Portage. La Reine, La Sarre, Languedoc and Guyenne came from the Falls to camp at Burned Camp, which the Chevalier de Lévis left this morning.

The Indians were bored and peevish, found the food bad, and wanted fresh meat. Consequently the young men yesterday killed fourteen oxen and today another four. The chiefs came to bear witness of their sorrow in this matter, that it was only their youth, and that they would reprimand them. The Nipissings, Algonkins, and Potawatomis are the only nations not taking part in this St. Bartholomew of the oxen, which they called an insult to their father. They have been told that they will be pardoned for this. It is a case of making a virtue of necessity.

Five hundred workmen ordered to work all night portaging over the carry.

꒰ JULY 31 : Today two brigades and four light companies under the orders of M. de Bourlamaque, colonel, M. de Bernetz, lieutenant colonel, M. de Montredon, commanding the Battalion of Béarn, have been ordered to pass over the Portage, which was ac-

Journal for 1757

complished by six in the evening. One has no idea of the difficulty involved in moving a considerable amount of artillery, 250 bateaux, food for six weeks for one thousand men, all this without horses or oxen, by men's arms alone. Also, they cannot appreciate in Europe the merit of the operations carried out in America. The hardships cannot be imagined, and it is impossible to give a fair idea of it.

The Indians, who for several days impatiently endured their inactivity in a camp where there was neither wine nor brandy and where consequently they could not get drunk, left at three to go forward three leagues on Lake St. Sacrement, where they will wait for us. They have with them three hundred Canadians left from the three brigades which went by land. On their departure they left at their camp a cloak, a breechclout, and a pair of leggings hung in a tree as a sacrifice to the Manitou. Two Sulpicians and a Jesuit, missionaries with this army, asked if they would be permitted to say mass in a place where one sacrificed to the devil. Reply by the General of the army, military casuist, that it was better to say it there than not to say it at all.

Today they assigned the bateaux and distributed the provisions to the battalions and the militia, and loaded the provisions. Attached is the embarkation table.

Embarkation Table

Artillery with Royal Roussillon and Béarn	115	bateaux	1330 men
Provisions with Gaspé brigade	32		440
Field hospital	3		45
Headquarters and staff	7		100
La Reine brigade, composed of La Reine, Languedoc and the battalion of La Marine	42		870
La Sarre brigade, composed of La Sarre and Guyenne	30		657
Courtemanche's brigade	16		400
Total bateaux	245	Total men loaded	3842

		Men loaded in	
Plus parties with Indians	2	the Indians' canoes	300
	247	Total	4142

Among the artillery bateaux there are thirty-one pontoons made of two bateaux fastened together with a platform on top. These pontoons carry the cannon and mortars, mounted on their carriages. They are very well conceived for a lake with high shores like Lake St. Sacrement. There is also a bateau carrying an eleven-pounder and two little swivels that M. Jacquot, artillery lieutenant, has had made. I attach the plan of it to this journal. [Omitted in MS.]

M. Wolf, volunteer, arrived at five in the evening, sent by the Chevalier de Lévis to report to the Marquis de Montcalm on the first day's march. The detachment yesterday evening passed Bald Mountain,[64] which is the most difficult passage. Kanectagon, famous Iroquois hunter who leads the way, assures them that they will reach the rendezvous on the day set.

🙵 AUGUST 1: The Marquis de Montcalm left at Carillon a garrison of 100 men with 100 armed workmen, under orders of M. d'Alquier, captain of the grenadiers of the Béarn regiment, commanding said regiment since the death of M. de l'Hopital; a captain and 50 men at the Falls, holding a redoubt in the midst of the falls themselves; a captain and 150 men at the Portage, where there is part of our provision depot.

The army embarked at two in the afternoon in the following order, the brigade of La Reine, that of La Sarre, that of Courtemanche, militia, artillery, the field hospital, the provisions, a picket of Royal Roussillon. M. Jaquot's bateau headed the flotilla, composed of 250 sail. Halted at five o'clock at four leagues from Carillon beyond Isle la Barque, where the Indians who left yesterday and who waited for us took the lead in 150 birchbark canoes.

---

[64] Rogers' Slide on the west shore of Lake George, some five miles up the lake from the present town of Ticonderoga.

Journal for 1757

The sight was singular, even for a soldier accustomed to seeing European armies, but who could imagine the spectacle of fifteen hundred naked Indians in their canoes?

Lake St. Sacrement is some dozen leagues from Fort George, where it starts, to the falls. It is not more than a league at its widest place and a half-league at other places. It contains a very great quantity of islands. Two mountain chains border it, on the east and on the west, and I have had occasion to remark in passing how just is M. de Buffon's[65] observation on the relation between angles, salients, and re-entrants. Thus nature, for its great operations, is the same here as in the Old World.

August 2 : At two in the morning the Marquis de Montcalm reached the Bay of Ganaouské, rendezvous given to the land divisions. Three fires lighted on the shore, which was the signal agreed upon, assured us that the Chevalier de Lévis was there. He had arrived yesterday at two in the afternoon, after a march which the heat, for the last six weeks as great as in Italy, the continual mountains, fallen trees, and the necessity of carrying everything on one's back had rendered extremely painful.

Several Indians were sent out scouting, the army halted. Provisions were issued to the troops who came by land, to give them an equal share.

Since we were within range of enemy scouts, for the fear of discovery, all shooting was forbidden, as well as lighting of fires or beating the drums. The French, who are overconfident, shot, lighted fires, and what is more, sounded horns as if on a hunting party. These are, I believe, the first horns that have yet resounded through the forests of America.

The Chevalier de Lévis, at the head of his detachment, again started the march through the woods at noon, and proceeded to a little bay located about three leagues from the Bay [of Ganaouské] to facilitate the disembarkation of the water army. This went ashore at noon and after several halts reached a place two leagues

---

[65] Famous French naturalist of the day.

from the fort, where it went into bivouac. Scouts were at once sent to examine the vicinity of the fort, its position, that of the enemy and a proper inlet for landing the artillery.

At ten in the evening two enemy barges came scouting and approached the place where the Indian canoes were drawn up. Those who were within range uttered the usual cry and pursued the English, who ran away to the south shore where they abandoned their barges and took to the woods. The Indians lost two men and captured three prisoners. According to their depositions the enemy had just received a reinforcement of twelve hundred men. They had known the day before that we were on the march to attack them. The prisoners were massacred that very night by Indians, relatives of the [two] dead.

At midnight received news from Montreal by M. de Bellestre, lieutenant of La Marine, who had returned from the Miamis and who brought us seventeen Indians, Weas and Miamis.

August 3 : In the middle of the night the Marquis de Montcalm gave orders to approach Fort George at daybreak. One of the prisoners had said that at the signal of a single cannon shot all the troops in the camp would rush to arms. The cannon had just been fired, and some Abnaki scouts warned us at the same moment that the enemy were on the move. Consequently, the order to march to meet the enemy was given. The army got under way, the Chevalier de Lévis forming the advance guard with his detachment and all the Indians, in case they came out against us, or to invest the place, if they did not come out. There were left for boat guards two men per boat under the orders of Sieur Privat, lieutenant colonel. At three in the morning the army started moving. The Chevalier de Lévis commanded the advance guard with his detachment and all the Indians; the brigades followed in column by battalions, the Marquis de Montcalm at their head. This march of more than three leagues was made through mountains and almost impassable forests.

The Chevalier de Lévis arrived and took a position on the road from Lydius, investing Fort George in all this area, the body of

Journal for 1757

the army formed the rest of the investment. The Marquis de Montcalm, having gone himself to the advance guard, realized that he could not attack the enemy's defenses without committing all the colony forces. At the same time, as the position the advance guard held, although the best possible for cutting off communications, was not a battle position and was too far away from the siege, the provisions, and other supplies, the Marquis de Montcalm sent an order to the Sieur de Bourlamaque to select a place to camp the army, the left resting on the lake, the right on some inaccessible ravines, and to take there at once the two brigades of La Sarre and Royal Roussillon. These brigades went into camp in the afternoon and immediately went to work making fascines and gabions.[66] The Marquis de Montcalm, with the brigade of La Reine and that of Gaspé and St. Ours, militia, remained in bivouac within supporting distance of the corps of the Chevalier de Lévis.

All day long the Indians in the cleared area around the fort fired their guns from the shelter of tree trunks. They were answered by a few discharges of musketry and cannon. There were seven killed or wounded.

During the day they killed nearly 150 oxen, and they brought 25 [live ones] to the Marquis de Montcalm, telling him that they were to drag his guns in place of those which they had killed at Carillon and the portage.

At three in the afternoon the Marquis de Montcalm notified the commander of the fort that humanity obliged him to warn him that once our batteries were in place and the cannon fired, perhaps there would not be time, nor would it be in our power to restrain the cruelties of a mob of Indians of so many different nations. He answered that his troops were determined to defend themselves to the last extremity. During the parley the Indians appeared in a great crowd in the space around the fort and an Abnaki speaking bad French but very clearly, shouted, "Ah, you won't surrender; well, fire first; my father will then fire his great guns; then take

---

[66] "Fascines" were lashed bundles of faggots, "gabions" were bottomless wickerwork baskets to be placed in position and then filled with earth. Both were standard materials for use in a siege.

care to defend yourself, for if I capture you, you will get no quarter."

I do not wish to omit an act of the famous Kisensik, of whom I have already several times had the occasion to speak. Charged with going from the road to Lydius to report to the Marquis de Montcalm that the advance guard was in position, I was hard put to find him, seeing that he was on the move amidst mountains heavy with timber, where everything is road because there is no road at all. I encountered Kisensik, to whom I told the trouble I had in finding the General in woods which were unknown to me. "I am going," he told me, "to look for my son who has been wounded. Except for that I would willingly be your guide." "The surgeon who dressed his wound," I replied to him, "assured me that the wound was light." He answered me, "Well, I am going to guide you, the service of Ononthio demands it. I shall see my son afterwards, so that there may be no mistake." This Indian, thinking and acting thus, is almost the only one of his kind. *Rara avis in terris*.[67]

AUGUST 4 : At daybreak the troops in the advanced position on the road to Lydius drew near to the lake. The Marquis de Montcalm led the brigade of La Reine into the camp picked by Sieur de Bourlamaque. The grenadier companies and the light companies of the Chevalier de Lévis' detachment returned to their battalions and the van of the siege was composed of the seven battalions and the brigades of St. Ours and Gaspé. The Chevalier de Lévis, with the brigades of La Corne, de Vasson, de Repentigny and de Courtemanche, Villiers' volunteers, and all the Indians, was ordered to cover the right of the army, to send scouts on the road to Lydius, to watch the enemy on this side, and to make them believe, by continuous movements in this area, that we occupied all this line of communication, for it was quite impossible to invest the whole place.

At eleven in the morning all the army was in position, and the Marquis de Montcalm, having decided to open the trenches this

---

[67] "A rare bird in the land."

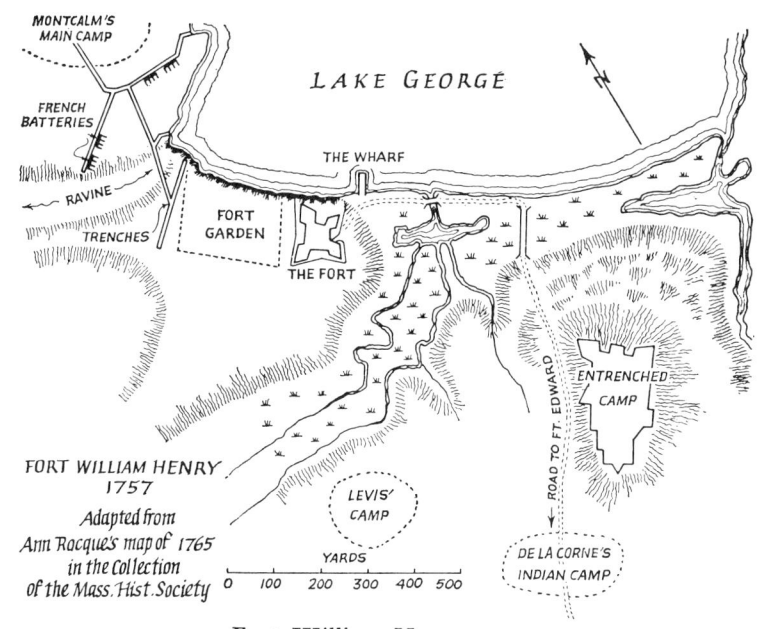

Fort William Henry, 1757

same night, went with the engineers and the artillery officers to reconnoiter the area where the attack was to be made and to look for battery positions. It was decided to make the attack from the north and to emplace two batteries, one to work directly against the north bastion, and the other to cross its fire onto the same front, both at the same time to deliver ricochet fire on the defenses. With respect to disembarking the artillery, what was thought easiest and quickest was to bring the pontoons at nightfall to the little cove that adjoined the supply depot for the trenches and to unload them in turn. The Marquis de Montcalm has put the Sieur de Bourlamaque in charge of the conduct of the siege.

During the day the Indians peppered away at the fort. The English used the time to make a second defensive line inside the first, to get water in, to take the roofs off their barracks and storehouses,[68] and to throw into the lake their firewood and useless

---

[68] Both Fort William Henry and Fort Carillon had roofs of wooden shingles. In case of serious attack these would be removed for fear of fire.

planks. The Indians, who, seeing this from a distance, believed that they were throwing away valuable things, came to complain to the Marquis de Montcalm of what the enemy was doing and asked him for troops to make them stop.

This afternoon a large number of workers have been employed in making practicable the road from the camp to the trench supply depot, and eight hundred others, protected by six light companies, in opening the trench at 350 toises from the fort, and at starting a parallel, the two projected batteries, and the communication of this parallel with the batteries. They took full advantage of the terrain and overcame the difficulties that the fallen trees and stumps which covered it presented. The work advanced well, and by daybreak was under cover everywhere except at the right battery, where the work progressed more slowly because it was more difficult. They also got twelve cannon ashore at the depot, as well as a few mortars and the necessary munitions. The enemy's fire was not very heavy this first night.

August 5 : At four in the morning the daytime workers relieved the night force, improving the trenches and working hard on the left battery. That on the right, the communication trench having been only started, they left for the following night. They only continued to improve the part of this communication trench which had been commenced.

Since the garrison is two thousand men and consequently strong enough to make sorties, and the way through the woods is very difficult, we camped close enough to the trenches to be able to support them. However, since the troops in this position were much bothered by the enemy's fire, and some were killed in their tents by cannon balls and bombs, the Marquis de Montcalm had the camp of La Sarre brigade pulled back, and shifted that of the Royal Roussillon at an angle behind the brigade of La Reine, which remained in its initial position.

Kanectagon, who left on the third to capture a prisoner on the Lydius road, returned today. Yesterday he ran into three men, one of whom was captured, one killed, and the third escaped. He

Journal for 1757

brought back here the prisoner and the jacket of the dead man. In the lining we found a letter dated the fourth at midnight, which General Webb, who is at Fort Lydius, wrote to Lieutenant Colonel Monro, or to any other officer in command at Fort George. He informed him that he could not send help until he had been joined by the militia of the colonies, which he had ordered to march at once, that a Canadian captured on the fourth by one of his parties, told him that the French army was eleven thousand strong, that it had a considerable artillery train, and that it had surrounded the fort entirely for a distance of five miles, that he informed him of these details so that, if the militia he had sent for arrived too late for him to march to the aid of the fort, the commander might see to obtaining the best terms he could.

This letter, fortunately fallen into our hands, determined the Marquis de Montcalm to expedite still more the construction of the batteries. The number of workers has been increased, and they expect to be in shape tomorrow to fire the guns of the left battery, which are six cannon and a mortar.

The Indians, instead of remaining camped with the Chevalier de Lévis and of making continual reconnaissances, spent all the day at our camp, showing a great impatience to see the big guns fired and going to fire some shots from the gardens which are around the fort. A few of them even, in imitation of our trenches which they had just seen with the greatest curiosity, approached the gardens by moving dirt and taking cover. This shooting doubtless inconvenienced the enemy, bothered their workers and artillerymen, and probably even killed a few of them, but it was not the real objective. The great usefulness of these Indians to us should be to overwhelm small parties on the Lydius road and neighboring woods, to intercept all couriers and convoys not of great size and to warn us of major movements which might be made at Fort Lydius in time for us to be prepared, and not be taken by surprise.

The Marquis de Montcalm summoned a general council which was held at five in the evening. In this council he complained that the Indians had not remained at the camp of the Chevalier de Lévis, that the reconnaissances were not being made, that it appeared that his children had lost their spirit, that there no longer was any agreement among them, that they neglected to carry out his wishes, that instead of following his orders, they went into the cleared land around the fort and exposed themselves unnecessarily, that the loss of several Indians killed in these shootings had been extremely painful to him, the least among them being precious to him, that it doubtless was of advantage to inconvenience the English by musketry fire, but that this was not their principal object, that their real occupation should be to keep him informed of all the moves of the enemy, and at all times to keep on the line of communication scouting parties, whose size and direction of march were arranged among all the nations, that with this in view they should all reassemble at the camp of the Chevalier de Lévis, that there they would find all their requirements, ammunition, and food, that even the missionaries were going to take their post there, and that it was there that the Christian Indians would find them, that the Chevalier de Lévis would explain to them there the wishes of their father and that he himself would always be ready to listen to advice and representations of their chiefs; that, finally, in order to restore their spirit, to get them back again on the right path, to wipe out the past and to brighten the future with the light of good fortune, he would give them two belts and ten strings of wampum.

The Marquis de Montcalm added that he had received with pleasure the oxen they had made him a present of, but as he was very different from those of them who thought only of the present, he would think of the future and would know how to foresee it, and so he had reserved them for their future needs, and specially to give soup to their sick and wounded.

Then he gave them the news, of the contents of General Webb's letter and of the measures that he planned to take in consequence.

The Indians took the belts and strings, promised to observe better in the future the wishes of their father, to act according to his orders and together, to separate no more, to remain all together at the camp of the Chevalier de Lévis, and to spend most of their time scouting. They then added that on their side they had something on their minds, that no one told them anything any more, that their chiefs were not told of the movements being made, that not only was their advice not followed, but that the reasons for not following it were not even revealed, that they were no longer consulted on reconnaissances, but that as though they were slaves it was attempted to make them march without having consulted with their chiefs and agreed with them. "My Father," they said, "thou hast brought into these places the art of war of this world which lies beyond the great ocean. We know that in this art you are a great master, but for the science of the craft of scouting, we know more than thee. Consult us and thou will derive benefit from it."

The Marquis de Montcalm replied that the things of which they complained had only happened because of a few of those mistakes inevitable in the tumult of such important happenings, that by his method of acting with them in this and in the preceding campaign they should appreciate how much he was conscious of their talents, what value he placed on their advice on reconnaissance, and that he liked to follow it and to consult with their chiefs, that he was going to take the very best measures so that in the future there would be no more similar mistakes, and that nothing should interfere with the happy conduct of affairs.

He ended by telling them that tomorrow the cannon would start to fire. This news produced great joy in the assembly, which broke up very contentedly.

As it was noted that the English vessels showed much activity, the bateaux guard this night was reinforced with three companies of grenadiers.

A thousand workers employed this night in the trenches finished the left battery, hauled the guns there, finished the communication trench to the right battery and very much advanced the work on this battery.

᛭ AUGUST 6 : At six in the morning the left battery, which consists of eight cannon, three of which are eighteen-pounders, and a nine inch mortar, started firing. This battery fired, either along or at an angle, on the defenses fronting on the lake, the west face of the fort, and the anchorage where the vessels were.

The day workers were employed at completing the right battery and improving the communication ditch leading to this battery.

Today some bateaux arrived here from Carillon. During the last few days ten Mohawks appeared at the portage but did no other harm than killing a horse and an ox. M. Iché, cadet, went in pursuit of them.

During the night five hundred workers finished the right battery and drove a trench forward on the center line of the west bastion. They completed 150 toises of work. They also repaired what had been damaged at the west battery by the enemy's fire.

AUGUST 7: At six in the morning the right battery, which consists of two eighteen-pounders, five twelves, one eight, two seven inch howitzers and a six inch mortar, commenced to fire. It fired a little obliquely on the front attacked and by ricochet on the entrenched camp.

Two hundred daytime workers improved the communication trench started during the night.

At nine in the morning, after a double salvo from the right and left batteries, the Marquis de Montcalm sent me to carry to the fort's commander the letter of General Webb which was intercepted on the fifth. I walked out of the trenches, with a red flag[69] carried before me, accompanied by a drummer beating his drum and an escort of fifteen grenadiers. The English cried out to me to halt at the foot of the glacis, an officer and fifteen grenadiers came out to me and asked what I wanted, upon which I said that I had a letter from my general to deliver to the English commander. Two other officers came out from the fort, one of whom remained under guard of my grenadiers, and the other, having blindfolded me, led me first to the fort, and then to the entrenched camp where I handed to the commandant the letter of the Marquis de Mont-

[69] Since the French flag was white, they used red for a flag of truce.

Journal for 1757

calm and that of General Webb. Much thanks for French politeness, expressions of pleasure at dealing with so generous an enemy. Such is the gist of the reply of Lieutenant Colonel Monro to the Marquis de Montcalm. Then they led me back again, eyes blindfolded all the time, to where they had taken me from, and our batteries started firing again when they judged that the English grenadiers had had time to get back into the fort. I hope that General Webb's letter, the gist of which I gave above, persuades the English to surrender the sooner.

From the beginning of the siege the enemy unceasingly went to hide various things in the woods on the south shore, and to watch our movements from there. Several Indians fell on one of these parties, killed and wounded a few, and made two prisoners, from whom we learned nothing.

The Sieur de Villiers with his volunteers and some Indians went sniping around the enemy's entrenched camp. The enemy made a sortie, were forced back, and the shooting lasted a very long time. We had twenty-one Indians and Canadians killed or wounded in this useless affair. The English, they say, lost an even greater number.

Today the officer whom the Marquis de Montcalm had sent to take from Carillon to Montreal the English captured during the last affair on the lake, has returned and brought us news from France, Louisbourg, Quebec, Niagara, and La Belle Riviére. I put off to another time the details of that part of the news which [do not] concern this continent. It is the only part that should have a place in this journal composed for Europeans.[70]

This night the workers continued the trench started the previous night, which they carried to within about one hundred toises of the fort. They also started at the end of this trench another parallel for a battery and for musket men who will fire at the parapets on the front being attacked.

The Indians and Canadians this night were placed in the fort gardens, lying prone in front of the workers. The trench guard consisted of seven light companies and three companies of grena-

[70] Showing that Bougainville evidently had plans for publishing this journal.

diers. Thus we were ready to receive the enemy if he had wished to make a sortie. Around eleven o'clock two English soldiers, who came, they said, to desert, but rather, I believe, to see what we were doing, fell into the ambush of our Indians who captured them both, one having his shoulder broken by several gunshots. After this discharge all the mountains around the fort resounded with the cries of the Indians whose chiefs named themselves and answered. This little adventure perhaps discouraged the enemy from a sortie that they were about to make.

The cold is as sharp during the night as the heat is extreme during the day. The forests and the proximity of the lake doubtless occasion this unpleasant temperature.

ಌ AUGUST 8 : Because of the shape of the terrain and in order to avoid bad places [the works] this night came to a marsh about fifty toises across. To get out of it it was necessary to proceed with the trench for eight or ten toises entirely in the open. Although it was daylight, in order to speed the work it was decided to make this passage like that of a wet ditch of a fort.[71] The workers went ahead with such ardor that it was finished that very forenoon, in spite of the brisk cannon fire and musketry of the enemy, and this allowed us to contrive in the marsh, by means of fascines and corduroy, a roadway capable of supporting artillery.

At four o'clock Indian scouts reported that a considerable body of the enemy were coming on the road from Lydius. The Chevalier de Lévis at once went there with the largest part of the Canadians and Indians. The Marquis de Montcalm followed him with the brigade of La Reine and three companies of grenadiers. The other three and the brigades of La Sarre and Royal Roussillon remained under command of M. de Bourlamaque to cover the trenches and the encampment.

St. Our's brigade was also sent on guard.

[71] A wet ditch of a fort was passed by the besiegers by construction of a causeway. Fascines were thrown in and sunk by stones and earth until they were above the water surface. The exposed side was shielded by a parapet of gabions, and, if exposed to fire from the front, two parapets and overhead cover were provided. A dry ditch was crossed by digging a trench with overhead cover where needed.

Journal for 1757

At half-past five the Marquis de Montcalm reached the Lydius road, where he joined the Chevalier de Lévis.

Unfortunately the news of the march of the enemy was false. An Indian took fright and thought that he saw it. The promptness of our movement at least served to show the Indians that with reason they could depend as much upon the vigilance as upon the valor of the French forces. At the end of the day all the troops were back in their camp and the work did not suffer at all.

This night they worked up out of the marsh by a trench giving communication to a parallel which was opened on the crest of a slope which bordered this marsh. It is from this parallel, about 150 toises long, that they should take off to establish the breaching batteries. The work was well advanced the same night, despite the fort's fire which had never before been so lively.

The trench guard consisted of seven light companies and three companies of grenadiers. Thirty Iroquois had also asked to mingle with the grenadiers in order to act as scouts and warn them in case the enemy should wish to make a sortie.

&~ AUGUST 9 : Two hundred workers were ordered to improve the work during the night. At seven in the morning the fort raised a white flag and asked to capitulate. Colonel Young came to propose articles of capitulation to the Marquis de Montcalm. I was sent to draw them up and to take the first steps in putting them in operation.

In substance the capitulation provided that the troops, both of the fort and of the entrenched camp, to the number of two thousand men, should depart with the honors of war with the baggage of the officers and of the soldiers, that they should be conducted to Fort Lydius escorted by a detachment of our troops and by the principal officers and interpreters attached to the Indians, that until the return of this escort an officer should remain in our hands as a hostage, that the troops would not serve for eighteen months against His Most Catholic Majesty nor against his allies, that within three months all French, Canadian, and Indian prisoners taken on land in North America since the commencement of the war should be returned to French forts, that the artillery, vessels, and all the munitions and provisions would belong to His Most Catholic Majesty, except one six pounder cannon which the Marquis de Montcalm granted Colonel Monro and the garrison to witness his esteem for the fine defense they had made.

Before signing the capitulation the Marquis de Montcalm assembled a council to which the chiefs of all the nations had been summoned. He informed them of the articles granted the besieged, the motives which determined his according them, asked their consent and their promise that their young men would not commit any disorder. The chiefs agreed to everything and promised to restrain their young men.

One sees by this action of the Marquis de Montcalm to what point one is a slave to Indians in this country. They are a necessary evil.

I think that we could have had these troops as prisoners at discretion, but in the first case there would have been two thousand more men to feed, and in the second one could not have restrained the barbarity of the Indians, and it is never permitted to sacrifice humanity to what is only the shadow of glory.

At noon the fort was turned over to our troops from the trenches, and, the garrison leaving with its baggage, it was necessary to let the Indians and Canadians in to pillage all the remaining effects. Only with the greatest trouble could the provisions and munitions be saved. The English troops were to remain in their entrenched camp until the next day. Despite a guard from our troops that we had put on it, the Indians could not be stopped from entering and pillaging. Everything was done to stop them, consultation with the chiefs, wheedling on our part, authority that the officers and interpreters attached to them possessed. We will be most fortunate if we can avoid a massacre. Detestable position of which those who are not here can have no idea, and one which makes the victory painful to the conquerors.

The Marquis de Montcalm went himself to the entrenched camp. He there made the greatest efforts to prevent the greed of the Indians and, I will say it here, [also] of certain people attached to them from being the cause of misfortunes far greater than pillage.

At last by nine in the evening it appeared that order had been re-established in the camp. The Marquis de Montcalm even was able to arrange that, beyond the escort agreed upon by the capitulation, two chiefs from each nation should escort the English as far as the vicinity of Fort Edward. I had taken care upon going into the English camp to advise the officers and soldiers to throw away all wine, brandy, and intoxicating liquors; they themselves had realized of what consequence it was for them to take this precaution.

At ten in the evening I was sent by order of the Marquis de Montcalm to carry to the Marquis de Vaudreuil the news of the surrender of Fort William Henry and the capitulation.

I reached Montreal the eleventh at four in the afternoon. The news I brought caused a sensation, all the more agreeable because a courier who left Fort William Henry thirty-six hours before me and had arrived only three hours previously had caused uneasiness there, saying that the enemy still held out, something which to the Canadians appeared extraordinary and disturbing. Several, however, were not pleased by the news because the English were not taken prisoners and we had not at once marched against Fort Lydius. These same people had always advised against taking prisoners, the colony not being in condition to feed them. Doubtless blood was necessary to content them, but pray God that the French be not inclined to such wishes. In regard to the enterprise against Fort Lydius, invincible obstacles prevented us from thinking of it, the lack of munitions, and provisions, the difficulty of a portage of six leagues without oxen or horses, with an army worn out by fatigue and bad food, the departure of all the Indians of the Far West who have five hundred leagues to go over lakes and rivers which freeze and prevent them remaining longer, the flight of almost all the domesticated Indians, the necessity of sending back the Canadians for the harvests already ripe, sixteen hundred men assembled at the fort whose capture they think so easy, these then are the reasons which stopped the further advance of the King's army.

If the wheat survey successfully made in July had been ordered in April, as the welfare of the colony demanded, our campaign would have started six weeks earlier, the enemy would not have had time to render his defense so strong, the difficulties outlined above would not have existed, and I dare say that today we would have had Fort Lydius. But this wheat survey was against the interest of the Commissary of Stores, and this Commissary of Stores is only the dummy of the great society to which the Governor General himself belongs. It is thus that they serve the King in the colonies.

AUGUST 12–31: A great misfortune which we dreaded has happened. Apparently the capitulation is violated and all Europe will oblige us to justify ourselves.

During the night of the ninth to tenth the guard we placed in the entrenched camp of the English did everything it could to prevent disorder. They had decided to have the garrison march out during the night, because it was known that the Indians almost never acted during the night. But the warning that was given that six hundred of these barbarians were in ambush at the moment caused a contrary order to be sent. This warning, however, was false. At daybreak the English, who were inconceivably frightened by the sight of the Indians, wished to leave before our escort was all assembled and in place. They abandoned their trunks and other heavy baggage that the lack of wagons prevented their carrying away, and started to march. The Indians had already butchered a few sick in the tents which served as a hospital. The [domesticated] Abnakis of Panaomeska,[72] who pretend to have recently suffered from some bad behavior on the part of the English, commenced the riot. They shouted the death cry and hurled themselves on the tail of the column which started to march out.

The English, instead of showing resolution, were seized with fear and fled in confusion, throwing away their arms, baggage, and even their coats.[73] Their fear emboldened the Indians of all the

[72] Now Old Town, Me.
[73] The troops retained their muskets, but according to Jonathan Carver, who served as a sergeant at the siege, they had no ammunition.

Journal for 1757

nations who started pillaging, killed some dozen soldiers, and took away five or six hundred. Our escort did what it could. A few grenadiers were wounded. The Marquis de Montcalm rushed up at the noise; M. de Bourlamaque and several French officers risked their lives in tearing the English from the hands of the Indians. For in a case like this the Indians respect nothing. Add to that, that a great number of English soldiers, hoping to put them in a good humor, had given them rum which, despite all our warnings, they had kept in their flasks. Finally the disorder quieted down and the Marquis de Montcalm at once took away from the Indians four hundred of these unfortunate men and had them clothed. The French officers divided with the English officers the few spare clothes they had and the Indians, loaded with booty, disappeared that same day. Only a few domesticated ones remained.

The same day the army moved its camp to a place in front of the entrenched camp facing the road from Lydius. The demolition was started.

᠅ AUGUST 11–13 : They continued the demolition with much difficulty, the fort having been solidly built.

᠅ AUGUST 14 : The Marquis de Montcalm sent Sieur Hamilton, English officer, with Sieur Savournin, lieutenant in La Sarre regiment, and an escort of thirty men to Fort Edward, charged with carrying two letters addressed, one to General Webb, the other to Milord Loudoun. In the first he explained to General Webb how the tumult had occurred and advised him that the next day he would send back all the English that he could gather together halfway on the road to Fort Lydius, where he prayed him to come and look for them. In the same way he told Milord Loudoun the details of the disorder occasioned by the Indians, of his attempt to stop it and to carry out [the provisions of] the capitulation; that he, [acting] in good faith on his part expected that he [Loudoun] would observe it scrupulously, adding that the least infraction on the part of the English would bring unpleasant consequences.

᠅ AUGUST 15 : In the morning the Marquis de Montcalm sent

off with an escort of three hundred men four hundred English ransomed from the Indians. Halfway to Fort Edward they found a like detachment of their [British] nation, to whom our escort delivered them. They had with them the cannon accorded Lieutenant Colonel Monro by the capitulation. This same day the demolition was completed.

৫৬ AUGUST 17 : Madness and indecent folly on the part of the Canadians. Officers and men leave without permission. It was necessary to fire over their heads to stop them. La Sarre brigade camped at the Falls under orders of the Chevalier. The rest of the army at the head of the Portage with the Marquis de Montcalm. Portaging was started on the seventeenth and pushed along with great vigor.

৫৬ AUGUST 19 : Béarn goes to take up again its former camp and the work at the fort. The same day all the army sang a *Te Deum*.

Meanwhile,[74] the Indians arrived at Montreal in a crowd with about two hundred English. M. de Vaudreuil scolded them for having violated the capitulation. They excused themselves and put the blame on the domesticated Indians. They were told that they must give up these English, who were captured unfairly, and that they would be paid for them, two kegs of brandy apiece. But this ransom was not greeted with enthusiasm. The Canadians bought the English plunder from them.

They did not spare the brandy, and this liquor, the god of the Indians, abounds in their camp. They get drunk, and the English die a hundred deaths from fear every day.

৫৬ AUGUST 15 : At two o'clock in the presence of the entire town they killed one of them, put him in a kettle, and forced his unfortunate compatriots to eat him.

I would believe that if immediately upon their arrival, the Governor had stated to them that until all the English were given up,

[74] The August 12–31 entries through the first paragraph of the August 19 entry are based on reports, since Bougainville reached Montreal on the eleventh and remained until the twenty-second.

there would be no presents, nor even any food, that under the most severe penalties he had forbidden the citizens either to sell or to give them brandy, that he himself could have gone to their cabins and snatched the English away from them. I believe it, accustomed as I am to think like a European. I have seen just the opposite, and my soul has several times shuddered at spectacles my eyes have witnessed.

Will they in Europe believe that the Indians alone have been guilty of this horrible violation of the capitulation, that desire for the Negroes and other spoils of the English has not caused the people[75] who are at the head of these nations to loosen the curb, perhaps to go even farther? The more so since one today may see one of these leaders, unworthy of the name of officer and Frenchman, leading in his train a Negro kidnapped from the English commander under the pretext of appeasing the shades of a dead Indian, giving his family flesh for flesh. That is enough of the horror, the memory of which I would hope could be effaced from the minds of men. *Heu fuge crudeles terras fuge littus iniquum.*[76]

On the twentieth I finished the dispatches reporting our expedition to the court. The Marquis de Montcalm, busy with other matters, had charged me with writing the details to the ministers. The courier left on the twenty-first to carry these dispatches to Quebec and the flute *Fortune* is ordered to sail at once.

AUGUST 22: I left again for Carillon where I arrived on the twenty-fifth. The portaging of the provisions taken in the fort and the English artillery and ours was almost finished. The troops went at this work with the greatest of spirit.

Herewith the tables of the English garrison, the artillery, munitions, and provisions found in Fort William Henry.

RETURN OF THE GARRISON
REGULAR TROOPS

Detachment of Fiftieth Regiment		*Detachment of Sixtieth Regiment*	
Lieutenant Colonel	1	Lieutenant Colonel	1
Captains	5	Captains	1

[75] The interpreters and Canadian leaders of the Indians.
[76] "Ah! Flee the cruel lands, flee the cruel shore."—Vergil.

Lieutenants	13	Lieutenants		1
Ensigns	6	Ensigns		2
Surgeons	2	Sergeants		7
Sergeants	22	Corporals		5
Corporals	24	Drummers		1
Drummers	11	Soldiers		104
Soldiers	507		Total	122
Total	591			

MILITIA

New Jersey Regiment

Colonel	1
Captains	2
Lieutenants	2
Ensigns	3
Sergeants	20
Drummers	7
Soldiers	267
Total	302

New Hampshire Regiment

Lieutenant Colonel	1
Captains	5
Lieutenants	5
Ensigns	3
Sergeants	12
Drummers	3
Soldiers	202
Total	231

Massachusetts Regiment

Captains	13
Lieutenants	21
Ensigns	8
Sergeants	23
Corporals	19
Soldiers	714
Total	798

Detachment of New York Regiment

Captains	1
Lieutenants	1
Sergeants	4
Drummers	1
Soldiers	50
Total	57

Detachment of Two Independent Companies

Captains	1
Lieutenants	3
Sergeants	5
Drummers	1
Soldiers	103
Total	113

Rangers

Lieutenants	2
Ensigns	1
Sergeants	4
Soldiers	88
Total	95

Journal for 1757

DETACHMENT OF ROYAL ARTILLERY

Captain	1
Lieutenant	1
Corporal	1
Cannoneers, bombardiers	21
Clerks	4
Total	28
Engineers	2
Total Garrison	2339

RETURN OF ARTILLERY FOUND IN THE FORT

- 23 Cannon, eight of them bronze
- 1 Iron howitzer
- 2 Mortars
- 17 Swivels
- 35,835 pounds of powder
- 2522 solid shot
- 542 Shell
- 1400 pounds of bullets
- 1 Chest grenades
- 6 Chests fireworks
- Some grapeshot of different sizes

RETURN OF PROVISIONS

1237 barrels of salt pork weighing 230 pounds and credited to the Commissary of Stores at 170 pounds net.

1737 quarters of flour of about 200 pounds, credited to the Commissary of Stores at 180.

Incidentally, there is a great difference between the English salt pork and ours. The latter is infinitely better. The difference comes from the fact that in the English colonies the pigs live in the woods, while in Canada they are fed domestically.

RETURN OF SOLDIERS KILLED AND WOUNDED DURING THE SIEGE

Regiment	Killed	Wounded
La Reine	–	6
La Sarre	–	3

Royal Roussillon	1	4
Languedoc	2	1
Guyenne	1	3
Béarn	1	1
La Marine	1	1
Militia	4	3
Indians	5	18
Cannoneers	2	–
Total	17	40

Only one officer was wounded, M. Lefevre, lieutenant of grenadiers of the Royal Roussillon regiment. On the fourteenth they broke the head[77] of a soldier of La Sarre who was wanting in respect to the Sieur de Langis, officer of colony troops.

The same day they made a man of the Royal Roussillon who had sold brandy to the Indians run the gauntlet.

᛫ AUGUST 29: The Marquis de Montcalm left Carillon and turned command of the army over to the Chevalier de Lévis, with orders to complete the portaging and to go with a large detachment to reconnoiter the end of the bay and the Chicot River. The Chevalier de Lévis will then leave with the battalions of La Reine, La Sarre, Languedoc and Guyenne which he will establish at St. Jean and at St. Therese to continue the work on this fort and on the roads. The Sieur de Bourlamaque with the battalions of Royal Roussillon and Béarn will continue to work on the fort of Carillon and will end the campaign there on the defensive.

Aoussik came back on the thirtieth with three prisoners captured near Boston.

At the end of this month the Indians had their farewell audiences. They have given up all or almost all of the English taken at Fort William Henry. They have each received complete outfits, varying according to the rank which each holds in his village. They have in addition [been] given what are called village presents, which consist of tobacco, vermilion, lace, and brandy.

[77] That is, executed.

Journal for 1757

At Lachine, the assembly place for the departure, they were swimming in this liquor, drinking it by kegfulls and not leaving the keg until they fell down dead drunk. In their eyes there could be no better death than that of dying of drunkenness. Their paradise is drinking. I prefer that of Mohammed.[78]

Before leaving Montreal an Ottawa killed a Frenchman on a farm belonging to the General Hospital.

The Marquis de Vaudreuil demanded the murderer. The nations turned him over to the Sieur de St. Luc who had gone to Lachine to look for him with a detachment of thirty men.

The head chief of the Chippewas himself brought him to Montreal where he was put in the dungeon. The nations have left convinced that his trial will take place and that he will have his head broken. The Marquis de Vaudreuil has settled the differences which existed between the Chippewas and the Foxes. The two nations accepted his mediation and departed friends.

SEPTEMBER 1–10: We reached Montreal September 1. The road from St. Jean to La Prairie is now impassable. Until they give the waters of this great flat plain a place to drain off, they will never succeed in making a road. We came by St. Therese.

The English at last ransomed from the Indians have been sent to Quebec where they are arming several packet boats to take them to Halifax. In addition to the English taken at Fort William Henry, the King has also ransomed the prisoners captured on Lake St. Sacrement during the affair of July 24, who, according to the laws of war of this country, belonged to the Indians.

The Chevalier de Lévis arrived here on the eighth, after having established at St. Jean the battalions of La Reine, La Sarre, and Languedoc, and that of Guyenne at Chambly. These battalions will be kept busy with necessary work. Before leaving Carillon the Chevalier de Lévis sent a detachment to reconnoiter to see if the enemy had made any movement toward Fort William Henry, and he himself with six companies of grenadiers, a light company,

[78] Houris!

and one hundred Canadians went to reconnoiter the bottom of the bay. He demolished some works the English had raised there and burned the huts of an old camp.

According to the news from Niagara and La Belle Rivière, there is nothing to report except Indian raids on the frontiers of the English colonies, all of which resulted in a few scalps. It would also appear that all the Indians of this region sigh over the destruction of Oswego, where they used to find trade goods at a low price, all they needed and more. On the other hand, all the things they use are sold at an excessive price at Frontenac, Niagara, and La Belle Rivière. Moreover, these posts are badly supplied with food and merchandise. The Indians realize this difference only too well. Let us hasten, then, to supply these posts abundantly and to take measures that the trade there will be more beneficial.

Again the interest of a few private traders amounts to nothing in this business; it is the political interest and the preservation of the colony that must be thought of.

The Shawnees and the Delawares have reported that the Cherokees have been asked by their allies, the Choctaws, to enter also into the alliance of Ononthio, and for permission to settle in La Belle Rivière, and that half of the Choctaws would come there this summer.

Negotiations of the Five Nations to detach the Mohawks from alliance with the English and to make them withdraw from them.

Four Acadians escaped from the Carolinas. They say that the English in Carolina have only a garrison of forty men in their capital, local militia, that this region would be very easy to ravage, the habitations are scattered, that the English have had a fort built in the Cherokee region on the waters of the Mississippi.[79]

Some Ottawas at thirty or forty leagues from Fort Duquesne seized three hermits of some kind, whom they have sent to Montreal. For eleven years they had lived alone in these mountains, having left a monastery established in Virginia forty years ago.

---

[79] Fort Loudoun on the Little Tennessee River some twenty miles above its junction with the Holston.

Journal for 1757

These are probably some Anabaptists chased out of Alsace, where they had taken refuge.

By news from Acadia we learn that M. de Boishebert has gone to Isle Royale with a party of his Acadians. The others made up a detachment of fifty who entirely defeated forty-five English near Beauséjour, killed twenty-seven of them, and took eighteen prisoners.

Deserters from Fort Edward inform us that General Webb has released the militia and that he is now employed in raising defensive works around the fort.

SEPTEMBER 9 : Courier from Quebec. Although the ship *St. Patrice*, loaded they say with four thousand quarters of flour, has arrived, people are dying of hunger.

Sickness still continues. The two Berry battalions suffer much from it. The four replacement companies for La Reine, and a like number for Languedoc arrived in the last few days.

News from Isle Royale. M. Dubois de la Motte is constantly in the harbor of Louisbourg with his squadron. That of the English is at Halifax.

SEPTEMBER 10–22 : I left Montreal on the tenth and reached Quebec the twelfth. The Marquis de Montcalm arrived there two days after I did. We have just received news from Isle Royale, dated August 20. At the moment of writing the English appeared in sight of the island. Nothing certain as to the strength of their squadron, or the size of their landing force. M. Dubois de la Motte since his arrival has placed batteries at the places most favorable for a landing. If the English fleet is much superior to ours, the latter will, they say, remain in port and use the 11,500 men on its ships to defend the place. We anxiously await news of an event decisive for the two countries. I would not know how to stop from asking myself why the government of Louisbourg, threatened with an immediate siege and not having anything for a vigorous defense, sent the two Berry battalions here. One could ask the same question in the case of the two sixty-four-gun ships, the *Bizarre* and the

Célèbre, useless in this harbor, useless even to the country for the provisions they consume, whereas they would have been able to decide an affair in our favor. But they had superior orders to come here in order to assemble the inhabitants of the lower river and to give asylum to all the colonists who escaped from the enemy. For the court had believed that the colony would be overrun and taken by eight hundred men, of whom four hundred were Indians and four hundred dressed and painted like Indians, who under pretext of trading would come to Quebec, set it on fire, massacre the inhabitants and from there carry carnage and fire to all the rest of the country. The project had been given consideration in England, and it was thought that the English might adopt it.

The two King's ships set sail the nineteenth. They have been ordered to proceed to Louisbourg. The sixteenth on board the *Bizarre* four sailors wishing to empty a cask full of sea water, serving as ballast, as soon as they had pulled the bung, two fell dead on the spot, the other two are in the hospital, very sick. One can well judge the power of the poisoned vapor. Besides the sojourn of these vessels here has placed a heavy burden on us. They ate up food of all kinds, and the scarcity was extreme. They continued to give out only four ounces of bread a person, and it is doubtful if this ration can be furnished all winter at this rate. The harvest is the worst they have ever seen in this country. Besides animals are lacking. There are almost no more oxen left. It is calves that they are eating now. The English know our situation perfectly. It has not been possible to conceal it from all these prisoners who had the run of the place and whom they are going to send to Halifax.

From the first of this month up to the twentieth they have given notes for paper money brought to the treasury. It is upon these notes that they are going to distribute the letters of exchange. Twelve million have been taken to the treasury. One must suppose that at least a million more in private hands, consisting of a million in card money, 500,000 livres in beaver notes, 600,000 livres of species in gold and silver. That makes today more than seventeen million circulating in a country where in 1730 they had barely 800,000 livres. Whence has come this quantity of money, so great-

Journal for 1757

ly increased in so short a time? From the enormous sums paid out by the King in this colony. From the time of M. Hocquart, when the King's expenses amounted to two million, the ministry was hard put to make payments, and one year they were obliged to suspend payment of the rents of the Hotel de Ville. Today they spend nine million and the court is not at all surprised by it. M. Bigot has known how to accustom them to it.

&ep; SEPTEMBER 20 : The Marquis de Montcalm reviewed the Berry regiment; the two battalions must have lost nearly two hundred men by the epidemic which still continues. In the last twenty days there have died four nuns, four chaplains, and generally fourteen or fifteen people a day. On the nineteenth, twenty-two died. It is some sort of plague contracted on board the ships. I see the same thing happen each year and I am astonished that they do not seek the remedy for this evil. Ventilation put in the ships would at least diminish the cause.

&ep; SEPTEMBER 22–25 : I have had occasion while walking along the banks of the river to note the following. In the rocks which border it the seams are not horizontal, a few are absolutely vertical. But all in general incline to the horizon and in different directions. This condition of the rock seams can, I believe, be attributed only to the movements of the tides and the difference in direction of their inclination to the sinuosities that they have given the river. I have noticed that at low tide the sand, the primary material of these rocks, seems even divided into different wavy and more or less vertical bands. Moreover, this observation holds for both sides of the river in all the length of its course, subject to movement of the flow. It is also general for the islands distributed over this region. I do not claim that one cannot find horizontal rock seams. But what rule is without its exception?

It is all the more simple to attribute this more or less vertical inclination to the impulse of the tide, since in the Lakes Ontario, Champlain, St. Sacrement, where there is none, I have observed the rock layers always parallel to the horizon, and I have distinguished the different kinds of earth arranged in the order indicated by M. de Buffon. I would like to know if anyone has made the same observation in other rivers subject to ebb and flow.

They are going to hold a court-martial, by express order of the King, to examine the conduct of the officers who in the last war in 1754 surrendered Beauséjour. These officers are M. de Vergor,[80] who was in command, and Jacquot,[81] artillery officer. They have been under arrest since the twenty-fourth, and, according to a custom of La Marine, all the soldiers of that garrison who are here are in prison. They will appear before the court-martial. M. de Sermonville, adjutant of Montreal, has arrived here to commence the procedure and make the first inquiries.

For several days there has been a continual and violent northeast wind. No ships, no news from Louisbourg; I foresee evil in this delay.

SEPTEMBER 26: Yesterday the *Societé*, 120-ton ship from La Rochelle, was wrecked on the flats of Beaumont, three leagues from Quebec. Five men, including the captain, were drowned. The cargo was wine and brandy for the account of various merchants and powder and scarlet cloth for the India Company. They hope to save most of it. This ship perished precisely where the *Toison d'Or*, three hundred-ton, Bordeaux ship, loaded with wine, brandy, and part of the effects of the Berry regiment, was shipwrecked July 25 at the St. Lawrence Point. The shoals, with which the river is filled, and the navigation, the most dangerous there is, are Quebec's best defense.[82]

News from Carillon. Everything is peaceful. No English have appeared in this region since the capture of Fort William Henry. As to the exact state of provisions actually in the storerooms of this fort there is flour and salt pork enough to feed until July 1 the troops who will remain in the field until the end of October, the

[80] De Vergor not only made an abject surrender, but also succeeded previously in looting the King's stores in the fort. In 1759 it was his inattention that allowed Wolfe's men to gain the Plains of Abraham without any French resistance.

[81] Error: The name of the other officer was Rouer de Villeray.—Bougainville's note.

[82] He forgets that Phips had no difficulty in bringing his fleet up the St. Lawrence in 1690, a feat which Admiral Saunders duplicated in 1759.

Journal for 1757

garrison that will spend the winter there, and for a body of three thousand men, if they wish to send them in the spring up until July 1.

◈ SEPTEMBER 27 : News of three ships very near here. The courier left yesterday, carrying an ordinance which taxes wheat at seven livres per minot until November 15, [a tax] which hitherto has been at six livres. The purpose of this ordinance is to get the inhabitants to thresh without delay. The inhabitants of Montreal have just been put on a half-pound of bread. Everything is short, flour, rice, salt pork. The *Bristol*, four hundred-ton ship, loaded with wine, brandy, and dry goods, entered the harbor this evening.

◈ SEPTEMBER 28–30 : The ship the *Liberté*, carrying complete clothing for 3200 men and 60 recruits, entered the harbor today. At first it, as well as several others, had a cargo of wheat and salt pork. The order came to unload in order to take on another cargo. It is the result of some intrigue among the subordinate ministers. We suffer from its effects. The cause is unknown to us; we can only suspect it.

They are giving out bills of exchange for the notes. They are in three maturities as usual. The only change is that only a quarter is payable the first year, the rest by halves in the two following.

The epidemics continue to make great ravages. The first battalion of Berry left the city. It is established in winter quarters in the parishes of Beaupré, Beauport, etc. The soldiers will be fed by the inhabitants, whom the King pays for this purpose.

◈ OCTOBER 1–10 : News from Montreal. Misery commences to make itself felt. The harvest is of the very worst in this government, which usually is the granary of Canada.

The Sieur de Bellestre, lieutenant of La Marine, has been sent off with eight officers, twelve cadets, two hundred Indians, fifteen soldiers, and thirty Canadians to go and raid in the direction of Albany. This detachment is too large for taking a few scalps and too weak for a stroke of this importance. Sieur Charly is charged to go on ahead to secure the approval of the Five Nations of this detachment going through their country and of getting some of their young men to join.[83]

‿ OCTOBER 10-13 : The Marquis de Montcalm went with MM. Pellegrin, Montbelliard, and me to visit the northern coast from Quebec to Cape Tourmente.[84] We have discovered on this cape an emplacement suitable for a battery of four cannon and two mortars. They would be safe from assault, this country being almost inaccessible, and they could shoot at vessels making the passage for almost a quarter-hour. They are forced to pass within range of this battery. It would cost little for its construction. From this promontory as far as Beauport it is impossible to make any landing. The Falls of Montmorency alone are an almost impassible barrier. I conclude that, since the south side is likewise impracticable for a landing because of the woods that cover it and the numberless rivers which cut it up, and because moreover, in order to besiege Quebec it is necessary to cross the river, the English can only double the point of the Isle d'Orleans and come to anchor in the Beauport basin in sight, but out of range of, the cannon of the place [Quebec]. Several redoubts placed from Pointe de Lessay up to the little river St. Charles, a good [defensive] work already half built at the General Hospital, and defensive lines from this work to the Plains of Abraham, on the one side, and on the other, lines to the lower city, cutting off a peninsula around which the River St. Charles flows, in order to shorten the front of these lines; these works, easy to build, quickly and with small cost, which three or four thousand men could hold, would, I believe, make the city entirely safe. There are no other ways of defending it except by preventing the enemy from approaching it. The fortifications are so ridiculous and so bad that they can be taken as soon as they are besieged. We have located the sites for almost all the redoubts. I do not think that the English are planning any enterprise against

[83] This is the expedition that raised havoc at German Flats on the Mohawk, where the Palatines hoped for neutrality. The village was entirely destroyed, but Fort Herkimer, just across the Mohawk, was not attacked.

[84] A point on the north shore of the St. Lawrence just below the Isle of Orleans.

Journal for 1757

Quebec. But they could be foolish enough, and prudence would demand taking measures so as not to be surprised in this case. The Marquis de Montcalm goes to make this proposition to the Marquis de Vaudreuil. Probably his advice will not be followed. He will have done his duty.

Sieur de M—— was ordered to build at Quebec a certain work for two hundred livres and would have done it. A colony officer, who here performs the function of engineer, asked eighteen thousand livres for the same work. One can see how economically the King is served here.

The Marquis de Vaudreuil has come here to hold the court-martial on the matter of the surrender of Beauséjour. From time to time a few merchant ships are leaving to look for cargoes in the islands.

The Chevalier de Lévis has received orders from the Marquis de Vaudreuil for the light companies which are due to form the garrison at Carillon to leave St. Jean on the twelfth; that the regiments of Royal Roussillon and Béarn, as well as the colony troops camped at Carillon should leave on the twentieth; that La Reine starts moving so as to reach Quebec the twenty-fourth; Languedoc, the regions above this city on the twenty-fifth; La Sarre and Guyenne the twenty-eighth, the first for the parishes around Montreal, the second for Chambly and the neighboring parishes. Thus, all the troops can be in their winter quarters by November 1.

OCTOBER 14: The Commissary of Stores having reported in a council held at M. Bigot's that he had only fifteen hundred quarters of flour, that the searches made on the south shore would produce only two thousand hundredweight, that the government of Montreal could help Quebec only to the extent of six hundred, it has been decreed that, commencing November 1, the weekly issue of provisions to the soldiers will be: four pounds of bread, two pounds of peas, six pounds of beef, two pounds of salt cod, and that in December they will start to issue horse meat, which will be continued in January and February. They will save the salt pork for a reserve. Fortunately there is in the colony, independent of privately held provisions, five thousand hundredweight of salt cod.

The Marquis de Montcalm proposed: first, the return of one or two battalions to Louisbourg; second, to disperse soldiers out into those villages where there are none at all. Since the inhabitants feed them in their homes at the rate of ten sous a head, which the King provides, the food consumption is less; third, to make bread with oatmeal and most of it bran, it will only be less white; fourth, to have new searches made in the countryside by the officers and soldiers of the regulars and of the colony. He cited the example of the Marshal de Belle-Isle in Provence in 1746. Finally, he proposed that the higher officials should set an example of frugality by reducing their tables to a single course, and he has started to do it for his own. There are times when magnificence is a crime against the state.

ঔ৯ OCTOBER 15: M. de Pontleroy, named chief engineer for New France by the court, arrived at Quebec. The brigantine which brought him left Bordeaux the beginning of August, loaded with provisions for the squadron of M. Dubois de la Motte at Louisbourg. It arrived there September 14 and left again on the twenty-seventh for Quebec. It carries 200,000 pounds of powder, 250 quarters of salt beef and some soldiers of the Berry regiment.

The first appearance of the English the nineteenth, twentieth, and twenty-first of August before Isle Royale was not followed up. They appeared again September 16 to the number of twenty-three sail. A frigate even came close enough to Cap Noir to receive a few cannon shot from it; our troops took up their posts, but the enemy withdrew. M. Dubois de la Motte talks of sailing back to France. If the enemy were enterprising, he could after the departure of our fleet, try to seize the city and perhaps would succeed, if the parapets facing the harbor had not been reinforced. His first broadsides would knock them down and the city would be all opened up. It would need only a favorable wind and courage.

On September 25 there was a violent hurricane at Louisbourg. The *Tonnant*, eighty guns, and the *Abenakis*, thirty-six, have been badly damaged. The former was fouled by the *Glorieux*, seventy-four, and the frigate went ashore.[85]

By the latest news from Europe we learn that the Prussian King, beaten, forced to raise the siege of Prague, sharply pursued and confined in the Lusace; the Prussian duchy invaded by the Russians; the Prince de Soubise with twenty-four thousand French and allied[?] troops on the way to deliver Saxony; Marshal de Richelieu on the Rhine at the head of forty thousand men, overawing the German princes; Cumberland beaten and pursued by Marshal d'Estrées. Our garrisons in Ostend and Niewport, fine beginnings these. But all this money used up to relieve the house of Austria, to destroy the equilibrium in Germany and the north, would it not have been better spent in overwhelming, by a strong naval force, the British Navy, its merchants, and its colonies?

Dispatches from the Minister of Marine acknowledge the receipt of the letters of April 24, [show that he] believes we have an abundance of everything. On this subject there is much malpractice in the bureaus.

News from Montreal of the thirteenth. Thirty Onondagas arrived, men, women, and children. They ask for powder and ball. They say that they have built many bateaux at Schenectady, that Colonel [Sir William] Johnson is there. Indian information; if it is true, the English perhaps are thinking of reoccupying Oswego.

One hundred and fifty Acadians have arrived here. Hunger drove them out of the woods. They come to augment our misery by their own.

ဢ OCTOBER 17–31 : During a walk I took along the riverbank to Samos and Sillery; two houses, one situated a league from Quebec and belonging to the seminary, the other a Jesuit house a half-league from the first, I had occasion to observe further the arrangement of the rock strata. In this area all the strata are absolutely vertical. The layers, thin and clearly distinguished, are at

---

[85] This same storm sank one and dismasted twelve of the British fleet which was keeping Louisbourg under observation.

first sight at a right angle with the course of the river, and besides these first there are others, equally vertical, which are parallel to them. In all this place the rocks which border this precipitous shore are of the same nature and the same shape as the strata the water covers at high tide.

I also am fascinated by the way at low tide the infinitely small brooks falling from the heights of the banks keep their course under the waters of the river, following the beds they have hollowed out there, and in which one clearly notices the conformity of the angles, although nevertheless great winds and high seas often make them change, a striking image of the effect that currents produce in the ocean and the formation of the different mountain chains.

Sillery was one of the first settlements made in Canada. There is a little chapel dedicated to the archangel Michael. They have hung up there a wampum belt which the Hurons offered him one year to get him to come on the warpath with them.

News from the Far West. That from Louisiana is of the month of April. All is peaceful there. They have had no news from the ministry for eighteen months.

According to letters from Fort Duquesne of September 7, the Indians of La Belle Rivière perform miracles. Since the beginning of the campaign they have brought back more than two hundred prisoners or scalps. They desolate the English countryside through the great number of horses and cattle that they either kill or carry off. There are few people near Fort Cumberland. The deserters assert that the English have not any project planned for this year, but that an attempt against Fort Duquesne is under consideration. Report that the English have a camp at Skaendoka,[86] a Pennsylvania village where they have sent a scouting party.

The news from Niagara is of September 17. The construction there is practically finished, the only thing left to do is to face with stone. The Indians are so strongly disposed in our favor that M. Pouchot believes the next spring, if we furnish Niagara abun-

[86] Perhaps Schahandoana, the Indian name for Wyoming, on the Susquehanna River.

Journal for 1757

dantly with powder and trade goods, we can unleash nearly three thousand Indians on the English colonies. What a scourge! Humanity shudders at being obliged to make use of such monsters. But without them the match would be too much against us. They have brought to Niagara a German family, seized four leagues from Philadelphia at Tolback.[87] All the prisoners assert that if the French should appear in Pennsylvania, this province would make itself an independent republic under the protection of France. I had told this to M. de Vaudreuil when he arrived here, but he did not believe me, or at least he acted as if he had not. According to the news received by M. Pouchot, the civilian Governor of Pennsylvania offers to let the Indians pass freely into Virginia, provided that they spare his province. What can one do against invisible enemies who strike and flee with the rapidity of light? It is the destroying angel.

M. Pouchot has been warned that the English have a plan to surprise some one of our forts where there is trade with the Indians. For this they must use Indians of the Five Nations. The commanders of all the posts have been warned.

☙ OCTOBER 20–25: I have again been to visit the north shore as far as the Falls of Montmorency, showing Sieur de Pontleroy around. The river which forms this fall is much shut in by high banks. The shore of the right bank is also raised above the bed, as for the place where the fall commences, it is above the level of the river. It is ——— feet high and consequently is not higher than that of Niagara which is ———.

I have found about six or seven hundred toises of river [bank] with the rock strata perfectly horizontal.

The latest letters from Carillon tell us that a party of enemy Indians killed at the Falls three of our men of our advanced post.

The court-martial to try the officers and garrison of Beauséjour and Gaspereau assembled for the first time on the twenty-second at the house of the Marquis de Vaudreuil, who is the president of it. Since by the letter from the King which ordered it to be held,

---
[87] Unidentified.

the Marquis de Vaudreuil has full authority over its composition, he has asked for three officers of regulars although the case is not mixed. On the twenty-fourth the court declared Sieur de Vergor, who commanded at this post and the garrison, free from any reproach and ordered an inquiry on Sieur de Villeret, who surrendered Gaspereau.

The next day but one he was also declared free from all reproach.

According to the latest news from Carillon a sergeant and three grenadiers, who were part of a patrol, were killed on leaving camp by some Indians hidden behind the trees. M. de Bourlamaque arrived here the thirtieth, and all the troops have split up to go into their winter quarters.

᥉ NOVEMBER 1–30 : On the third they started to use sleighs. I do not know if this snow will last. It is early and a source of further misery because it makes it necessary to feed the cattle and fowl, who no longer can find pasturage.

᥉ NOVEMBER 5 : The *Robuste*, Captain Rosier, left here as a packet boat for Plymouth, carrying 106 English prisoners.

᥉ NOVEMBER 6 : The *Sauvage* and the *Diamant* left for Rochelle. The ship *Deux Frères* left the seventh at daybreak. It is time they did, for on the sixth we had minus eight degrees [15°F.].

By news from Carillon we have learned that one of our parties of Iroquois brought back two scalps taken near Fort Lydius, where the enemy was still in camp on the twenty-sixth.

᥉ NOVEMBER 8 : One hundred and fifty Acadians arrived here from Isle St. Jean. The harvest failed there, the same as here; they also are eating up their animals in order to keep alive.

The smallpox made great ravages this year. Generally it comes only every twenty years; however it now has reigned here for two. It is the Acadians and British prisoners who have brought it.

This year ninety-six thousand livres were paid for tools. Sieur Mercier, commandant of artillery, made, they say, a thirty per cent profit along with a contractor. *Regis ad exemplum totus com-*

ponitur orbis.[88] It is thus that the state here spends twelve million a year.

Through the return of M. de Langy, who went to escort MM. Schuyler and Martin, we have received a letter from Lord Loudoun. He raises several difficulties in executing the capitulation of Fort William Henry, but he appears determined to observe the article calling for not serving for eighteen months. He puts forward several obstacles against the return of the prisoners; this would not be of great consequence to this country. For the last seven or eight years the English have not taken any prisoners in America except the Baron de Dieskau, his aide-de-camp, Sieur de Bellestre, ensign of colony troops, Sieur de la Force, Canadian who was with M. de Jumonville, two militia officers, a woman, and forty-one soldiers and militiamen.

The Marquis de Vaudreuil, unnecessarily, solely because he is a timid man and one who neither knows how to make a resolution nor to keep one once made, had had brought from Carillon to St. Jean, two hundred quarters of flour, which makes twenty-eight thousand less rations for the start of the next campaign.

On the twenty-seventh there was news from Michilimackinac, dated October 25 and 30. The Indians there seem to be satisfied with the campaign and with us. They are building at St. Jean a new bark of sixty-ton burden.

DECEMBER: News from Niagara of November 12. Kouevidy [Korrendy?], famous chief of the Five Nations, is to go to war against the English. The smallpox has made great ravages again among the Indians of the Far West. A number will be forced to winter at Niagara.

News from Carillon, dated November 21. The enemy appeared there on the fourteenth in small numbers. On the nineteenth about three hundred showed themselves at the edge of the woods. A post of a sergeant and fifteen men, who were covering the wood choppers and charcoal burners, showed good spirit and fell back without loss. M. Wolf, sent out from the fort with sixty men, speeded

---

[88] "The world shapes itself after the pattern of its ruler."—Claudian.

up their retreat. The enemy disappeared after having set fire to a charcoal kiln.

Deserters said that there were six hundred men in garrison at Fort Lydius and four hundred Highlanders in barracks on the island which is opposite to it. They said also that there was talk of re-establishing Fort Anne on the Chicot River.

M. de Bellestre's detachment has returned after having destroyed the Palatine village on the Mohawk River. The Indians pillaged and burned everything. They brought back much plunder and 150 prisoners among whom was the mayor of the village. We had only three men lightly wounded. The Acadians die in crowds. Their past and present misery, the greed of the Canadians, who try only to squeeze out of them all the money they can, and then refuse them the goods so dearly bought, are the cause of this mortality.

Up to the present the winter has been mild with little snow. They would still have been able to get a ship off to Europe on the twelfth, which is almost phenomenal.

M. de Rigaud's detachment has cost 1,200,000 livres of extraordinary expenses. Acadia, where we have almost nothing any more, still costs 800,000 livres annually.

Journal for 1758

ಈ‿ December 12, 1757–March 1, 1758 [a summary]: On the ninth they started to issue horse meat to the troops. The women of Montreal went and threw it at M. de Vaudreuil's feet. He yielded and consequently, the soldiers at La Marine regiment the next day at pay assembly refused to take any. It was necessary to have recourse to the Chevalier de Lévis, whose voice quieted the unrest. They will not boast of his having this duty, the more so since all unrest is contagious in a country where one breathes independence.

The party of Indians commanded by Sieur de Langis took twenty scalps and three prisoners at Fort Lydius. They learned nothing. An English detachment has again come to Carillon; their expedition ended in killing some oxen. There was at this fort the start of a mutiny which the excellent conduct of Sieur de Hébecourt quelled. One of the most mutinous had the pox. They had him given a triple dose of mercury to put him out of the way of doing any harm.

MM. de Contrecoeur and de Maurepas have made an examination of the supply of grain, which is enough to assure subsistence until May 31.

The commissioners made the inhabitants take oath that they were making an exact declaration. The bishop has relieved them of this oath. News from Louisbourg of November 6, which gives us European news of September 24.

Order of the King to forbid games of chance. They have been playing them with frenzy and indecency. The Intendant has been the top performer; he has lost 204,000 livres.

A citizen of Quebec owed a debt to a member of the Great Society. He was unable to pay it. They assigned him the housing and feeding of a large number of Acadians. He let them die of hunger and cold, got all the money they had, and paid off his extortioner creditor. What a country! What morals!

News from Acadia says that the Indians and Acadians from time to time make a few excursions. The Indians we have in this region might amount to five or six hundred.

We still have at Pekondias, Miramichi, the St. Jean River, Cape Sable, and Isle St. Jean, about four hundred families of Acadians.

According to the latest news from the Illinois,[1] the English are setting up posts in this region which gives umbrage to Sieur de Macarty, commandant of this post.

News from Fort Duquesne of January 1, the governor of Virginia,[2] whom the Indians call "The Big Saber," is trying to negotiate with the Delawares, Shawnees, and Choctaws with the object of keeping them neutral. There should be a great amount of trade goods at Fort Duquesne to guard against this threat. The King has sent a lot of it for which he surely paid dearly. It is stolen and always will be stolen in transit.

The Jesuits have secured permission from the Marquis de Vaudreuil to send a missionary and a dozen converted Abnakis to La Belle Rivière. The Delawares and Shawnees protest that instead of trade goods and soldiers they are sent a black robe and some apostles.

We reached Montreal on February 22. The Indians of La Presentation are asking for Abbé Piquet back again. Question to

---

[1] Kaskaskia, Cahokia, and Vincennes, part of the Louisiana colony.
[2] Robert Dinwiddie.

Journal for 1758

decide; is it necessary to put French garrisons in the Indian missions, or [should one] leave their conduct solely to the missionaries?

The expenses are becoming so considerable, and the prices are so high that the Intendant has judged it proper to issue one hundred-pistole notes.[3]

❧ MARCH 1–13 : I visited the Indians of Sault St. Louis, by whom I have been adopted. Some tobacco and vermilion which went along on my visit made it most agreeable. It is not fitting for a chief to go to see his warriors with empty hands. We sang the war song. Then Onoregueté, the chief of the Turtles, which is my family, and head chief of the Sault, came to me to pay the compliments of the nation and declared to me that hereafter they were no longer my brothers, my relatives as I used to call them, but that they were my children.

The next day two hundred of them, along with a score of Canadians, left for a raid between Albany and Saratoga.

The party of Indians from La Presentation made a raid between Fort Coharie[4] and Schenectady. It has been relieved by another party from the same village which is now in the field. An additional third party leaves shortly to go to the same region.

News from St. Joseph River and Detroit dated January 4. The Indians who came to the army during the last campaign have lost many people from smallpox. Their custom in such a case is to say that the nation which called upon them has given them bad medicine. The commanders of the posts must dry their tears and cover the dead. Beautiful opportunity to make memoirs. It is a mourning which will cost the King dearly.

❧ MARCH 13 : M. de Boishebert left for Quebec with orders to embark for Miramichi as soon as navigation opens. He will take a detachment of 150 men, Acadians, Canadians, and colony soldiers, which, added to what is already in this region, will make up a body of six hundred men destined to go to Louisbourg. And if this body is not needed there or cannot get there, M. de Boishebert

---
[3] A pistole was ten francs.
[4] Kouri, Indian name for Fort Herkimer at German Flats.

has orders to annoy the English in the St. Jean River region, where they have three forts, guarded by free companies, Boston militia.

M. de Boishebert, the most junior captain of this colony, owes his reputation to the fact that since the taking of Beauséjour, while M. de Vergor surrendered this fort most unseasonably, and while M. de Villaret did not know enough to burn the one at Gaspereau, he, following the advice of Father Germain, burned that of St. Anne, where he commanded, and which was incapable of any defense. He has since kept to the woods in the canton of Miramichi and St. Jean River, without the English going there to look for him. He is an inactive officer with little intelligence, and who has only the talent, common to all the people in this country, of getting rich at the expense of the King.

MARCH 16: News from Carillon of the sixth. Sieur Wolf was well received at Fort Lydius. The commandant has replied that he would have the letters of the Marquis de Vaudreuil and de Montcalm sent on to Lord Loudoun at New York.

Sieur de Langis Montegron has taken a prisoner, and, the Iroquois who make up his party not wishing to remain any longer, three Ottawas, who were more patient, have put to rout a convoy of thirty-one sledges and taken two scalps.

MARCH 19: News from Carillon of the fifteenth. Sieur de Hébécourt, commanding at this fort, having been warned by two Abnakis that they had discovered some fresh tracks, sent out scouts whose report was that there was a great English body marching from the direction of St. Frederic. M. de la Durantaye, arrived the night before, left with his two hundred Sault St. Louis Iroquois. MM. de Montegron, de Force, lieutenant of La Sarre, and d'Avesine, sub-lieutenant of Béarn, joined him. Our advance guard fell on the enemy, who then first discovered them, and delivered a discharge at point-blank range. But the main body having come up and M. de Langis having turned the enemy, the detachment under command of Captain Rogers was entirely defeated. The Indians brought back 144 scalps and took seven prisoners. We had

Journal for 1758

two cadets wounded, a Canadian wounded, three Iroquois and a Nipissing killed, eighteen Iroquois wounded, almost all severely, [and] an Abnaki whose arm it was necessary to amputate.[5]

According to the report of prisoners at Albany and Fort Lydius, there are movements of supplies and men which seem to indicate an offensive action on this frontier.

However it also appears that they will again attempt the expedition against Louisbourg. They say that a lieutenant general is coming to this continent, Lord Rothes[?]. Is he coming to relieve Lord Loudoun, who is only a major general? Or will one act against Isle Royale, while the other takes charge on the mainland? According to the tally of the English forces, there are twenty-three battalions of regular troops here, which on a full strength basis would make twenty-three thousand men. That is a lot of men. For my part, I do not doubt but that they will make the greatest efforts and that this campaign, lost or won on their part, will be the last.

ஃ MARCH 24: A party of seven Abnakis from Misiskoui have penetrated, always hunting through the woods, to within twenty leagues of Boston. They have looted and burned a country house, killed three men, and brought back the wife and children. One Abnaki was slightly wounded.

ஃ MARCH 30: Sieur de Montdardier, young man of quality from Languedoc, lieutenant in the Berry regiment, having conducted himself unworthily of his name, threw up his position and was reduced to teaching reading at Cape Moraska.[6] He wished to go to Gaspé, but was assassinated by a deserter from the same regiment, who later died in the woods from hunger and cold.

ஃ MARCH 31: Great council held with the Sault St. Louis Iroquois. Two of their wounded have died and several others are in

---

[5] This was Rogers' "Battle on Snowshoes." With 180 men he attacked what turned out to be only the advance party of a French and Indian body of from 250 (Lévis' statement) to 600 (Rogers'). Rogers lost at least 120 men, but claimed to have killed 150 and wounded as many more of the enemy.

[6] Kamouraska on the south shore of the St. Lawrence opposite Murray Bay.

danger. The Marquis de Vaudreuil has covered their dead, and promised some Panis[7] or slaves to replace them.

APRIL 1: At nine in the evening there was an aurora borealis accompanied by a luminous band which crossed the sky from north-northeast to south-southwest. It ended on the south by a trail of fire which seemed to form a tail to it.

APRIL 3: News from Carillon. M. Wolf arrived with thirty Abnakis. He penetrated as far as the Massachusetts River,[8] on the shore of which he burned a house. Two officers of regulars, volunteers in Captain Rogers' last detachment, came to Carillon to surrender, after having been lost in the woods for six days.

I continue to study the way in which these rapid fortunes are made here, which have no other parallel than those of Rue Quincampoix.

APRIL 4–15: The thaw has come soon enough. The snow has melted, and since the beginning of this month the high ground of this island has become bare. At Lachine four men sowed on the fourth and since then they have sowed in various places. On the sixth there was an open channel in the river opposite this city, although on the tenth they still were crossing on the ice three leagues downriver.

APRIL 12: Indians from Sault St. Louis came here from their village by canoe.

News from Niagara by which one learns that a party of Indians left there on the warpath, that the Governor of Pennsylvania held a big council at Philadelphia, in which he very much exaggerated our distress in every way, promised marvels to the Five Nations and the Delawares, to whose chiefs he distributed forty gorgets and medals. He only asked their neutrality. A chief of the Five Nations has given up to M. de Vassan, commander at Niagara, [his] gorget and English medal. M. de Vaudreuil found all this news

---

[7] Pawnees literally, but the word *"pani"* became the Canadian word for any Indian slave.

[8] Another transcript says Massachusetts Bay.

Journal for 1758

very good, and I for myself find it bad. First, I note that all winter only part of the Indians have come, proof of their coolness, since last year they were here all the time. Second, the English will perhaps succeed in detaching the Indians from our alliance and then La Belle Rivière is lost. Why will one permit that the so great sums spent on them by the King should be useless? That two-thirds of what he sends should be stolen? And the other third sold by the commandants instead of being given? Why put at Fort Duquesne as commander a man who drinks too much and under him drunkards and fools? Why as the result of an intrigue of the junior officers' mess have they relieved M. de Pouchot,[9] whom the Indians adore, and replaced him with a man whose Spanish arrogance has no sympathy for their character and who makes them wait in his antechamber and then has them announced by his servant?

They trust to the good fortune of the Chief and this confidence in truth is as blind as fortune and as the Chief.

❧ APRIL 15–25 : The distress increases. The people of Quebec are reduced to two ounces of bread. There was a mob of women at the door of M. Daine, lieutenant general of police.

News from Frontenac by which one learns that the Mohawks on November 10 answered a belt that the Iroquois of Sault St. Louis had sent them in July. By this answering belt they promised neutrality and invited their brothers of the Sault to send deputies to a great assembly of the Five Nations that they would hold at the house of the Onondagas.

Colonel [Sir William] Johnson is active among the Five Nations. He has a good chance to paint for them a picture of our distress.

News from La Presentation which tells of the return of a party of Indians from this mission with three scalps and the departure of another of eighty warriors with Sieurs Lorimier, Jr., and Sacepée. The weather is terrible. Cold, snow, rain; they don't know when to sow, and a great deal of grain is being consumed.

The garrison of Chambly, composed of three companies of the

---

[9] Pouchot was removed from command at Niagara to make room for a fortune-hunting Canadian officer who later went to the Bastille with Bigot's crew. Vaudreuil found it necessary to restore Pouchot to the command early in 1759.

Guyenne regiment, no longer has anything at all to eat. The Marquis de Montcalm has answered their call for help, has sent nets and lines so they could live on fish and industry. Now is the migration time of the passenger pigeon, true manna of this country, but lead is lacking and they have not learned how to prepare iron to take its place.

℈ APRIL 25–30: M. de Chabert left to go to negotiate with the Five Nations and the Delawares. He is taking them eighty thousand livres of trade goods, thirty thousand livres of gifts, and has with him some armorers destined to be paid by the King and established in their villages.

The vessels that wintered at Sorel reached here on the twenty-ninth. Navigation thus is entirely established.

℈ MAY 1–12: On the second a convoy of twenty-five bateaux left for Niagara and Fort Duquesne. Sieur d'Espinassy, lieutenant of the Corps Royale, has gone off to take charge of the artillery and fortifications at Niagara. Good officer, skilled in his trade, too recently from Europe to take advantage of this mission.

News from La Presentation and Frontenac. A few Indians of the Five Nations wished to go to strike a blow against the Chien Nation. We prevented them, in order not to distract their hatchet from the English.

℈ MAY 3: News from Quebec. Great want; the people reduced to two ounces of bread. The soldiers to a half-pound instead of a pound of beef or horse meat, a half-pound of salt pork, and a quarter-pound of salt cod.

℈ MAY 5: A courier left carrying an order to La Reine regiment, which cannot find enough to eat at Quebec, to leave for Carillon. The three battalions dispersed in quarters in this government have orders to form light companies of soldiers whose hosts can no longer feed them and to have them go with La Reine.

℈ MAY 6: News from Carillon. M. de Langy's detachment has brought back four scalps. We cannot doubt that the English are getting ready for an expedition against Louisbourg.

Journal for 1758

ࡄ MAY 7 : Courier from Quebec. No news of ships in the river.

ࡄ MAY 9 : News from La Presentation. Eighty warriors from this mission have taken forty-six scalps and three prisoners on the Mohawk River. One Iroquois killed, one wounded. The English are building a fort at Tioga,[10] burned by M. de Bellestre last fall.

The storehouse keepers at Chambly, St. Jean, St. Frederic, Carillon, dismissed. The thefts too glaring, rules to prevent them useless if they do not inflict any punishment at all. *Si prohibita impune transienduntur, neque metus ultra neq: pudor est.*[11]

M. de Montgolfier, grand vicar, has told me that most penitents believe that stealing from the King is only a petty offense, and that each Easter the King makes them a present of what they have taken.

News from Quebec. The first ship for France set sail the 4th under command of Sieur de Boucherville, merchant captain.

ࡄ MAY 12 : News of Quebec of the ninth. No ships in the river. At the time the courier left there was a heavy wind from the northeast. Many of the inhabitants have not been able to sow, although the King has had three thousand minots of wheat distributed in the Quebec government.

ࡄ MAY 12–20 : I am told by surest way that there are only four officers to whom the King's affairs can be confided without any fear of rapine; Benoit, Repentigny, L'Ainé, Le Borgne. [This sentence is in English just as printed.] There then was nothing in this colony to save [it from the fate of?] Sodom.

News from Louisiana of August 26. They have had nothing at all from France, and the Indians of this region are very discontented. The English have built a fort called Loudoun on the River of the Cherokees, who have struck against us. A few years ago this nation proposed to us to enter into alliance and to build cabins in our country. This opening was neglected and the English have profited by it. This place is, however, of the greatest importance

---

[10] He probably means German Flats, not Tioga in Pennsylvania.
[11] "It is a shame if forbidden things are done without bounds or punishment."

to us because of the nearness of Mobile, which we have been thinking of making the center of the Louisiana colony.

The Illinois people sent a great shipment of flour, Indian corn, beans, and peas to La Belle Rivière, which fortunately puts them in shape to get along without help from us this year.

Great unrest among the Indians of the Far West. The Menominees besieged the fort at the bay for three days and destroyed a French family in Wisconsin.

The Ottawas have evil designs. The Potawatomis seem indisposed. Finally [the relations of] all these nations [with us] are on the decline. What is the cause of it? The great loss they have suffered from the smallpox, the bad medicine the French have thrown to them, the great greed of the commanders of the posts and their ignorance of Indian customs? They are merchants that favor and intrigue while charged with a business most important to the safety of the colony. Besides the English have sent a wampum belt to all the nations, and they make them the finest offers. To these ills which foretell still greater ones to come a prompt remedy is needed, one still easy to apply, but which they will not do or will do too late.

News from St. Frederic and Carillon. The English have carried away four men from the vicinity of St. Frederic, they have killed two near Carillon, and have captured or killed seventeen men who crossed to the other side of the river to cut wood. They believe from an examination of the tracks that it was Mohawks who made this strike.

M. de Langis has returned with three prisoners who have no information. He left again at once with all the Indians we have in this area to go and reconnoiter the major moves the enemy is reported to be making from Albany to Fort Edward.

M. Desandrouins arrived here on the sixteenth. On the thirteenth, when he left Quebec, there was no news of any new ship in the river, although for several days a continual northeaster has been blowing. Our situation is most critical. They are no longer distributing bread at Quebec.

Journal for 1758

May 16: Courier from Quebec. No news of ships up to the fourteenth. The first ship dispatched for France left on the seventh. M de Boishebert on the ninth. He will arrive too late to be of any use at Louisbourg. He should have been sent over the ice. How Caesar would have suffered in this country!

The Five Nations have had the Marquis de Vaudreuil warned that the English were going to rebuild the forts at Tioga,[12] Bull,[13] and William Henry to prepare the way for the re-establishment of Oswego, that they [the English] were making them great threats. In the council held today, the sixteenth, with their envoys they have asked the Marquis de Vaudreuil for a powerful assistance, one which will warrant them to declare in our favor. What can we answer to this and what can we do, we who are dying of hunger? The expression is literal. Many people keep alive only by fish and fast when they catch none.

Order to La Reine regiment to stop at St. Jean. Return of workmen who left Quebec for the works and artillery at Carillon. The shortest lived follies are the best. Eighteen hundred rations uselessly consumed. All [Indian] trade has just been made exclusive. The insatiable Grand Society is an abyss where everything is swallowed up.

Kisensik with twenty-five Nipissings leaves for Carillon. He is going to make red with English blood the ashes of his father, dead last fall. His father was presented to Louis XIV, who gave him with his own hand a gorget with an inscription on it which said it was a gift of the King. Kisensik has not wished to take this gorget yet, he wishes to earn it by new deeds. Since Indians believe that the period of mourning is a fatal time during which they cannot succeed in their undertakings, the Nipissing chief appeared in mourning garb before the Marquis de Vaudreuil, who raised him up, giving him the equipment of a warrior.

May 21: Courier from Quebec. No news of ships. The dis-

---
[12] See the entry for May 9, 1758.
[13] A stockaded fort on the portage between the Mohawk River and Lake Oneida.

tress is so great that some of the inhabitants are reduced to living on grass.

🦢 MAY 22 : News at last at half-past ten in the morning of vessels reaching Quebec. We learn that the Minister sent off three convoys from Bordeaux for this colony. The first, composed of twelve vessels and a frigate, set sail on March 7. Two ships got separated from it off Ouessant, two on the Grand Banks, and on the evening of May 19 the other eight with the *Sirene* and an English prize anchored at Quebec.

We have received 7500 quarters of flour, 2400 of salt pork and beef in the following ships:

The *Prudent* The *Providence* The *Aimable Marie* The *Charmante Manon* The *Brave*	For the Commissary of Stores
The *Aigle* The *Cheval Marin* The *Tason*	For Gradis, contains munitions and merchandise
The *Licorne*, frigate	Commander, Sieur Beaussier de Chateauvert, [who] has for his own account 600 quarters of flour.

No letters from the Minister of War, seven from the Minister of Marine to M. de Montcalm, the most recent, February 10. The latest letters from private citizens are of the end of that month.

The news from Europe well proves the truth of the Greek proverb which says that it is better to have an army of deer commanded by a lion than an army of lions commanded by a deer.

🦢 MAY 23 : A courier left for Quebec with orders to the battalions of Languedoc and Berry to start moving. La Reine will move at once to Carillon. They also made the artillery workman return. If no more than this convoy get here, we have only enough to prevent dying of hunger. The two other Bordeaux convoys should have left, one ten days after the first, and the other ten days later.

֍ May 25 : Courier from Quebec. News from Louisbourg. Arrival of two ships at that port.

| The snow *Acadien*
 The schooner *Retraite* | } | Flour, salt pork, beef, Indian corn, and a few artillery munitions. |

We know that the *Charmante Narcisse* and the *Soleil*, ships of the first convoy, put into Brest. We fear that the *Charmante Lilique* and the *Foudroyant*, ships of the same convoy, very richly laden, have been captured.

M. de Beaussier is in the port of Louisbourg with five warships. Several ships have arrived there loaded with munitions and provisions and a fine battalion of foreign volunteers. They announce the coming there of the Second Cambis battalion. They have up to now from Isle Royale seen only those eight [British] ships which they know wintered at Halifax. Great uncertainty of the destination of these immense preparations being made by the English. Are they thinking of Isle Royale, Quebec and Canada, or our [West Indies] islands? Several merchants and traders have suffered great losses through the capture of almost all the ships which carried to France the product of this country.

֍ May 26 : Courier from Quebec to announce the arrival of two ships.

| The *Babillard* | 250 quarters |
| The *Soleil* | 1500 quarters |

One from the first convoy, the first forming part of the second contingent which it left behind in the clutches of five English privateers. We actually have 10,000 quarters of flour and salt pork in proportion. This on the basis of a pound and a half makes 130 days' rations for 12,000 men, and on a one pound basis, 200 days. This computation is made on the assumption that they make 240 pounds of bread out of each quarter of flour.

> MAY 27 : News from Carillon. Letters of General Abercromby announce the departure of Lord Loudoun, and that he has succeeded him in command. He proposes an exchange of prisoners which we do not care to accept, since it would partly annul the capitulation of Fort William Henry. The enemy has a Highland regiment and several free companies [rangers] at Fort Edward. They are continually sending off a great number of war parties. Of the seventeen soldiers missing from the affair of May 4, ten are prisoners or wounded.[14] M. de Langis has been in the field since the seventeenth with twenty-five Indians.

> MAY 28 : A continual northeaster gives us hope.

> MAY 29 : News from Detroit. M. de Muy very sick. The Hurons, a nation always suspected and troublesome, have bad ideas in their heads. We should today send there the officer who is to replace M. de Muy.

News from Fort Duquesne of April 11 and May 7. According to prisoners there is talk of an enemy march toward the Ohio with four thousand men and wagons. The English Indians have twice killed three men within range of the fort.

Our Indians always seem to have good intentions. They would like some French regular soldiers (which they will not get). Since March 2 they have taken 140 prisoners or scalps to Fort Duquesne.

At Fort Duquesne they fear lest the English attack the convoy from the Illinois.

News of Niagara of May 20. Sieur d'Espinassy, who has got there, has found the artillery in great disorder at this fort and at the one of Frontenac. The garrison of 130 men too small to work usefully on the fortifications.

Several war parties of Missisaugas are out. M. de Joncaire, who for some time has been with the Five Nations, gives assurance that all the Iroquois have been at war. An intelligent man who is with him claims that these various parties have been striking toward La Belle Rivière and that their policy is to spare the Schenectady

---

[14] See the entry for May 12–20, 1758.

region, in order to cover themselves in case of an eventual reconciliation with the English.

᠁ MAY 30 : Courier from Quebec. He reports that the ship *Lion d'Or*, fifteen hundred quarters flour, fourteen hundred salt pork, has run aground on Île aux Lièvres.[15] They expect to save the cargo.

Order to Languedoc battalion to leave its quarters on June 3, to the third battalion of Berry to leave the same day from Quebec, and the second battalion of Berry on the fifth from its quarters.

Several robberies made from the convoy to La Belle Rivière where some quarters of salt pork arrived full of rotten wood.

The people of Quebec put on four ounces of bread.

Arrival of a party of Abnakis returning from hunting, where by chance they took three scalps and brought back several exiled Acadians who were working in a mill in the Massachusetts country and whom they were going to kill, when these latter, terrified, made themselves recognized as French by the cry of *"Vive le Roi."*

᠁ MAY 31 : Arrival of M. de Langis at Montreal. He took three scalps on the road from Albany to Fort Edward.

᠁ JUNE 1 : Council with the Iroquois of the Lac des Deux Montagnes, who came in three bands to avoid, they said, confusion and drunkenness. They offer to go to war wherever their father wishes.

᠁ JUNE 2 : News from Carillon of May 30. The party of forty Nipissings lead by Kisensik met near the falls of the Chicot River, on the right bank, a party of eighteen Indians and five English. It took four scalps, two English and two Indian, and nine prisoners, two English, two Delawares, four Mohawks, and a Mahican.

The two prisoners' stories are so conflicting that they cannot make anything out of them.

Courier from Quebec reports another ship from Bordeaux in the river, the *Zélindor* with barrels and goods for the King. It had

[15] About twenty-five miles upstream from the Saguenay.

a considerable leak, having struck a shoal near Quebec. They also say that there is a brigantine from Louisbourg in the river.

A boat with provisions at last reached Chambly where they were in the last stages of famine.

At this post and at St. Jean the plundering of provisions has been extreme, although under most critical circumstances. It was the fault of the commanders. It has not been remedied there. I do not know for what reason. At the beginning of winter Sieur Desandrouins left at St. Jean many tools, wheelbarrows, planks, etc. for the work started at this fort. They burned them all up during the winter; expense to the King of making them again. It is thus that this colony is ruining France.

We continue to have much to suffer from the insolent and shabby bearing of these people and the favoritism of the Chief.

News from Carillon of the thirtieth. Kisensik's party upon going off to war found the track of an enemy detachment composed of eighteen Indians and five English. They took four scalps and nine prisoners, seven of them Indians. The prisoners' stories varied. All the time, however, through their reports it seemed to me that the enemy has offensive plans on the Lake St. Sacrement frontier.

News from Quebec. In the river the *Zélindor* with food and goods for the King.

JUNE 3 : Courier from Quebec. Arrival of the *Judith* gives us grievous news of the second convoy which presumably has been captured almost entirely. They also say that the *Foudroyant*, ship in the first convoy carrying recruits and all the King's presents for the Indians, was wrecked on the coast of Newfoundland.

Part of M. de Boishebert's detachment returned through lack of food. He continues on his way with the rest.

Our northern fisheries have been most profitable.

JUNE 4 : At St. Jean there is assembling a party of eighty Indians from the Sault and the Lake to go raiding toward Lake St. Sacrement. Kisensik arrived at Montreal with nine prisoners that the Indians wanted to kill. The Abnakis objected. Lively squabble was quieted.

Journal for 1758

∂∾ JUNE 7 : The Béarn companies in garrison in this city left to camp along the road to Lachine in order to repair it. Useless work in that it is started too late, will be finished too soon, a wasted expense for the King, but it will be an opportunity for gain for the [grafting] officials.

Why haven't they sent oxen and wagons for the portage at Chambly which must be made by all troops? It is because such foresight would be useful only to the good of the service.

∂∾ JUNE 15 : Determination of the Marquis de Vaudreuil to assemble at Carillon an army of about five thousand men and to detach the Chevalier de Lévis and De Rigaud with a corps of sixteen hundred men and Indians to execute a special operation.

Order to the regular troops to go to Carillon where La Reine is already.

Departure of Languedoc from St. John	the 11th
of 3rd battalion of Berry	the 12th
of Monsieur de Bourlamaque	the 13th

The 2nd Battalion of Berry is on the march.

Order to Guyenne to leave Chambly	the 15th
Royal Roussillon to leave its quarters	the 16th
La Sarre	the 18th
Béarn	the 20th

M. de Lévis' detachment is to be four hundred regulars, to wit: a sixty-four-man light company from each battalion, the two Berry battalions furnishing one between them, four hundred from La Marine regiment and eight hundred Canadians.

This corps is to go by way of the Oswego River, the Mohawk, and the Hudson.

Its object is to cause the Five Nations unanimously to take up the hatchet against the English and then to march in concert to ravage the shores of the Mohawk River and to capture some of the forts in this region, if the opportunity presents. This is what the Marquis de Vaudreuil believes should come about, because he doubts nothing, but which will not happen at all, but which they will say has happened. Besides this undertaking is that favored both by the Canadians and the elite of the Indians.

The region of Carillon, although really threatened, abandoned to the regular troops and their general, will have to take care of itself. They would willingly let the regulars be short of everything, even hope for a reverse for them, if it did not have too grievous consequences for this colony.

JUNE 13 : M. de Langis left for Carillon with eighty warriors. A few Indians carried away a Canadian near Lake St. François. It is suspected that an Iroquois, chased away by Father Gourdon, missionary at this post, and returned to the Five Nations, carried out this coup.

News from Detroit. M. de Muy, who commanded there, is dead. M. de Bellestre temporarily in command.

News from Fort Duquesne and Machault.[16] They talk of enemy moves against these posts.

The Chevalier de Villiers is on the march from the Illinois country leading to La Belle Rivière the convoy asked for.

They write from Louisiana that they are short of powder and merchandise.

JUNE 16 : The *Rhinocéros*, flute loaded with salt pork and supplies is in the river.

Arrival of the promotion list for the colony as of May 1, 1757, caused much discontent because there is a quantity of injustices, without any basis to excuse them.

Arrival of a courier from Louisbourg overland, having left December 5.

[Some] "*Têtes de Boule*" brought here by the Nipissings. These Indians, also called "*Gens des Terres*," live deep in the woods, are great hunters, mediocre warriors, have neither government nor policy, trade more with the English of Hudson's Bay than with us. Their dialect is a corrupt form of Algonquian. They have few

---

[16] Fort Machault at Venango, present Franklin, Pa.

Journal for 1758

ideas and few words, no foresight for the future. In case of necessity when the hunt is unproductive, they eat their old people, who very peacefully allow themselves to be killed. They have asked the Marquis de Vaudreuil for a gorget, their chief having died.

JUNE 17: Departure of courier carrying dispatches for France and orders for the frigate *Sirene* to set sail with the first favorable wind.

News from Carillon. Many parties in the field. Two soldiers deserted from La Reine. It is feared that memory of the discomfort of last winter and the prospect of the next have caused this desertion.

Mob of women come to demand bread from M. de Vaudreuil or from the Commissary and the Judge complain that at the storehouse wheat sells for twenty sous a pound. Promise of M. de Vaudreuil to distribute one hundred pounds of bread instead of seventy-five.

JUNE 18–19: News from La Belle Rivière. M. de Vaudreuil tells the Marquis de Montcalm nothing. It appears that the enemy is marching on Fort Duquesne with five thousand men and five hundred Indians, Catawbas, Cherokees, etc., that M. de Ligneris, who has had two men killed at the entrance of the fort and a sentinel almost carried away, is much alarmed, that he has asked for aid from M. de Vassan, commandant at Niagara, who has sent him one hundred men from his garrison, by this reduced to twenty or thirty. They are not doing anything following this news. Luck and a chapter of miracles.

The Delawares attached to the English have asked our [Delawares] for neutrality. Ours answered that they were devoted to us and would always remain so.

News from Carillon of the seventeenth. M. de Bourlamaque arrived there with Languedoc on the thirteenth. Berry has gone through a tempest and suffered a sort of shipwreck.

M. Wolf with thirty soldiers and six Indians defeated an enemy party which was quite near our Portage. He killed seven men and captured three, including an officer of the Fifty-fifth regiment. He left at once to carry to General Abercromby the Marquis de Vaudreuil's answer to his dispatches.

Enemy news according to the prisoners. Attack on Carillon projected. Abercromby going to Fort Edward with his regiment, that of Murray, of Lord Howe, the Scottish Highlanders, and five companies of Rangers, fifteen to twenty thousand militia, ordered out and ready to march. They expect Blakeney's and Webb's regiments. They are going to build an entrenched camp on the ruins of Fort George.

From this I infer either the project of attacking Carillon or at least that of re-establishing themselves at the head of Lake St. Sacrement.

JUNE 20 : Courier from Quebec, six ships in the river, four from Bordeaux of the third convoy which left May 2 under escort of a warship and two frigates, and two from Bayonne. Their cargo is dry goods for private merchants, eighteen hundred quarters of wheat, and much Indian corn.

JUNE 22 : Arrival at Montreal of the light companies of the regulars who are to be in the detachment of the Chevalier de Lévis. La Reine, having left for Carillon before the project was planned, is not furnishing any of it. We furnish:

The Chevalier de Lévis		Brigadier	
M. de Senezergues		Lieutenant Colonel	
M. de Raymond with M. de Béarn, making the detail of the troops.			
La Sarre,	67 v.[?]	MM. de Boischatel,	Captain
		de Savournin)	Lieutenants
		Lenoir)	
Royal Roussillon,	67 v.	du Cros	Captain
		St. Alembert)	Lieutenants
		St. Privast)	
Languedoc,	67 v.	Duchat	Captain
		de la Miltiere)	Lieutenants
		Clericy)	
Berry,	67 v.	de Cadillac	Captain

Journal for 1758

		de Guernier)	Lieutenants
		Beaupré)	
Béarn,	67 v.	de Pouchot	Captain
		de Pinsen)	Lieutenants
		de Costebelle)	
Guyenne,	67 v.	de Carnier	Captain
		de Fouquet	Lieutenant

Left Montreal for Carillon.

ৡ~ JOURNAL OF THE 1758 CAMPAIGN, STARTING JUNE 23 : I see with grief the growing misunderstanding between our leaders.[17] The Marquis de Vaudreuil this evening at ten o'clock gave the Marquis de Montcalm two obscure and captious orders. If our general was charged with them, they were so worded that any unfortunate results could be blamed on him, no matter how he acted. He returned them to M. de Vaudreuil with a memoir justifying his action in so doing. Great reluctance of M. de Vaudreuil to give him other clear and simple [directives]. He is especially attached to a preamble [he wrote] in which he says that he deliberated with our general on all the affairs of the colony and took his advice on everything. I admit that he should have done it, that the position, the successes, the reputation of the Marquis de Montcalm, what is more, the orders of the King, required it. But as he never consulted him about anything, had never informed him of the news, nor of his plans, nor of his measures, the Marquis de Montcalm has positively declared that he will never allow this preamble to stand at the head of his instructions as a monument against his reputation. If the Canadian general [Vaudreuil] had insisted, our protest against this false assertion was ready. It is more than enough that a base jealousy should impede the result of zeal and talent, without suffering still more as a black, senseless intrigue associates one with follies over which one may groan but cannot stop.

Orders at last changed; our departure decided.

[17] The weak, vain, intensely jealous, but well-intentioned Canadian-born governor and the excitable, impulsive Provençal general clashed continuously, and their mutual animosity increased. Vaudreuil was largely to blame, but Montcalm's too openly expressed contempt fanned the flames.

🙵 JUNE 24 : Left Montreal at nine o'clock with M. de Pontleroy, chief engineer of New France, who at last has obtained, after much argument, permission to carry out his duty and to visit the works at Carillon. He has a good and honest heart, he is open in his speech and true in his conduct. He knows his profession well, [has] enough of the experience of routine and of war which make a good combat engineer. It was with great difficulty that consent was obtained that an honest and clearsighted man should go to disclose the dishonesties with which favor allows an ignorant man to enrich himself. M. de L[otbinière] is a relative and courtier [of Vaudreuil].

Slept at La Prairie.

🙵 JUNE 25 : Left at five o'clock; stopped at the Little Montreal River where we went by boat to within three-fourths of a league of Chambly. Walked the portage as far as the fort. M. de Beaucourt had it built on the left bank of the Sorel River. Four stone bastions, a large enough parade ground inside, the finest fort in Canada until M. de Pouchot built Niagara; and, something almost unbelievable, M. de Beaucourt stole nothing from the King in getting it built.

From Chambly to St. Thérèse on horseback; from St. Thérèse to St. Jean by boat. We slept there.

Two rapids in the Sorel River, one between Chambly and St. Thérèse and the other between St. Thérèse and St. Jean. When peace comes, see if, by removing rocks, the navigation cannot be made easier.

Communication from Montreal to St. Jean at present slow, difficult, costly. When peace comes see if it is necessary to make the road from La Prairie to St. Jean directly through the plains, or from La Prairie, or, going lower down, from Longueuil to Chambly, and from this fort to St. Jean, overland,[18] or by following the river; or if it not be more advantageous, in case it were possible, to make a canal from La Prairie or from Longueuil to St. Jean.[19]

---

[18] Both these roads exist today.

[19] The Richelieu River was canalized instead one hundred years later in 1858.

Journal for 1758

Several rivers in this region, excellent lands, useless on account of flooding, would be drained by the canal, would become a granary sufficient to feed a great army.

The Marquis de Vaudreuil has given the Marquis de Montcalm a list of the colony officers assigned to the Carillon region. It is a disgrace not to be employed in the expedition of the Chevalier de Lévis.

JUNE 26 : Courier from Montreal at three in the morning. The *Bizarre* is in the river. News that Louisbourg is besieged. Landing made at Gabarus on the eighth, "day fatal to the State." Such is the term [used by] M. Franquet in his letter to M. de Montcalm. How were they able to make this landing without resistance on our part with only sixty or seventy barges, which could mean 3500 men at most, a barge not being able to carry more than fifty?

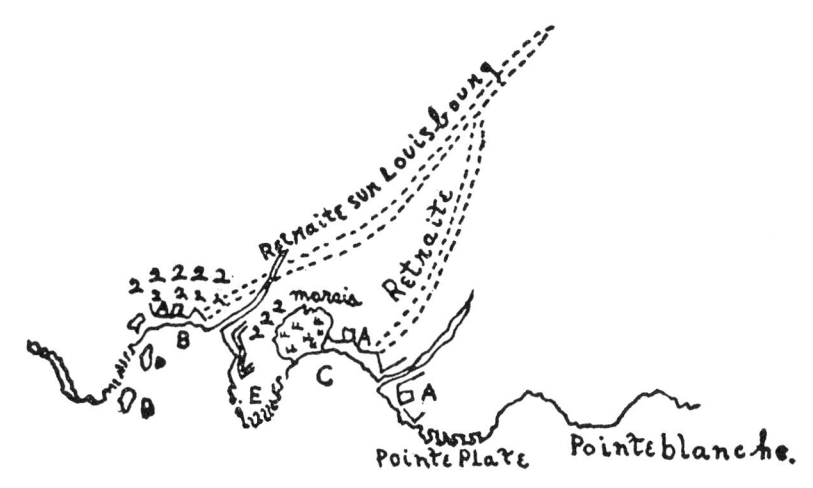

A. *Batteries*
B. *Anse aux Sables*
C. *Anse de Gabarus*
D. *Cormorandière*
E. *Lieu où s'est faite la descente*

Such is a sketch of the Gabarus coast. They say the landing was made at the place marked E. But why did not the troops charged with defending the works at this point, after the first artillery and musket fire, charge the English with the bayonet and overwhelm them? Why did not the other nearby troops also charge?[20] The bad feelings between the two corps and the greed of M. Prévost,[21] who controls M. de Drucour, will make the King lose Louisbourg. I say the greed of M. Prévost, and here is why.

The King's storehouses are behind one of the points of attack. From them they take almost all the goods to the storehouses of private citizens. They surrender the place soon in order to secure under the capitulation that the citizens keep their property and can either send them to France or sell them to the besiegers. The Commissary reports an inventory of only what remains in the King's storehouses at the surrender, and makes no mention of the goods carried into the city, which go to his profit. M. B[igot] did the same in 1745. He got the inhabitants to request the commander to surrender, and the commander consequently surrendered under the pretext of not being able to restrain revolting inhabitants, as well as a mutinous garrison. M. Prévost, pupil of M. Bigot, follows at a great rate in the footsteps of his master.

The Marquis de Vaudreuil is told that official mail has been sent overland from Louisbourg.

M. de la Houlière, commandant of Salces, in Roussillon, former major of the Lyonais regiment, holding a brevet of colonel, arrived at Louisbourg on the *Bizarre* to command the French troops there. I do not know if he was well received or whether their discontent [at his appointment] will injure the service.

They also write that they have sent us two St. Malo vessels loaded with provisions for Louisbourg. Either they have an immense supply there or they figure that [the city] will soon be taken. One puts up a poor defense when, only just attacked, one has the thought of being conquered.

M. de Boishebert left too late, doubtless will amuse himself fur-

---

[20] Wolfe managed to land a few light infantrymen at a critical point guarded by a small redoubt which the French forgot to garrison. The British held against the French counterattack, then received reinforcements and broke the French defense into rout.

[21] Commissary in charge of all supplies at Louisbourg.

ther in his Indian trade at Miramichi. However once he has arrived at Isle Royale, keeping to the woods with his Acadians, the Micmacs, the habitants of Isle St. Jean, the habitants and garrison of Port Toulouse and of Port Dauphin, from whom he will form a body of fifteen hundred to two thousand men, he would be able to harass the enemy's movements and then advance from Gabarus to the trenches which are a long league apart, and to co-ordinate through previously agreed on signals the attacks from outside with the sorties of the besieged; but I greatly fear that nothing of this sort will be done and that the city will be taken.

They write, furthermore, from Louisbourg, that the English ought to keep on the defensive on Lake St. Sacrement and to attack the Ohio country. I do not know what trust will be given this warning. Perhaps they will like to believe it, in order to leave the forces of M. de Montcalm weak.

Left St. Jean at half-past eleven. Northeast [wind] took us to Pointe au Fer where we passed the night. I do not enter into details of a route already described in my journal of the preceding campaign.

§► JUNE 27 : Left at daybreak. On the lake met Ignace, chief of the Lorette Hurons, sent by M. de Bourlamaque to advise of the enemy establishing themselves at the end of Lake St. Sacrement on the ruins of Fort George. Perhaps they plan to march against us, or simply to re-establish this fort. Also met a convoy of bateaux that were sent back to St. Jean to take the colony troops to Carillon. There was on these bateaux a detachment of militia from Montreal which was returning there. They are too good to be left to us. They are destined to the favored army [that of Lévis]. We have those from Quebec whom even the Canadians scorn.

Held up by heavy wind from southwest at Isle aux Chapons where we spent the night.

This evening and every night there have passed several canoes of Indians, Algonkins, Nipissings, Iroquois of the Lake,[22] who

[22] Christianized Iroquois who had taken up residence at Caughnawaga and at the Mission of the Lake of the Two Mountains, where the Ottawa River enters the St. Lawrence.

were returning to Montreal and from there to their villages with nineteen prisoners they had taken, M. de Langy at their head, at an island in Lake St. Sacrement. They promised M. de Montcalm to come and join him as soon as they had seen [to] their fields of Indian corn. Remains to be seen if the Marquis de Vaudreuil will not persuade them to march [instead] to the Iroquois country. This chimerical expedition toward Schenectady, as the courtiers call it, perhaps will cause the end of the colony. We must march at once against the enemy with the Indians, the best of the Canadians, the regulars, and the colony troops. They will not yet be ready for a defense. Persuaded, according to the report of prisoners, that shortage of provisions renders us unable to assemble an army, they are less on their guard and do not think of accelerating their works. An unexpected and vigorous attack will bowl them over and will end the campaign in this direction. The Marquis de Vaudreuil then could busy himself either with sending aid to the Ohio, or with his supposed negotiations with the Five Nations. But who knows if he wishes for any decisive success for the colony if the Marquis de Montcalm is the agent?

M. de Bourlamaque has sent M. de Hébécourt with a French detachment and Indian guides to reconnoiter the end [head] of the bay.

JUNE 28: Held up all day by a violent southwest wind.

JUNE 29: Left in a calm at three o'clock. The heavy weather and contrary wind caught us at the heights of the Bouquet River; forced by the southwest wind to fall back to Isle aux Boiteux.[23]

I noticed in all this part of the lake, whose shores are rugged and rocky, that the rock beds are horizontal, and the salient angles almost everywhere equal to the re-entrants. At twelve or even fifteen leagues from St. Frederic there commences a mountain chain which on the north side extends to the country of the Five Nations, and on the south crosses New England and extends almost to the sea.

[23] Unidentified.

Passed the day at Isle aux Boiteux, the contrary wind continuing with the same force.

June 30 : Left at three in the morning with a northeast wind, reached St. Frederic at eight, where we stopped until eleven to give M. de Pontleroy time to look over the fort and the surrounding countryside.

At three in the afternoon reached Carillon.

There we found the eight battalions of French regulars very weak by themselves because of the quantity of bad recruits, still further weakened by the volunteers for light infantry duty that had been drafted for the detachment of the Chevalier de Lévis, forty men of La Marine, thirty-six Canadians ready to go to war, and fourteen Indians; provisions only for nine days, and for an emergency, 3600 rations of biscuits.

The strength of the enemy increases every day at the head of Lake St. Sacrement, their portaging [of supplies] well advanced; one thousand horses and a proportional quantity of oxen in use: depositions of prisoners unanimous on their intention to lay siege to Carillon and to start their movements early in July. Twenty to twenty-five thousand men destined for this expedition according to their report.

There is our situation!

The Marquis de Montcalm this evening sent a courier to the Marquis de Vaudreuil to make a report [of conditions]. M. de Bourlamaque's letters should already have made him aware of them. Will he persist in his blind [belief] in the security of this frontier? Does he stubbornly hold to this Don Quixotry of the Schenectady [expedition]? Will he at least hasten to forward to us the provisions, the Indians, and the reinforcement of the colony troops that he has promised us? The enemies [of Montcalm?] may well get him [Vaudreuil] to announce that he will come to war himself. Let him come, let him see, and, I will add with all my heart, let him win!

The small number of Indians that we have here, realizing the need we have of them, are extremely insolent. This evening they wished to kill all the General's hens. They forcefully take away barrels of wine, kill the cattle, and we must put up with it. What a country! What a war!

M. de Hébécourt returned two days ago from the end of the bay, found no tracks in this region.

❧ JULY 1 : General assembly this morning at daybreak. Seven battalions advanced: La Reine, Guyenne, and Béarn to occupy the head of the Portage; La Sarre, Royal Roussillon, Languedoc, and the second battalion of Berry to occupy the right and left banks of the Falls of Lake St. Sacrement. The third battalion of Berry came to place itself in the camp La Reine has left between Fort Carillon and a redoubt which commands the junction of the river from the end of the bay and that from the Falls.

This movement, doubtless rash, was necessary to give prudence to the enemy, to impose on them, to make them lose the idea which they have of our great weakness and at the same time to prevent them from grabbing the Portage all of a sudden, something they could do by an advance on the lake of only ten or twelve hours.

The Marquis de Montcalm went this morning with MM. de Pontleroy, Desandrouins, Jacquau, and de Hébécourt to reconnoiter the surroundings of Fort Carillon in order to select a battlefield and the place for an entrenched camp. We lack man power, and perhaps time is also lacking. Our situation is critical. Action and audacity are our sole resources.

Council with a dozen Ottawas who wanted to return to Montreal and from there to Michilimackinac. With breechclouts, mitasses, shirts, guns, the Marquis de Montcalm has held them. They have promised to do him the favor of [forming] a war party and waiting until other Indians come. Great good fortune that they are willing to stay.

This evening there arrived a convoy bringing thirty thousand rations, that is to say provisions for seven or eight days for our present number.

Sent off a courier to the Marquis de Vaudreuil.

Journal for 1758

JULY 2: It has been decided to occupy the heights which dominate Carillon with an entrenched camp, with redoubts and abatis,[24] the left resting on the Rivière de la Chute and the right on the one going to St. Frederic; to build in addition a defensive work in rear resting at its left on Carillon, and on the right on a great redoubt which will flank an abatis extended up to the river. But to carry out these works strong arms are needed, as well as the arrival of the colony troops, and time granted us by the enemy. All that can be done at the moment, and which is being done, is to lay out the works and get the troops at the Falls and the Portage to make as many fascines and palisades as their camp duties will permit. The third battalion of Berry, which is in the fort, can furnish only eighty to ninety workers. How to do it with so few people?

Council with the Iroquois, the Nipissings, and the Ottawas. They again have come to ask to be allowed to leave for Montreal. It was merely in order to show how good they were and to get blankets, mitasses, etc., etc. They have promised to stay until other Indians come.

The Marquis de Montcalm has gone to camp at the falls to be near the head of the Portage and [possible] enemy movements. One of our advanced guards met an enemy scouting party. Shooting by both sides. The Mohawk took to flight.

JULY 3: M. de Raymond, captain of La Marine, arrived with 118 men, 80 Canadians, the rest soldiers of La Marine. M. Mercier also arrived to take command of the artillery. He brought letters from the Marquis de Vaudreuil which announced the arrival of powerful reinforcements and of the detachment of the Chevalier de Lévis [which had] been destined for the Schenectady expedition, which the American General called off. I do not know whether he went so far as to send no one at all to the Five Nations or to the Ohio. That would be the case of saying that the extremes are touching. Here they feel certain that M. de Longueuil will go to carry a message to the Five Nations, accompanied by a detach-

---

[24] An entanglement of felled trees in front of the defensive works.

ment which at once will go on to the Ohio under orders of M. de St. Ours, lieutenant. This news appears certain, although M. de Vaudreuil has written nothing about it to our general.

A convoy of merchant ships and a few warships arrived at Quebec. The latter, destined for Louisbourg, brought to Port Toulouse[25] the battalion of the Cambise regiment which reached Louisbourg overland and did not enter the port because the siege had started.

The King having judged it proper to employ me in America as *"aide-marechal des logis"*[26] of his troops, under orders of the Marquis de Montcalm, the Marshal de Belle-Isle has sent him the commission.

News from Niagara. The Indians continue to do well. No letters have been received from M. de Ligneris which indicate that he fears being attacked. The Illinois convoy at last reached Fort Duquesne.

JULY 4: Duties, guards, and patrols as usual. Our position, very risky, obliges us to [take] the greatest precautions.

Bridge at the Portage with a little redan[27] to cover its head.

Bridge below the Falls to allow communication [between] troops camped on the two banks of the river.

This evening there departed, under orders of Sieur de Langy, a detachment of about 150 men, 104 of them volunteers from our [regular] battalions, 25 Canadians, and a score of Indians. A fact worth noting and one which does us honor is that in this detachment, a captain and seven lieutenants of our regulars march under the orders of an ensign; M. de Langy has only this rank. His orders are to go and observe the location, the number, and the movements of the enemy at the end of Lake St. Sacrement and to make prisoners if it is possible.

A sad ceremony almost made the detachment fail to depart. An

---

[25] A small port on Cape Breton Island some forty miles southwest of Louisbourg.
[26] A senior staff appointment with no exact modern equivalent, but much like chief of staff.
[27] A V-shaped defensive work.

Journal for 1758

Iroquois, in cold blood and for no apparent reason, publicly assassinated one of his brothers with a knife. The murderer at once fled. The Indians hunted him everywhere to kill him. He has three other brothers, one of whom came and wishes to avenge the dead man on the assassin. They do not know how this affair will end. They pardon murder committed by drunkards. A drunken man is a sacred person. According to them it is a state so delicious that it is permitted, even desirable, to arrive at; it is their paradise. Then one is not responsible for his acts. But ordinarily, they themselves calmly punish cold-blooded murderers with a speedy death neither proceeded nor followed by any formalities.

It was necessary to cover the dead man with an "ouapon," that is to say a complete outfit given his family. Six strings of wampum have dried their tears, cleared their throats, and put the warriors in shape to go off to war. Today I commenced the duties of my new position.

Detachment of 130 men who took the bateaux to St. Jean returned yesterday.

Received advice from St. Frederic that on the third and the fourth M. de Lusignan had indications of enemy parties on the right bank of the river [Lake Champlain] opposite St. Frederic, and on the left [bank] in the bay behind the fort.

👉 JULY 5 : Arrival of three captains of the colony [troops] with about 150 Canadians and soldiers of La Marine.

Formation of two companies of volunteers drawn from our battalions, under orders of Sieur Bernard, captain in the Béarn regiment, and Sieur Duprat, captain in that of La Sarre.

Departure of the Indian murderer with his two brothers. They go home to mourn the dead man and perhaps to avenge him.

Detachment sent to Pelée Mountain[28] returned without having seen anything.

The first division of the Chevalier de Lévis' division should reach St. Jean today. They assure us that the promised aid will join us.

At five o'clock in the evening Sieur de Langy's detachment

---

[28] Rogers Rock on Lake George.

returned, having seen on the lake a great [body] of enemy barges which could only be what it was, the advance guard of their army, led by Colonel Bradstreet and Major Rogers.

Orders [given] at once to the troops at the Falls that at a general call by drum beat, they should spend the night in bivouac and should commence to clear away the [camp] equipment. The same order sent to the Portage [with additional instructions] to send out detachments to the north and south to observe the landing of the enemy. Consequently Sieur de Langy has been detached with 130 volunteers to take post between Mont Pelée and the lake, and Sieur de Trépezac, captain in the Béarn regiment, supports him with three light companies. One hundred and fifty men under orders of Sieur Germain, captain in La Reine regiment, posted at Contrecoeur's camp, a patrol of grenadiers and volunteers on the south side. Bernard's volunteers sent to Bernetz River,[29] which comes through the mountains with which this country is covered to empty itself into the [River] of the Falls, to furnish warning in case the enemy wishes to get in our rear by [going] behind the mountains.

Sieur de Bourlamaque has not thought it desirable to have his [camp] equipment sent away. He fears such action would have an appearance of timidity. However, all the troops, even the veterans who are preparing for battle, are getting rid of their [camp] equipment.

During the night exchange of shots between Sieur Germain's patrols and those of the enemy, who have put scouts ashore.

JULY 6: The troops under arms; enemy barges seen on the move around four o'clock in the morning; sending back the [camp] equipment of the battalions at the Falls and their bateaux to Carillon; orders to Sieurs de Pontleroy and Desandrouins to mark out immediately the abatis defenses on the heights [as] determined the first of this month; to Sieur de Trécesson to put the third battalion of Berry to work there with their flags.

Sieur Germain returns to camp after having fired at those barges

[29] Trout Brook.

Journal for 1758

which passed within range of him. Bernard's volunteers fall back also after having fired a few times.

The enemy army started to disembark at Contrecoeur's camp around nine o'clock.

Sieur de Bourlamaque retreated in good order and without losing a single man, although in the presence of the enemy. He joined up with the Marquis de Montcalm, and the five reunited battalions crossed the River of the Falls, destroying the bridge, and with the [battalions] of La Sarre and Languedoc, took up battle position on the heights situated opposite and on the left of this river.

Strength and Composition of the English Army

Major General Abercromby, man of more courage than resolution, more of sense than of dash and of objectives; age has lessened in him the fire necessary for the execution of great undertakings. He reflects sufficiently, operates slowly and with too much precaution. He expresses himself with difficulty, talks little, writes better than he speaks, Commander in chief.

Milord Howe, brigadier general
Milord Gage, brigadier general
Sieur Spithall,[30] brigade major
Colonel Bradstreet, commander of barges

Troops of Old England
Two battalions of Scots
Two battalions of Royal American regiment
Young [sic] Murray's regiment
General Blakeney's regiment
Milord Howe's regiment

Militia of Different Provinces
Militia of New York
of Long Island
of New England
of Rhode Island
of Connecticut
of Jersey
of Massachusetts

---

[30] Unidentified. Captain Moneypenny was probably the acting brigade major.

Four companies of Rangers or woods rovers of Major Rogers with Indians incorporated in these companies
A body of Colonel Bradstreet's soldier-bargemen.

Artillery and Engineers

All these militia form an army of twenty thousand men as one would not doubt after the act published March 24, 1758, in the different colonies, given herewith:

For the New York contingent.

"An act for raising, paying, and cloathing two thousand, six hundred and eighty effective men, officers included, for forming an army of twenty thousand men with the forces of neighboring colonies to invade the French possessions in Canada, in conjunction with a body of his Majesty's regular troops; and other purposes therein mentioned.

New York. Printed by I. Parker, at the new printing office in Beaver street. Publish'd the 24th March, 1758." [The journal gives both the English original and a French version.]

One can deduct from this number what must be left for guard of a few forts of this frontier and of the depot left at the farther end of Lake St. Sacrement.

However the 350 man detachment, which Sieur de Langy led, abandoned by the few Indians who served it as guides, went astray in the mountains and after twelve hours marching came into contact with an English column which was proceeding toward the Bernetz River. About four o'clock in the evening we heard a great [burst of] musketry fire and we perceived an hour later the remains of this unfortunate detachment pursued by the English. A few companies of grenadiers at once crossed the rapids at the Falls to lessen the [pressure of] the enemy's pursuit, and several of our people, favored by their fire, got across by swimming. We lost out of this detachment, Sieur de Trépezec, dead the next day from his wounds. Sieur Bonneau, captain in Guyenne, La Rochelle, lieutenant in the same regiment; Bernard, lieutenant in La Reine, Jaubert, lieutenant in Béarn, and 150 soldiers or Canadians killed or prisoners.

Journal for 1758

The enemy suffered a considerable loss there in the person of Milord Howe, who was killed. He was brigadier general and had showed the greatest talents, although still in his youth. He had above all in the greatest degree those two qualities of heroes, activity and audacity. He it was who had projected the enterprise against Canada and he alone was capable of executing it. He was marching toward us when Sieur de Trépezec's detachment ran blindly into his column. At the first shots he ran up and was killed dead. His death stopped the advance. The disheartened English gave us twenty-four hours' delay, and this precious time was the saving of us and of the colony.

The body of Milord Howe was taken to Mutton Island[31] and embalmed. He was buried at Albany where they erected a superb tomb. Most glorious for him is the regret of his compatriots and the esteem of the French.

Around six o'clock in the evening Sieur Duprat had warned the Marquis de Montcalm that the enemy was pushing toward Bernetz River with sappers and that their plan evidently was to throw up a bridge. The Marquis de Montcalm ordered him to fall back and not to hesitate to retire himself on to the heights of Carillon, the enemy by the route they had taken being able, by going around a few mountains, to get between us and the fort. The army entered the camp at Carillon toward eight o'clock in the evening. The companies of grenadiers and volunteers formed the rear guard.

This same evening a party of the enemy's regular troops and their light troops came to occupy the two banks of the Falls River extending as far as the Bernetz River and took up defensive positions there. General Abercromby with all the militia occupied Contrecoeur's camp, the Portage, and took up positions there.

JULY 7 : The army was all busy working on the abatis outlined the previous evening by the third battalion of Berry. It [the army] was covered by the grenadier companies and the volunteers. Even the officers, ax in hand, set the example, and the flags were planted on the works.

[31] An islet near the outlet of Lake George, now called Prison Island.

It [the line] had been, as we have said, traced the evening before on the heights, about 650 toises in advance of Fort Carillon.

The left rested on a steep slope eighty toises from the Falls River, the summit crowned with an abatis. This abatis flanked a gap behind which we were going to place six cannon to cover it as well as the river.

The right also rested on a height whose slope was not so steep as that on the left. The plain, between this height and the St. Frederic River, was flanked by a branch of our entrenchments on the right, and should have been [covered] by a battery of four guns which was finished only after the action of the eighth. Moreover, the cannon of the fort were directed on this plain as well as on the landing place they could use on our left. The center followed the sinuosities of the ground holding to the high ground, and all parts gave each other flanking [support]. There were, to be sure, several places there, as well as on the right, subject to enemy cross fire; but this was because they did not give us time enough to raise traverses. These kinds of defensive works were made of tree trunks, lying one on top of the other, and having in front overturned trees whose cut and sharpened branches gave the effect of *chevaux-de-frise*. The army worked with such ardor that the line was in a defendable state the same evening.

Between six and eight in the evening the light companies of our troops, [who had been] detached with the Chevalier de Lévis, reached camp. They had been most diligent, advancing day and night despite contrary winds to join their comrades, whom they knew were about to be attacked; they were received by our little army with the same joy as were Caesar's legions by those Roman cohorts blockaded with Cicero by a multitude of Gauls. The Chevalier de Lévis arrived in the course of the night.

All day long our volunteers exchanged shots with the enemy's light troops.

General Abercromby himself, with a large party of militia and the rest of the regulars, advanced as far as the Falls; he got over [the portage] several barges and some pontoons, each mounted with two cannon. His troops in the course of the day raised several

Journal for 1758

defensive works, one in front of the other, and the nearest to us was not a cannon shot from our abatis.

The army slept in the open along the entrenchments.

JULY 8 : They beat to arms at daybreak so that all the soldiers could know their posts for the defense of the works, according to the attached disposition which was nearly the same as that where they had worked.

List and Composition of the French Army, July 8, 1758

The Marquis de Montcalm, brigadier general
Chevalier de Lévis, brigadier
Sieur de Bourlamaque, colonel
Sieur de Bougainville, chief of staff
Chevalier de Montreuil, brigade major.

	La Reine	365
Brigade of La Reine	Béarn	410
	Guyenne	470
Brigade of La Sarre	La Sarre	460
	Languedoc	426
Brigade of Royal Roussillon	Royal Roussillon	480
	1st Bn. Berry	450
2nd Bn. Berry detached as guard for Fort Carillon except grenadier company which served in the line and made		50
Troops of La Marine		150
Canadians		250
Indians		15
	Total	3526

At the left of the line were the battalions of La Sarre and Languedoc and two of the light companies [which] arrived the night before. Bernard's and Duprat's volunteers guarded the gap formed by the River of the Falls.

The center was occupied by the battalions of Royal Roussillon, the first Berry and the remainder of Chevalier de Lévis' light companies.

La Reine, Béarn, and Guyenne defended the right and in the

plain between the escarpment of the right [flank] and the St. Frederic River,[32] they had placed the Canadians and the troops of La Marine who were also protected by abatis.

Along the whole front of the line each battalion had behind it a company of grenadiers and a light company in reserve as a support for the battalion as well as [available] to go where necessary.

The Chevalier de Lévis was charged with the right. Sieur de Bourlamaque with the left, and the Marquis de Montcalm remained in the center to be within range of all parts.

The disposition determined and understood, the troops immediately went back to work; part were busy perfecting the abatis, the rest at constructing the two batteries mentioned before and a redoubt intended to protect the right.

This morning Colonel [Sir William] Johnson arrived at the enemy army with 300 Choctaws, Delawares, and Iroquois, and Captain Jacob with 150 more.

Around ten o'clock we saw them as well as a few light troops on the mountain which is opposite Carillon, the other side of the River of the Falls. They let off a great fusillade which did not interrupt our work at all; we amused ourselves by not replying.

Half an hour after noon the English army advanced on us. The grenadier companies, the volunteers, and the advanced guards fired [a volley], fell back in good order, and re-entered the lines without losing a single man. At the same moment, at an agreed upon signal, all the troops were under arms at their posts.

The left was first attacked by two columns, one of which tried to outflank the defenses and found itself under fire of La Sarre, the other directed its efforts on a salient between Languedoc and Berry.

The center, where Royal Roussillon was, was attacked at almost the same time by a third column, and a fourth carried its attack toward the right between Béarn and La Reine. These different columns were intermingled with their light troops and better marksmen, who, protected by the trees, delivered a most murderous fire on us.

[32] Lake Champlain.

Journal for 1758

At the start of the affair a few of the enemy's barges and pontoons advanced down the River of the Falls. Bernard's and Duprat's volunteers, posted in this area, received them in fine style; Sieur de Poulhariez, at the head of the company of grenadiers and of a light company of Royal Roussillon also appeared there and, the cannon of the fort having smashed two of these barges, they withdrew and did not appear again during the action.

The different attacks, almost all afternoon and almost everywhere, were made with the greatest of vigor.

As the Canadians and colony troops were not attacked at all, they, from the defenses which sheltered them, directed their fire against the column which attacked our right and which a few times came within range. Chevalier de Lévis in succession sent Sieur d'Hert, captain adjutant, and D'Hainaut, also captain in La Reine, to order the more active of them to make two sorties and to take this column in the flank.

This column, composed of English grenadiers and Scottish Highlanders, returned unceasingly to the attack, without becoming discouraged or broken, and several got themselves killed within fifteen paces of our abatis. Chevalier de Lévis twice ordered the Canadians and the troops of La Marine to make sorties and take them in the flank.

Around five o'clock the column which had spiritedly attacked Royal Roussillon, threw itself against the salient defended by the Guyenne regiment and by the left of Béarn.

The column which had attacked La Reine and Béarn with the greatest fury threw itself there again with the result that this attack threatened danger. Chevalier de Lévis went there with a few troops from the right, at which the enemy was only shooting [and not really attacking]. The Marquis de Montcalm also ran there with a few reserve troops and the enemy met a resistance which finally cooled their ardor.

The left continually withstood the fire of the two columns which tried to penetrate in this area, in which their supply depot was [located]. M. de Bourlamaque had been dangerously wounded there around four o'clock and Sieurs de Senezergues and de Privat, lieutenant colonels of La Sarre and Languedoc, made up for his absence and continued to give the best of orders. The Marquis de Montcalm went there several times and was attentive to getting reinforcements there at all moments of crisis. For, throughout the entire affair, the grenadier and light companies of the reserve always ran to the most threatened places. Around six o'clock the two columns on the right gave up the attack on Guyenne and came to make another attempt at the center against Royal Roussillon and Berry and finally a last effort on the left.

At seven o'clock the enemy thought only of retreat, covered by the fire of the light troops, which was kept up until dark.

During the action our abatis caught fire outside several times, but it was put out at once, the soldiers courageously passing over the back of it to stop the progress [of the flames].

Besides munitions of powder and ball they constantly sent up casks full of water and Sieur de Trécesson on this occasion has, both himself and his battalion, rendered the greatest service by their activity in getting munitions up to us as well as [the] refreshments so necessary in such a long fight.

The darkness of the night, the exhaustion, and the small number of our troops, the forces of the enemy which, despite his defeat, were still infinitely superior to us; the nature of these woods in which one could not without Indians involve oneself against an army which had four or five hundred of them; several defensive works the enemy had raised one behind the other from the battlefield [back] to their camp; here were the obstacles which prevented us from following them in their retreat. We even thought that they would try next day to take their revenge, and consequently we worked all night to secure defilade against the neighboring heights by traverses, to perfect the abatis of the Canadians and to finish the batteries on the right and left [which were] commenced in the morning.

ಕ್ಕ JULY 9 : The day was devoted to the same work and to burying our dead and those the enemy had left on the field of battle.

Our companies of volunteers went out, advanced up to the Falls, and reported that the enemy had abandoned the posts at the Falls and even at the Portage.

꙳ JULY 10: At break of day the Marquis de Montcalm detached the Chevalier de Lévis with the eight grenadier companies, the volunteers, and some fifty Canadians to find out what had become of the enemy army.

The Chevalier de Lévis advanced to beyond the Portage. He everywhere found signs of a hurried flight. The English have since told me that the affair got under way before the dispositions were entirely completed, that hurry had occasioned a sort of disorder, augmented subsequently by the death of a great number of officers; when they withdrew in the evening, they expected that it would only be to take better measures and to return with cannon and better disposition [of troops]; that the order to re-embark had greatly surprised all the regular troops; that the militia alone had rejoiced at it. He moreover said to me that they were only a body without a head since the death of Milord Howe.

Wounded, provisions, abandoned equipment, shoes left in miry places, remains of barges and burned pontoons; incontestable proof of the great loss our enemy had suffered. We estimate it, from what we have seen and their prisoners [stories], at five thousand men killed or wounded.[33] If one should believe some of them and [take account of] of the speed of their retreat, their loss would be considerably more. They lost several principal officers, Milord Howe, chief staff officer and colonel of a regiment, the commander of the New York troops, and several others.

The greatest part of their Indians, especially those of the Five Nations, remained as spectators at the tail of the columns. They doubtless awaited the outcome of a combat which the English believed could not be doubtful.

The Act of March 24 announces the general invasion of Canada, and these same terms are expressed in all the commissions of their

---

[33] The actual British loss was 1,610 killed, wounded, and missing, while the French lost 377.

militia officers. Justice is due them that they attacked us with the greatest of determination. It is not common that defenses are attacked for seven hours and almost without any respite.

This victory which, for the moment, has saved Canada, is due to the sagacity of the dispositions, to the good maneuvers of our generals before and during the action and to the unbelievable valor of our troops. All the officers of the army have so conducted themselves that each of them deserves a personal eulogy.

We had forty-four officers and nearly four hundred men killed or wounded.

List of Officers Killed or Wounded in the July 8 Battle

Sieur de Bourlamaque, colonel, dangerously wounded
Sieur de Bougainville, chief of staff, slightly wounded by a shot in the head.

La Reine	D'Audin, lieutenant, killed; De Hébécourt, captain, Le Comte, captain, Massiac, lieutenant, Filord, wounded.
La Sarre	Chevalier de Moran, captain, Chevalier de Mesnil, captain, Adam-Champredon, killed; De Beauclair, captain, Fourmet, lieutenant, wounded.
Royal Roussillon	Ducoin, captain, killed.
Languedoc	De Fréville, captain, Chevalier de Parfournu, lieutenant, killed; De Basserode, captain, Marillac, captain, Douglas, captain, Blanchard, lieutenant, De Courcy, lieutenant, wounded; Chevalier d'Arenne, sublieutenant of engineers, an arm cut off.
Guyenne	Patris, killed, St. Vincent, captain, dead of his wound; La Bretèche, captain, De Restauran, lieutenant, wounded.
Berry	De La Breme, captain, De Pymeric, lieutenant of engineers, killed; Chateauneuf, captain, Carlan, captain adjutant, Chavimont, lieutenant, wounded.
Béarn	Pons, lieutenant, Douay, lieutenant, killed; Malartic, major, De Montgay, captain, Kergus, captain, wounded.

Journal for 1758

La Marine　　　De Nigon, lieutenant, De Langy Montegron, ensign, wounded.

General Reflection

Bayle[34] says somewhere, "It is unfortunate that men are such that when writing history one has the appearance of making a satire."

Special Observations

1. In this occasion we must recall what Caesar said: "Up to the present I have fought for glory, but today for my life." For us there is no retreat, no quarter; either conquer or perish. Moreover and above all, never [was] the situation more critical for the commander. If the enemy took measures to cut us off, by portaging barges, from communication with St. Frederic, what could we do? We should have only five days supplies. It would be necessary to abandon Carillon and to retire to Fort St. Frederic. Soon afterwards one would still be forced to abandon this [latter] position; a road half a league long would take barges behind St. Frederic into Lake Champlain. One would then have said that by this retreat, necessary in the eyes of every soldier, the victory and the country had been handed over to the English. Another precipice open at our General's feet, if he was stubborn at Carillon.

Today [now] that the enemy are on the run, everybody wishes to associate himself with the success. Every man who aspires to the command of armies ought, upon entering on that career, deeply engrave in his mind this truth perfectly expressed by Tacitus: *Inquissima haec bellorum conditio est; prospere, omnes sibi vindicant; adversa, uni imputantur.*[35]

2. Our defeat would bring on the loss of the colony. The French [regular] troops destroyed, Carillon taken, what troops, what place could stop a victorious army, almost as large in numbers as all the inhabitants of Canada together?

The sensible people of this colony realize it perfectly and can-

---

[34] Pierre Bayle (1647–1706), the French philosopher.
[35] "It is a most unfair condition of war; when all goes well, all claim credit for themselves; when badly, it is blamed on one alone."

not conceive for what reason it [the colony] has thus been put on the edge of the precipice.

3. At the start of the affair it was necessary for Sieur de T[récesson][36] to fire from the ramparts of Carillon on a large number of Canadians, who were fleeing toward the boats. One of these fugitives was wounded by the discharge and the others turned back to hide in the shelter of their abatis or remained crouching behind stumps. It is true that these were not Canadians of the good sort.

4. At the first sortie which the Chevalier de Lévis ordered the Canadians and colony troops [to make], Sieur Raymond, who commanded them, called for men of good will to follow him. A small number stepped forward with Sieur Nigon, an officer come from France in 1757 and placed in La Marine regiment. These volunteers advanced; the enemy fired on them once, all disappeared. Sieur de Raymond returned alone, and Sieur de Nigon, wounded by a shot in the thigh, scarcely found anyone who would bring him back.

It was the same on the second sortie; Sieur Denys la Ronde, lieutenant, was the only one who followed M. Raymond. *Note:* Many soldiers of La Marine (Among them is a great number of very good ones.) wished to share with the regulars the risks and the glory and fought in our defenses. It was there, and beside the Chevalier de Lévis, that Sieur Langy Montegron was wounded.

5. From the start of the affair, orders were given to an artilleryman to hold a bateau ready to set sail and to guard it under the pretext that the Marquis de Montcalm wished to send dispatches to Montreal. Can one think ill of Sieurs Mercier and de Lotbinière for having thus taken precaution to save for the colony their talents so precious to it? *Note:* Subsequently someone has produced a sketch in which appear the fort, the defensive lines, the battle, the movement of troops. On one of the bastions [of the fort] there is shown a man who, arm passed through the painter of a bateau, watches the affair through a telescope.

6. Since the landing of the first British troops, Sieur de L[otbinière] was busy only in putting his cash box in order and mak-

[36] Commander of the battalion of Berry garrisoning the fort.

ing the wisest provisions so that the fruit of his labors should not be lost for everybody.

They commenced to lose that keen confidence in the special Providence which makes miracles for Canada alone. The eve of the battle, the speculators offered brandy at nine livres per velte; today it sells at fifty livres.

7. When the French had won the battle, confidence returned to Sieurs M[ercier] and de L[otbinière]. They regained their Canadian spirits and busied themselves only in ways of taking away from the French [regular] troops the glory of an action which it appeared difficult to attribute to anyone else. But with envy as with love, one must be ingenious. These gentlemen have, on this occasion, swept away designs which doubtless would not have been understood by people who were not as moved as they by maxims of evangelical patience.

8. When it was demonstrated that the enemy was after Carillon, and that, after an almost general clamor, the Marquis de Vaudreuil for a time let his favorite chimera of Schenectady escape from his arms; one no longer doubted but that all the forces of the colony would fly to the threatened frontier. It is remarkable that only the French light companies [from the Schenectady expedition] reached Carillon in time to fight, and that the first parties of Indians and colonists did not come until three days after the retreat of the enemy. *Note 1.* The Marquis de Vaudreuil, even after having decided to send the colony forces to Carillon, never believed that the enemy would come there. Also skillful courtiers loftily were saying that it was unfortunate that a panic among the French caused the beautiful secret expedition against Schenectady to fail. In truth, how could anyone believe that the enemy had offensive intentions on this frontier? M. Prévot had written from Isle Royale that they [the English] would hold to the defensive there [the Champlain frontier]. *Note 2.* The news which showed the enemy's intentions reached Montreal the evening of the twenty-eighth [June]. All the daytime of the twenty-ninth was devoted to placing gracefully on the shoulders of Ononthio[37] the

[37] Vaudreuil.

cordon rouge[38] which arrived the previous evening. On the thirtieth it was decided to send us great reinforcements.

Order to the light companies of the regulars to leave, and to the eight hundred militiamen of Montreal, assembled and ready to start on the secret Schenectady expedition, to return home. There would always be time enough to get them back.

9. We had believed that this aid would reach our landing place, rowing vigorously, without hesitation or reflection. Our eyes often turned toward the shore, and every moment people were heard to say: "There are bateaux, the Canadians are coming, see the Indians!" But the Frenchman is imprudent and the Canadian thinks it over. They did not expose themselves, and if Sieur de Rigaud had arrived on Lake Champlain while the enemy still were in front of Carillon, he would not have believed it wise to advance to St. Frederic. He would await orders. Was it not serving the colony well to keep a door open in the rear? *Note:* Sieur Marin had proposed at St. Jean to jump into the boats without any delay, to reach Carillon with only hard bread or flour paste, to make, while coming ashore in the woods, Indian cries, of which the English have great fear, and to try by this unforeseen attack to break the line of the enemy if they had us blockaded. But this advice was that of a young man more zealous than wise. Nestor often was obliged to stop the impetuosity of Achilles and Ajax.

10. In mid-June Sieur Wolf, officer of our [regular] troops, was sent to carry letters from the Marquis de V[audreuil] to General Abercromby.

It was a matter of exchange of prisoners.

The English held our ambassador until the ninth, the day of their retreat; they sent him back with the answer that the King of England had declared the capitulation of Fort William Henry null.

When Sieur Wolf reached Fort Edward, the English General asked him where MM. de Montcalm and de Lévis were. "They expected them at Carillon when I left," he replied. "I am better informed than you," replied Abercromby, "the Marquis de Mont-

[38] The *Croix de St. Louis*.

calm is at Montreal, the Chevalier de Lévis should be on the way with a big detachment for a secret expedition against Schenectady, I know it without question."

11. Pierre and another Iroquois of La Presentation, charged by the Marquis de Vaudreuil to negotiate secretly with the Five Nations concerning the secret expedition, had so faithfully concealed their negotiations that they had kept them secret from Abbé Piquet, their priest. On [his] return from the great town of the Five Nations, Pierre said in open council to the Marquis de Vaudreuil:

"Ononthio, thou hast charged us secretly to negotiate in the greatest secrecy with the Five Nations. The bowels of the earth are not more closed than have been our mouths on this occasion. We reach the great town; we carry thy word secretly to the chiefs in council. For whom have we been taken in these cabins? For whom hast thou thyself taken us? The young men, the children who play ball games, even the English know that thou wishest to make a secret expedition in this direction. My father, thy secret has been badly guarded by others than ourselves." *Note:* One is obliged to render justice to the Marquis de Vaudreuil, however, in that he had kept the greatest silence concerning the secret expedition. At least he told the Marquis de Montcalm of it only at the moment when it was necessary to pull the light companies out of our battalions.

12. The Marquis de Vaudreuil was unquestionably well assured of the wish the Five Nations had of taking up the hatchet against the English.

It is true that there were in the English camp before Carillon two or three hundred of them with Colonel [Sir William]. Johnson; but these were only curiosity seekers.

Continuation of the Journal

On the news that the Canadians had seen or thought that they had seen several English barges at the entrance of Lake Champlain, orders [were given] to Sieur de Carlan, lieutenant in the Languedoc regiment, to go with one of Sieur Jacquau's boats and a few others to cruise for a few days in front of Otter Creek and to make reconnaissances in this river.

⁊ JULY 11: All the army went into camp between the defensive lines and the fort, the flag side, along the flats. The two Berry battalions camped on the ridge of Carillon between the fort and the hospital.

Arrival of M. de Rigaud with several colony officers, many Canadians and Indians. Compliments from them on the victory, more forced than sincere.

⁊ JULY 12: Council held to reunite and bind together the Indians of the different tribes: Iroquois, Abnaki, Hurons, Ottawas, etc. They are desolated for not having been at the battle. Much booty lost and the chance to acquire a great name through taking a prodigious number of scalps. They would have had enough of them to adorn all the cabins of all their villages. These are their trophies, their obelisks, their arches of triumph; the monuments which attest to other tribes and consign to posterity the valor, the exploits of the warriors and the glory of the cabin. The Indians say haughtily that it was the Marquis de Vaudreuil who kept them, and whatever may have been his reason, it was he that caused their arriving too late. They are in a very [bad] humor over it.

It is the custom in America that troops who have had a success themselves sing the *Te Deum* for it, and I approve this custom strongly. Clovis had himself baptized and thanked God for his victory at the head of his troops on the battlefield of Tolbiac. The army took up arms today and sang the *Te Deum*. Never has a victory been more especially due to the finger of Providence.

⁊ JULY 13: Thefts and robberies by the Abnakis especially. Of all the Indian tribes, the Abnaki is that in which the young men have the least submission to the old men and the chiefs, either in peace or in war.

Council held with the chiefs to take them to task for these disorders. Great difficulty, almost impossibility of stopping them.

The interpreters are often the cause. Great defect in the makeup of this country that it is not officers, that is to say, men who have the sentiments of such as well as the name, who serve as interpreters. It was [not?] thus formerly. Now this function, which gives the greatest control over the Indians, is given up to vile souls, mercenaries, cruel men, who are occupied only in retaining their control over the Indians, from which they draw a great profit in countenancing all their vices and even in furnishing the means of satisfying them.

Strange situation [that] of the French officer. He is forbidden to prevent Indian pillaging by the only ways that would stop it. The Indians know it, abuse it, take all their provisions. It is necessary to watch them, say nothing, and reduce oneself to bacon and water.

Continuation of council to regulate detachments and scouting expeditions. Work [on defenses] recommenced. First to improve the defensive works and to finish the right and left batteries.

Arrival of the colony in a crowd, the militia levies, both the active and the reserve; everybody comes.

Departure of twenty-three Abnakis to make a raid.

Letter of the Marquis de Vaudreuil. Series of captious dispatches. Snare set maladroitly, in truth, for one is warned and on his guard.

Ononthio says: "Fine victory; one must profit from it, I send you all the forces; almost certain opportunity of making the enemy leave their position at the end of Lake St. Sacrement, to enrich the colony with their artillery, barges, munitions, and provisions, etc."

What means does Ononthio give to chase away from their position twelve to fourteen thousand men who are dug in and who have supplies of all kinds for two or three months? An army without doubt superior in numbers, well supplied with provision, with artillery, with means for making portages,[39] in condition to keep the field for a long time? No; neither provisions, nor means of making portages [do we have].

---

[39] That is, with wagons and horses or oxen.

ADVENTURE IN THE WILDERNESS

State of the Army of Carillon
July 13

French battalions	3528
La Marine and militia	2671
Indians	470
Total	6669

Note: This report is taken from the list signed by the Commissary for today's pay[muster]. One knows that for this distribution the number is on the high side; and that in the matter of cheating what is minor in Europe is done in a big way here. Some Canadians and Indians are called back, the first for August 15 for the harvest, and one knows that the others never remain in a camp after they have made a coup.

But this gives a good way to achieve the desired goal.

Here is something for the instruction of men of war: to send out during a fortnight big parties on the [lines of] communication to intercept convoys of provisions which are not sent. The only convoys which are going from Fort Edward to the end of the lake are almost all of wine, spirits, and provisions that the sutlers of the different corps take to the army on their own account.

What then is the object of the letters of the Marquis de Vaudreuil, and why, lacking provisions, does he persist in sending, after this action, this crowd of travelers who serve only to occasion a fearful consumption [of provisions]? In order to be able to write to the Court: The Marquis de Montcalm has beaten the enemy. They retired to the end of Lake St. Sacrement in consternation and disorder. At once I sent him all the forces of the colony in order that he should chase them from their position and should reap benefit from his victory. He could not; he has not done it.

That is the objective. Such is the dirty trick of this year. That of the preceding year was to say: He could [have] taken Fort Edward, I had given him the means, he did not wish to.

꙳ JULY 14–24 : The defensive works of Carillon and the project of the outer works to be built there have been outlined. They

Journal for 1758

are going to occupy themselves for the rest of the campaign working on them. The works have been outlined by Sieurs de Pontleroy and Desandrouins. They will also try to finish the fort.

Sieur de Lotbinière, under the pretext of restoring a shattered constitution, left the fifteenth for Quebec. Several people think that it is a pretense of one who has not been able to remain with those who see clearly.

He proposed to trace a meridian at Carillon; for this man, great engineer among astronomers, (I have in my hands a letter from M. Duhamel, great physician, and the member of the Academy of Sciences, most skilled in culture of trees and fields, who writes me that M. de Lotbinière is a very good engineer.) is no more than an astronomer among engineers.

Council upon council with the Indians; mosquitoes a thousand times more troublesome than the real ones. Cruel war by them on sheep, poultry, wine, spirits, and on all such things.

M. de Courtemanche finally left on the tenth with a detachment of nearly six hundred men, more than four hundred of them Iroquois, Abnaki, and Ottawa Indians.

He takes his route by the end of the bay to get onto the [line of] communication and to commence by carrying out the great projects of M. de Vaudreuil. He is going to fall, without their knowing it, on a fort the English built this year halfway from Fort Edward to Lake St. Sacrement to serve as a depot and for safety to their convoys. His advance guard attacks some fifty men at a little distance from this fort called Halfway Brook.[40]

Three hundred men came out to support them. The Indians fell upon them precipitately, instead of letting them get involved in the woods; took fifteen or twenty scalps, eight prisoners, returned the twenty-first at full speed and demanded [to be allowed] to go home. One Iroquois was killed and two wounded.

According to the prisoners' depositions, the enemy, to the number of twelve to fifteen thousand men, are established at the end of Lake St. Sacrement. They have there a considerable mass of provisions, and their plan appears to be to pass the rest of the campaign

[40] Near present Glens Falls, N. Y.

there without thought of rebuilding a fort there. Seven hundred men guard the fort at Halfway Brook. Only convoys of rum, beer, and other spirits pass there.

[Sir William] Johnson has gone off again with all his Indians; a body of three thousand men and five six-pounders have followed him toward the Mohawk River. Perhaps they fear lest we wish to take up again today the secret expedition of Schenectady. Perhaps also for the rest of the campaign they will offer us a demonstration of an offensive in order to force us to hold forces there and, during this time, the body which marched toward the Mohawk River will make, without opposition, dispositions for the re-establishment of Oswego.

General Abercromby is still with the army. Will he return to attack us here? Will he wait to determine the outcome of the siege of Louisbourg and the time of our harvest, for which he knows we are obliged to send back the Canadians? At all events we are preparing to receive him as well as a very bad position, without a superior naval force, can permit us to.

The English give us knowledge and examples which we do not know of or do not wish to profit from. The lakes and rivers are the only outlets, the only open roads in this country; also should England commence to have a real navy on Lake Ontario, this navy, if we let them have a few more months, would chase us out of the Far West.

How would it be possible for us to prevent the capture of Niagara, which is the key to it? Carillon is a bad place, St. Frederic, St. Jean, Chambly do not even deserve the name of bad forts. [Yet these are] nevertheless the only barriers which close the way to Montreal and Trois Rivières to the enemy. If we wish to avoid the loss of the colony which, this time again, was saved only by a miracle, (and one will always be necessary to save it in the state it always is whenever attacked) the only way to assure ourselves the possession of Lake Champlain and St. Frederic River is by a strong naval force. I hear of chebecs, half galleys, bateaux like that of M. Jacquau, of officers, and of experienced crews. Then all portaging of barges will be useless for the English: they are destroyed as soon as they appear. Then it is necessary that under shelter of a fort built in some place at the end of the bay, they build up a naval force such as ours. But how will they sustain this fort at a distance from their other places? Besides it is easy to prevent a new establishment near us: *Principus obsta*.[41]

For this we have enough strength, but not to conquer. *Note:* Here is what the Marquis de Montcalm is writing since July 1 by almost every courier to the Marquis de V[audreuil]. He already had often spoken to him of it; but as the danger was not too urgent, one could not hope that clear reasoning which had only the proof of logic [behind it] could then affect him much.

The twenty-three Abnakis returned with a few scalps taken between Albany and Fort Edward.

Sieur Otlas, colony cadet, sent to reconnoiter the end of Lake St. Sacrement. He got within five leagues of it, returned and said: "I have discovered ——" Thus are reconnaissances made here by most of these gentry.

The 18th M. de Rigaud goes to take up station at the Falls with a party of Canadians and troops of La Marine. Chevalier de la Corne on the nineteenth occupies the Portage camp with almost all the rest. Sieur de St. Luc arrived the sixteenth with the Nipissings, Algonkins, Iroquois of the Lake, and it was necessary to hold a council. All the Indians are disheartened at not having been at the affair of the eighth. When they get an idea in their heads, they hold it a long time and strongly; they go to the bottom of it, dream of it, make magic. Here is a great victory brought off without them. They think perhaps that we are in a state that we can dispense with them; and, from what one can believe, they conclude that it is so and it puts them in [bad] humor. The interpreters provoke them further and always exhort them to go back [home].

The Marquis de Montcalm solemnly covered the Iroquois dead and consoled the wounded with outfits. He proposes that they remain and is refused. The throat is stopped up, the ears closed, the sight troubled; much repetition and useless words from all quarters.

[41] "Principle opposes."

They at last explain themselves by complaining that they have not been received as usual; that it seems that the victory won without them has made the French overproud, that they believe that they can get along without them [the Indians], etc., etc. That is what they thought. It was easy to get them in good humor again; everything is patched up; they have almost all agreed to remain.

About a hundred left the twenty-fourth to return to Montreal with a promise of returning and arranging the coming of their warriors in such a way that there will always be a certain number with the army up to the end of the campaign.

Such should be the object of the Marquis de Vaudreuil so that the army should never be without Indians, instead of sending them all together. Were there a thousand in a war party, if four scalps were taken, they all would go home.

JULY 23 : MM. Schuyler and Martin, who have had permission to go to their country on parole, sent back by General Abercromby, under escort of a lieutenant of Scottish grenadiers and thirty men.

Propositions by the English General to the Marquis de Montcalm to establish a cartel to exchange prisoners taken in all quarters.

The Marquis de Montcalm sends the matter on to the Marquis de Vaudreuil, observing that, since the French prisoners taken on this continent before the capture of Fort William Henry should be free under the terms of that capitulation until the two courts have decided on the validity, the cartel ought to apply only for French prisoners taken subsequently.

The English flag of truce sent back to their army and MM. Schuyler and Martin to Montreal. It was necessary to hide them from the Indians; no precaution can hold back their young warriors.

Note: The English officer asked the return of a picture of Mrs. Bever left on the battlefield, her husband, a colonel, having been killed. It was in the possession of Sieur d'Aubrespay, captain in the Béarn regiment, who at once gave it back to him.

Journal for 1758

M. Rigaud de Vaudreuil, Governor of Montreal, brother of the Governor General of Canada, like him, born and baptized in this colony, advised him [D'Aubrespay] to sell the picture [at a] very high [price]. One would not be embarrassed in France at the answer made him by [D'Aubrespay,] a person of quality, an officer, and a Frenchman.

M. de St. Luc left the twenty-fourth with a detachment of nearly four hundred Indians and two hundred French, that is to say Canadians.

He also passed by the end of the bay. All had been planned for this detachment to start on the twenty-second. Games of lacrosse between the Iroquois and the Abnakis delayed the departure. There were at stake one thousand crowns worth of belts and strings [of wampum]. This game is played with a ball and sticks curved in the shape of a crosier. The ball is placed between the two sides; each of them has a goal and the object is to get the ball to one's goal while preventing the antagonists getting it to theirs.

ஃ JULY 25 : New dispatches from the Marquis de Vaudreuil. He still expects that the detachments, the convoys cut off, the march of the Canadians, the remembrance of their defeat, fear, confusion, will make the English abandon their position at the end of the lake; that they will even leave behind in order to withdraw quickly, and because the colony needs them, provisions, barges, pontoons, cannon, mortars, cannon balls, bombs, artillery train, and field carriages, etc., etc. The Marquis de Vaudreuil is so sure that this will happen that he notifies the Marquis de Montcalm that he has put off the departure of the frigate which should carry the news of the victory of the eighth, so that it can carry at the same time that of the flight of the enemy. He assures him that this will give the King great pleasure. I don't know what Fontaine was thinking of when he wrote the fable of the milk jug. Why isn't he here? What milk jug! and on whose head!

Scouts have discovered beyond Camp Brulé a great number of corpses on litters. These doubtless are wounded that the enemy abandoned in their retreat. General Reflection: One often will be obliged to interrupt oneself to remember that that which is not probable is often so, and it almost always is in this country.

❦ JULY 26 : M. Mercier leaves for Montreal. He doubtless has [private] business there. Such is the way of the colony. The Indians come to make a coup and go home. The militia men do the same; also the officers of La Marine. For the next fortnight they will all come to ask to leave under pretext of poor health, of business, of trade, of commerce, of bills of exchange. They will have completed three weeks or a month of campaign. In truth that is very long.

List of the Regiments of the Troops of Old England That Were in North America, January 1, 1758, According to an Almanac Printed in New York

Second Battalion of the 1st Regiment, or Royal Scots	Colonel James St. Clair, lieutenant general
17th Regiment	Colonel John Forbes
22 Regiment	Colonel Edward Whitmore
27 Regiment	Colonel Philip Bragg, lieutenant general
25[35] Regiment	Colonel Thomas Otway, lieutenant general
40 Regiment	Colonel Peregrine Thomas Hopson
42 Regiment	Colonel John, Lord Murray, major general
43 Regiment	Colonel James Kennedy
44 Regiment	Colonel James Abercromby, major general
45 Regiment	Colonel Hugh Warburton, major general
46 Regiment	Colonel Thomas Murray, major general
47 Regiment	Colonel Peregrine Lascelles, major general
48 Regiment	Colonel Daniel Webb

Journal for 1758

55 Regiment	Colonel Lord Howe, brigadier general, killed
	James Donaldson
62[60] Regiment or Royal American	Colonel James Abercromby

has four battalions of one hundred men at full strength; four colonels commandant, to wit: John Stanwix, brigadier general, James Prevost; the second and fourth vacant; four lieutenant colonels: Henry Bocquet, Frederick Haldimand, John Young, Sir [John] St. Clair.

A regiment of Highlanders [77th], newly raised; of two battalions: lieutenant colonels commandant Archibald Montgomery, Simon Fraser.

Total—20 battalions, which complete make: 20,000 men.

4 independent or ranger companies, 400 men—at New York. 3 in Carolina. 1 in Bermuda. 1 in Bahama Islands. 2 companies of royal artillery: colonel commandant, William Bedford.

Troops from old England are still arriving for the siege of Louisbourg. Whatever be the result, will they recross the ocean or will they leave them in this country? The more northern provinces only this year have furnished twenty thousand militiamen. What strength in comparison with our weakness! Besides, these provinces abound in food and provisions of all kinds. Should this great body once get a head, what will Canada become?

French Forces in North America

12 battalions, full strength (they never have been)	6000 men
Soldiers of La Marine regiment, about	3500 men
2 companies of artillery	120 men
This year after the enemy's retreat, the Marquis de Vaudreuil had marched the militia levies, both the active and the reserve, here: militia men arrived	2108

In addition four battalions at Louisbourg can be of no aid to Canada, nor can the troops of La Marine.

All the western posts must be manned. Then, to be able to put on a campaign there remain ———.

Departure of M. Bellot, captain in Guyenne regiment, to go hunt our recruits at Quebec. He carries there dispatches for France.

JULY 28 : Nothing new, much panic in the advanced camps. In 1756 when the same troops occupied the same posts, it was necessary to establish there a detachment of regulars, who were relieved every four days, in order to put an end to false alarms.

JULY 29 : Certain people are talking a lot about going home. They never made war in Canada before 1755. They never had gone into camp. To leave Montreal with a party, to go through the woods, to take a few scalps, to return at full speed once the blow was struck, that is what they called war, a campaign, success, victory. They assembled in ——— a body of ——— and the object of this army was to destroy the Foxes.

It is the first and only campaign of the Marquis de Vaudreuil. It is where he educated himself in the difficult art of Mars. The success was brilliant and instructive. They took an old man whom they tied to a stake and who, according to what I have often heard the governor general tell, made very comical faces while they were burning him. The Marquis de V[audreuil] still laughed at the memory of it.

The Chickasaw War for which detachments left Montreal, Detroit, the Illinois, New Orleans [and] joined themselves together on the Mississippi, cost the King more than two million and lasted a year, ended in a road started to take artillery in front of enemy villages surrounded with palisades, in two or three prisoners, and a few belts of wampum.

Now war is established here on the European basis. Projects for the campaign, for armies, for artillery, for sieges, for battles. It no longer is a matter of making a raid, but of conquering or being conquered. What a revolution! What a change! One would believe that the people of this country, astonished at the novelty of these objects, would ask some time to accustom themselves to it, some more time to reflect on what they have seen, still more to

Courtesy Fort Ticonderoga Museum

Diorama showing a portion of the French defenses at Fort Carillon.

Courtesy Fort Ticonderoga Museum

Montcalm congratulating his troops
on the successful defense of Fort Carillon.

Journal for 1758

efface their first ideas, become false ideas, dangerous, prejudiced from infancy, and still much more time to learn [new] principles, to draw conjectures, to put themselves to the school of experience. On the contrary, townsmen, bankers, merchants, officers, bishops, parish priests, Jesuits, all plan this [war], speak of it, discuss it, pronounce on it. Everyone is a Turenne or a Folard.[42]

Great misfortune for this country; it will perish, victim of its prejudices, of its blind confidence, of the stupidity or of the roguery of its chiefs.

This oracle is more sure than that of Calchas.[43]

JULY 30 : Departure of four bateaux for Montreal.

M. de St. Luc returned, having struck the twenty-eighth at noon. His troop, in ambush between Fort Edward and Halfway Brook, destroyed a convey of forty to fifty wagons escorted by an ensign of Blakeney's and fifty men. Several women, children, sutlers made the trip together. All were captured or killed. We had an Iroquois killed and two wounded. The Iroquois always lose someone. It is [because] they are the bravest of all the Indians. Sarégoa, their war chief, is the one who led the undertaking. When, in a detachment, the Indians are the most numerous, they lay down the law and decide without appeal. Good fortune when he among them who is the leader has a good head, and Sarégoa's is well organized.

The prisoners' statements are almost the same as those of the twenty-first. The enemy, to the number of ten to twelve thousand men, established at the end of Lake St. Sacrement, occupy the neighboring islands with detachments.

It is not certain if they wish to rebuild the fort or simply to stay there [for] the campaign, [or] if their project is to come again to attack us, or [hold to] the defensive.

According to the latest news that has been received from Louisbourg, the place still holds out.

Indians are in camp. Great business buying up the loot they

---

[42] French soldier and military writer (1669–1752).
[43] Greek soothsayer of the time of the Trojan War.

have taken. Brandy is the specie which facilitates sales. Few people here [are] scrupulous [in the use of] this article.

JULY 31: Arrival of a courier from Montreal. Letters from the Marquis de V[audreuil] as usual, that is to say, vague, ridiculous, or captious, not answering at all to reason, to facts, to proof.

News from Belle Rivière, all is quiet there.

They say at Montreal that on the day of the battle eighteen hundred Canadians or soldiers of La Marine were here, and that now we are twelve thousand men. It is necessary to explain how this can be said and proved.

Report of Soldiers of the Colony and Militiamen Who Were at Carillon on July 8 at Noon

Arrived July 1	110
With M. de Raymond, colony captain	118
With MM. de la Naudiere, St. Ours, Gaspé, captains, the fifth	180
With M. de Gannes, captain, the sixth	183
Total	591

From which it is necessary to deduct about 140 men, sick, detached to take the bateaux to St. Jean, killed, or captured in the battle of the sixth.

There remain 451 soldiers of La Marine, or Canadians present when the affair of the 8th started.

On the eighth at four o'clock M. Duplessis, lieutenant, arrived with 85 men.

Boisvert, clerk to Commissary of Stores, with 168 men.

A large part went to the field of battle.

It is a long way from this number to eighteen hundred.

1. A certain number of habitants of the better sort have been ordered to go to war; they enter them on the rolls, they equip them accordingly, there they are ready to leave. Then they offer them the choice either of engaging at a very low pay to go to the western sea, the bay, etc., or to "march to the fire [i.e., go to the battle front]"; that is the term which they use here and which one finds very expressive. Their choice does not take long, nor is it

doubtful. They engage to go to the [western] posts and it is said that they are [gone] to war. The [muster] rolls attest it.

2. The Commissary of Stores needs people and even in great numbers for his supply trains. Instead of determining the necessary number and of drawing them from the entire body of militia and volunteers for all the campaign, they order some militiamen to war, put them on the army rolls, then they exempt them from going on the condition that they will make two or three trips for the Commissary of Stores without pay. Hence it follows that the army appears numerous, [but] that really only the worst sort of men march to it, and the parishes are crowded.

Tantum potuit suadere malorum auri sacra fames.[44] If the people in power tolerate such abuses, decisive for the ruin of the colony, it must be that they are profitable for them; if they do not know about them why are they in office?

Report of Battalions, Militia, and Colony Troops, July 31, 1758

Regular troops		3528
La Marine soldiers		1112
Militiamen		2108
	Total	6748
Indians, about		300

Council with the Indians. Ceremony of covering the killed Iroquois. They ask to return to Montreal and promise to come back. However, they are leaving a small number of them here.

August 1: Departure of about 150 Indians. There still remain here fifteen Iroquois of the Sault and seven of the Lake, a few Algonkins and Nipissings, a few Abnakis, six Hurons, and all the Ottawas, in all about 150 Indians.

Arrival of thirty or forty Missisaugas.

Reconnaissance on Lake St. Sacrement by the Chevalier de Lévis as far as Isle la Barque. Detachment marches by land at the same time.

Courier sent to Montreal. Arrival of a deserter. The news that he gives of the enemy the same as above.

[44] "So much does hunger for gold make one the slave of evil."

꿿 August 2 : One will find it odd that today when the impossibility of undertaking this campaign and [making] the siege of Fort Edward is clearly demonstrated, they continue to bring here the artillery trains and other munitions, to make handcarts, wheels, and tools necessary for portaging in case of siege. One will not be more surprised when they learn the reason for it.

Sieur Mercier and Company have the contract for the transport of artillery and other portages relating to military expeditions, of the furnishing of tools, carts, wheelwork, etc. That tells it all.

Note: In 1757 M. Mercier paid his workmen for ninety-eight thousand livres of tools without holding back the four percent, proof that he was paying them for his own account. The Intendant passed on to him thirty-six percent of the profit.

All of the hatchets were of plain iron without steel [edges], also all bent like pancakes at the first blow. The colony just missed destruction through the poor quality of the hatchets. Where would we have been without our abatis? It was M. Mercier who was the contractor for them [the hatchets] who received them.

Note how here everything is directed *ad majus lucrum*![45]

One will object that it is always advantageous to place here the requirements for [making] a siege; that if one does not make one this year, they will serve for the next campaign.

The objection would make sense in the other world [in Europe], but not so here. At the end of the campaign they will take back to Montreal and even to Quebec the equipment and artillery munitions which have only just arrived here. The carts, tools will be burned during the winter because nobody will take care of them. New wagons, new furnishings to make for the next campaign.

In general all this is contracted for and that is why all the furnishings are detestable and the expense enormous. The King gets nothing firsthand. The chiefs, the protégés, the protégés of the protégés, all these must make a profit on everything the state buys. The Indians and the soldiers complain of the bad quality of the food, the food comes on contract, and this is the only country where the government authorizes the Commissary of Stores to

[45] "To the greatest profit."

Journal for 1758

furnish bad [food]. The deerskins, the tanned shoes, the tobacco are of a bad kind; the deerskins, the tanned shoes, the tobacco come on contract. The coats, breeches, mitasses, are of poor material, too short, too tight; the coats, breeches, mitasses come on contract. The hatchets, shovels, picks are almost always useless; the hatchets, shovels, picks come on contract.

Still this is not all. These contractors use the King's workmen and their pay is charged to the King's account. One could continue on this subject at length.

Under the agreement of the King with the Commissary of Stores, he [the King] is obliged to furnish him everything necessary for the conveyance of provisions. If a private party had made such an agreement as this with anyone, civil law would have at once forbidden it. Here criminal justice should play its role.

When troops are not in a fort, when in camp or marching, then the Commissary of Stores no longer furnishes the rations; it is up to the King to feed them. Since the Commissary of Stores alone has the provisions, he sells to the King at his own price and the conveyance is contracted for. The camps at the Falls and the Portage fall into this category.

In a fort that is being built, horses are necessary for haulage. It would be very simple if the King had some that he fed, as well as men paid to care for them. It is not so. The supply of horses goes on contract. The holder of the privilege has horses for which the King pays by the trip; a few individuals have some also; the holder of the privilege takes them, pays owners seven livres, ten sous per day, price fixed by the Intendant, gets himself paid by the King for them on a trip basis, and, by this arrangement, each horse earns from twenty-two to twenty-four deniers[46] per day. *Note:* They made the King pay Sieur Lot[binière]'s carters like carpenters and other workmen from the beginning up to July 1. They presented the certificate to M. de Pontleroy who refused to sign it. He even wrote the Intendant to ask his directions in this respect.

Seven horses from the tenth to the thirty-first have earned at

---

[46] A denier was 1/240 of a livre. I suspect an error here, as the sum named seems too small.

Carillon, 6748 livres, 7 sols, 8 deniers, according to signed and paid certificates.

They earn almost as much winter as summer: then the cost to the King [is] 120,000 livres per year.

2. I have said by this arrangement; I explain myself. M. Lotbinière's clerk was ordered to execute a certificate for more trips than the carters actually made, with the result that each horse earned at least twenty livres and it was M. de Lotbinière who signed the certificates. Now that he is gone, it was necessary to reveal this secret inequity to M. de Pontleroy, and the proofs one has of them are authentic and certificated. Furthermore the King pays for all the trips the horses make for the Commissary of Stores and there is time still to make many [such]. What horses! Those of Castor and Pollux were only jades alongside of them.

M. de Lotbinière and Company thus have the horse concession for the works at Carillon. Now it is he who makes the money there and who pays the various expenses in his quality as engineer.

It is then quite true to say that this land will perish after having ruined France through the monstrous abuses of these privileged select.

Departure of a courier for Montreal.

August 3: Council with Missisaugas.

Arrival of a score of Abnakis from Panaouameské [Panaomeske]. Council with them.

Courier from Montreal gave us news of Louisbourg. The trenches were not opened until June 28.[47]

August 4: Departure of M. Marin for the end of the Bay with a party of 219 Indians and 225 Canadians. They took food and equipment for this number of men. Several sold this after having received it and returned asking for more. There is no accounting, no [muster] roll. For of these 444 men equipped under pretext of [going with] this party, there are not perhaps 300 of them who went. Whoever will claim that it is possible to remedy this abuse will prove that he has never come into this country.

---

[47] That is, the actual siege operation initiated.

Journal for 1758

Work [on the fort] continues. They led the Canadians there, half an hour later almost all disappeared and one no longer knew where to find them again. In all ways they are, most of them, more undisciplined, more lazy than the Indians, and lack much to equal the latter in war.

Why not punish them? cries some European. Punish a Canadian! M. de Vaudreuil would prefer to lose a battle, and he would not fail to write the court, as he has already done, that they are treating harshly people from whom one gets all one wishes with gentleness.

AUGUST 5 : Titus used to say that he had wasted his day when he had lived through it without according a favor. A European here has employed his well if he has lived through it without learning of a peculation or a new roguery.

When the troops marched toward this frontier, they ordered the habitants near the Chambly portage to bring their carts there. The Commissary of Stores has had paid to those who had not brought their [own] food with them the ration, one livre, ten sous. Well! said a habitant, this same Commissary all winter gave us only ten sous a day for feeding a soldier and he secures us one livre, ten sous for the same ration. The order of the Marquis de V[audreuil] was precise in this respect.

When the Canadians are in the army, they suffer the same reduction in ration as the rest of the troops, but the Commissary of Stores does not make the deduction because of economy; it goes entirely to his profit. It is in this colony that Juvenal would cry out: *Difficile est satyram non scribere: nam quis iniquae tam patiens gentis tam ferreus, ut teneat se.*[48]

Nothing new in the army.

AUGUST 6 : Courier from Montreal. Letters from the Marquis de Vaudreuil in which he cautions the Marquis de Montcalm that the colony owes its safety to the Indians, that these tribes require much gentleness and complaisance, that they complain in

---

[48] "It is difficult not to write a satire: for who is so tolerant of this wicked race, so iron [of character] that he can contain himself?" Bougainville substituted "race" for the "city" of the original.

open council that he [Montcalm] has treated them harshly and [they] have declared that they will no longer return to war in this region, as long as he commands there.

Here then is a grievance that can be held against the Marquis de Montcalm. In everything else his conduct is irreproachable. The facts speak [for themselves] and what they say is clearer than the day. This sole motive, enveloped in thick, dark clouds, is the motive which offers material for reproach. It is with Indians and interpreters as with pagan oracles which their priests cause to say that which they judged is apropos, that which was favorable to their interests, to their views, or conformed to the wishes of those who paid them or whom they wished to flatter.

A few Indians of Sault St. Louis have been told to complain of the French General; they have complained of him, or at least the interpreter has, in council, rendered the words of the complaint. However, these so discontented Indians have, a thing unheard of at this season, made up two considerable war parties and without going home, and a certain number of them in addition go off in a third detachment with M. Marin.

The facts are in all tongues, but their language is not understood, one supposes what he wishes.

Today Sunday, respite from the works. A few Indians of M. Marin's have returned; saying they were indisposed.

₰ AUGUST 7–12 : I have been sent by the Marquis de Montcalm to the Marquis de Vaudreuil with orders to smother, if it is possible, this leaven of discord which was fermenting and which perhaps would have hurt the good of the service. Thus our General still makes the advances. The public interest controls his actions, and he constantly has in mind this word of Themistocles: "Strike, but listen ———." It appears that the Marquis de V[audreuil] has rather followed in all these bickerings the prejudices of subalterns interested in making trouble, rather than his own ideas. In this affair, however, it is self love and a jealousy of rivalry, foundation upon which marplots build, which possess him. The appearances are that my trip has not been unfruitful. I hope that it proves true.

Journal for 1758

M. Péan has left for Quebec, whence he will go to France on Captain Canon's flute, which is ready to set sail. He will carry the news of our victory. He will lack at his recital only the ability to say: "I saw it." The pretext for his trip is a rheumatic pain in his arm, which needs the aid of the waters [of a spa]. The true motive is the necessity of getting there first and feeling out a new minister who could yet change.

So that the Marquis de V[audreuil] will not be alone, Sieur Mercier comes to take the place near him that Péan occupied. It is very necessary that M. the Intendant, always should have a resident near the person of the Governor General. M. Martel, former keeper of [King's] stores at Montreal, member of the Great Society, goes to France with him. He goes to see how he will there invest the immense sums extracted from this unfortunate land.

The Commissary of Stores has loaned me seven men to take me from St. Jean to Carillon. They have told me that they were summoned for military service, then selected from all the draftees, turned over to the Commissary of Stores to handle his bateaux, that it was their fifth or sixth trip, and that none of them had yet been paid. The Commissary of Stores pretends that this roguery is due to his clerks who have charge of the transport.

The Menominees have sent to Montreal as prisoners the seven Indians of their tribe who this winter assassinated a French family at the Bay. Three have been flogged in the city square. The other four must come to war to expiate their crime.

This submission of an independent tribe, distant more than five hundred leagues, does great honor to the French name.

M. Marin returned the tenth. He encountered Rogers with five hundred men, supported by Major Putnam[49] at the head of 250 men, of a new corps composed of picked men, called light infantry, under the command of Sieur Gage, brigadier general. The game was not even. Our people withdrew in good order, leaving on the field of battle thirteen dead, five of them Indians, and bringing off their wounded to the number of ten. They took five pris-

---

[49] Israel Putnam (1718–90) of Bunker Hill fame. He narrowly escaped being burned by the Indians on this occasion.

oners, including Major Putnam. A large part of the Canadians in M. Marin's detachment were of the bad sort. They claim that the militia commander gave him these because of professional jealousy. Besides, business of concern for society of the post[?] has estranged M. de Rigaud from his brother-in-law.

AUGUST 10–12 : Five hundred militiamen of the Montreal government left to go home. Order to stop at St. Frederic to cut wood for the garrison.

Departure of the great part of the Indians. There remain seventy-five, to wit:

Iroquois	9
Abnakis	18
Micmacs	2
Nipissings	4
Missisaugas	42

M. Wolf, sent to carry to the English General the Marquis de Vaudreuil's propositions concerning the exchange of prisoners, has returned on the twelfth with an answer from this General which seems to indicate that he has not understood the meaning of these proposals. The Marquis de Vaudreuil sent me to this person [General Abercromby] to present to him plainly the Governor General's intentions. The Englishman made no change in his answer. It appears that he wishes to keep our soldiers which he believes we need; he speaks only of exchanging the officers. The justice is agreed to of the Marquis de Vaudreuil's condition to continue to hold sequestered, pending a decision of the two courts, the Canadians and soldiers taken before August 9 that we claim should be returned under [the terms of] the capitulation of Fort William Henry. This condition, however, serves as a pretext for the difficulties he is making.

I was received and treated with the greatest politeness. The English say that the Canadians are even more cruel than the Indians. I do not believe that they are thinking of rebuilding Fort William Henry.

M. de Longueuil has returned from his embassy to the Five

Journal for 1758

Nations. He stopped at the mouth of the Oswego River. The Indians warned him that he could not go beyond there without running great risks. They came there to confer with him and told him that they were going to send deputies to Montreal. The English, to the number of five or six thousand men have already rebuilt Fort Bull. They portaged the material necessary to rebuild this, which was at the head of the Oswego River. It seems that the Five Nations have consented to this re-establishment. The Onondagas alone were opposed to it. All these Indians would be enchanted to see Oswego re-established, and I think that it will be this year. We have, in truth, done nothing which could prevent these Indians regretting this countinghouse where the trade was advantageous to them.

ఏ AUGUST 17 : Departure of the rest of the militia designated to be sent back. They have withdrawn the Portage camp back to the Falls. There remains a post of 200 men in a redoubt; this post is relieved every twenty-four hours. It keeps a scouting party on Lake St. Sacrement. The army is reduced to 1,933 men of the colony, 600 of whom are militiamen and 200 sick. Workmen, cannoneers, about 250.

	Combatants	Hospital at Carillon	Other Hospitals [?]	Absent or detached	Servants
La Reine	370	17	23	7	13
La Sarre	436	14	15	0	9
Royal Roussillon	460	14	12	0	12
Languedoc	418	20	23	15	9
Guyenne	393	23	32	5	0
Berry	723	77	48	0	12
Béarn	393	8	24	9	21
	3,193	173	177	36	76

Total 3,623 reduced to 3,193 combatants.

There appeared near St. Frederic an enemy party that carried away a habitant.

ఏ AUGUST 19 : Departure of thirty Abnakis to go and raid between Albany and Saratoga, and of twenty-three Iroquois who turn their steps toward Connecticut.

ᛞ AUGUST 20 : Some thirty Missisaugas were due to leave with M. Marin. One of them, a sick man, made medicine, [and said] that it was necessary to sacrifice a dog in order to cure him. The dog was bought, put in the kettle, the feast was made, a senator made magic, and the sick man died.

ᛞ AUGUST 21 : Departure of M. Marin with some fifty men, twenty of them Indians, in a canoe on Lake St. Sacrement.

Cross planted at the foot of the entrenchments with this inscription:

> "Christian! It was not Montcalm and his prudence,
> Nor these felled trees, the heros, their exploits,
> Which dashed the hopes of the bewildered English;
> It is the hand of thy God, conqueror on this cross."
>
> *Quid dux? Quid miles? Quid strata ingentia ligna?*
> *En signum! En victor! Deus hic, Deus ipse triumphat.*[50]

ᛞ AUGUST 22–23 : Return of the Iroquois and Hurons of M. Marin's party. They did not wish to go beyond Isle la Barque. They had been told only of a scout and not of raiding. If they had been warned of it before leaving home, they would have acted differently. M. Marin went by land with ten Missisaugas and three Frenchmen to attempt an adventure at the end of Lake St. Sacrement.

Arrival of a convoy of twenty bateaux.

ᛞ AUGUST 24–31 : The Marquis de Montcalm sends off to war M. de la Miletiere, officer in the Languedoc Regiment, adopted by the Indians. destined by the Marquis de Vaudreuil to follow the trail of M. de Joncaire, whose niece he married, with sixteen Iroquois of his clan who had asked for him as leader of an expedition. He leaves, reaches the Falls. M. de Rigaud holds him up and makes

---

[50] "Who the leader, who the soldiers, what great battle lines [gained the victory]? Behold the sign! Behold the victor! It was the Lord himself who triumphed."

Journal for 1758

representations to the Marquis de Montcalm: it is an attempt against the rights of the colony to send a French officer with Indians. It is Catiline who disguises himself as a woman in order to be able to enter into the mysteries of the good goddess. The Marquis de Montcalm replies gently to the remonstrances, but insists on the departure of the detachment. It is believed that it will leave; no, the affair remains unsettled for two days and during this time there is intriguing with the Indians who finally say that they have changed their minds and no longer wish to go.

Thus it is that the King is served. Arrival of a deserter. The result of his deposition is that the enemy are working at cleaning up the Chicot River in order to go afterwards to besiege in Lake Ontario a French fort which can only be Frontenac; that they have built and launched on Lake St. Sacrement a bark of eighteen guns, that they have a very large lime kiln, that their entrenchments have battlements throughout, which proves that their purpose is to have a body of troops in huts pass the winter in these defenses. It also appears that the reinforcements they will receive, either from Louisbourg, the Fort Duquesne [expedition], or from German Flats, will determine a new attempt on their part on Carillon. We await them steadfastly and we are constantly working to make our position better. The soldiers are in the best of spirits and ardently desire the return of the enemy. They are sure of victory. It is a fortunate presage of success.

Return of Sieur Marin. He remained three days in ambush around the enemy's camp without finding occasion to take either a scalp or a prisoner.

Departure of Sieur de Sabrevois, ensign of colony troops, with a small party to try for an adventure between Fort Lydius and Lake St. Sacrement.

Two Iroquois who sulked in their huts have also gone off alone in the same direction.

Arrival of a few Iroquois. The Missisaugas asked to leave, and one could scarcely refuse them; they have been here a long time.

I have been with forty volunteers and a few Indian guides to reconnoiter a road [by which], after disembarking an hour and a half from Carillon toward St. Frederic, and passing through the back country, [one could] fall on the Contrecoeur camp. I found it to be 11,562 three-feet paces; from the place where I disembarked and the Bernetz River 6,200 paces. I passed it almost dry-shod. I always kept a quarter-league on my right the mountain chain which extends the length of Lakes St. Sacrement and Champlain, behind which passes the Mohawk road.

Courier from Montreal; no news from Louisbourg. A Spanish ship, loaded at Bordeaux, arrived at Quebec.

SEPTEMBER 1 : Courier from Montreal. The enemy detachment which left Lake St. Sacrement on July 12, is afloat on Lake Ontario and was within two leagues of Frontenac when the courier left to carry this news to Montreal. There is, and with reason, the greatest uneasiness. There are only forty men in the garrison in the fort which is the depot of the artillery, of the munitions of war, and the provisions for [all] the Far West. The vessels are not armed, their rigging has been used on M. Péan's schooners, and if these vessels, in no condition to get away, fall into the hands of the enemy, what will prevent them from seizing Niagara, the garrison of which is as weak as that of Frontenac? They well know it; the same Indians of the Five Nations, who have without fail advised them of the weakness of the post and the garrison of Frontenac, will not have left them in ignorance that there were only thirty men at Niagara. These two forts were their trading posts. Their fidelity was assured. M. Duplessis, major of Montreal, eighty years old, left with fifteen hundred men to go in that direction [toward Frontenac]. Assistance has also been sought from Quebec, but one does not know what effect this tardy succor will produce.

Thus at last behold the arrival of the evil so much predicted. The enemy open their eyes, sense the advantage which numbers and abundance of everything gives talents, even limited [ones]. What an opportunity they have against our misery and folly!

We would not be in these critical circumstances, if, after taking Oswego, its river had been made navigable, and we had built on the location of Fort Ontario[51] or at Cayuga Bay,[52] or at least at Niaouré Bay a post capable of holding five hundred men, as was several times proposed; if one throughout the campaign had only kept well armed vessels cruising in the vicinity of the Oswego River; if only Frontenac and Niagara had been put in a state of capability of resisting a sudden raid, considering the weakness of the post or the lack of defenders. If only in this campaign after the affair of the eighth and the retreat of the enemy, instead of sending us here a useless and transient troop, which has served only to consume without result a great quantity of provisions, one had at once sent to the ruins of Oswego a body of fifteen hundred or eighteen hundred men, supported by well-armed vessels, which could have arrived before the enemy, who only left Lake St. Sacrement on July 12, have filled the port, barred the river, and ended the campaign in this position. Then in case of an enemy attack, they would have only their superiority [in numbers], and not [the benefit of] our negligence for which there is no remedy, while wisdom corrects inferiority of force. But all these reflections on the past are good only for readers yet to come. Resources are needed, not elegies and philippics.

New ships at Quebec. News from France as of June [has] little consolation; from Louisbourg as of July 25 can give a few rays of hope to spirits which are readily fooled.

A few Iroquois and Abnakis took a scalp and two prisoners near Fort Number Four,[53] situated at the head of the Connecticut River above the mouth of the Black River. This fort is of horizontal timbers with four cannon and one hundred militiamen for a garrison. It, however, is less exposed than Frontenac, since one can get to it only through the woods.

By the latest news from Fort Duquesne it seems that we are about to be attacked there.

Today the eight battalions with their flags worked on the defenses which have been almost entirely rebuilt. Attacked on all

[51] The most easterly of the three forts at Oswego.
[52] Sodus Bay, twenty-six miles southwest of Oswego.
[53] Charlestown, N. H.

sides and forced to divide our weak forces, it is necessary to supplement [small] numbers by skill. These works will have five trees for a base, four above, three, two, and one. It would be wished that a ditch could be built around, but it is feared that ledge will be found too soon.

I have proposed occupying Mutton Island with a dug-in, hidden battery. I asked for the labor of two hundred Canadians for three days, work which would in no way interrupt that of the Carillon camp.

After I had been twenty-four hours on the island [I would be] safe from musket fire, it would need cannon to drive me away; if the enemy let me have fifteen days, I would sustain a siege of Troy there.

For the execution of this project I asked for M. Jacquau who shares it with me and who alone is able to build a battery such as we conceive, four poor cannon, munitions and provisions for two months, and fifty men, determined like M. Jacquau and myself not to surrender. We would have dugouts for food, powder, and charcoal sheltered from bombs. The construction is new and without precedent, for since the island forms an ellipse with the greatest diameter of fifteen toises and the smallest six, all the engineers exclaim of the impossibility of making anything tenable, since the parapets alone, being three toises each, use up the six toises. From this position, one can without inconvenience fall back on Carillon, the post at the Portage, and the camp at the Falls after having barred, plugged up, and rendered impracticable the river of that name [Falls]. The enemy would be obliged either to besiege me in the formal way, and this would not be an affair of one day, or to land above the Burned Camp or Contrecoeur's camp; then he would have a portage of three leagues to drag to our works, and, in case of a repulse, the cannon; a part of the munitions and provisions would remain with us. Besides the consolidation of our forces in one place, these obstacles to the march, the operations, the advance of the enemy would put us in position to send eight hundred to one thousand men to the Marquis de Vaudreuil when he should ask for them, or without his asking. *Note:* The advan-

The Montcalm Cross—a replica of the cross Montcalm erected after the defense of Fort Carillon.

Fort Ticonderoga today.

Journal for 1758

tage of a reinforcement sent at once to the Marquis de Vaudreuil would be to establish without delay a strong point at La Presentation or at the Cedars which would calm the alarmed colony, [thus] given the means to make there all the preparations for an autumn or spring expedition according to the enemy's actions. In this latter case I would wish to set up my depot above the rapids,[54] in order that transport of munitions and provisions would not hold me up the moment navigation becomes practicable.

I do not know if this project will be carried out. If it is turned down it is doubtless because the masters of the art [the Royal Engineers] will find more disadvantages than I, a novice, see or believe to see advantages.

§∽ SEPTEMBER 2–4 : M. Wolf was the morning of the second to carry to General Abercromby the Marquis de V[audreuil]'s answer on the subject of the exchange of officers, which he refuses absolutely unless the soldiers are included. He returned here the third with a dispatch of the English General to the Marquis de V[audreuil], the contents of which we do not know.

When I was sent to the English camp, I bet with Captain Abercromby, the General's nephew and aide-de-camp, that Louisbourg would not be taken [by] August 15. He wrote me by Monsieur Wolf that the place had surrendered July 26 and included with his letter a New York gazette, dated August 28, which gave details of this surrender and the articles of capitulation. Despite this newspaper and his letter, which copies it literally, I believe the news false and published in their colony to encourage the citizens and the soldiers. According to them Louisbourg surrendered the twenty-sixth at discretion, if I may say so, and according to letters we have had from there of the twenty-fourth, the place was still only being fired at from two hundred toises.[55] They had made entrenchments to resist the assault; all the streets were barricaded, the houses loopholed, the wharves fortified; everything, then, pro-

[54] In the St. Lawrence.

[55] Six hundred yards, a range then considered excessive for fire on a walled city under siege.

claimed the resolution to conquer or perish. The surrender included, said this gazette, the inhabitants of Isle Royale, St. Jean —— and Father Germain, missionary of this region, had not known of it on August 7, the day he wrote [us] here that Louisbourg was defending itself well.

Besides, if this place had been taken July 26, ships or longboats, or even people on foot would certainly, before September 1, have brought the news to Quebec. A thousand other circumstances make me persist in believing that the New York gazette is false and deceitful. I am keeping this newspaper and Captain Abercromby's letter.

M. de Sabrevois, ensign of the colony troops, returned the fourth from a scout made by land with ten or twelve men to the end of Lake St. Sacrement, has reported that the English camp is much diminished, that it seemed to him less numerous than ours at Carillon, that there were not more than 150 or 200 barges. From another point of view M. Wolf, who has viewed the camp from about a league out in the lake in full daylight, and whose eyes they did not blindfold, on a night visit to be sure, until [he had reached] the foot of the defenses, but after he had landed over several rows of bateaux, insists that all appears exactly the same as at his first trip to the camp. It seems to me that even supposing that MM. de Sabrevois and Wolf deserve equal degrees of confidence in ordinary circumstances, in this it is necessary to believe the report of that of the two who certainly has viewed [matters] cooly because the flag he carried sheltered him from all danger.

Some people pretend that the young Canadian has only said what his superior compatriots have told him to say and that consequently they would recall [troops] from this frontier, which is no longer threatened, doubtless to march to the aid of the other frontier. To arrive there, one passes and stops at Montreal, and that is the point of the affair, for after September 8, they will not issue any more letters of exchange on the treasury. In effect M. de Rigaud writes to Monsieur, his brother, that it is the only reconnaissance which, up to the present, has been well executed; that the enemy are no longer in force at Lake St. Sacrement, and that

Journal for 1758

thus it is no longer necessary to leave here those that are here. *Note:* They have given so short a period to the receipt of paper money for conversion into letters of exchange [because] first, in order to hide the enormity of the expense, since for four months they have not paid any of those who work for the King; second, in order that the partisans and friends of the G.S. [Grand Society], who appreciate the danger to the colony, who fear the devaluation of the paper money, should have better opportunity to convert it into letters of exchange in a period when business is not yet concluded [for the year] and when the officers, all traders, are with the army. The Marquis de Montcalm has asked the Intendant to assign each year to the French troops, a fund of eight thousand livres in bills of exchange of the first term.[56] This request was all the more reasonable since our funds are at once paid in coin by the War Department treasurer to the treasurer of the colonies. The Intendant flatly refused. *Note:* Since we have been in Canada our pay has decreased by almost a sixth; instead of paying us in coin as in the first years, for the last eighteen months they have paid in paper; they have reduced a part of our field allowance. Meanwhile everything here has reached such an excessive price that one would hardly believe it. I speak of the necessaries of life. He who wished to list the vexations of all sorts which overwhelm us here, would produce an elegy, the strength of which few people would appreciate.

I have written a letter to Montreal to be shown to the Marquis de Vaudreuil in which I say that in his place I would immediately make at La Presentation, if there is still time, or at least at the Cedars, all preparations for an expedition, fall, winter, or early spring; I would hold back all the *voyaguers* and employees of the Far West, gaining two thousand excellent men; I would have it said to the Indians of these regions that they should come themselves to look for their requirements in Montreal, where I would give them these instead of selling them; I would detain all the fishermen of the River and Gulf of St. Lawrence whom I would make

---

[56] These bills of exchange were not currently payable in France, but had varying maturities.

into sailors on Lakes Ontario and Champlain; I would even take upon myself, to fulfill the same objective, the holding for the winter of a few of the merchant ships now at Quebec; their crews, rigging, and masts would serve for the navy on the lakes; I would at once order Sieur Levasseur to employ all his workmen in building at St. Jean and at La Presentation, chebecs, half galleys and brigs; I would have assembled quantities of bateaux, birch canoes, and I would buy up all those privately owned; I would employ for service and for military work all the workmen of the towns and countryside; I would order the officers who should march to war with them to take command of the militiamen of the countryside; I would bring up all the companies of regulars and colony troops to sixty men, incorporating in them the elite Canadians who would serve the whole campaign with pay furnished by the King or even by the parishes; this mixture would give each troop good shots, good canoemen, and good workmen of all kinds whose mutual emulation would make into excellent warriors; I would put order and discipline into the convoys of the Commissary of Stores which would bring out better men; finally, for the economic employment of these men and of time I would try to avoid any critical position.[57]

The Indians have asked to leave. These gentry do not like bad news. Wampum belts, a war song sung by the Marquis de Montcalm, a pig given for a feast, a shot of brandy, these inducements have held them. They have promised to remain another week. Their number is about one hundred.

SEPTEMBER 5 : Continuation of work on the defenses by all eight battalions. I believe that they would have been able to find enough earth to have made a ditch in front which would have improved the defense of the [log wall] works, would have protected them from [being set on] fire, which would have spared us taking them down this fall and remaking them in the spring. But

---

[57] These thoughts, impossible of execution with Vaudreuil in control, show how sound a thinker and planner Bougainville was.

Journal for 1758

it was believed that the enemy would not have given us time to finish them, and that, if only partly complete, in case of an attack they would be more [useful] to the attackers than to us.

They are arranging to withdraw the camp at the Falls, that is to say they are taking to Carillon the [palisade] stakes, oars, sweeps, fire wood that the troops at this camp made, and that today they are going to start blocking the Falls River by a dike within cannon range of the fort. I am charged with this work which is nothing but a beaver dam made of trees lying in the water, trunks and branches, and bound together by various lines of piles, driven to water level. A few Indians who were hunting along the sides of the Pendu River[58] have been attacked by an enemy party; one Indian was slightly wounded, the others ran away to Carillon. M. de St. Luc followed the enemy's tracks with almost all the Indians in camp and returned, two hours later, to tell us that they [the tracks] seemed to be those of some thirty men, several of them in French shoes, the rest Indians. Thirty of our men will leave tomorrow morning to run after this party which they expect to meet the day after, and not on their guard, provided that they then do not expect to be pursued.

M. de Charly, stepson of M. de Noyan, commandant at Frontenac, left today for Montreal.

ࢬ SEPTEMBER 6: News from Quebec which announces the capture of Louisbourg, from Montreal telling of that of Frontenac.

Louisbourg really surrendered July 26 as Captain Abercromby wrote me. We are absolutely in ignorance of the details of the siege and of the surrender. Along with this place it has cost France six or eight warships. If M. de Drucour had been more public-spirited and less occupied with his private interests he would have spared it this fate. Really [with] these ships, kept in the harbor, unable to save the place, the futile honor of a little longer defense was not worth their sacrifice. I think that if Isle Royale is returned to France, there is no need of a fortress, but only a simple post

---

[58] Probably East Creek across the lake in Vermont.

with a commander and one hundred men for the police of the fisheries. Regardless of what works they erect there, the place will be taken because they do not know how to prevent a landing; thus it is an enormous expense for the fortifications, its upkeep, and that of a great garrison which will fall a complete loss.

I would recall to Canada the companies detached to Louisbourg, which would make a strong and good increase to the colony troops. Since we have no other details at all, I attach hereto the principal articles of the capitulation according to Captain Abercromby's letter.

The place surrendered the twenty-sixth under the following conditions:

1. The garrison will be prisoners of war and taken to England in British vessels.

2. All the artillery, munitions, provisions, and arms will be turned over to commissioners of his British Majesty.

3. The Governor will order the troops in Isle St. Jean and its dependencies to surrender themselves on board such vessel as the Admiral will send to receive them.

4. The traders and their clerks who have not born arms will be sent to France, etc.

We are informed here that the city of Louisbourg ransomed itself from all pillage and confiscation for the sum of 150,000 livres, that all the inhabitants were [left] in peace in their houses and in the enjoyment of their possessions up to the time of embarkation, and that the Admiral had hanged an English soldier who stole from an inhabitant.

On the twelfth they received from Montreal a journal of M. de Boishebert which contained details of his maneuvers since July 8, the day he reached Isle Royale, until the thirtieth, the day he left.

It appears by this journal that he always kept very close to the rear of the English camp, that he was not at all or only slightly inconvenienced, that his detachment was weak and of mediocre spirit, that in a word, it would have been better to spare the King the five or six hundred thousand livre expense by not sending him at all to Isle Royale. He has gone to make a raid in the direction of Fort George,[59] in the vicinity of the St. Jean River.

☙ SEPTEMBER 6–12 : Detail of the capture of Frontenac. Sieur d'Espinassy, lieutenant of engineers, arrived the twenty-second at Frontenac, having left Niagara the twentieth in the bark *Marquise*. The purpose of his trip was to select limestone to face the works at Niagara. The evening of the twenty-second the chief of the Iroquois of La Presentation came to warn M. de Noyan that the English were coming in force to attack him.

The night was passed putting in shape the few cannon there were on the ramparts. The garrison was only eighty men; two barks were armed, with only ten or twelve men apiece as crews; the four or five others were unrigged.

Thursday the twenty-fourth in the evening the enemy landed a few troops. Friday all their army, which was four thousand men,[60] landed and opened a trench quite near the fort. Saturday they came on in column, supported by four twelve-pounders and two mortars, to take position in the entrenchments we had started in 1756 to cover Frontenac.

They easily made it into a parallel and commenced to fire. During the night of Friday to Saturday the two barks were attacked by about thirty English barges, which were repulsed with a loss of a score of men on their side. Saturday passed in cannonading by both sides. The night of Saturday to Sunday the English established a breaching battery; the barks left the fort to try to dismount this battery by their fire, but they were so annoyed that it was necessary to abandon them.

The breach being found practicable on Sunday at the right hand bastion, part of the guns dismounted, the powder magazine exposed, the barks out of action, and the garrison unable to resist an assault, M. de Noyan surrendered at nine o'clock in the morning. The garrison was made prisoners of war and sent off the next day

---

[59] Either Fort St. George, near present Thomaston, Me., or Fort George, near Brunswick, Me.

[60] Actually it was about three thousand.

to Montreal to be exchanged. The English conducted themselves with the greatest humanity, I will say, even with much politeness. We had seven or eight men killed or wounded. Our greatest loss is:

1. That of the barks which should have been saved, provided that they could not save the place and that Friday there was a northeast wind suitable to put them in safety.

2. That of nearly eighty pieces of artillery captured at Oswego which remained at Frontenac, one does not know why or how. In truth we spiked[61] them but they are nonetheless lost to us.

3. That of many munitions and provisions destined for supplying the Far West, an irreparable loss under the present circumstances.

The English took away the *Marquise* and a snow of sixteen guns, and burned the other vessels. There they are again, masters of Lake Ontario. Pray God they do not at once go to Niagara. The Marquis de V[audreuil] has sent orders to Sieur de Montigny, captain of La Marine, to get there with five hundred picked men with the greatest speed.

The Marquis de V[audreuil] having also summoned the Marquis de M[ontcalm] to confer on the actual state of the colony, this general left Carillon incognito the evening of the sixth, with Sieur de Pontleroy, who was also sent for. I followed him this trip. Arrived the evening of the eighth at St. Jean. A few days before there was a panic there because of eighteen militia deserters from Carillon who were thought to be almost an English army. Three or four hundred Chambly and La Prairie men assembled at St. Jean to oppose the advance of this enemy whose march had certainly been secret enough as far as St. Jean.

Reached Montreal the ninth and left again the thirteenth. The Marquis de M[ontcalm] during this interval gave the Marquis de V[audreuil] three memoirs; one on the Lake Ontario frontier, one on that of Lake Champlain, and the third on the defense of Quebec

---

[61] A cannon was put out of action by driving a hard-tempered steel spike into the touchhole and breaking it off flush with the barrel. Then a new touchhole had to be drilled, a time-consuming operation.

and the operations and general regulations to be carried out. These three memoirs are attached hereto. [Not with MS]

It has been decided that M. de Pontleroy will go to establish an entrenched post at Frontenac, abandoned by the enemy, that they will at once build two vessels of twelve guns and will assemble on this frontier a body of three thousand men, either to undertake to drive the enemy from Oswego, provided they are not there in force, or to end the campaign in this region and labor on projected works. Reading the Marquis de M[ontcalm]'s memoirs will show what has been his advice on these various objectives. As for myself, I constantly bear in mind these verses of Ovid:

> *Principiis obsta; sero medecina paratur;*
> *Cum mala per longas convaluere moras.*[62]

The Marquis de V[audreuil], appreciating the critical position of the colony, is determined to send to France an officer to render an account to the court at the end of the campaign. He has condescended to choose me for this important and delicate commission. I would only congratulate myself if I felt I had as much talent to execute it well as I have zeal and good will.

SEPTEMBER 12 : A courier arrived from Quebec who informed us of the arrival in the river of a ship of the convoy from La Rochelle, the *Prince de Condé*. The captain of this ship writes that he saw the *Gédéon* and the *Deux Amis*, vessels of the same convoy, captured.

The same day in the evening Sieur Godefroy, captain of colony troops, arrived from Detroit. He spent August 31 at Niagara and they then did not know that the English were at Frontenac, and September 9 was at La Presentation, whence Sieur de Montigny had not yet departed. Sieur Duplessis' detachment was in very bad shape, almost naked, badly armed, many sick, no bateaux. Until they change the method of militia command they will never get any good out of it.

[62] "Resist beginnings; too late is medicine prepared when disease has gained strength through long delays."

Leaving Montreal the thirteenth, we reached Carillon the sixteenth. Nothing of moment happened during our absence. The work on the defenses has been finished, a battery was built on the right; rest from work the thirteenth and fourteenth.

The tenth there was an alert for the whole army. The occasion: eight barges that were taken for 30, 60, 140, innumerable; the post at the Portage fell back; the enemy landed; the companies of volunteers were sent forward; they saw nothing; the posts resumed normal routine.

᠊ SEPTEMBER 15–25 : They have been working to close the interval between the redoubts of the second line by a ditch and palisades. They also started the covered way and the glacis. The soldiers work at this with great speed because for this work they are paid by the toise and not by the day. The fort would have been finished long ago if they had followed this method. Sieur de Lotbinière never wished it. It was not in the interest of the holder of the canteen privilege that the work should be finished promptly.

᠊ SEPTEMBER 13 : Three hundred men were sent out on Lake St. Sacrement under orders of Sieur de Repentigny, captain of colony troops.

He returned the seventeenth without having seen anything.

᠊ SEPTEMBER 24 : Arrival of a convoy. News from Montreal which gives us some from Lake Ontario. Sieur Langy-Levrault, who was sent from La Presentation to scout the regions of Niaouré Bay and Oswego, reported that there were no English at these two places, that he had seen near Oswego the remains of barges and one of our burned barks and much scattered rigging. I would, however, like some direct news from Niagara. Perhaps the English army, content with its Frontenac expedition, is busying itself today with solidly establishing Fort Bull. This location would fulfill for them the objective of Indian trade just as well as that of Oswego, only it would not give them the key to the colony through the ability to be masters of Lake Ontario by means of a navy superior to ours. But also, since we cannot contest with them for this fort on the highland, its re-establishment will do them no good in the

Journal for 1758

peace treaty. I doubt that this [peace treaty] will be made this winter. France usually makes a peace of little benefit, because she never makes it at the right moment. Her moment was at the end of 1756. Now is the best time for England, and England will make the most of it. Our navy is wiped out and this objective alone caused this war; it is wiped out without costing the English any dismemberment, since Louisbourg will balance Port Mahon; the English will make peace this winter. Besides, the King of Prussia today is perhaps pressed to hold his own. He can sustain himself only by continual victories; once beaten, it is as if he had never conquered.

The Marquis de Vaudreuil is busying himself with sending great convoys to Niagara. We also have retaken possession of Frontenac and Sieur de Pontleroy has gone there to make an entrenched post. The builders ought to start the three barks there. They tell us of a reinforcement here of Canadians and Indians. I believe it very useless: First, I do not think that the enemy will return; second, when they do return we are enough in number to receive them well and to prevent their making any progress. The season has advanced and every day will more and more increase our strength.

SEPTEMBER 25–30 : The evening of the twenty-fifth a deserter from the fourth battalion of the Royal Americans arrived. The following is his statement. On September 21, the day he deserted, the Lake George army was composed of five to six thousand men, the Forty-fourth and Forty-sixth regiments, the regiment of Young-Murray, the fourth battalion of the Royal Americans, one of Scots, two regiments of militia, some New England levies, five companies of rangers and four hundred men of a light infantry corps. The twentieth they had heard of the arrival at Albany of five regiments from Isle Royale, which were marching to the lake. They expected winter clothing for the entire army, such as was necessary for cold weather operations; there were twenty-four cannon from six to twenty-four pounders, twenty or twenty-five mortars, several of large caliber, a bark carrying twelve four-pounders, five bateaux mounted, one with two guns, the four others with one, with twenty-four oars. For the last three weeks they worked at putting the barges in shape to move, and the camp gossip was that they were going to come to attack us the beginning of October, and that the General's intention was to take us under formal siege. They have taken to their camp an immense quantity of provisions; already they have built a storehouse 350 feet long to hold them, and they are building a second similar one. These two storehouses are inside the fortified camp, as well as such a multitude of little houses that the camp seems like a city. Every day convoys arrive escorted by twelve or thirteen hundred men and every few miles between Fort Edward and Lake George they have made [stockaded] posts into which they would throw their convoys in case of attack; in the post at Halfway Brook there are eight hundred men, half militia, half regulars; at Fort Edward fifteen hundred, the first battalion, Royal Americans, a hundred Scots, the rest militia.

The deserter has heard nothing said of the corps under orders of Colonel Bradstreet since the news of the capture of Frontenac, for which they made a rejoicing in the camp. Nothing from the Ohio, nothing from Europe, except that the King of Prussia had taken several places. He believes that all the troops from the siege of Louisbourg have remained in the New World, part in garrison at Louisbourg itself, another part at Halifax, the rest on the way to join the Lake George[63] Army.

What to make of this statement, supposing it true in all points? One can draw from it almost with equal basis the following alternative, either that General Abercromby wants to come to attack us next month or simply that his intent is to make all preparations at the lake to attack this frontier at the beginning of next spring, and to leave as a guard for these preparations a body of two or three thousand men who will winter at Lake George in huts and defenses built there. Here is the reasoning. What to conclude for action? To act as if the enemy should really come in the course of a few days, and that is what our General is doing. The camp at the Falls was withdrawn the twenty-ninth in order not to risk losing

[63] *Sic*, instead of the usual St. Sacrement.

equipment in a hurried retreat, and not to carry back to the army an indication of consternation, and to give us here fourteen hundred men more, who will be employed on necessary work. Everything is being put in shape, food, artillery, defensive works, bateaux, both as much at Carillon as at St. Frederic; each knows his post and his task, and this certainty of not being surprised produces confidence. Departure of a courier to carry this news to the Marquis de V[audreuil] and take him the deserter.

Return of a party of colonists who have learned nothing. They pretend that one of their men deserted while near the enemy, which made them abandon their canoes and return hotfoot.

𝕊 SEPTEMBER 28 : Seven English barges advanced to Mutton Island and lay to there for some time. They fired at them some from the Portage post, and they withdrew at nightfall.

𝕊 SEPTEMBER 29 : The Falls camp was withdrawn and the soldiers of La Marine re-entered the lines. The guard at the [log wall] defenses has been increased; two hundred men under orders of a captain of grenadiers, go all day long to patrol the Falls and its vicinity. A company of volunteers takes post by day at the Portage, whence it scouts the two shores of Lake St. Sacrement. At nightfall all withdraw into the defenses, except night patrols guard against all surprise. They have formed from the soldiers of La Marine two companies of volunteers under orders, the one of Sieur de Montesson, the other of Sieur Marin, to do duty with the volunteers from our battalions.

𝕊 SEPTEMBER 30 : I was sent to take soundings in Lake St. Sacrement from the Portage to Mutton Island. The gentlemen of La Marine pretend that even an unloaded bateau cannot pass there. I found a channel by which one could take a vessel of one hundred tons to the very foot [head actually] of the Portage. It is with such truth as this that they make almost all their reports. Now we see the amount of confidence that one may put in them. This same day I climbed a mountain from which the view is both beautiful and instructive. One sees all the shape of this country, the theater of the war, the course of the waters from the end of the bay, those of Lake St. Sacrement, the junction of these two waters beneath Fort Carillon, which, after having flowed for some time through a narrow bed, form Lake Champlain, whose beginnings one sees beyond St. Frederic. One sees also the different mountain ranges which cover this country, one of which running almost north and south is part of the Appalachians, which end at the Gulf of Mexico at one extremity, and at the Gulf of St. Lawrence at the other. Among these mountains the observer follows the sinuosities of the different passes which serve as roads to the Indians and through which it is necessary to pass when one wishes to go by land from St. Frederic or Carillon to Forts George, Edward, Saratoga, etc., and vice versa. Moreover, to follow these obscure routes one must have an Indian or a compass for a guide. In the latter case besides one must be perfectly informed of the location of the principal places, of the forts, and of the course of the lakes and rivers.

OCTOBER 2 : An English flag of truce arrived carrying dispatches from General Abercromby for the Marquis de Vaudreuil on the subject of the surrender of Frontenac. He asks that in consequence of this that English prisoners be returned in number equal to those French prisoners sent back to Montreal on parole under the conditions of this exchange, or that the French be returned to him.

The flag of truce bearer was stopped at Contrecoeur's camp by a detachment of the company of volunteers who mounted guard at the Portage. The Marquis de M[ontcalm] sent me to keep him company, and I spent the night with him. He brought me a basket of Bristol beer from Captain Abercromby, to whom I have sent one of Pacaret wine; a necessary and good example to set in this barbarous country, not only on account of humanity but because of politeness between enemies at war.

Captain Abercromby sent me the latest news from Europe, which is not favorable; the Battle of Crevelt; that near Olmütz; and in the first, one can suspect either treason or at least unpardonable negligence; the Count of Clermont recalled, the Marshal de Riche-

Journal for 1758

lieu succeeding him; the troops under orders of the Duke of Marlborough passed to Emden; the Dutch on the point of declaring for us; the Turks threatening the Russians with invasion; Denmark ready to attack Sweden; Spain alone motionless in the midst of this conflict of the universe; an English squadron departed from English ports under orders of Admiral Anson to descend again on the coasts of France. Our navy, then, is wiped out, military discipline banished from our armies; discouragement has dried up our courage, we have no more generals, for not by changing them every day do they become better; intrigue at court and in the cabinet has then taken sole hold of the tiller of affairs.

Talent, understanding, resolution, virtue, wise and decisive undertakings, it is a fact that France knows you no longer; she owes her safety only to some lucky chance; but who will return her glory to her?

As regard to this continent I would willingly conclude, after my conversation with the bearer of the flag of truce, that we shall not be attacked this autumn at Carillon; that a body of troops will winter at the end of Lake St. Sacrement; that Bradstreet has not gone to Niagara; that the Ohio [Fort Duquesne] was attacked at the end of September by a corps of six or seven thousand men under command of Brigadier Forbes, and that a part of the English troops from the siege of Louisbourg returned to old England; that Pitt still rules and rules well.

The truce officer also told me that the English have reunited the Cherokees with the Mohawks and the Oneidas, and that, as a token of the reunion, the chiefs of the two nations have taken wives from each other's villages. Up until now they have been irreconcilable enemies.

ओ OCTOBER 4: Three English barges advanced into sight of Mutton Island, lay to there some little time, but the post they saw there prevented them approaching land.

The evening of the fourth a courier from Montreal. News from Niagara. Sieur de Montigny arrived there with the first convoy seven days after leaving La Presentation. It was only eleven hours before that Sieur Vassan, commander of this fort, had learned of the capture of Frontenac. Its [Niagara's] garrison was forty-one men. The Indians started to act up and prepared to ruin and to burn what could not be defended in case of attack. Bradstreet missed the most beautiful chance of dealing a mortal blow to Canada.[64] Let us hope that the danger we have escaped will serve as an example to us not to abandon, in the future, a fort which is the key to the country to a troop more merchants than soldiers and ones who will not even suffice to line the ramparts of one of the bastions.

I forgot to say that even today, despite the urgency of extreme danger, instead of stocking convoys with articles for the defense of the frontiers, the Grand Society, more powerful even than the Governor, in preference sends to Niagara and Toronto things necessary for trade. Everybody sees it, knows it, the cry is general. What matter that to these brokers who enjoy the authority? Separated from the throne by fifteen hundred leagues, up to now sure of impunity, because they have dared to make accomplices even as far as within the sanctuary of the supreme power, they have accustomed commerce, private parties; the people see it all, suffer all, and [continue] to be the instrument of their fortune.

In the last ten years the country has changed its condition. Before that time one was happy there because with little one [still] had in abundance all things necessary for life; one did not wish to be rich, one did not even have the idea of wealth; no one was poor.

Verres[65] came; in building the structure of an immense fortune he associated in his peculations with several people necessary to his views or his pleasures. The amount of money increases in the colony and, consequently, the price of commodities.

The earlier simplicity blushes at first because it finds itself vying with a most affected superfluity; luxury comes in and with it corruption of customs, of feelings, avarice, greed, the spirit of graft. The way to pay court is to seem to want to make a fortune. Delicacy as to means is publicly mocked, treated as folly. The example

---

[64] He did indeed, but Frontenac alone was his directed objective, and his force was exhausted by the rapidity of the operation.

[65] A Roman magistrate, notorious for his misgovernment of Sicily. Bougainville means Bigot.

of the leader produces the usual result, that is to say, many imitators. Everybody wants to trade; conditions are all confused; trade, wiped out by exclusive privileges and by the all-powerful [holders of] the privileges, groans, complains, but its powerless voice, stifled, cannot make itself heard. It is necessary to submit to a law which is going to destroy it.

To what cannot man accustom himself? Force of habit extends even to enduring grief. Extortion has raised its mask, it no longer knows limits. Enterprises increase, multiply; a single society eats up all the interior commerce, the exterior also, all the substance of the country that it devours. It plays with the lives of men.

The inhabitants, worn out by excessive work, consume in pure loss to themselves, their strength, their time, their youth. Agriculture languishes, the population decreases, war comes, and it is the Grand Society which through outrages useful to its interest alone furnishes the ambitious English with the pretext of lighting the torch. An exhausted colony cannot sustain the fatigue and the expense. The peculators do not tire at all. The peril of Canada which becomes that of the state, makes no change in their method; this dried-up land can no longer furnish anything for their greed. Well! It is the wealth of the state itself they wish. All is put underway to rob the King; means which one cannot give names to, because up to now, no one has thought of them. At last, unheard of thing, this Society, a law to itself, is the true Commissary General, itself it sets the prices. They traffic with our subsistence, with our life. Is there no remedy for this evil which is so extreme? And is it necessary that one man alone should exhaust the finances of France, abuse our dangers and our misery, and compromise the glory of the nation?

News from the Ohio as of August 29: M. de Ligneris writes that his latest scouts have reported to him that the enemy, after having advanced six leagues beyond Fort Cumberland, retraced their steps. I prefer to believe that the English army has taken a different route from that of Braddock, as the flag of truce bearer has told me. Time will tell. In any case, the abandonment of Fort Duquesne would be, to my mind, under the present circumstances, more advantageous than harmful to the colony: it is the branch which exhausts the trunk [of the tree]. How, during such a shortage of men, of provisions, and of means, to maintain so distant a post, the occasion and cause of immense expenses, that is to say, a waste without limit? At a council of war, if since 1757 they had wished to hold one, I would have offered the advice of blowing up Fort Duquesne and of considering Niagara as the barrier in those regions and thus drawing back my center defenses. But would they have consented thus to abandon the opportunity of prodigious riches for the Grand Society?

Two Acadians have brought back word to Quebec that they saw in the Gulf of St. Lawrence a fleet of twenty-eight sail of which five were ships of the line flying a red flag. This news deserves confirmation. I would not be surprised that the English had sent this fleet to sieze our returning vessels and that they would even ravage the settlements of the lower river.

The season of year no longer permits trying an enterprise against Quebec.

According to the schedule of the price of provisions, wine is today 690 livres a cask, brandy 50 livres per velte; a calf costs 100 livres, a sheep 60 livres, a pound of beef 1 livre, 5 sous; they ask 400 livres of extra allowance a month for officers, still they will find little [relief] with these prices. How will an officer live? A captain has 2,700 livres of pay and a lieutenant 1,250. Things necessary to clothe oneself are proportionally just as expensive as are provisions. Murmurs, even discontent, are extreme throughout the army. One's eyes are open and the brightness of too penetrating a light strikes them; one sees oneself the victim of an insatiable greed of a few people who do not even hide their purpose. They have usurped everything: provisions, trade, enterprise. They are the tyrants of the price schedules and would take away our very lives if they could tax the air we breathe. The chief of the finances, [Bigot] who is either the author or the accomplice of these infamous monopolies, has not, does not, and will not make any regulations to stop them. All my prayers are that Heaven will preserve in the troops that spirit of patience which up to now has restrained them from idle complaints.

They have built a new battery at the defense line which covers all the lowland [on the right].

On the sixth arrived at St. Frederic five hundred Canadians that the Marquis de Vaudreuil made march because of the statements of the latest deserter. The seventh the Chevalier de Lévis went to St. Frederic to find some useful work on which they can be employed until their departure.

It is feared that the English are setting up an establishment at Gaspé. If they do, it is astonishing that they have not done so earlier; if they do not, they then are ignorant of the advantage of this position and the [best] use of their forces.

The Grand Society sent agents fifteen to twenty leagues out to sea to buy up the cargo of all the ships coming to Quebec. Thus making themselves masters of all the provisions and merchandise of the country, these insatiable bloodsuckers set prices and hold our very life at their discretion. Also they write from Quebec that a great number of families are escaping to France. I say "escaping" because it is here a matter of fleeing from an enemy a thousand times more dangerous than the English. How now! Will the cry of this crushed people never reach the foot of the throne?

In consequence of the capitulation of Louisbourg the English have evacuated from Isle St. Jean the four thousand inhabitants who were there. One would never have thought the number would be so great. However, I would have considered it a great victory to bring back into the interior of the colony these people that it supported at great expense and to use them here, either as workers on the lands of habitants serving with the troops, or as canoemen to carry goods, and thus ease the load on the farming population. But in this country one has no exact price schedule of any article relative to the government, be it civil, political, or military, because it is to the interest of our Verres to fish in troubled waters.

On the fourth for the first time it snowed, but only a little. Then the weather became fine again; it is magnificent, and if the English do not take advantage of it to come and attack us we can no longer count on them this autumn.

On the seventh Sieur de Langy Montegron left for the end of the bay for a raid with a detachment of forty men, twelve of them Indians. It was five or six days ago that the Marquis de Montcalm negotiated with the Indians for this detachment. What a race! And how one complains of being forced to use them. We still have about thirty in camp who wage war on the poultry, sheep, and wine barrels. They are very clever thieves, all the more so because they are sure of impunity.

On the eighth the Chevalier de Lévis returned from St. Frederic. He found 950 Canadians, and this detachment is composed of the good kind, almost all *voyaguers*. One recognizes them easily by their looks, by their size, and because all of them are tattooed on their bodies with figures of plants or animals. The operation is long and painful. The figure is outlined by pricking the skin with a needle and printed in by burning powder in the holes. One would not pass for a man among the Indians of the Far West if he had not had himself tattooed.

They tell us another one thousand or twelve hundred Canadians and eighty Indians are coming. The first will be employed in digging a ditch around St. Frederic with a double palisade, one in the ditch, the other on the berm, until we have news of the enemy which will allow us to send them back.

Almost all the Indians of the Sault and of the Lake have gone alone and without French leaders to attack Colonel Bradstreet's force.

From the third to the twelfth different bodies of Canadians kept arriving at St. Frederic; today, the thirteenth, they total 1,950. They are employed on the ditch being made around the fort and on surrounding the outer houses with a palisade. Yesterday about 150 Iroquois or Abnakis arrived. They do not propose to stay here very long. As soon as there is news of the enemy, which we expect on Sieur de Langy's return, the Canadians and Indians will be dispensed with.

Journal for 1758

On the eleventh Sieur Coutrot arrived from the post at the bay [Green Bay], which he commands, with four Menominees and four Short Ears [Ottawas]. The name of these last comes from the fact that they wear their ears like Europeans, that is to say, as nature made them without artificially lengthening them.

On the twelfth news from Quebec. They have learned that the English are established at Gaspé, in Penouille Bay, that they have taken there a fort and houses, all prefabricated. In a week at most the establishment was completed.[66] They did the same at Beauséjour and at Halifax. The very same day, so as to say, in the evening sees a fort and a village erected where in the morning was only grass. Their fleet consisted of nine ships of the line and thirty transports.

Thus behold Canada surrounded on all sides. I have heard it said of the English that they would always first seize the crown of the hat, which would let them make themselves masters of the brim. Only peace can save this colony today. I cannot conceive how France has failed to make at Gaspé a solid establishment and a strong place.

It is the doorway of Canada and its location is infinitely preferable to that of Louisbourg as the key to the colony, as a depot, and as a trading center for all the fisheries. My fear, now that the action of the English has made us realize the importance of this place, is that the English, supposing that they are willing to make peace this winter, will wish to require that France shall not make any establishment at Gaspé.

The same courier informed us that the *Aigle*, King's ship of fifty guns, was wrecked on August 8 on the Shoals of Quincampoix, eight leagues from Mécatina.[67] The crew was saved and had for sustenance since the day of the wreck only thirty quarters of wheat thrown up on the shore by the waves.

This ship carried recruits, provisions, munitions, and the clothing for our battalions. The ship *Légère* has been sent to look for

---

[66] A false report. Gaspé was raided but not occupied.

[67] On the south shore of Labrador about halfway between Anticosti and the Strait of Belle Isle.

this unfortunate crew. It is doubtful if the season will allow bringing them back to Quebec. The officer sent in a shallop by the *Aigle's* captain to bring this sad news has been continually held up by the weather.

Since the greatly excessive prices of provisions and of all goods, shameful result of a visible monopoly, has raised a great unrest in the minds of the officers, today deprived of almost all existence without going into debt, the Marquis de Montcalm has assembled the troop commanders, two captains and two lieutenants per battalion. He has told them of the representations that he has made and continues to make in their behalf to the Intendant, that he proposed to him methods of making subsistence possible, especially to the lieutenants whose pay is absolutely insufficient. He added that he has also reported to the court the present state of affairs and begged an increase, either in pay, or in ration allowance; that he hoped his remonstrances [would have effect], that, moreover, the true soldier was not only he who could face danger, but also he who knew how to be firm in the face of difficulties and troubles of all sorts; that grumblings were superfluous, produced no remedy, could become contagious and incendiary; that obedience and devotion to the King, to the country, and to his superiors was like the glass in a mirror which the lightest breath would tarnish.

I confess that up to now part of the officers have lived as in the depths of peace and the greatest abundance, that their gambling has been enormous, their table covered with delicacies, and that finally, at the expense in truth of their patrimony or of their creditors, luxury, good cheer, the easy life, alone seem to occupy those whose only object should be glory. But alas! I say it with bitterness in my heart, desire for glory, fine sentiments, emulation, honor, what has become of you?

Our soul is disgraced; vile interest alone is the cause and objective of our conduct. One almost blushes in doing a good deed, solely for the glory of having done it.

Our ears are no more shocked by this which shocked those of our fathers. They say ——

Journal for 1758

End of Journal

☞ CONTINUATION OF THE JOURNAL FROM OCTOBER 18 TO NOVEMBER 3 : I left Carillon on the eighteenth; I visited in passing the works built to make St. Frederic safe from a sudden attack. They consist of a palisaded fort, a palisade at the foot of the berm,[68] an enclosure around the houses, a powder magazine inside the fort, the repair of the ramparts, that is to say, of the banquette, to allow fire from the ramparts. This place in its present state need fear no sudden attack; it is always something to force the enemy to bring up his artillery; but the artillery once in position, it would be necessary to surrender.

I remarked at St. Jean in passing the necessity of establishing a good hospital there and considerable body of barracks.

I reached Montreal the twenty-first. They were in the greatest consternation there. They believed the enemy [to be] at Carillon or ready to return there, and this on the report of several Iroquois and the depositions of prisoners made at Fort Duquesne in the adventure of which I am going to give the details.

I took with me a prisoner captured by Sieur Langy Montegron between Fort Edward and Albany. His statement positively contradicted what they believed so firmly at Montreal. He declared a project formed by the enemy to abandon their position at the end of Lake St. Sacrement, part of the troops already withdrawn, a great many empty wagons sent to the English camp; the undertaking by Colonel Bradstreet, a great expediter of transport, to remove within a week the barges, artillery, munitions, and provisions. Because of this deposition, which the early approach of winter and the inaction of the enemy render so reasonable, the Marquis de Montcalm took it upon himself to send back the greatest part of the Canadians, needed at home for their fields, which they had not previously had time to tend. Moreover, all the useless consumption [of supplies] under our present circumstances is a lost battle. They will tremble still more at Montreal over this

---

[68] A narrow ledge along the top of the wall which forms the inside face of the moat, and from which the parapet rises.

action. They imagine Carillon, abandoned by its best defenders, attacked and taken. I was on the point of starting back, and the Marquis de Vaudreuil hesitated as to whether he should not order the released Canadians back again. Several days later, however, events proved the wisdom of the actions of the Marquis de Montcalm. Wolf, sent to the English camp to carry the dispatches by which the Marquis de Vaudreuil announced the execution of the capitulation of Frontenac, found the camp almost struck and the army ready to leave it.

It was useless to make any mystery about it to him, for he had seen everything; besides, they made no bones about it. Two days later one of our parties will find the camp absolutely abandoned, the defensive works, the storehouses, the huts burned and still smoking. A deserter arrived at Carillon at the same time says that the enemy during the night had buried bombs and shot and sunk their bark and part of their barges, doubtless to save having to portage them next spring. Acting on this report, the Marquis de Montcalm sent a detachment with some specialists to try to unearth their artillery caches, to find and haul out the bark and the barges. This detachment found twenty quarters of salt pork, two hundred barrels of lime, the location of the bark, fifty sunken barges, and several other caches in a neighboring swamp.

He also sent off several little war parties so that the Indians might be of some little use before their departure. The withdrawal of the army was set for November 1 and the days to follow. Berry and La Reine, destined to winter in the Quebec government, left Carillon on the first and second, on the third, Languedoc, whose quarters are in the Trois Rivières government; and on the fourth, fifth, and sixth, La Sarre, Royal Roussillon, Guyenne, and Béarn, who have theirs at that of Montreal.

The soldiers of La Marine in the same way have departed in accordance with where they are quartered. The Marquis de Montcalm should leave on the fifth.

The garrison left at Carillon consists of four hundred men, three hundred regulars and one hundred of La Marine, under command of Sieur de Hébécourt, captain of colony troops, the same who commanded there last winter. There remain there also some sixty Indians, as much for hunting as for scouting, and about the same number of Canadians.

This so prompt retreat of the enemy from Lake St. Sacrement is somewhat strange. It is difficult to divine the reasons for it. What I know is that it has been very favorable to us and that the enemy ended this campaign as they started it, in not doing us a hundredth part of the harm they could have.

The Marquis de Montcalm, before leaving Carillon, received the Intendant's answer to his representations on the disproportion between the officers' means and the excessive cost of provisions.

M. Bigot in his letter asserts certain principles on the trade of the colony, pretends that he can tax neither the merchandise nor even the eatables, bread excepted, that he can no longer buy at current prices wine, meat, and bread for the account of the King and resell them to officers at a lower price. However, in view of the too well-demonstrated impossibility of an officer living today on his pay, he takes it upon himself to increase it by fifty sous a day for captains and thirty for lieutenants.

It would have been worth more to reverse this, perhaps even giving the four livres to the lieutenants alone, for a captain has much more resources. It has also been ruled that the forced economy will be paid by the Commissary of Stores on the basis of a livre per ration. The hitherto contrary practice was a crying injustice.

When I arrived at Montreal, a deputation of Onondagas had been there for two days.

In the course of the first councils they referred to the words of M. de Longueuil on his visit to their villages and confirmed them by the strings of wampum and the belts he had given them in this connection; a customary ceremony among them [but] very useless in the final analysis. Other belts to cover our dead in this campaign.

In the succeeding councils the Marquis de Vaudreuil reproached them for not having warned him of the English project against Frontenac, of not even having closed the road to them, as they were bound to by their promises and their belts.

Vague answers, phrases empty of meaning, long discourses, new promises, nothing positive. They sent them off with fine presents. Note that this embassy was composed only of Onondagas who spoke only for themselves and never in the name of the Five Nations.

Abbé Piquet returns to La Presentation. Quarrels with the military commander there had estranged the two. He claims that in Indian missions only priests are needed. Is he right? Or rather is this a pretention of ecclesiastical despotism? It is certain that he himself formed this establishment, that since his departure affairs have gone badly there, that the Indians ask for him back again.

So it is proper then to send him back. He has not, however, won his case entirely. There will always be a military commander there. The former one, it is true, has been recalled and M. Benoist, who replaces him, is the most honest man in the colony and joins to honesty, knowledge, understanding, and zeal.

The English send many belts into the villages of the Far West; their promises are as considerable as our misery is great. The disaffection has already commenced. If wise measures are not taken by sending the most skillful [emissaries] there at once, there is everything to fear.

I return to the affair of Fort Duquesne of September 14.

The English court having sent the order to attack Fort Duquesne, they held in Carolina and Pennsylvania a body of seven to eight thousand men destined for this operation, under command of Brigadier General Forbes. But the order was not to make this attack before the end of October, in order that the Indians, little accustomed to remain long in the same place, would have left a permanent camp and that at the same time, their long sojourn there in the continual waiting for a nearby invasion, would have resulted in a great consumption of things of all sorts.

The English army then did not have to leave its quarters until very late. Only at the end of July did General Forbes send a body of two thousand men under Colonel Bukley [Bouquet], to open up a route different from that of Braddock, shorter and less difficult. This body built in sequence three forts to establish and ensure this communication.

Journal for 1758

Colonel Bukley [Bouquet] at the end of August detached Sieur Grant, Major of Montgomery's Highlanders, with eight hundred men to make a night assault on the Indian camp at Fort Duquesne. The march was made without discovery, but when he came in sight of the camp the fires that the Indians were accustomed to make opposite each of their cabins had gone out.

A major of the Virginia forces, whom he ordered to attack with four hundred men, got lost and returned without doing anything. As daylight was near, Major Grant contented himself with setting fire to a storehouse situated on the left of the camp and placed himself with his troop on a mountain which dominated the fort.

At the first movement the surprised Indians fell back to the other side of the river, but the soldiers of La Marine and the Canadians quickly fell from all directions upon the enemy who, astonished by an attack of a sort new to them, made no resistance. Disorder seized them; the officers were not listened to; an engineer who had gone ahead to reconnoiter the fort was killed and his escort dispersed or destroyed.

The Indians, reanimated by this initial success, crossed the river again, attacked from their side. It was no longer anything but a precipitate flight on the part of the English, who were pursued until noon.

Almost all the officers were captured or killed, and one could say that this detachment was entirely destroyed. One circumstance lessened the good of this affair, it is that the very same day the Indians left to return to their villages without anything being able to stop them. One then is still very worried over the fate of Fort Duquesne which, according to all probability, will have been attacked by the end of October. If the attack is not successful for the English, the remains of their troops will winter in the forts built by Colonel Bukley [Bouquet] and provisioned with this in mind.

The body of Canadians who marched under M. Duplessis' command to reoccupy Frontenac, in order to pass the winter there and build barracks, has fallen back to La Presentation. It was reduced to sixty or eighty poorly equipped men, the winter quarters were difficult to build, the wood necessary for construction distant, and they could not go to look for it without much trouble and loss of time. They decided to build them [winter quarters] at La Presentation and to put off to spring the re-establishment of Frontenac.

News from the lower river. The English, whom they said had taken to Gaspé prefabricated houses and blockhouses, with a view of establishing themselves there, have withdrawn completely after having destroyed the habitations, as well as those of Mont-Louis[69] and having unsuccessfully planned similar action against Miramichi.

It seems that they have really established themselves at St. Jean River. A body of four thousand men have, they say, landed there and built a permanent fort.

Father Germain and his Indians abandon the place and fall back on us. They say that they will establish themselves at Mont-Louis to the number of eighty cabins. They also expect M. de Boishebert with the rest of his detachment, part having returned.

NOVEMBER 3–11 : I left Montreal on the third in a bateau taking five English officers to Quebec, where I arrived on the evening of the sixth, after having been shipwrecked below "*Les Ecureuils.*"[70] I passed the night stranded on a rock raised more than six feet above the low tide mark, I had been forced to abandon the bateau which the high seas had smashed and to reach shore at daybreak, making more than three-quarters of a league through the water, since the tide had started to rise. There already was ice along the edges.

It has been decided that I will embark on the ship the *Victoire*, eighteen-gun privateer from St. Malo, belonging to the Commissary of Supplies. The other vessels carrying dispatches are the *Outarde*, King's flute of twenty-six guns, and the *Hardi*.

Left the sixth; the cold has been extraordinary for the season; the eighth, ninth, and tenth it got down to minus 14 degrees [1 °F.].

[69] On the extreme northern portion of the Gaspé Peninsula.
[70] On the north shore some twenty-six miles above Quebec.

Journal for 1758

The Berry regiment, which was coming to its quarters, has been dispersed, held up in the ice.

The bateaux arrive, one after the other, several remain caught in the shoals [ice floes?], and the men come by land. Already they know of five frozen to death and every day they bring in some who are frostbitten. They are very worried about three bateaux that have been seen caught in the ice of Lake St. Francis, and which they appear to be trying vainly to aid.

Languedoc will have trouble reaching its winter quarters, for the Sorel River is almost frozen over. It is also said that La Sarre, Royal Roussillon, Guyenne, and Béarn have been scattered over Lake Champlain by a furious storm. One waits news with the greatest of alarm, as well as news of the Chevalier de Lévis, whose bateau no one has seen. In Europe one could not conceive this sort of danger and the horror of finding oneself dying of hunger and cold.

Meanwhile the ice floes are forming as well as the ice along the shore, and one begins to find that the ships are too late in leaving. The Marquis de Vaudreuil's dispatches do not come; here are four days of a fine southwester lost, and who can say what will happen if they still delay a little more?

Perhaps one cannot leave, perhaps at Cape Moraska one will be caught in the ice. Such an unfortunate business is not without example here. What a country! What a voyage! One should be a civilian!

On the eleventh the Marquis de Vaudreuil's packets at last came, and we go aboard this evening.

No news from Fort Duquesne.

If the wind does not veer to the northeast, tomorrow at five in the morning, time the tide starts falling, we set sail. *Sic te Diva potens Cipri, etc.*[71]

Journal of Trip from Quebec to France
November, 1758

I embarked on the eleventh at midnight on board the *Victoire*,

---

[71] "So may the goddess of Cyprus [Venus] guide you."

privateer built at St. Malo, designed for twenty-four guns but carrying eighteen, of 150 ton burden. We have a crew of 55, several of them Canadians, skilled pilots of the river, destined to bring the Commissary of Supplies' ships back here in the spring.

Two local pilots are charged with taking the vessel to Île aux Coudres.

Hoisted sail at five o'clock in the morning, wind southeast, and tide falling, in company with the *Outarde*, King's flute, of 600 tons burden, carrying twenty-two guns, and the *Hardi*, merchant ship of 150 tons. These two vessels and ours carry in triplicate the packets for the court. On board the *Outarde* are nearly forty passengers, among them M. Doreil, army commissary intendant, MM. de Carlan, de la Bretèche, officers wounded at July 8 affair and who are going home because of their wounds, and M. de Goffreteau, also a captain in the Berry regiment. I am the only passenger in the *Victoire*.

While passing through the Traverse I noted how important a battery built at Cape Tourmente would be, one such as we had examined and suggested at the end of last fall in a memoir concerning the defense of Quebec and of the river. I do not know whether they will carry it out. They have adopted part, a little late in truth, that of defending the descent [of the Traverse] by redoubts and lines. M. de Pontleroy has started to locate and mark them out. The unlooked for snow of the first part of the month forced him to interrupt this work.

Without contradiction, if the terrain would permit, a fort would be still better, or, best of all, the suggested battery and a fort on the dominating heights. It would suffice to prevent an army landed higher up[river] from undertaking anything against this battery. This location is one of those where a small number [can] stop a multitude.

I would also like two forts, one on the western point and the other at the eastern end of the Isle of Orleans.

The *Outarde* anchored two leagues above the Traverse not daring, in her capacity as a navy ship, of making it on a falling tide. The *Hardi* followed us.

Journal for 1758

☞ NOVEMBER 12–13 : At two o'clock the wind swung to the northwest. We continued on the way and came to anchor at Île aux Coudres in eight fathoms. The river pilots left us and the control of the ship returned to Sieur Gilbert, a man familiar with the lower river and the one who worked the fisheries of the stations below.

During the night our anchor failed to hold, it was only noticed later after we had already drifted considerably. We were so nearly ashore that the rudder touched bottom. At once another anchor was lowered. But the wind coming on shore and striking us abeam, we were in the greatest danger of our lives if the wind had increased, for these shores are perpendicular and rocky. We remained three hours in this critical position. Then, having experienced several squalls, we managed to profit from the following maneuver: we raised one of our anchors, we hung on the other, all the crew at the ready. At the first squall we cut the cable and by means of the rudder, which thrust the ship ahead, and the falling tide we gradually went about, after which we hauled the sails; little by little the wind filled them and pushed us on our way.

Some time later, the wind becoming north-northeast and northeast, it was necessary to go about and to return to gain the anchorage at Île aux Coudres, or La Prairie[72] where we anchored in eleven fathoms, alongside a ravine which marks the best anchorage.

This adventure, which could have been well-nigh fatal to us, is sad in that it made us lose an anchor; only three more remain, one of which is of little use. God save us from losing another and from all other danger! When will we be so fortunate as to gain the open sea? The cold is excessive here and we cannot have any fires. We look forward to the sea air, it will be milder.

There should be two forts here, one at Les Éboulements[73] at Pointe aux Bouleaux, the other at La Prairie. With these two forts, the battery at Cape Tourmente and the two forts on the Isle of Orleans, one could no longer fear an attack on Quebec.

☞ NOVEMBER 13–14 : At six in the evening the *Outarde* ar-

[72] Unidentified.
[73] A settlement just north of the eastern end of Île aux Coudres.

rived and, having dropped her anchor to moor alongside us, the cable broke and the current drove her on us. We scarcely had time to veer our cable to avoid her. The danger was great, for a ship such as ours to be struck by a vessel the size of the *Outarde* would have broken us, with both wind and current driving here strongly.

This afternoon our pilot from Île aux Coudres came aboard to bring us sand. I sent letters by him to Quebec and Montreal.

At seven in the morning the snow *Prince de Condé* appeared at the head of Île aux Coudres. The wind being weak and barely giving her steerageway, she just missed being carried by the current into the rapid, vast, and rock-strewn gulf, almost inevitably fatal to any ship carried there. Finally she escaped it and came to anchor below us. The wind came from the west and southwest but too weak to allow us to breast the tide, which is of prodigious force in these quarters.

During the calm we saw many white porpoises.

NOVEMBER 14–15: M. Salomon, captain of the *Outarde*, sent his gig for me and I dined on board. The company is numerous, consequently a great number of useless hands, much burden when it is necessary to maneuver.

The captain of our ship has assigned his crew their quarters in case of combat. We have been obliged to put two cannon in the hold, having only enough people to serve sixteen. My place is on the quarter-deck.

At five o'clock, the southwest wind having freshened and the tide falling, we set sail, a full moon in a clear sky allowing us to steer in sight of land. The *Outarde*, as a King's ship and thus forbidden to sail in the river at night, remained at anchor. The *Hardi* and the *Prince de Condé* also remained.

At nine o'clock we made the crossing to the south from Cap aux Oies[74] to Cap au Diable,[75] which is eight leagues. From this last cape to Cape Moraska we met a great amount of ice, already

---

[74] Just east of Les Éboulements.
[75] On the south shore due east from Île aux Coudres.

quite heavy, formed in the almost still waters of many bays which edge this coastline.

🙢 NOVEMBER 15–16 : Half an hour after midnight we left the dangerous passage between Isle Verte and Isle Rouge.[76] Upstream from both are shoals and the channel between the two is difficult to keep to, the start of the tide drawing one to the Isle Verte shoal, and its end toward that of Isle Rouge. It is a case of fearing as they say: *Incidit in Scyllam cupiens vitare Caribdim.*[77]

At five o'clock we had passed Bic[78] and consequently were out of soundings, Bic being the last anchorage. A good wind going down the river. The southwest winds continued brisk up to ten o'clock. Then they calmed, and all the rest of the day we could only steer the ship with the foresail and the fore-topsail. The current, however, always made us descend a little.

🙢 NOVEMBER 16–17 : Little wind for twenty-four hours. At first calm, the ship without steerage way. At five o'clock a little southwest breeze, freshened at half-past nine, under four main sails and mizzen topsail; weather foggy and raining.

Our day's run estimated at twelve leagues. At noon we found ourselves passing by Mont-Louis. It is there the dwellings were that the English destroyed this summer. During the night and morning we met several icebergs.

🙢 NOVEMBER 17–18 : The wind steady to west and northwest; nice fresh one. At two o'clock we set the studding sails, upper and lower, steering E¼SE and ESE. Good fresh wind all night until four in the morning. Since then little wind up to noon. Then we found ourselves passing Anse aux Griffons, five leagues above Gaspé.

From the seventeenth to the eighteenth, Saturday, the winds ranged from west to southwest by north; fairly fresh. We made several tacks, the weather very cloudy. At noon we thought we were ESE of Pointe de Forillon, about fifteen leagues from Gaspé.

[76] Two islands near the mouth of the Saguenay River.
[77] "He falls upon Scylla when eager to avoid Charybdis."
[78] On the south shore forty miles below the mouth of the Saguenay.

ʒ❧ NOVEMBER 19 : Imperceptibly the wind shifted to southwest, fairly fresh. Our route has been southeast and we count on having made thirty-eight leagues; the weather cloudy and foggy, at noon it cleared. The observation gave [a latitude] of 48° 15′.

ʒ❧ NOVEMBER 20 : After the observation we steered SE ¼ S expecting to be midway between Cap Ray[79] and Cap Nord,[80] and consequently passing beyond Cap à l'Anguille[81] and that of Ray. But the horizon being foggy, they were mistaken on the estimate of the run, for violent currents which pass between Anticosti and Isle du Petit Nord or of Newfoundland and which attract [one] into Baye St. George[82] and a strong sea from the south, to which enough attention was not paid, cast us farther to the north than we thought. Through a clearing at three o'clock we clearly saw Cap à l'Anguille which bore S 5°W. The wind was then west-southwest and we had the cape of the entrance of Baye St. George [before us].

We came up into the wind; but as the captain saw that he could not double Cap à l'Anguille, he went about at four o'clock to run to the NW and at eleven o'clock, the wind coming from west or northwest we tacked and this morning at eight o'clock the aforesaid cape lay to the east about four leagues. At noon that of Ray bore NE¼E at nearly the same distance.

We would run a great risk if we entered Baye St. George: First, the wind strengthening and night preventing view of the shore, we could be driven ashore. Second, in 17—— Sieur ———, one of the most skilled pilots of this route, having thus got into this bay, was caught in the ice, lost his ship, and the crew was forced to winter in Newfoundland. What a pitiful situation! Such are the dangers of all sorts of this navigation, one of the most difficult there is. Better two thousand leagues in the open sea than two hundred leagues between [two] shores.

[79] The southwestern tip of Newfoundland.
[80] The northern tip of Cape Breton Island.
[81] On the coast of Newfoundland.
[82] Just north of Cape Anguille.

Journal for 1758

In general, the surest way to sail out this gulf is to come, when the weather permits, to seek the Isle aux Oiseaux.[83] One then finds oneself in the middle of the channel and able to take advantage of whatever wind may come. Good northwest [wind], 18°.

👉 NOVEMBER 21 : The winds have been from north to northwest, good and fresh, all sail set. Steered to the south until two o'clock, then every four hours we took a quarter [point] east, in order to gain the open sea and a good distance from Cap Ray.
Estimated run SE 1°E, 56 leagues.
Estimated latitude on Koulen's Dutch map cy[?], 45° 11'.
Estimated longitude same, 305° 33'.

👉 NOVEMBER 22 : Wind northwest, very fresh, all sail set until three o'clock, when they furled the topgallant sails and took in all the reefs in the topsails. They furled them at eight o'clock and brailed up the mainsail and we remained under foresail; the sea very rough and rolling, the wind estimated E 5°N and according to our altitude [observation] we have made ENE 3°E 64 2/3 leagues.
Observed latitude, 46° 17'.
Estimated longitude, 329° 54'.

👉 NOVEMBER 23 : Winds north-northwest very fresh up to midnight, when they hauled to the west and afterwards from southwest to south. Weather very cloudy; some hail. Yesterday at two o'clock we hauled our mainsail aboard and set our topsails, fully reefed. This morning the main yard broke. We repaired it. We steered E¼SE and made according to our reckoning E¼NE 4° 30' E 57 1/3 leagues.
Estimated latitude, 46° 35'.
Estimated longitude, 333° 30'.

👉 NOVEMBER 24 : Winds continued south to southwest very fresh until 6 o'clock, when they swung to west and west-northwest, high wind; weather very cloudy and rain until midnight. We steered E¼SE, but not being able to hold [our course] be-

[83] Bird Rocks, north of Cape Breton and west of Cape Ray.

cause of the sea and the tempest, the captain eased off against the waves.

At noon: course estimated E 5°N, 57 1/3 leagues.

Estimated latitude, 47°.

Estimated longitude, 337° 40′.

Since we are taking a course north of the Azores, we must expect greater seas and still heavier winds. In this season especially navigation is frightful there, but it is faster than by the southern [route], and one runs less risk of meeting enemies. We are suffering in this miserable hulk more than one can express. The rolling is horrible and continual. One does not know where to put himself nor how to keep himself [there]. One is in danger of breaking his neck at any instant. The shock of the waves, which follow each other almost without respite, flood us with this vile salt water. Add that there is no question of [boiling a] kettle; that our beasts and fowl die in flocks. I do not speak of the dampness nor the cold which one must endure without a fire and all day in the open air. Detestable position and one which would be a punishment well proportioned to very considerable crimes. Ah! As Horace said with reason: *Illi robur et aes triplex circa pectus erat, etc.*[84]

NOVEMBER 25 : Winds north-northwest, always violent and with squalls, the seas very high; the weather very obscure. Continuation of tempests and torments. We always steered E ¼ SE so that we estimate E ¼ NE 4° E, 54 2/3 leagues.

Estimated latitude, 47° 22′.

Estimated longitude, 341° 40′

Tonight I noticed that in the tossing of the waves, the sea appeared luminous, even brilliant. What is the cause of this phenomenon? But rather what is the cause of the light or of the colors? Those who account for it in the movement of particles have an easier way to explain the preceding phenomenon.

"Do not all fixed bodies," says Newton in his *Optics*, "when heated to a certain point give off light? Is not this emission caused

[84] "Oak and triple bronze were around his breast [who first dared launch his ship on the sea]."

Journal for 1758

by the vibrating movement of their particles? Do not all bodies containing much earthly parts, sulphurous ones especially, shine all the time that their particles are sufficiently agitated, whatever may be the cause of it; warmth, friction, percussion, putrefaction, vital movement, etc.? For instance the water of the ocean shines at night during a violent storm."

Other philosophers indicate other causes for this phenomenon. *Non nostrum inter vos tantas componere lites.*[85]

ঌ NOVEMBER 26 : Same punishment as on preceding days. Northwest winds, very violent and squally; hail. Nightime especially frightful. Steering ESE. Estimated [course] E 5°N, 65 2/3 leagues.

At noon observed sun at 49°, but doubtful observation because of high seas and little sun.

Estimated latitude, 47° 40'.
Longitude, 346° 29'.

ঌ NOVEMBER 27 : This night we were horribly tossed about. An imagination most prolific in troublesome ideas could not come within a hundredth of outlining the unbearable details of our position. The despotic rolling tyrannizes not only our life, our movements, our attitudes, our rest; one must struggle against it for each morsel one wishes to eat or whatever need one has to satisfy.

The winds have continued from northwest to north, high wind with violent squalls until midnight, when it calmed, and a little afterward the wind veered to northeast, fairly fresh, the sea still very high, the weather very unsettled. At noon we made an observation.

Latitude, 49° 8'.

By our reckoning we were only at 47° 40', the run according to our reckoning having been only eastward at most.

The run, corrected since leaving the gulf is E¼NE 5°E, 367 leagues before the wind.

Corrected longitude, 347° 34'.

---

[85] "Not for us to settle such great contests between you."–Vergil.

> NOVEMBER 28: It was calm up until eight o'clock in the evening, when a very brisk south wind came. We kept our topsails until midnight and then remained under our lower sails. This morning at eight o'clock brailed up and furled the mainsail and continued under the foresail.

At noon reckoned the run NE ¼ E, 20 leagues.
Estimated latitude, 49° 42'.
Estimated longitude, 349° 12'.

A sailor died and was cast into the sea this morning. These burials are done without expense or ceremony. Here one dies as he has lived.

> NOVEMBER 29: Southeast winds prevailed, great tempest with squalls. Frightful night, fearful rolling, no [safe] position to take, the blows of the seas wet down every part of the ship. Add further to this more than distressing condition, the chagrin of seeing us going backward rather than advancing, and one will find that Pantagruel most rightly cried out in a similar situation: "Oh, three and four times happy the gardener who plants cabbages, for he always has one foot on the ground and the other is only away from it the length of the blade of the shovel."

We brailed up the foresail and lay to under bare poles. At eight in the morning the winds calmed and veered southwest; hoisted the two lower sails and the topsails, fully reefed, steered SE; but the sea being very rough and the ship straining much, it was necessary to strike the topsails.

The weather squally.
Run reckoned N ¼ NE, 20 leagues.
Observed latitude, 50° 42'.
Observed longitude, 349° 30'.

> NOVEMBER 30: Southwest winds prevailed, quite fresh, the sea very rough. Under small sails we steered from SE ¼ E to E up to six in the morning. The wind then came south and south-southeast; violent tempest which obliged us to brail, strike all sails, and remain under bare poles. Oh God! The sea has no end for us, even its shores are missing. Just as vast is that sea of sad reflections

Journal for 1758

through which the imagination wanders or stops and holds. But there is no remedy at all. One must overlook these troubles, this anguish of mind of all sorts, as the fable says that Saturn overlooked the stones.

Run reckoned E, 19 2/3 leagues.
Latitude, 50° 42′.
Longitude, 350° 59′.

ᛞ DECEMBER 1 : We had placed hope in the new moon which comes this evening, for does not a drowning man seize a rotten plank? Vain hope; the tempest continued from the south to southeast; the sea very high. We remained under bare poles, lying to from ESE to ENE up to midnight, when we went on the other tack.

This night St. Elmo fire appeared on our foremast, warning and sign of storm, say the sailors. Oh, that this gloomy fire no longer shine for me!

Run reckoned WNW, 8 leagues.
Estimated latitude, 51° 35′.
Estimated longitude, 350° 30′.

ᛞ DECEMBER 2–5 : The winds have all the time continued from southeast to east, storm continual or almost so. We remained lying to or under topsails, sometimes with bare poles, sometimes with two jibs. How long time is in so violent and critical a condition! Friday the crew made a vow and subscribed for a solemn mass upon first reaching land in order to secure a change of weather. Let one judge by this action of these irreligious people how bad our situation was!

> Oh Neptune! in these times of fear and horror,
> Why thy foaming waves spew out their fury,
> Does't thou wish to plunge the world into primary chaos?
> The sun is lost in a profound night;
> Thy long roarings make the air shudder,
> And even up to Heaven thou showest Hell.

Ah! I would be tempted to pardon Aeneas the tears he poured

forth in the storms he endured. A hero can indeed be one and yet be fearful of drowning.

This contrary weather according to our reckoning made us fall back sixty-eight leagues. According to all the navigators, and we have a great number of them [on board], it is most extraordinary that a southeast wind should last so long, especially in a continuous tempest.

From Monday evening until 2:00 P.M. Tuesday we at last had some rest, calm weather, fine sun, we revived. Gentle [sun]light, we see thee again! and it is with a transport of joy which is felt but cannot be expressed. We utilized this day in airing out the ship which was poisoned by the mixture of bad odors of all sorts which were concentrated below decks.

꙳ DECEMBER 6 : South winds prevailed, nice and brisk, the weather cloudy. We steered ESE 5 E.
Run reckoned, 38 leagues.
Latitude, 49° 42′.
Longitude, 349° 31′.

꙳ DECEMBER 7 : South winds prevailed. Very brisk. At night, storm appears, fearful sea. A wave flooded our false deck four fingers deep. The alarm at this blow was greater than the harm, for they cried out that the side planks were stove in. Had this been so, we would have certainly perished. Knowledge of the structure of a ship is like that of anatomy. Both are most proper to compare [with each other]. I would say not only cautiously but also meticulously. What preserves our life at sea? A displaced nail puts it in danger, just as a broken vein [in the brain], so as to say, destroys the human body.

Since midnight we remained under the foresail. Wind swung to southeast.
Estimated run 5°N, 61 leagues.
Estimated latitude, 49° 58′.
Estimated longitude, 354° 13′.

꙳ DECEMBER 8 : Southwest to west winds prevailed, very

fresh; rain up to 6:00 P.M. when wind shifted to northwest, still very fresh; the sea very high from the south.

Estimated run E 3°N, 43 leagues.
Observed latitude, 51° 15′.
Estimated longitude, 357° 34′.

℘ DECEMBER 9 : Northwest to west winds prevailed, good and fresh, the seas always high, the waves from south-southwest.

Estimated run 5°S, 73 leagues.
Estimated latitude, 49° 46′.
Estimated longitude, 3° 12′.

℘ DECEMBER 10 : West to northwest winds prevailed, always good and fresh, and the waves high and abeam.

Estimated run ESE 5°E, 69 leagues.
Estimated latitude, 48° 46′.
Estimated longitude, 8° 14′.

℘ DECEMBER 11–14 : It seems that we must experience evils of all sorts. The latitude observed Friday at noon was so different from what our reckoning gave us, that we feared that we had been carried north by violent currents. Consequently we switched until Thursday more to the south than to the east. We also judged that our compass bore too much north and in the direction of our course we added for error to the sixteen degrees of variation. Sunday at midnight we sounded and found fine sand, speckled with black and muddy, at seventy fathoms. All the soundings we made up to Monday noon were sixty to seventy fathoms, and all of the same sort, except two which showed a bottom of heavy gravel mixed with shining stones of various colors. Now these two bottoms agree equally with those of the approaches to Belle-Île in the Cul-de-Sac and to those of the Sorlingues at the entrance of the Channel. Since we had always switched to the southeast after Friday's observation, it was quite simple in accordance with these soundings, to believe ourselves in the vicinity of Belle-Île and we so thought. The always foggy sky did not permit us to take an observation during all this time.

From Monday midnight until Wednesday at 2:00 A.M. we had a frightful tempest of west-northwest winds. We had to remain under bare poles without being able to raise any sail to make sight of land. The boltrope of our mainsail was broken away by a blast of wind and it was no small operation to brail it [the sail] up, we could not even bind it up entirely. The force of the wind made the ship heel way over and sometimes it had difficulty in coming back. The sea soon increased and became frightful. The waves overwhelmed us, they came on from all directions. Our false deck was almost stove in. Still that was not the worst risk. We had hoped to keep well at sea, but the wind beat us abeam and our drift [downwind] was at least half a league per hour. How long thirty hours are in such a situation! Death lay before our eyes, and what a death! For cast ashore in such a tempest there would be no hope of safety. The sailor makes vows when there is no other resource; they made them then. The crew vowed to go in procession, barefooted, and clad in shirts, to hear the mass already promised on Wednesday, December 1, at the first land the ship should reach. Wednesday at about two o'clock in the morning the wind died down and the sea gradually fell. A fine moon appeared and dissipated the mist. Wednesday morning, a clear day with a northwest wind, we headed southeast to make land between Belle-Île and Île d'Yeu.

At noon we shot the sun, but what was our surprise to find ourselves at 49° 55' of latitude, twelve leagues west of Les Sorlingues and sailing headlong into the Bristol Channel! Without this observation what would have become of us? And why with such false compasses were we not lost a thousand times? We must have been north of 55° of latitude, fortunate in such stormy weather and long nights of not being lost on the coast of Ireland, fortunate to have secured this observation which warned us just as we were entering the Bristol Channel, or, one might say, the wolf's jaws.

Now how to shape our course with such compasses! We allowed two quarters of error to the north and for further safety in the afternoon we headed south-southwest to raise the coast of England. We met three ships, one of three masts to leeward and we

Journal for 1758

bearing east, and two to windward, brigantines, the first sailing east-southeast and the second east. The sight of these vessels did not make us change our course at all. Since our purpose was to make for Ouessant and to make land east of it, at four in the afternoon under a northwest wind we headed south, reckoning that with our compass error it would [actually] be southeast, which was found correct by the landfall which we made Thursday morning three or four leagues and NE ¼ N of Ouessant.

The heavy mist and the calm then did not allow us to proceed and caused us keen alarm. Without a pilot, so near a coast with many rocky shoals in weather so obscure that we had to fear lest the wind should drive [us on them] after dark. And sad experience had taught us that a furious blow always followed these calms so unusual at this time of year. At daybreak we saw to windward a little single-masted vessel that the mist soon hid from our eyes. The log ends here.

Supplement and Corrections to the Journal for 1758–59

ON JUNE 3 the British with 24 ships of the line, 20 frigates, and two fire ships and about 150 transports entered Gabarus Bay.[86] The same day they fired on the defenses made to prevent this landing.

The fifth and sixth they tried in vain to make this landing.

On the eighth at four in the morning two ships and six frigates, moored very close to shore, delivered a continuous fire on the defenses until eight o'clock. The landing force in 250 barges in two divisions, under command of Generals Hamerst [Amherst], Wolfe, and Whitmore; that of General Wolfe made its landing in a place accounted impracticable. The French troops, only too fortunate in not being cut off in their retreat, re-entered Louisbourg the next day with a loss of about eighty men killed or captured.

The night of the seventeenth to eighteenth the enemy opened the trenches. There then were in the port of Louisbourg five ships

---

[86] At Louisbourg.

of the line [and], the *Apollon* of 50 guns, the *Fidèle* of 40, the *Echo* of 32, the *Arethuse* of 36, the *Chevre* of 12, the *Biche* of 10, and four merchant vessels. They closed the port entrance by sinking the *Apollon*, the *Fidèle*, the *Biche*, and the four merchantmen. The other ships remained at anchor in the harbor, useless spectators and of more harm than benefit to the defense.

Of all possible actions they took the worst, for the landing made, the capture of the city was inevitable. Either the ships should have tried to get back to France, or have followed the advice of brave Beaussier of leaving on the fourth and of going to burn the transport vessels at the entrance of Gabarus Bay. The English warships could not have prevented their doing this. They had the imprudence of putting themselves at the bottom of the bay, the wind being favorable, but we had the still greater stupidity of not profiting through this mistake.

The place surrendered July 26. On the twenty-fourth the *Arethuse* escaped; this same day bombs set three of our warships on fire. The night of the twenty-fifth to twenty-sixth one thousand men in sixty barges went to capture two others in the harbor itself. The crews were ashore and there was no officer on board. Of these ships they seized and held the *Bienfaisant* and burned the *Prudent* which carried Chevalier Desgoutes, squadron commander.

During the siege we had 1,500 men killed and the English lost 3,400.[87] Three sorties were made, one of 1,500 men, the other 1,200, the third 600. The number of our prisoners, soldiers, habitants, and sailors comes to about 8,000 men.

At the start of the campaign the English, not believing that Louisbourg would hold them up so long, expected, immediately that it was taken, to come and besiege Quebec. Their plan was to establish their supply depot at Gaspé and their warships were to cruise between Gaspé and the Seven Islands.[88] The frigates with the transports would have ascended the river, anchored at the

---

[87] The actual British losses were 195 killed and 363 wounded.

[88] On the north shore of the St. Lawrence seventy-five miles west of the west end of Anticosti.

Journal for 1758

capes, and the troops would have landed in barges at St. Joachim.[89]

Louisbourg being taken only at the end of July, they gave up the Quebec expedition and formed the plan of establishing themselves at Gaspé.

On August 10, hearing of the Battle of Carillon, they sent six thousand men to New York.

On August 28 six warships, one a three-decker, two frigates, a fire ship, and eleven transports, having on board a landing force of fifteen hundred men, twelve houses all prefabricated, and eighteen cannon, set sail from Louisbourg and reached Gaspé before September 4. The warships anchored off the landing place and the transports farther into the bay, even to the entrance of Penouille.[90]

Admiral Hardy commanded the squadron and General Wolfe the troops. On the fifth they summoned Sieur Reval, commander of Gaspé, to surrender, but he had been dead for three days, and all the inhabitants had hidden in the woods at the sight of the English squadron. Two habitants who came with their families to surrender, showed the place of refuge of the others. Thus from that very day the English took possession of Gaspé, where there were about sixty inhabitants, eight houses, and a great storehouse serving as a store for the fur trade with the Micmacs of the Bay of Chaleurs. There were there at that time four thousand hundredweight of salt cod, two shallops full of fur, and four hundred muskets of which the English took possession.

On the tenth they started defensive works at the landing place, but their houses were still on shipboard.

On the eleventh they detached a frigate, a fire ship, and six transports carrying 300 troops to go to destroy the habitations and the camp at Miramichi, where there were 150 men, but as they were warned of the design of the English, they had time to prepare to receive them. They moored two bateaux, each mounted with three cannon and three swivels to bar the Miramichi River a league

[89] On the north shore of the St. Lawrence opposite the east end of the Isle of Orleans.
[90] Unidentified, except it must have been in Gaspé Bay.

above the camp and put everyone at these two places. The English, seeing these dispositions, did not dare to do anything.

They have since destroyed the Mission of Mont-Louis, where there were a few houses and a church.

During the first part of October, under orders from Louisbourg, they withdrew from Gaspé, one cannot guess for what reason, for their intention on leaving Louisbourg was to have one thousand men winter there.

Canadians and Frenchmen, although having the same origin, the same interests, the same principles of religion and government, with an urgent danger facing them cannot agree among themselves; it seems that these are two bodies which cannot be amalgamated together. I even believe that a few Canadians pray that we do not succeed, hoping that all blame will fall on the French.

Oswego

A few people say that the English had purposely let this fort be taken; a subtility as ridiculous as that of the Athenians who wondered if King Philip did not let himself die purposely in order to deceive them.

It would have required much eloquence to persuade so many people to surrender themselves prisoners unnecessarily and to expose themselves to all the cruelties of the Indians.

The Indians and the Canadians alone took Oswego [they say].

The ease of this expedition according to [these] people, the Marquis de Vaudreuil, and the bishop who took it, they say, with his clergy; doubtless as Joshua took Jericho with three trips around the walls.

Eagerness of Canadians to leave as soon as the expedition is completed. With other troops and other orders from the court, a garrison left at Oswego, a sudden march of the army against Fort Bull, which is within twelve leagues, and against the troops of Colonel Bradstreet that one would perhaps have met on the way.

Bad administration of provisions; giving abatements to the companies or private parties who are charged with their furnishing and transport.

Canadians glorious as if they were beggars and without interest.

V[audreuil], when he has conceived an idea becomes enamoured of it as Pygmalion did of his statue. I pardon this to the latter, for his was a chef d'oeuvre.

After the affair of M. de Dieskau, the Five Nations, seeing how they had treated the Mohawks and fearing the resentment of the French, sent ambassadors who proceeded as far as La Presentation. They sent to make excuses and disavowed [the actions of] their young men. They were received with firmness by the Marquis de Vaudreuil who assured them that he would have treated as enemies all those of them that he found with the English. They gave him belts as assurance of neutrality and to tell him that he should not make war in their regions, that he could at Oswego, but not to carry it farther west. These speeches were accepted and cemented by two belts.

Abbé Piquet and M. de Joncaire were the intermediaries of this treaty.

However, the Marquis de Vaudreuil has had ambassadors with the Five Nations all winter. The Oneidas accompanied M. de Lery and have appeared disposed toward us. For three months we have been waiting the answer of a few of our ambassadors. M. de Joncaire is charged with counterbalancing Colonel [Sir William] Johnson's negotiations.

The Marquis de Montcalm should not ignore the fact that the Iroquois are not in a favorable mood toward the English, since they have maltreated the Delawares, their nephews.

Journals for 1759–60

The prisoner is called Pierre Morfi [Peter Murphy!], born at Boston, was captured between St. Frederic and Carillon, is of Inglison's [Nicholson?] regiment, Boston militia, which regiment is all alone at a camp five miles from St. Frederic and has been there for two weeks, having been sent there from St. Frederic where they have been a month cutting timbers to build a fort on the rock of St. Frederic which is undermined.

At St. Frederic there are about ten thousand men, not including his regiment, to wit: five thousand Boston militiamen and they expect another two thousand more from the same province. There are men from Rhose [sic] Island, Hampshire, Connecticut, and New York. There are four regiments of regulars. Rogers is there with one thousand rangers. There are also many Indians of several tribes.

He does not know the name of the General, who is from Old England.

There are five vessels, one of 22 guns, one of 20, one of six 24-pounders, our two chebecs,[1] and a floating battery of three 24's.

[1] Abandoned and sunk by the French in September, when cornered by Captain Joshua Loring.

There are in the gun park about thirty bronze pieces, At St. Frederic there is the big fort and three little ones and six blockhouses of six cannon each.

The army is at St. Frederic with many barges lined up in a stockaded enclosure; Rogers is at Point Hocquart with one thousand men. His [own] regiment of one thousand men occupies the camp at Postnam Point.[2]

Then there are about three thousand men at Carillon, fifteen hundred of them regulars and the rest militia, as well as our third chebec.

There is still a regiment camped at different posts from the Falls to Contrecoeur's camp.

General Hamerst [Amherst] was at Albany when they left with two Scottish regiments and the headquarters staff. At St. Frederic they are every day expecting him [to come] with much artillery.

They expect any day to come to Isle aux Noix[3] and attack this post.

He has not heard them speak of a junction with M. Murray,[4] nor if there will be an army at Oswego.

For a long time there has been no news from Europe. All winter they counted on peace, now they do not count on it any more.

Quebec Truce—Death of Montcalm

[This must have been dictated by Bougainville at the Lorette Camp, September 21, 1759]

Here is a short history of my doings, the details of which circumstances will not let me give.

I reached Quebec May 10, after having been for ten days in the ice between Cap Nord and Cap Ray. The Bordeaux fleet arrived there three days after me, and on May 23 the advance of the English squadron was at Bic.

Then all prepared for the defense of this so exposed frontier.

---

[2] Unidentified. Putnam?

[3] An islet eleven miles north of Rouses Point. In 1760 its little fort, commanded by Bougainville, was New France's last defense on the Champlain frontier.

[4] Brigadier Murray, who was occupying Quebec at this time.

The troops assigned to this defense were five French battalions and about five to six thousand militiamen. M. de Bourlamaque, with the other three battalions and a thousand Canadians, was charged with covering Montreal on the Lake Champlain side, and the Chevalier de la Corne, with twelve hundred men of La Marine and the militia, on the Lake Ontario side. MM. de Vaudreuil, de Montcalm, and de Lévis had returned to the capital.

On June 3 I was detached with five companies of grenadiers and five hundred militiamen to build redoubts and lines from the Falls of Montmorency up to Quebec. My camp was enlarged day by day up to the twenty-eighth, as the entire army came to occupy it, and as the English army, arrived a few days before, landed on the Isle of Orleans and two days later put a body of three thousand men at Pointe Lévis opposite Quebec. From this time on the English tried several maneuvers to make us abandon our position. The batteries established at their Pointe Lévis camp smashed and burned the city. In mid-July the troops camped on the Isle of Orleans moved to the left bank of the Montmorency Falls, while we occupied the right. Mr. Wolfe there put nearly fifty guns which, through the shape of the terrain, swept all the plain which was held by the left of our army under command of the Chevalier de Lévis. The Marquis de Montcalm was at the center, and I was in charge of the right under the Marquis de Vaudreuil.

On July 31 the enemy anchored three vessels broadside in front of our camp on the left, one with sixty guns; their artillery and the batteries at the Falls delivered upon us for ——— hours a fire of which there are few examples, for in this space of time there were nearly four thousand shot, bombs, or grenades thrown. At two in the afternoon the troops at Pointe Lévis got into their landing craft and came at four o'clock to land and form column of attack opposite our left, while the troops camped at the Falls came down [to the shore] to attack at the same time. The Chevalier de Lévis had made his dispositions to receive them, and the Marquis de Montcalm had joined him with a party of troops from the right and center. The enemy was repulsed with a loss of six or seven hundred men, and, in retreating they burned two of their anchored vessels.

Journals for 1759-60

The Chevalier de Lévis then was sent to defend the Lake Ontario frontier, threatened by a considerable army which was coming after having taken Niagara.

Meanwhile, several English vessels had passed up above Quebec, and measures were taken to prevent their inroads on our communications. August 5 the number of these vessels was increased and a landing force of fifteen hundred men was put on board them. I then was detached with a company of grenadiers, a light company of regulars, and one of militia to guard the communication of the army and of Quebec with the vessels from which the provisions were drawn, and with Montreal. There were about five hundred men spread out over these lines of communication, and they were to be under my orders. I followed the English squadron as far as Pointe aux Trembles, where it anchored. This parish is seven leagues [upstream] from Quebec. I there assembled about 250 men and I had three-quarters of a league from me on my right a troop of 150 volunteer cavalry under command of M. de la Rochebeaucour, organized at the start of the campaign, instructed and disciplined by this officer, who has served with the greatest of distinction.

The afternoon of August 8 the enemy anchored broadsides before the landing place at Pointe aux Trembles a frigate of twenty-two guns and several bomb ships which fired on the shore. The landing place was a smooth beach without any covering heights or any defenses; I had not had time to make any. Their first landing was made at low tide; their troops, to the number of fifteen hundred men, formed there and marched against me. The cavalry was advanced on my right and I might have had three hundred men in action. This first attack did not succeed and they re-embarked. My horse was hit.

They came on a second time to the attack at high tide and were again pushed back with a loss of three hundred men killed or wounded.

On the tenth the enemy camped opposite me on the south shore. My detachment was increased by a company of grenadiers and two hundred militiamen.

On the seventeenth the enemy made a night movement in barges and landed at Deschambault,[5] seven leagues above me. I at once marched there with my two companies of grenadiers, my light company of regulars, one hundred cavalrymen, and sixty militiamen, and I forced them to re-embark.

Then they broke camp, took to their boats again, and their squadron went downriver and anchored opposite St. Augustin, three leagues below Pointe aux Trembles and four above Quebec. I followed them there. The next night they were reinforced with about one thousand men and came to attack me from ten in the evening until half-past twelve. They made a great bombardment from their ship's cannon and muskets, attempted a landing without success on my left, and never dared set foot ashore.

These efforts on their part proved that they had designs on our communications, a thing essential to us, but difficult to guard, [we] being obliged to follow on foot with much inferior forces the movement and rapid advances of their vessels and barges.

At the beginning of September the English evacuated their camp at the Falls, went to Pointe Lévis, and the largest part of them went on board the squadron which was opposing me. Then I was given the five grenadier companies, Duprat's volunteers, three light companies of our regulars, and a few militia light companies, which gave me a corps of fifteen hundred men, in addition to the various posts I had placed along the shore.

The English anchored opposite Cap Rouge, three leagues from Quebec, where I went. They made several moves to keep me on the move and a few offensive demonstrations.

Between the night of the tenth and that of the twelfth the troops camped on the Isle of Orleans, those at Pointe Lévis, and on the ships entered their barges and surprised a post half a league from Quebec.[6] I was not informed of it until nine in the morning. I

---

[5] Some forty miles upstream from Quebec. The British here destroyed a supply depot, where was also deposited the personal baggage of many of the French officers.

[6] The post above Wolfe's path leading from the Anse de Foulon to the Plains of Abraham.

marched at once, but when I came within range of the battle, our army was beaten and in retreat. The entire English army advanced to attack me. I retreated before them and posted myself so as to cover the retreat of our army [toward Montreal], to join with it, or to march again against the enemy if it was judged proper.

The Marquis de Montcalm died the next day of his wounds. He had conducted a campaign worthy of M. de Turenne, and his death caused our misfortunes. It was believed necessary to abandon the Beauport camp all standing and to withdraw behind Jacques Cartier River, eleven leagues [upstream] from Quebec, which the enemy at once besieged.

I took it upon myself (and the Marquis de Vaudreuil approved) to remain with my corps at Cap Rouge and Lorette. There I reassembled the remnants of our army and got provisions into Quebec.

On the eighteenth I marched with six hundred men to throw myself into [Quebec], and the Chevalier de Lévis, arrived the evening before from Montreal, advanced the army to get within range of attacking the English. I was only three-quarters of a league from Quebec when I learned that the city had surrendered. It had been bombarded for sixty-eight days. I was forced to retrace my steps, for the English army moved to march against me.

Such was the end of what up to this moment was the finest campaign in the world. We spent three months in bivouac. Just the same, the English hold only the [outer] walls and the King [still] holds the colony.

Memoir Since November 15, 1758

I LEFT QUEBEC November 15, 1758, in a privateer of eighteen guns, called the *Victoire*, to go to report to the court on the situation in Canada and to beg aid.

The crossing was fifty-two days, the weather detestable. Two vows made by the crew attest that it was not nice; almost captured within sight of land, we escaped the privateers only through risking shipwreck on the Sorlingues.

My trip was fortunate for me since I obtained a brevet of colonel and the Cross of St. Louis. This last favor was granted me by His Majesty himself, the Marshal de Belle-Isle having proposed me only for a brevet of colonel. Mme de Pompadour showed me the greatest kindness, and, as she was then the First Minister, I often worked with her over the object of my mission. I did not succeed anywhere nearly so well for the common cause as for my personal interest.

M. de Berryer who, from lieutenant of the Paris police, had been made Minister of Marine[1] never would understand that Canada

[1] Mme de P[ompadour] must render account of it to God. They say that the cause of her favor toward him was because he had served her as a spy against M. d' Argenson, whose creature he was.—Bougainville's note.

was the barrier of our other colonies and that the English would never attack any other until they had chased us away from that one.

The result proved the truth of this proposition.

This minister loved parables and told me very pertinently that one did not try to save the stables when the house was on fire.[2] I then could obtain for these poor stables only four hundred recruits and a few munitions.

I had proposed sending to Canada only the necessary aid in munitions and provisions, and since we were informed that the enemy would attack in the spring of 1759 with three armies, by the St. Lawrence River, by Lake Champlain, and by Lake Ontario, waiting until these three armies had reached the three frontiers and then landing four thousand men with arms of all sorts for a great number in Carolina. On arrival they would summon to freedom the Germans that the English treated as slaves in their colonies, after having attracted them there under the allurement of advantageous concessions; we would arm part of them, we would send arms and munitions to the Cherokees, Indians of this region, implacable enemies of the English, would offer neutrality to the Pennsylvanians, people of the Quaker sect, who do not make war at all because of religious principles, and [then] would have marched to the north. This diversion would have forcibly released Canada. We would support the troops which made it according to the success they had had. If possible we would have made the English colonies the theater of war; come the worst these troops always had an assured retreat to Louisiana, where since 1759 they would through precaution have sent provisions and established subsistence depots.

This project, proposed to Mme de Pompadour and by her to a committee of ministers, was agreed upon. It was only a question of finding the funds necessary to implement it; the King's coffers were empty. Mme de P[ompadour] did everything possible to find two million, engaging herself for this sum. Her efforts were fruit-

[2] Bougainville is said to have replied, "At least, Monsieur, no one will say you talk like a horse."

less and the project failed. The Duke de Choiseul wanted me to head the expedition, although I begged off on account of my youth and small experience.

The Marshal de Belle-Isle granted all the favors the Marquis de Montcalm sought for his little army, and told me in open audience that, had it been possible to make a brigadier into a marshal of France, the King would have given this favor to the Marquis de Montcalm.[3]

I took my leave at the end of February and went to Bordeaux to board the *Chézine*, twenty-six-gun frigate, part of the fleet of twenty-three sail that Sieur Cadet, Commissary of Stores of Canada, had fitted out to carry provisions there. At Blaye I reviewed the four hundred recruits destined for the colony; they embarked there on the Commissary of Stores' fleet and we set sail at the end of March.

A week later I left the fleet and continued alone. We were held up twenty-two days between Cap Ray and Cap Nord, caught in the ice, and we reached Quebec May 10. The rest of the fleet arrived there several days later, and soon we had news of the English army and fleet which were coming to besiege Quebec.

Since the generals were at Montreal, I went there at once to give them the dispatches and instructions of the court. The campaign started the end of May. The Marquis de Montcalm and de Vaudreuil went to defend Quebec with an army of ten thousand men, four thousand of them regular troops and the rest militia. The Count de Bourlamaque was charged with the Lake Champlain frontier, and the Marquis de Rigaud with that of Lake Ontario.

The campaign did not end as happily as it began; it cost us Quebec, Carillon, St. Frederic, Niagara, Frontenac, and the Marquis de Montcalm. This general was killed at the battle lost on September 13 before Quebec, and the colony was brought to bay.

These then were the frontiers of the Quebec region: a little fort hurriedly built at the Jacques Cartier River;[4] Isle aux Noix organ-

---

[3] Montcalm was, however, made a lieutenant general at this time.
[4] On the north shore of the St. Lawrence some twenty-eight miles above Quebec.

ized for defense on Lake Champlain, and a fortified island[5] in the midst of the rapids which on the Lake Ontario side form the head of the St. Lawrence River.

During the 1759 campaign I was almost always on detached duty in command of the companies of grenadiers and volunteers guarding the army's communications with its supply depots, which were eighteen leagues away. I had several special advantages, I even hoped to throw myself into Quebec to defend it after the battle. Ramezay, King's lieutenant, who commanded there, never wished to give me the opportunity, in spite of my several proposals; he surrendered September [18], although the evening before I had got into the place a provision convoy under La Rochebeaucour, commanding the volunteer cavalry, and, already arrived myself on the Heights of Charlesbourg, I would in the night of ––– to ––– have thrown myself into the city with eight hundred grenadiers and volunteers. This man surrendered without having tried a cannon shot, and the enemy not even having started their trenches.

In the month of March, 1760, I was sent to Isle aux Noix to defend it; Desandrouins, engineer officer, was charged with the defense of Fort Lévis at the rapids, and the Marquis de Lévis left to besiege Quebec, the snow not yet having melted. The speed of his march surprised the enemy. Murray, Governor of Quebec, came out [of the city] with his troops, was well beaten on the same terrain where we had been September 13, 1759, lost his field artillery, and was forced to re-enter the place. They at once started the siege, that is to say that in order to be open to no reproaches in case aid came from France, they started the trenches in the snow and put in position a dozen twelve-pounders (there were no others) against a place defended by a numerous garrison and more than one hundred cannon of heavy caliber.

The arrival of an English squadron decided the matter, it was necessary to raise this siege of a sort, leaving Bourlamaque with a body of troops to follow along the river the movements of Murray,

[5] Fort Lévis, on a very small island near present Ogdensburg, N. Y.

whose troops had been reinforced. The Marquis de Lévis prepared some defenses at Isle Ste Helene, opposite Montreal.

In the month of August I was besieged at Isle aux Noix which I had strongly entrenched, and I evacuated it on the twentieth day by order of the Marquis de Vaudreuil; I retreated through the woods to St. Jean. Two days later we had to shut ourselves up in Montreal, General Amherst already having arrived on the island of that name, after having taken Fort Lévis; Murray having landed there on the other side, after having forced Bourlamaque to fall back there, and the army which had laid siege to Isle aux Noix occupied Longueuil and La Prairie,[6] ready to join the other two.

It was more than was needed against a paltry town, overpowered on all sides, which had only a shirt and ten or twelve bad cannon; we were reduced to less than three thousand men.

I was charged by the generals to carry to General Amherst the articles of a general capitulation for Canada.

The country [itself] was well-treated, the English well-knowing that it would remain theirs; the troops badly, since the English General demanded that they should lay down their arms and not serve for the rest of the entire war.[7] We presented a memoir to the Marquis de Vaudreuil containing sharp protests against these humiliating conditions and the offer to attack the enemy at once or to defend Isle Ste Helene. The Canadian General gave us written orders to lay down our arms, and at the end of the year we returned to France on English transports.

In 1761 there was question of a congress at Augsburg to negotiate peace. I was named to accompany the Duke de Praslin, plenipotentiary of France, and this mission prevented me from accompanying to Malta, threatened by the Turks, Bourlamaque, La Rochebeaucour, Desandrouins, and several other officers of those who had fought in Canada, whom the ambassador of the Faith had requested in the name of the Grand Master [of the Knights of Malta].

---

[6] Just across the St. Lawrence from Montreal.
[7] Amherst remembered the massacre at Fort William Henry, and, perhaps unfairly, held it against the French regular troops.

The congress of Augsburg did not come off, and I spent this year in useless attempts to obtain my liberty from the English court.

I got the *Académie des Belles-Lettres* of Paris to compose an epitaph for the Marquis de Montcalm, and I wrote to Minister Pitt to arrange to get it cut on the tomb of the General at the Ursulines of Quebec. The answer of this minister was most amiable and did him as much honor as it did the General and the French troops.

The year 1762 opened with great events and saw our ministry change. The Marquise de Pompadour, reserving to herself only the disposition of the favors of which she was the sovereign, had given up the helm of affairs. The Marshal de Belle-Isle was dead at his work. Pierre Berryer, after having sold a part of what remained to us of our navy, doubtless in order to have it accomplished sooner, had been made Keeper of the Seals. The Duke de Choiseul doubled as Minister of War and of Marine, and gave that of Foreign Affairs to the Duke de Praslin, his cousin. In the month of January the Family Pact was announced; it was a start toward peace or at least for France to make war more vigorously.

Nevertheless, the loss of Guadeloupe and Martinique followed that of Canada.

The warrior Conflans had already seconded the politician Berryer in the project of destroying the French Navy. Havana was taken just after Martinique. The armies of France and Spain advanced slowly in Portugal, and our armies in Germany with difficulty maintained a sorry defense. Frederick [of Prussia] alone was on top of things.

Louis XV, impelled by the repeated losses suffered by his kingdom, strongly desired a peace which his conquests in the previous war had not prevented him from desiring and granting. With the King of Sardinia as intermediary, Bussy first, and Stanley, then Nivernois and the Duke of Bedford, were sent to Paris and to London to treat for a peace difficult to conclude, unless France determined to give up considerable.

I spent the spring and part of the summer this year at Versailles, very well-treated by the Duke de Choiseul and his family, torn by internal bickerings. At last I obtained a half-liberty from England, that is to say, permission to serve in Europe only and for the month of July. I was sent with private instructions to the Marshals d'Estrées and de Soubise. I remained with the army with the Count de Stainville until the end of August. He sent me off to report to the court the situation of our armies.

During my absence someone started an atrocious piece of malice against me among the household of the Duke de Choiseul. The pretext for it was a too intimate relationship with a lady of importance of which they accused me. The Duchess de G[ramont] received me very badly, and my disgrace with her has since continued. I took my position of going to the Minister's house only like anyone without a private liaison. He much wished to seek my entire liberty without restrictions from the Duke of Bedford. He had secured it, and I was already under orders to go to Dunkirk to take command of a body of two thousand men destined to join those who were to sail from Brest, under command of the Count d'Estaing, when peace was signed at Fontainbleau and London.

They did me the honor of offering me the governorship of Cayenne, but I declined, then having [in mind] a project which I have been permitted to carry out.

England, mistress of Canada by the peace treaty, of the sea by a navy incomparably stronger than those of all the powers of Europe combined, seemed to me to desire further only establishments in the South Seas.

Seizing with them the sources of silver, she would effect this project of universal monarchy falsely imputed to Louis XIV. Anson had advised his country to establish itself in the Falkland Islands, which their position rendered the key to the South Seas. What else had the English to do in the interval of such a peace than to grab a supply base which put them at the first outbreak of war in the position of being the arbiters of Europe? I believed that France should anticipate them, and I obtained leave to make, at my own expense and that of MM. de Nerville and d'Arboulin, one my cousin and the other my uncle, exploration of these islands and an establishment which would assure France its possession. Thus in former times the zealous were granted permission to sell their property for the trip to the Holy Land.

I left St. Malo September 22, 1763, with the frigates *Aigle* and *Sphinx*.

APPENDIX

Extracts from Bougainville's Letters

THE FOLLOWING EXTRACTS have been translated from René de Kerallain's *La Jeunesse de Bougainville* (Paris, 1896).

Letter to his brother.
August 28, 1756
[Two weeks after fall of Oswego]

I do not have an instant to myself. Scarcely do we have the time to eat and sleep. This campaign is indeed rough; the General [Montcalm], who was in the campaign in Bohemia, finds this one even more fatiguing. I forgot to tell you that I have become an epigraph writer. On the ashes of Oswego we planted a cross and a post with the arms of France. On the cross I gave for a motto: "*In hoc signo Vincunt;*" on the post: "*Manibus date lilia plenis.*" That may be very bad—well and good; in war as in war.

Letter to his brother.
July 3, 1757

I passed my time [last winter] in reading, meditating, and writing. This ennui which torments me has been turned to the profit of my soul. You will see a memoir I sent Madame Herault for the Minister. It is only the germ of ideas which need to be developed.

Appendix

... My portfolio is full of observations on the customs of the Indians, their language, the quality of the country....

Letter to Madame Herault.

June 30, 1757

... He [Montcalm] is under the orders of a man, limited, without talent, perhaps free from vice, but having all the faults of a petty spirit, filled with Canadian prejudices, which are of all the most foolish, jealous, glorious, wishing to take all credit to themselves. He no more confides in M. de Montcalm than in the lowest lieutenant....

I will say only that we expect two sieges and a battle, that your child shudders at the horrors which he will be forced to witness. It will be with great difficulty that we can control these Indians of the Far West, the most ferocious of all people, and great cannibals by trade. Listen to what the chiefs said to M. de Montcalm three days ago. "Father, do not expect that we can easily give quarter to the English. We have young men who have never yet drunk of this broth. Fresh meat has brought them here from the ends of the earth. It is most necessary that they learn to wield the knife and to plunge it into an English heart." Behold our comrades, dear Mama; what a crew, what a spectacle for a humane man.

To his brother.

June 30, 1757

We have nearly 8,000 men, 1,800 of whom are Indians, naked, black, red, howling, bellowing, dancing, singing the war song, getting drunk, yelling for "broth," that is to say blood, drawn from 500 leagues by the smell of fresh human flesh and the chance to teach their young men how one carves up a human being destined for the pot. Behold our comrades who, night and day, are our shadows. I shiver at the frightful spectacles which they are preparing for us.

To his brother.

August 19, 1757

My health is robust, since these extreme fatigues have not hurt it too much, although the day we invested the place [Fort William Henry] I thrice fell down fainting from exhaustion. . . .

Letter to Madame Herault.

September, 1757

Would you believe that this abominable action of the Indians at Fort William Henry has accomplices among people who call themselves Frenchmen; that greed for gain, the certainty of getting very cheaply from the Indians all the goods they had pillaged, are the primary causes of a horror for which England will not fail to reproach us for a long time to come? Thank Heaven our own officers are blameless in this respect; several risked their lives on this occasion; they divided up everything they had with the unfortunate English, and these latter say that if ever they have occasion to besiege and capture us, there will be two capitulations, one for the French troops, and the other for the Canadians. These are frightful truths, dear Mama. But spectacles still more frightful have befouled my eyes and left an ineffaceable bitterness in my soul. May the memory of these abominations vanish. What a land! What a people! . . .

To his brother.

September 17, 1757

They [the English] openly praise it [the actions of the French regulars], but these savages and these others, worse than savages, are our allies, and their infamy soils our glory. My brother, we all have rankling hearts so much so that, in a moment of indignation, the officers of our troops [the French regulars] wished to ask to be allowed to carry on the war alone and refused as companions-in-arms the monsters capable of dishonoring us. Upon this occasion there passed interchanges of fury and of unbelievable meanness that one cannot record and I would from the depths of my heart wish to be able to forget. But unfortunately, I have seen and heard only too much myself. I go farther. The air one breathes here is contagious, and I fear lest a long sojourn here makes us acquire the vices of a people to whom we communicate no virtues. . . .

Appendix

Letter to Madame Herault.

April 21, 1758

I learned from the Sault St. Louis Indians, who always keep up contact with their Mohawk brothers, of a fine scene that happened during the last campaign. While we were besieging Fort William Henry, Johnson, Dieskau's conqueror, arrived at Fort Edward at the head of 800 provincials, Mohawks, and Moraigans, a sort of bastard tribe, all in war paint like his troop, tomahawk at his side, halberd in hand. He proposed to General Webb to march at once on the French lines. Webb said that he would do no such thing, that he did not wish to expose himself to a complete defeat in woods still red with English blood. Johnson replied that these same shores of Lake George would be as fatal to Montcalm as they had been to Dieskau, that French bones would cover this battlefield, and as for himself, he swore by his halberd and tomahawk he would conquer or die. General Webb was not moved. Johnson then called to witness the Belgian [*sic*] lion, tore off one of his leggings and hurled it at Webb's feet. "You won't do it?" said he — "No." Tore off the other legging. "You won't?" Hurled a garter. "You won't?" Hurled shirt, tomahawk, and halberd down, and galloped off with his troop who had imitated his actions entirely. Where is Homer to paint such scenes more than Greek?

Letter to Madame Herault.

February 20, 1758

... God knows we do not wish to disparage the value of the Canadians. ... In the woods, behind trees, no troops are comparable to the natives of this country.

... the Governor of Montreal enjoyed a trading post which was worth immense sums to him. This line of business will never be known to the Minister for the colonies. Letters from Paris say that they intend to have this M. de Rigaud replace M. de Kerlerec in Louisiana. It must be then that this government needs only a wig stand. What a man! The Intendant, who gave me this news, cannot believe it.

Adventure in the Wilderness

Letter to his brother.

April 21, 1758

Without Montaigne, Horace, Vergil, Tacitus, Montesquieu, Corneille, the conversations and kindness of my General, ennui would have consumed me.

Montcalm to Marquis de Paulmy.

[probably November 1, 1757]

My Lord, you are acquainted with Sieur de Bougainville, one of my aides-de-camp. It will not have escaped you that he has spirit and talent. I can assure you that he has a military mind indeed and in adding experience to the theory he already has, he will become a person of distinction. You could use him in Europe upon his return in the various senior staffs of the army and send him into the various parts of the world where the King will be obliged to carry war. After having told you of his talents for his profession, I believe that I can assure you of the soundness of his heart and of his inviolable attachment to you, my Lord; and I look on him as one of those to whom the Ministry of War should pay the most particular attention. Whatever general you should assign him to, will thank you; as for myself, I shall always ask for first call on him whenever I am charged with a particular task. . . .

Index

For the purpose of conciseness there have been omitted from this index all reference to entirely minor personages and to most minor places, unless some noteworthy event took place there. Cities have received the same treatment.

Abercromby, General James: 208, 214, 229, 230, 269, 280, 282
Abnakis: 10, 24, 42, 43, 44, 46, 49, 83, 84, 86, 105, 136, 143, 145, 158, 159, 199, 209, 243, 245, 247, 255, 258, 263, 267; christianized, start massacre, 172; thieveries of, 242
Acadia: news from, 66, 88, 181
Acadians: 58, 180; near starvation, 88; famine drives to Quebec, 116; driven by hunger, 189, 192
Acapas (Catawbas): 89
Adventure of French soldier: 52
Agramont: 39
Albany: riot at, 90; neutrality of Dutch at, 106
Algonkins: 24, 122, 145, 154, 219; of the lake, 136
Amalecites: 43, 143

Amenities: Bougainville sends wine to British, 282
Amherst: assails Montreal, 326
Aoussik: dances at council, 123
Arpent: 15n.
Artillery: increased, 140; captured at Fort William Henry, 177
Attigué: British attempt to burn, 53

Ball at Bigot's: 78
Bateaux: capacity of, 61; artillery, 156
Bay: Bottle, 129; Ganaouské, 146; Niaouré, 19n., 28
Béarn Battalion: 12, 18, 19, 20, 23, 28, 29, 34, 37, 51, 64, 85, 95, 97, 98, 104, 108, 131, 154, 174, 178, 179, 187, 211, 222, 231, 232, 292, 297; delayed by high winds, 22; size of, 51; soldier of, scalped, 53; winter quarters, 62
Bécancour: 83

335

Beef: price of, 1757, 102; 1758, 286
Beer, spruce: 52
Behavior, Canadian, in battle: 238; at work, 259; Indian: 37, 114, 115, 127, 130, 132–33, 221–22, 245, 248, 288; in battle, 116
Berry Regiment: 138, 181, 184, 206, 209, 213, 222, 223, 226, 229, 231, 232, 234; losses of, 183
Bigot, François (The Intendant): 6, 31, 71, 78, 136, 183, 187, 218, 293, 296; his immense requisitions, 70; his gaming losses, 196
Bills of exchange: 185
Bleury, Sieur de: 48, 52, 63, 88; his convoy service, 42; brings 70 bateaux, 46; convoy at last arrives, 61
Bougainville, Louis Antoine de: 3, 18, 29, 31, 33, 63, 66, 68, 80, 82, 125, 130, 175, 178, 276, 278, 291; brief biography, vii–viii; summons Oswego to surrender, 26; reconnoiters Lake George, 37–40; adopted by Iroquois, 124; sings war song, 124; advises British keep liquor from Indians, 171; goes reconnoitering, 186; visits Sault St. Louis, 197; promoted, 224; observations on battle of Carillon, 237–39; plan for holding west, 271–72; to carry reports to France, 277; shipwrecked, 296; leaves for France, 297; trip down St. Lawrence, 297–301; terrible voyage, 304–11; observations on luminosity, 304–305; remarks on capture of Louisbourg, 311–12; remarks on Oswego, 314–15; subsequent career in Canada, 317–21; later career, 322–29; promoted and decorated, 322; proposes attack on Carolinas, 323; returns to Canada, 324; commands at Isle aux Noix, 325–26; secures epitaph for Montcalm's tomb, 327; malice against, 328; serves in Europe, 328; refuses governorship of Cayenne, 328; starts South Sea adventures, 329; Montcalm's testimonial, 334
Bourlamaque, Chevalier de: 3, 5, 21, 22, 104, 108, 111, 112, 113, 131, 152, 154, 159, 160, 161, 168, 173, 178, 192, 213, 219, 220, 221, 226, 227, 232, 318, 325, 326; commands at Oswego, 26; presents British flags to church, 30; wounded, 233; defends Champlain frontier, 324
Braddock, General (?): reported to have 1,000 regulars, 1757, 5
Braddock, General Edward: his papers, 67, 69
Bradstreet, Major John: 226, 280, 288, 291; report of bateau fight, 6; misses chance of Niagara, 283
Brandy: price of, at Fort Carillon, 102; price of, 286
Bread: scarcity and adulteration, 72; none at Quebec, 136
Breechclout: age when given Indian child, 21
"Bridging" of St. Lawrence at Quebec: 78–79
British: intelligence of, 5, 84, 109, 143, 245–46, 279–80, 291, 316–17; reports of moves of, 29; dispositions, 1756, 34–35

Cadet, Joseph: see Commissary of Stores
Caitas: 99
Calf, price of: 286
Campaign: 1756 ends, 51; 1757 commences, 104; 1757 troop departures, 120; troops open, 1758, 211; British close, 1758, 292; French close, 1758, 292
Candles, lack of: 56
Canestio (Conestoga?): 138
Cannibalism, Indian: 122, 143, 144, 150, 174; British, 174
Canteen, de Lotbinière's: alone has wine, 52; concession favors slow progress, 55, 278
Cape: Chat, 76; Diamond, 47, 49, 56, 59; Moraska, 199; Tourmente, 186
Capitulation of Canada: 326
Carillon, Fort, battle of: 228–34
Casualties, French at Fort William Henry: 177–78
Catawbas: 89, 105, 113, 119, 138; scalp Canadian, 91
Caughnawaga (Sault St. Louis): 9n., 32n.
Cayugas: 17, 73, 90, 106, 114
Cédres, Les: 94
Census of wheat: 119

Index

Ceremony passing Grand Banks: 17
Cherokees: 89, 105, 180
Chichicoy: 135
Chien Indians: 82, 107
Chickasaw War: 252
Chippewas: 9, 32, 36, 42, 66, 116, 121, 132, 136, 143, 179
Choctaws: 82, 89, 119, 180, 196, 232
Commissary of Stores (Joseph Cadet): 255, 256, 257, 258, 261, 293, 324
Convoy: cost of and bateau capacity, 61; brings supplies to Quebec, 206–207
Corlar: 67
Corps Royal: 136, 141
Council, Indian: 9–10, 11, 21, 38, 45, 50, 110, 115, 120–21, 122–23, 132, 144, 145, 146–48, 163–64, 222, 223, 242, 293; with Iroquois, 103–104; at Niagara, 106; at Onondaga, 106
Court-martial: of Major Robert Stobo, 67, 69; of Captain van Braam, 67, 69; clears de Vergor, 192
Cross erected: at Oswego, 28, 330; at Ticonderoga, 264
Crossing the Line: Grand Banks ceremony, 17
Cruelty of Indians: 40, 41, 114, 143
Customs, naval, in Canada: 17

Delawares: 31, 35, 44, 90, 91, 105, 107, 114, 120, 138, 143, 180, 196, 213, 232
Desandrouins, Sieur: 4, 41, 204, 210, 222, 226, 245, 326; reconnoiters Oswego, 25; sent to repair Fort St. Jean, 93; commands Fort Lévis, 325
Deschambault: skirmish at, 320
Detroit: Indian footraces at, 45; sending food to Fort Duquesne, 90; news from, 119
Dieskau, Baron de: 5, 30, 50, 193, 315
Discipline, lack of: 174
Dissension: between Montcalm and Vaudreuil, 260
Dogs, sled: 87
Doreil, Sieur: Bougainville awaits, 3; reaches Montreal, 7; returns to France, 298
Drucour, Chevalier de: 88, 103
Drunkenness, Indian: 179, 225
Dutch, Albany: neutrality of, 106–107

Earthquake at Montreal: 79
Embarkation assignments, 1757: 155
Equipment, issued for winter raid: 87
Escabian: 117

Famine: 136; at Quebec, 112, 181, 201
Firewood: requirements of a fort, 63; tools burned for, 210
Fish oil: plentiful but not used, 56
Five Nations: see Iroquois
Flat Heads: see Choctaws
Food: bad quality of, 6, 7; lack of, 70; carried voyage to France, 73; shortage, 89, 92–93, 107; scarcity at Quebec, 108; scarcity delays start of campaign, 108; arrival of, 113, 206; Illinois villages supply, 114
Fort Anne: 142
Fort Augusta (Shamokin): 107n.
Fort Bull: 205; burned, 67; rebuilt (as Stanwix), 263
Fort Carillon (at Ticonderoga): 50, 57, 61, 63, 108, 113, 118, 127, 130; garrison at, July 1756, 13; description, 33; disposition of troops at, 34, 130–31; description of roads, 34; temperature at, 42; progress of construction, 51, 55; report of raid from, 121–22; plans for defense of, 222–23; battle, 228–34; defenses rebuilt, 267
Fort Cumberland: 43, 53, 83, 105, 138, 285
Fort Duquesne: news from, 52–53, 82, 114; attack expected, 112; falls, 294–95
Fort Edward: see Fort Lydius
Fort Frontenac: 4n., 12, 13, 18, 19, 112, 208, 273; rumors of attack, 265; news of fall, 275
Fort George (Oswego): 27
Fort George (William Henry): 34, 35, 38, 39, 45, 46, 47, 48, 50, 56, 57, 59, 60, 61, 102, 108, 109, 113, 123, 130; described, 60–61; Indians plan raid, 75; winter raid prepared, 86–87; raided, 95–97; siege planned, 119; 1757 expedition, 156–70; invested, 159; surrender, 169; massacre, 172–73; British garrison at, 175–77; French casualties, 177–78
Fort Granville: 44; captured, 43
Fort Halfway Brook: attack on, 245

337

Fort Loudoun: 203
Fort Lydius (Edward): 5, 34, 35, 46, 48, 50, 57, 60, 61, 82, 97, 108, 130, 136, 141, 142, 163, 169, 171, 173, 174, 192, 198, 199, 247, 253; garrison at, 84; convoys from, 244
Fort Machault (Venango): 212
Fort Niagara: Pouchot commander, 90; to be rebuilt in stone, 90; news from, 91, 105–106, 109, 113, 114, 119, 137, 180, 190–91, 200, 208, 283; Bradstreet misses chance at, 283
Fort Ontario (at Oswego): 25; Ontario garrison retreats to, 26; for battle of Oswego, *see* Oswego
Fort St. Frederic (Crown Point): 10, 12, 48, 51, 63, 98, 130; description, 33, 291; fuel requirements, 63
Fort St. George (Maine): 137
Fort St. Jean: 109; description, 31; conditions at, 65
Fort St. Regis: 15, 112n.
Fort Shamokin: 107
Fort Ticonderoga: *see* Fort Carillon at Ticonderoga
Fort Toulouse: 99n.
Fort William Henry: *see* Fort George
Fort Williams: burned, 67
Foxes (Indians): 121, 145, 149, 179; with Iroquois, 107
Fronsac: 62
Frontenac, Count de: 16
Fuel: firewood requirements at Fort St. Frederic, 63

Gambling: forbidden by King, 196; Bigot's great losses, 196
Gaspé: Reported British attack, 66; British occupation reported, 289; British withdraw, 296; raid on, 313
Geology: Bougainville's observations, 183, 189–90, 191, 220
Germain, Father: 58, 59, 66, 198, 270; leaves Acadia, 296
Gifts, Indian: list of, 21
Gluttony, Indian: 127
Gradis and Co.: 113n., 116
Graft: *see* Peculation
Grand Banks: ceremony when passing, 17
Grand Society (Bigot *et al.*): 119, 196, 205, 261, 271, 284, 286, 287

Grappling Hooks: made, 84
Guyenne Regiment: 12, 18, 19, 20, 23, 28, 32, 33, 34, 64, 109, 120, 131, 141, 154, 178, 179, 187, 222, 231, 234, 292, 297; reaches Lachine, 29; size of, 51; winter quarters, 62; arduous trip of, 70

Half Moon (N.Y.): 35
Harvest of 1757: worst ever in Canada, 182, 185
Hérault, Mme: 330; Bougainville's letters to, 331, 332, 333
Hermits: seized by Indians in Pennsylvania, 180
Horse meat: issue of, 195; resulting riot, 195
Horses: de Lotbinière's, 63
Hospitals, field: approved, 89
Howe, Lord: 214; killed and buried at Albany, 229
Hurons: 42, 75, 83, 219, 242, 255, 264; always troublesome, 208

Ice, effect on shipping: 69
Illinois towns: supply food to Fort Duquesne, 204
Indian, civilized shopkeeper: 123
Indian, European dress of an: 103
Indian behavior: *see* Behavior, Indian
Indian child: kills prisoner, 21
Indian councils: *see* Council, Indian
Indian cruelty: 40, 41, 114, 142
Indian gifts: list of, 21
Indian magic: 55–56, 126, 130, 135, 155, 264
Indian religion: 133–34
Indians, a necessary evil: 170
Indians, character of: 41
Indians, control of: 36; difficulty, 331
Indian scout, action of: 49
Indians, food draws them: 73
Indians, list of those on Fort William Henry expedition: 150–51
Indians, mission compared to those of west: 45
Indians, policy for use of: Bougainville's thoughts, 59–60
Indian tracking ability: 54–55
Indian treatment of prisoners: 8–9, 41
Indian tribes: *see* Abnakis, Algonkins, Amalicites, Caitas, Cayugas, Chero-

Index

kees, Chiens, Chippewas, Choctaws, Delawares, Flat Heads, Foxes, Hurons, Iowas, Iroquois, Mahicans, Menominees, Miamis, Michilimackinacs, Micmacs, Missisaugas, Mohawks, Moraigans, Natchez, Nipissings, Oneidas, Onondagas, Ottawas, Potawatomis, Saginaws, Sauks, Senecas, Shawnees, *Têtes de Boule*, Tuscaroras, Winnebagoes

Indians, western: description, 118
Indolence: of work at Fort Carillon, 51
Inflated money: 271
Inflation: 182–83; difficulties caused officers, 286; Montcalm attempts to neutralize, 290
Intelligence, British seek: desire prisoners, 59
Intelligence, lack of: of British on Lake George, 130
Intelligence of British: 5, 57, 84, 109, 143, 245–46, 279–80, 291, 316–17
Intendant: *see* Bigot
Interpreters, Indian: 243
Iowas: 151
Iroquois (Five Nations): 12, 13, 17, 24, 27, 28, 36, 39, 41, 42, 43, 44, 46, 48, 51, 54, 56, 60, 73, 86, 89, 102, 103, 105, 106, 110, 115, 121, 122, 137, 138, 169, 180, 191, 202, 208, 223, 232, 241, 242, 245, 255, 264, 265, 267, 294; make approaches to French, 30; French attempts on, 30; assure Vaudreuil of neutrality, 30; return from scout, 37; council with, 74; French desire transit through, and food, 85; protest appointment of chief by Vaudreuil, 101–102; ferment among, 109; desire neutrality and open trade routes, 119; approval of transit through, sought, 185; attempts to incite, 211; murders brother, 225; at battle of Carillon, 241
Iroquois of La Presentation: 111, 113
Iroquois of the Lake: 89, 136, 209, 219
Iroquois of the Ohio: 91
Iroquois of the Sault: 10, 32, 89, 149, 199, 333
Isle au Castor: 82
Isle au Chapon: 64
Isle aux Coudres: 71

Isle aux Morpions: 129
Isle aux Noix: Bougainville defends Champlain frontier at, 325–26

Jansenism: 83
Jesuits: 83–84
Johnson, Sir William: 30, 90, 107, 109, 189, 201, 232, 241, 246, 315; inciting Five Nations, 12; his house, 32; chief of Indian affairs, 35; seeks aid of Oneidas, 95; gives belts to Iroquois, 106; anecdote, 333
Joke, Lord Loudoun's: 108
Joncaire, Chabert de: 17, 91, 106, 208, 264, 315; brings Iroquois to Oswego, 28; intermediary with Iroquois, 30

Kisensik: 25, 146, 205, 209, 210; speaks at council, 123; guides Bougainville, 160

Lac des Deux Montagnes: description of mission, 122
Lachine: 211; canal proposed, 14
Lacrosse: 249
Ladder, scaling: 71, 94
Lake Champlain: ice starts to break, 98
Lake George: *see* Lake St. Sacrement
Lake Ontario: navigation of, 22
Lake St. Sacrement (George): Bougainville reconnoiters, 37–40; description of, 41, 157
Languedoc Battalion: 34, 54, 62, 64, 69, 96, 97, 98, 109, 115, 118, 154, 178, 179, 181, 187, 206, 209, 213, 222, 227, 231, 232, 292, 297; rich soldier of, 55; winter quarters, 62
Leopard's sickness: 4; subsides, losses, 8
Letters of exchange: issue stopped early, 271
Lévis, Gaston François de: 3, 30, 50, 63, 72, 77, 131, 146, 152, 153, 154, 156, 157, 158, 160, 163, 164, 168, 178, 179, 187, 211, 221, 223, 225, 230, 232, 233, 235, 238, 240, 287, 288, 318, 325; commands Fort Carillon, 13, 121; leads land army against Fort William Henry, 149; calms a riot, 195; roster of his Mohawk Valley expedition, 214; feared lost in ice, 297; defends western frontier, 319
Long House: 101

Lorette, La: description, 75–76; Vielle and Jeune, 83
Losses: French at battle of Carillon, 236
Lotbinière, Michel de: 55, 58, 86, 245, 257, 258, 278; holds canteen concession at Carillon, 51; his horses, 63, 256–67; action in battle of Carillon, 238–39; an astronomer, 245
Loudoun, Lord: 29, 34, 35, 41, 57, 107, 110, 116, 173, 193, 198, 199, 208; arrival expected, 32; his joke, 108
Louisbourg: attack expected, 110, 118; expedition against, assembles, 116; British fleet has left, 137; French fleet at, 139–40; news from, 181, 273; besieged, 217–18; report of surrender, 269; remarks on capture, 311–12
Louisiana: messenger from, 99
Lusignan, Sieur de: commands at Fort Carillon, 81; immense profits, 102

Machicoté: 90, 105–106
Magic, Indian: 55–56, 126, 130, 135, 155, 264
Mahican (Moraigan): 35, 122, 209
Marin, Indian leader: 11, 12, 13, 23, 41, 127, 130, 135, 138, 240, 258, 260, 262, 264, 265; leads reconnaissance, 130; returns from raid, 141; reconnaissance of, 142; encounter with Rogers, 261
Marine Regiment, La: 54, 86, 120, 132, 144, 158, 185, 221, 225, 231, 238, 250, 254, 281, 292; increase in, 115; size of, July 1757, 152
Martel, Sieur: sent to make census of wheat, 119
Mass: ship's crew vow, 307
Massacre: 158, 174; at Oswego, 26n.; at Fort William Henry, 172–73, 332
Mataché: 15n.
Materials for fortification, lack of: 5
Medal, French for Indians: 11
"Medicine" Indian: see Magic, Indian
Medocktek: 137
Ménade: 106n.
Menominees: 8, 11, 13, 23, 24, 27, 46, 120, 143, 145, 149, 204, 261; described, 9; audience with Vaudreuil, 10
Mercer, Colonel Hugh: killed, 26
Mercier, Sieur: 12, 20, 22, 37, 86, 92, 93, 95, 141, 153, 223, 250, 256; his combustibles fail, 96; demands surrender of Fort William Henry, 96; action at battle of Carillon, 238–39; one of Bigot's crew, 261
Miamis: 152
Michilimackinacs: 115
Micmacs: 137
Mirimichi: news from, 137
Missisaugas: 75, 112, 113, 114, 116, 151, 152, 255, 258, 264, 265
Misunderstanding between Montcalm and Vaudreuil: 215
Mitasses: 87
Mohawks: 32, 35, 106, 141, 209, 223, 315
Money, fiat: issued by de Lotbinière, 51
Moneychanging: great profits at Fort Carillon, 58
Monro, Lieutenant Colonel: 163, 167, 170, 174
Montcalm, Marquis de: 3, 5, 7, 10, 12, 13, 14, 18, 24, 29, 31, 41, 53, 63, 64, 66, 68, 71, 80, 97, 111, 116, 117, 120, 122, 123, 124, 127, 130, 132, 133, 144, 145, 146, 147, 148, 149, 150, 152, 155, 156, 157, 159, 160, 161, 162, 163, 164, 165, 166, 167, 168, 169, 170, 171, 173, 174, 175, 178, 181, 187, 198, 206, 215, 217, 220, 221, 222, 223, 227, 229, 232, 233, 234, 235, 238, 240, 241, 244, 247, 248, 259, 265, 271, 276, 277, 282, 288, 291, 292, 293, 315, 318, 321, 324, 327, 330, 331; inspects defenses of Carillon, 36; reviews troops at Carillon, 52; excluded from Vaudreuil's planning, 86; small stature of, 115; inspects Chambly and St. Jean, 117; visits Indian missions, 122; examines camps, 134; his quick wit, 145; holds council at Ticonderoga, 145; reviews troops, 183; reconnoiters Quebec defenses, 186; proposes economies, 188; Vaudreuil tells him nothing, 213; sings war song, 272; plans to meet new attack, 280–81; attempts increase pay junior officers, 290; death of, 321, 324
Mont Louis: raided by British, 314
Montreal: earthquake at, 79; weather at, 91, 99; horse meat issued, 195; riot results, 195; surrounded, 326; Amherst assails, 326; surrender, 326

Index

Moraigons: *see* Mahicans
Morale: British at Oswego, 7
Murder: among Indians, 225
Muster roll: Indian method of making, 132

Natchez Indians: 100
Navigation: closing by winter, 69; erratic, 310
Navy, British on Lake Ontario: 4; effect of possible, 246
Neutrality: Oneidas seek, 110
New Jersey Blues: 143n.
News: from Europe, 29, 43, 48, 61, 100–101; 189, 282–83; from Fort Duquesne, 105, 138, 190, 208; from Louisbourg, 62, 188, 207; from Louisiana, 203; from Niagara, 90, 91, 105–106, 109, 113, 114, 119, 137, 180, 190–91, 200, 283; from the west, 114, 180, 190, 196, 208
Niagara: *see* Fort Niagara
Nipissings: 24, 44, 45, 48, 49, 103, 122, 123, 136, 145, 146, 148, 150, 154, 205, 212, 219, 223, 255; deputies reach Montreal, 4
Number Four (Charlestown, N.H.): 267

Oneidas: 94, 95, 106, 110, 111, 114, 143; fidelity suspected, 89; neutrality desired by, 112
Onondagas: 73, 91, 101, 104, 106, 120, 189, 293, 294; hold first place among Iroquois, 102; location their town, 106n.
Ononthio: 68, 145
Order of the day: examples, 18, 22–23
Oswego: 4n, 10, 11, 19, 24, 25, 26, 27, 45, 52, 110; description, 7; to reconnoiter, 12; preparations for expedition, 13; attack prepared, 19–22; attacked, 25–26; surrender, 26; destruction of, 27–28; effect of capture on Indians, 59; Indians regret destruction, 104; re-establishment feared, 107; brandy, Indians swim in, 116; Bougainville's remarks, 314
Ottawas: 31, 32, 36, 42, 102, 113, 116, 117, 118, 120, 125, 131, 132, 133, 143, 145, 151, 152, 179, 180, 204, 222, 223, 242, 245, 255; various subtribes listed, 126
Ouapon: 42, 225
Oxhides: as food, 137
Ox roast: 32

Palatines: 94, 110; hope for neutrality, 94n.; village destroyed, 194
Parker, Colonel of Jersey Blues: his defeat, 142–43
Pay: officers' increased, 293
Peace: signed, 328
Péan, Major Michel: 45, 72, 261
Peculation: 93, 172, 187, 192, 196, 203, 254–55, 256–68, 271, 284, 285, 286, 287; at Presque Isle, 107
Pigeons, passenger: 125, 202
Pillage: at Fort William Henry, 170
Piquet, Abbé: 16, 103, 122, 136, 196, 241, 315; reaches Oswego, 27; intermediary with Iroquois, 30; brings Indian delegation, 101; incites Oneidas to back French, 111; conflict with military at mission, 294
Pointe à Fer: 88
Pointe à la Peur: 129
Pointe aux Sables: 129
Pointe aux Trembles: skirmish at, 319
Pointe Chequamegon: 121
Pointe Scononton: 126
Policy: military of Montcalm, 42–43
Pompadour, Marquise de: favors Bougainville, 322; approves of Carolina attack, 323; retires, 327
Pontleroy, Captain de: 191, 216, 221, 222, 226, 245, 276, 279, 298; new Canadian chief engineer, 188; refuses to approve peculation, 257; to re-establish Fort Frontenac, 277
Port Toulouse: 137
Portage at Ticonderoga: 34, 59, 131
Portage collar: 87
Potawatomis: 45–46, 49, 55, 56, 57, 61, 102, 105, 114, 121, 131, 143, 150, 151, 154, 204; wisest of the Indians, 132
Pouchot, Capt.: 90, 105, 106, 114, 138, 190, 191, 216; commands at Niagara, 85; reports from Niagara, 137; relieved at Niagara, 201
Presentation, La: 112; description, 16
Presents for Indians: 117

341

Presque Isle: 8, 59; news from, 5; peculation at, 107
Prices of food: 102, 286
Prisoners: Indian treatment of, 8–9, 41; evacuated to Europe, 69; unconfined at Quebec, 72
Provisions: scarcity and poor quality, 10, 12; captured at Fort William Henry, 177
Putnam, Israel: captured by Marin, 261

Quebec: weather at, 71–80 *passim*; "bridging" of St. Lawrence, 78–79; Acadians driven there by hunger, 116; nervousness at, 117; recruits arrive, 121; no bread at, 136; improvements to defenses, 186; convoy breaks famine, 206–207; fall of, 318–21
Quincampoix, Rue de: 58

Ration, French: 18, 22, 187; ovens for bread, 18; description of, 19; ordered reduced, 63; size, 63; for winter expedition, 87; value and composition, 93; for Fort Duquesne, 105
Rattlesnake bite: cure for, 49
Records: conveniently burned, 86–87
Reine, La, Battalion: 33, 52, 64, 69, 70, 109, 115, 120, 131, 154, 155, 156, 159, 162, 168, 178, 179, 181, 187, 202, 205, 206, 214, 222, 231, 232, 292; size of, 1756, 52; winter quarters, 62
Reinforcements, troop: approved, 115; arrival, 138
Religion, Indian: 133–34
Review, end of campaign: 51
Rice: being distributed, 136
Rigaud, Pierre François de: 11, 18, 19, 23, 24, 26, 80, 86, 91, 92, 94, 95, 102, 110, 122, 125, 127, 131, 132, 134, 152, 211, 240, 242, 247, 249, 262, 270; commands Oswego advance, 25; presents British flags to church, 30; raids Fort William Henry, 86ff.; cost of the raid, 194; his jealousy of French, 264–65; commands on Ontario frontier, 324
Riot: soldiers, at Albany, 90; Lévis quells, 195
Rivers: Barbue, 47; Chicot, 33, 47; Otter Creek, 47; Richelieu, 216; St.

Jean, 58; St. Lawrence, voyage up, 13–17; "bridging," 78, 79; ice starts to break, 99; river open, 100; British warships in, 286; difficult navigation, 299–300
Road: Montreal to St. Jean very bad, 31; St. Jean to La Prairie, 65, 179
Rogers, Robert: 46n., 226; boats abandoned by, 46–47; whaleboats of, 51; raid near Ft. Carillon, 81–82; defeated near Carillon, 198; battle on snowshoes, 199n.; skirmish with Marin, 261
Roster: French Army, July, 1757, 152–54; Lévis expedition, 214; British Army, July, 1758, 227–28; July, 1758, 231; at Carillon, July, 1758, 244; January, 1758, 250–51; 1758, 251; Canadians at battle of Carillon, 254; July, 1758, 255; at Carillon, August, 1758, 263
Roubaud, Father: 136, 150
Rous, Captain: 58
Royal Roussillon Battalion: 34, 63, 64, 86, 95, 96, 97, 98, 104, 108, 130, 131, 154, 156, 162, 168, 178, 187, 214, 222, 231, 232, 233, 234, 292, 297; reviewed, 53; winter quarters, 62
Rozzio (Roggio): 129

Saginaws: 143
St. Catherine's Gale: 72
St. Francis: 83, 136
St. Luc, La Corne de: 23, 122, 136, 247, 249, 273; leaves for Oswego, 7; at Menominee council, 10; at ceremony, 117; raids British supply lines, 253
Sapinette (spruce beer): 52
Sarre, La: 12, 18, 19, 28, 31, 43, 63, 64, 65, 67, 97, 98, 109, 120, 131, 154, 156, 162, 168, 173, 178, 179, 187, 222, 227, 231, 232, 292, 297; winter quarters, 62; size of, 66
Sauks: 120, 149
Sault, The (Sault St. Louis, Caughnawaga): 9, 32; description, 124–25
Sault St. Louis Mission: visit to, 124; council at, 124; Bougainville adopted by Iroquois, 124
Sawmill at Carillon: 55
Scalping, near Fort Carillon: 53

Index

Scalps, multiplying: 142
Scarcity of food: 70, 89, 92, 108, 202
Scouting, British: active, 131
Season, growing: length of in Canada, 100
Senecas: 17, 35, 106, 114; reject British advances, 138
Seven Years' War (French and Indian War): résumé, xv–xx
Shamokin (Fort Augusta): 107
Shawnees: 90, 105, 114, 180, 196
Sheep, cost of: 286
Shipwreck in St. Lawrence: 184, 296
Short Ears (Ottawas): 289
Sickness: the *Leopard*'s, 4; from poor rations, 12
Sixtieth Regiment: recruited in America, 34
Skirmishes: 140, 141
Sledges: 92
Smallpox: 137, 192; rumors of, 5; Indian fear of, 8; great ravages, 1757, 192; hits western Indians, 193; ravages western Indians, 197
Snow, powdered: description, 75
Soldiers: French, indolence of, 51
Sowing: earliest in 1758, 200
Spruce beer (*sapinette*): 52
Stinking Bay (Baie des Puants): 8
Stobo, Major Robert: trial of, 67, 69; escapes and recaptured, 108
Strawberry, giant: after death of Indian, 134
Succession: if Canadian governor dies, 80
Sulpicians: 122
Superstitions, Indian: 126, 134
Supplies: shortage of, 83
Susquehanna Indians: 35

Tattooing: 288
Tax, on wheat: 73, 185
Te Deum: at Oswego, 28; at Montreal for Oswego, 29; for Fort William Henry raid, 100; King requests for Port Mahon, 117; Indians sing, 124; army sings at Carillon, 1757, 174; 1758, 242
Temperature at Carillon: 42
Testimonial: Montcalm's on Bougainville, 334
Têtes de Boule: 212

Theft of royal money chest: 85
Ticonderoga (Fort Carillon), Battle of: preparations for, 226–27; description, 227–34; defenses, 230; aftermath, 234–35; French losses, 236; Bougainville's observations, 237–39
Tioga: 91, 203, 205
Tomahawks: poor quality of, 6
Trade and commerce: completed for winter, 68
Traverse, La: 71; need of battery at, 298
Troops: Vaudreuil requests increase, 69
Truce, red flag of: 166
Tuscaroras: 111

Van Braam, Captain: trial of, 67, 69; escapes and recaptured, 108
Vapor, fatal: 182
Vaudreuil, Marquis de: 6, 7, 9, 11, 12, 20, 29, 30, 59, 77, 137, 144, 149, 171, 174, 179, 193, 196, 198, 205, 211, 214, 217, 218, 220, 221, 222, 223, 224, 239, 240, 241, 242, 243, 244, 245, 247, 248, 249, 254, 259, 260, 261, 262, 264, 268, 269, 271, 276, 277, 279, 281, 282, 287, 292, 293, 297, 315, 318, 321, 324, 326; ill at Trois Rivières, 80; recovered, 85; plans attack on William Henry, 119; holds court-martial on de Vergor, 187; women demand bread of, 213; misunderstanding with Montcalm, 215; his first and only campaign, 252
Vergor, Duchambon de: 198; court-martial of, 184; cleared, 192
Villiers, Coulon de: 11, 132, 141, 152, 154, 167, 212; to reconnoiter Oswego, 4; attacks Bradstreet's convoy, 6

Washington, George: at Fort Necessity, 67
Weapons: poor condition of Canadians', 94
Weather: early thaw, late freeze favor British, 58; at Montreal, 91, 99; at Quebec, 71–80 *passim*
Webb, Colonel Daniel: 135, 143, 163, 164, 166, 167, 173, 181
Wheat: census ordered, 119

343

Wild Oats (Wild Rice): 8
Wine: lack of at Carillon, 52; price of, 51, 55, 102, 286
Winnebagos: 118, 120, 151
Winter quarters: Vaudreuil makes assignments, 62-63; makes captious change in, 64; troops move to, 187

Wolf, Lieutenant: 22, 156, 193, 198, 200, 213, 240, 262, 269, 270, 292; burns vessel at Fort William Henry, 97
Wolfe, Brigadier James: 318
Women at Iroquois council: 103-104
Wool: 76

This translation of the American journals of Louis Antoine de Bougainville has been set in a machine adaptation of a seventeenth-century type design attributed to the Leipzig typefounder Anton Janson. The historical flavor of the Janson face complements the events and language of the text, while the time-tested readability of the Janson letter satisfies the practical needs of today's reader.

UNIVERSITY OF OKLAHOMA PRESS

Norman